EMILY

DICKINSON'S

POETRY

Stairway of Surprise

BY

CHARLES R. ANDERSON

HOLT, RINEHART AND WINSTON

NEW YORK

To

Gertrude Roberts Anderson

and

Robert Lanier Anderson

He shall aye climb
For his rhyme . . .
·But mount to paradise
By the stairway of surprise.

           –Emerson, *Merlin*

PREFACE

More than seventy years ago in the remote New England village of Amherst a little lady died at the age of fifty-five, unknown to the world and undreamed of as one of America's great poets. During Emily Dickinson's lifetime only seven of her poems had been published, and though a fairly large number had been shown to friends these were mostly light nature pieces, elegies, and expressions of thanks or sympathy, along with a fraction of her best work. Even the family was completely unprepared for the surprise discovery at her death in 1886. Her sister found hidden away in her bureau a mass of nearly two thousand manuscript poems, many of them copied out neatly in little 'volumes' and the rest in every imaginable state of composition, some revised, some unfinished, and some just fragments. This poetic legacy she described as her 'Letter to the World' that never wrote to her—namely, posterity.

The first problem in bridging the gap between a 'private poet' and her posthumous audience was an editorial one. How could these miscellaneous manuscripts be brought within the conventions of printing and made accessible to the modern reader, yet with all their uniqueness preserved? During the first half century after her death they were published piece-meal and inaccurately in a bewildering series of installments—probably the most unfortunate publication history in modern literary annals, but too well known to need rehearsing here. Then at long last, in 1955, a complete scholarly edition was issued that resolves the problem of a definitive text as well as can be hoped for, though it still leaves some difficult questions unanswered. (The two principal ones are considered in an appendix to the present book: Can manuscripts such as these be reproduced exactly as written, other than by facsimiles? Should the scholarly text, once established, be compromised in order to provide a reader's text free of distracting idiosyncrasies?) But these are problems for future editors. Meanwhile, readers of the Harvard Edition, the text followed here, can be assured that they finally have the poems of Emily Dickinson substantially as she wrote them. It is now evident that the real assessment of her poetic achievement must begin over again, and this is a task for the critic.

The second pre-requisite to reading a private poet, which must be undertaken before any significant interpretation can begin, is the winnowing and ordering process that the author never got around to. One of the salutary by-products of publication is a periodic house-cleaning in which the poems that failed to materialize, the unused fragments and unusable notations, are discarded. If the creator is also a severe self-critic, the discrepancy between the total body of writings and the best of them may be reduced to a minimum, with great advantage to the reader. But with someone like Emily Dickinson who published nothing and apparently destroyed nothing, the literary remains may include the miscellaneous sweepings of the poet's workshop, ranging all the way from splendid finished creations down to absent-minded scribblings. To cherish all of these indiscriminately is the surest way to render her poetic reputation a disservice. A close reading of her complete writings in the new edition brings two opposing impressions into sharp prominence: the excellence of her best poems and the mediocrity of the majority. Recognition of this is the first step towards that re-evaluation which now seems the great desideratum.

The whole duty of the critic will be to establish the canon of her highest achievement, to present the selected poems in an order that will make them most meaningful, and then to lead the reader as far into them as he can. But an initial problem often arises concerning a choice of texts, because of the state in which the manuscripts have come down. They consist of penciled jottings, worksheets or rough originals on scrap paper, semi-final drafts with suggested changes, and fair copies. For a good many poems, frequently the most interesting ones, two or more versions survive or at least a number of variant readings. (See Plates II, III, and IV, pp. 310-12.) Which text is to be preferred? In these instances,

Thomas H. Johnson, the editor of the variorum edition, was faced with the practical problem of choosing among the texts for principal representation, and he solved it by selecting 'the earliest fair copy.' But this rule of thumb was chiefly for the purpose of arriving at the chronological arrangement rather than the highest evolution of the poem as poem. So the reader must not make the mistake of assuming that the text there printed first and in larger type has any absolute priority. Johnson himself cites some cases that make exceptions to his rule. For example, poem No. 1437 (as numbered in the Harvard Edition) in its earliest form consists of a semi-final draft with a suggested change for the concluding lines; the next two manuscripts are fair copies that adopt it; but the latest fair copy rejects it and returns to the text of the semi-final. Others show that any such rule is arbitrary. For example, No. 228 exists in three fair copies written over a period of years, all variant, and the editor confesses that one text is as valid as another. One more that is simply baffling: No. 533 was written in all but final form in 1862, with a single line variant; then the poet went back to it in 1878, broke it down into a worksheet, and finally abandoned it in a state of chaos. Which is the 'final version'? Nor is there any way to tell which of the suggested changes at the bottom of the page she might have adopted. In illustration of this Johnson cites examples (Nos. 310 and 670) where the semi-final draft offers several variants of which the fair copy adopts some, rejects some, and adds others not even suggested on the earlier manuscript. Certainly all poems that got no further than semi-final drafts must be considered 'unfinished.' Nor is there really any way to be sure what changes she might have made even on a 'finished' poem as long as it remained in manuscript.

Because of her ambiguous character of being a poet yet not a publishing poet, one must simply accept the fact that Emily Dickinson did not leave any of her poems in final form, strictly speaking, nor indicate her preferences absolutely. For this reason I have felt free to choose any version and adopt any variant that struck me as best (with specific indication of choice made in the notes), though never making a composite text from several manuscripts. A few examples will illustrate my procedure. No. 585, 'I like to hear it lap the Miles,' exists only in a semi-final draft with four suggested changes; I have rejected one of these but accepted the other three as improvements (see p. 15). No. 1333 offers an unusually complex set of variants, which I have analyzed in detail (see pp. 79-81, and Plate IV, p. 312). For No. 675, 'Essential Oils are wrung,' I have chosen the version printed second as clearly superior (see p. 64). More complicated questions are raised by No. 311, 'It sifts from Leaden Sieves' (see pp. 159-62). This survives in four manuscripts representing two radically different treatments of the same theme, running to twenty and twelve lines respectively. I have reproduced the earlier and longer version, printed first in the Harvard Edition, for comparative purposes only; then the shorter version written many years later, with full commentary to show how much better a poem it is, though it might well escape the casual reader's attention since it is printed fourth by Johnson. This demonstration has been carried out in such detail to indicate the various decisions that must be made before the critic can even arrive at the business of selecting, arranging, and interpreting the best poems.

In undertaking this larger task a special method has proved helpful. Such an extraordinary number of unusually short poems, nearly two thousand with an average length of a dozen lines or less, poses a problem of approach. To survey the whole or concentrate on single lyrics runs an equal danger of scattering one's fire or pin-pointing too small a target. The chronological arrangement in the new edition has been useful in minor ways, but not for selecting or ordering the poems. There are no marked periods in her career, no significant curve of development in her artistic powers, no progressive concern with different genres, such as might furnish the central plan for a book on Milton or Yeats. Continuing the search for an order and a suitable body of poetry to interpret, one happily remembered her tendency to return again and again to a few fundamental themes or areas. This was recognized by her earlier editors, but since their groupings are quite unsatisfactory the critic must make his own by re-searching the entire canon. Thus the approach that suggested itself was a thematic one, and it only remained to find some really meaningful sequence for the groups.

The plan that finally emerged was to begin with her theory of art: her strategy of Wit, her way with Words, her exploration of Circumference and Center as the upper reach and lower limits of the poet's valid themes—then her theory of Perception, what use the poet can make of the external world. It is the purpose of this first section to set before the reader the kind of poetry she wanted to write and give him a way of reading it. The last of these esthetic issues, perception, is made the opening chapter of the second section on the outer world, since it leads directly into her attempts to take nature as her subject. The simplest of these are the poems trying to reproduce the variety of natural Forms; next, with her realization of how impossible this is, a group of more interesting ones on the Evanescence of these forms; then, with her discovery that the most important characteristic of matter is its motion, the highly original poems on nature as Process. If the external world eludes the poet's grasp he is thrown back on the inner world as his only reality, and the third section illustrates this with her treatment of the dramatic poles of human existence, Ecstasy and Despair, two themes that produced far better poems than any of the more moderate aspects of the inner life. Finally, since ecstasy and despair are inextricably related to spiritual strivings and misgivings, they lead inevitably to her thematic concern with man's knowledge of Death and his dream of Immortality, in the concluding section.

The categories here set up for the four divisions of this book—art, nature, the self, death and its sequel—are in no sense hard and fast or mutually exclusive. Some of the poems on the inner world are essential to her esthetic by defining her concept of reality. Some of her finest nature metaphors occur in poems dealing with despair or immortality. The only possible place for the fulfillment of love came to be heaven, reached through the grave. But these groupings clearly define the major areas of her achievement and provide a climactic order in terms of excellence. Within each group the interrelations of her poems are such that they illuminate one another, the language forming a rich spectrum, the images and ideas radiating out from a central vision.

Finally, in the large mass of undifferentiated manuscripts that has survived, this approach helps one to single out the successful completed poems, even frequently to point out that what are printed as two or more separate poems are essentially variant attempts to draft the same poetic idea. Winnowing her poems for the best, one finds that a great many can be reckoned as incomplete, about a third of the total if one includes not only the fragments and those that never progressed beyond semi-final drafts but genuine poetic flights that fall off into failure after a brave beginning. An even larger number though completed are not true poems, including both the occasional pieces and the verse aphorisms that are scarcely distinguishable from sententious passages in the letters. A fair number, probably fifteen per cent, are minor successes not sufficiently distinguished to linger over. Her really fine poems do not seem to me to number more than a hundred, her great ones about twenty-five, and these are the ones I have concentrated on. Since their full texts are included in this book, they constitute a select anthology of her best poems. A similar number are less successful embodiments of the same themes, and these have been worked into the discussion by the cluster method.

What follows is simply one person's reading of Emily Dickinson's highest achievement in poetry, with grateful acknowledgment to those who have paved the way and a strong hope that these chapters will send many readers back to the text to rediscover for themselves these remarkable poems. Having access to them at long last in their original form, one finds they are even more idiosyncratic and difficult than had been thought, but also bolder and more original. To give her poetry the serious attention it deserves is the real task that remains. To study it intensively, to stare a hole in the page until these apparently cryptic notations yield their full meanings—this is the great challenge to modern readers.

ACKNOWLEDGMENTS

Acknowledgment is hereby made to the following for permission to quote from ED's poems and letters: Millicent T. Bingham and the Trustees of Amherst College, the Harvard University Press, and Little, Brown & Company.

I wish to express my deep gratitude to those who have kindly read the MS of this book, in whole or in part, and made valuable suggestions for its improvement: Millicent T. Bingham, Stanley Burnshaw, Dudley Fitts, Thomas H. Johnson, and Jay Leyda. Also my warm thanks go to several colleagues at Johns Hopkins for criticisms of separate chapters: Don Allen, Richard Green, Arthur Lovejoy, Hillis Miller, Georges Poulet (now of Zürich), Leo Spitzer, and Earl Wasserman.

A special debt to former students is a pleasure to record. During seminars on ED at Johns Hopkins and at the University of Hawaii, they adopted my method of approach and techniques of analysis and then produced original papers on aspects of her poetry, some of unusually high caliber. Since these were in a sense communal projects, the authors have generously allowed me to draw on their results for my own interpretations of several poems. A list of these students follows, with the specific indebtedness indicated by numbers in parentheses referring to the pages of my book where these poems are discussed: Jean Akimoto (90), Carl Bain (182, 183-4, 247), Ralph Baldwin (172-3), Evelyn Castro (212), Diane DeTuro (194), Jay Levine (265-6, 275, 278), Frank Manley (199, 204, 275), Alan Roper (265-6), and Doreen Tam (215-6).

Set apart from all the others is my gratitude to Eugenia Blount Anderson for unfaltering support and counsel throughout.

CONTENTS

xvii

Four THE OTHER PARADISE
'*The White Exploit*'

APPENDIX

One:

THE PARADISE OF ART

'My Splendors are Menagerie'

I

WIT

Emily Dickinson approached language like an explorer of new lands. It offered her the excitement of adventure. It conferred the fresh wonder of discovering what no man had ever seen before. She used words as if she were the first to do so, with a joy and an awe largely lost to English poetry since the Renaissance. Also with a creator's license: coining with a free hand, boldly maneuvering her inherited vocabulary, collapsing the syntax, springing the rhythm, slanting the rhyme.

In youth words to her were colored balls to toss in the air, the play of exuberant spirits and a lively mind. Then with careful discipline she fashioned them into delicate instruments for recording her reactions to the sights and sounds of a curious world, for probing the mask of reality. As psychic pressures closed in upon her mature life, they became a burning fountain welling up from the heart's secret springs. And in their ultimate refinement, they were her gesture of hail and farewell to the life of the mind, to the death of the body. With her gradual discovery of the miracles of language came the discovery of her poetic powers. But she began as a wit, a precocious word-juggler, unaware she was a poet.

Wit is indispensable to the great poet, it might be agreed again today after the lapse of a hundred years or so. The ups and downs of this word's reputation from the Renaissance to the present offer a commentary on the history of our poetry. Through the seventeenth century it clung to its root meaning, denoting in the highest sense the sagacity of genius. At the peak of its favorable application to the literary artist it stood for the power of joining thought and expression with an aptness calculated to delight by its unexpectedness, according to John Locke in his *Essay Concerning the Human Understanding*. From this it has declined to its present low estate of a mere synonym for verbal cleverness, though the controversy over this word in modern critical circles shows the urgency of reviving its full complex of connotations. T.S. Eliot first raised the issue in his essay on Andrew Marvell, praising him because he 'plays with a fancy which begins by pleasing and leads to astonishment.' This quality he defined as a proper alliance of levity and seriousness, 'a tough reasonableness beneath the slight lyric grace . . . [whereby] the poem turns suddenly with that surprise which has been one of the most important means of poetic effect since Homer.' After tracing its mutations in eighteenth-century satire, he deplored the fact that it has become virtually extinct today. But he overlooked the one poet of the last century who most nearly fits his definition. The light and the serious meanings were never incongruous, in fact, nor was their fusion altogether lost sight of. Webster's dictionary of a century ago still tried to combine the two, quoting Pope as well as Locke to support its own definition of wit: 'The association of ideas in a manner natural, but unusual and striking, so as to produce surprise joined with pleasure.' In her own development as an artist, Emily Dickinson moved naturally enough from her early delight in being a verbal entertainer to the creation of a poetic idiom of great novelty and brilliance.

Her reputation as a local wit, dating from her earliest years, is amply testified to by family and friends. From the beginning she had a sense of her own uniqueness and a compulsion to be original as well as amusing. At the age of fourteen, explaining why she had not written sooner to an absent schoolmate, she said: 'I thought as all the other girls wrote you, my letter if I wrote one, would seem no smarter than anybody else, and you know how I hate to be common.' As a school girl of about this period she was humorist on the comic column of a magazine circulated in manuscript at Amherst Academy, and at Mt. Holyoke Seminary a few years later she amused the students by improvising funny stories. Afterward with her sister, brother, and his fiancée she formed a little coterie which considered itself an avant-garde, despising the literal, the commonplace, and the conventional. Her first experiments, though no specimens have come down, were apparently burlesque sermons and fanciful tall tales in imitation of the popular genres of American humor which she was familiar with from reading the pages of the Springfield *Republican*. Next she tried her hand at the Valentine letter of pretentious nonsense then fashionable among young people. The surviving examples in prose and verse show ingenuity in punning, Latin parody, and the juggling of clichés.

What is precocious in all this is her early compulsion to escape from the doldrums into which contemporary American writing had sunk, rather than any claim to the dubious distinction of being a child prodigy. Indeed, the maturing process was slow with her in many ways, not really complete until near the age of thirty. Throughout her twenties she remained a gay and high-spirited child, with 'Instincts for Dance– a caper part– An Aptitude for Bird,' as she described herself in a later poem. A similar strain of persiflage runs through many of her letters during this decade. The prose frequently slides off into a metrical pattern, and conversely the only five poems known to have been written before 1858 are more properly letters turned into verse to sharpen the banter. She was simply indulging in the acrobatics of composition, unconscious that she was developing verbal skills to suit her future needs. Her maturity as a wit came almost without warning or transition, just as her poetic maturity did, and at about the same time. Badinage and nonsense are suddenly replaced by penetrating observation and pithy comment. It was obviously as a wit rather than as a poet that she was admired by her small private audience, who cherished and preserved her sallies in prose and verse. But there was danger in this applause. It might have tempted her to pour too much of herself into this mold. Just as there is a tendency towards the sententious in her letters from the middle 1850's, that later became a distinct mannerism, so the poems after 1865 move more and more in the direction of the epigrammatic.

Apparently she even came to talk, as she wrote, in aphorisms. Her niece recalled evening conversations on the side piazza between her aunt and visitors: 'She loved to fence in words with an able adversary. Circumlocution she despised. Her conclusions hit the mark and suggested an arrow in directness, cutting the hesitancies of the less rapid thinker.... She loved a metaphor, a paradox, a riddle.' The sole recorded conversation with her supports this aptly. As transcribed by T.W. Higginson, after his visit to Amherst in 1870, it consisted of a veritable barrage of wit—epigram, epithet, conceit, hyperbole, aphorism—illuminative flashes that will be quoted throughout the following chapters wherever pertinent to her central themes. She permitted herself to go to the adventurous limits of her vocabulary, talking to him as she was on ideas of major concern to her, and to pirouette on a pin-point because she felt secure there, knowing the rest of the universe to be unstable. But he could only complain that her language was 'the very wantonness of over-statement,' 'a crowning extravaganza,' and so on. 'I never was with any one who drained my nerve power so much,' he concluded. 'Without touching her, she drew from me. I am glad not to live near her.'

This is reminiscent of the effect on conventional people of another witty talker, Samuel Bowles, with whom she frequently sparred as a fit adversary. Emily Dickinson's description of him might well apply to herself: 'You remember his swift way of wringing and flinging away a Theme, and others picking it up and gazing bewildered after him.' The only danger in all this was the temptation to become a virtuoso in words, delighting in the means to the neglect of the ends. But by the time she finally turned to writing as a career she had fashioned an idiom exactly suited to all her utterance. It was the language of wit, the words to match her thoughts and mask herself. In her serious work she never forgot that it was merely an instrument for rendering. In between times, practice pieces would serve to keep her fingers nimble and her mind alive. And on occasion the artist needed, quite simply, to take a holiday.

Her wit sparkled in its gayest form when she allowed it to play over the simple village world of which she was a part. Since she had no intention of writing novels, social satires, or autobiography as part of her serious art, she had an accumulated store of impressions that were lying around unused and only needing a receptive audience. Opening a correspondence in 1862 with Higginson, in a desperate search for literary counsel, she realized after the first few exchanges that she had found not the critic she needed but the perfect foil for her wit. He was an outsider yet kindly, concerned with expression though wedded to the conventional, interested but baffled. The extraordinary sheaf of poems she sent him had aroused his curiosity about the artist more than his admiration for her art. If he could not really serve as her preceptor in poetry he could at least be her 'safest friend,' as she later referred to him, a sounding board for the words that would articulate her self in relation to the society she had withdrawn from.

To his inquiries about herself, her family, her friends, she replied with a poetic autobiography unique in literary history. She had never had a photograph taken, she said: 'I noticed the Quick wore off those things, in a few days.' She would send him a pen-portrait instead: 'I . . . am small, like the Wren, and my Hair is bold, like the Chestnut Bur—and my eyes, like the Sherry in the Glass, that the Guest leaves.' When he asked for a brief sketch of her life, this is what he got:

> I went to school— but in your manner of the phrase— had no education. When a little Girl, I had a friend, who taught me Immortality— but venturing too near, himself— he never returned— Soon after, my Tutor, died— and for several years, my Lexicon— was my only companion— Then I found one more— but he was not contented I be his scholar— so he left the Land.
>
> You ask of my Companions Hills— Sir— and the Sundown— and a Dog— large as myself, that my Father bought me— They are better than Beings— because they know— but do not tell— and the noise in the Pool, at Noon— excels my Piano. . . . But I fear my story fatigues you—

It probably did not help him much when in a later letter, immediately after assuring him that her life had been 'too simple and stern to embarrass any,' she added: 'It is difficult not to be fictitious in so fair a place.' His reply candidly confessed his bewilderment. Grasping at some straw of fact, he decided that her solitude was all too real and formed a barrier to communication. 'It is hard to understand how you can live s[o alo]ne,' he wrote. 'Yet it isolates one anywhere to think beyond a certain point or have such luminous flashes as come to you— . . . you enshroud yourself in this fiery mist & I cannot reach you.'

Over the years he had prodded her on the dangers of seclusion, but her answers increasingly baffled him. When he finally visited Amherst in the hope of understanding his 'partially cracked poetess' better, he pressed the matter again, asking if she did not feel the lack of contacts with society. 'I never thought of conceiving that I could ever have the slightest approach to such a want in all future time,' she said, adding, 'I feel that I have not expressed myself strongly enough.' Her answer should have closed this line of inquiry for all time, but two years later he made one more effort to draw her out. 'Thank you for the "Lesson",' she replied; 'I will study it though hitherto'— but here she gave up prose as a

medium of explanation and quoted instead the central lines of a poem
she had just composed:

> The Show is not the Show
> But they that go—
> Menagerie to me
> My Neighbor be—
> Fair Play—
> Both went to see—

Higginson had just begun his long residence at Newport. His renewed
invitation to gregariousness seems to have stirred her memory of an
article in the Springfield *Republican*, satirizing the social season there
under the caption 'a Human Menagerie,' and prompted her to turn the
tables on the man of the world who found her withdrawal eccentric.
From her private window she could see the outside world as antic too.

Actually, until about the age of thirty she took a normal part in village
life, and even after her withdrawal she kept in touch with the world
through the frequent visits to her house of friends and relatives. But in
her letters she usually gave a special slant to this limited society too, as
in the following:

> An unexpected impediment to my reply . . . was a call from my
> Aunt Elizabeth— 'the only male relative on the female side,' and
> though many days since, its flavor of courtmartial still sets my spirits
> tingling.
> With what dismay I read of those columns of kindred in the Bible—
> the Jacobites and the Jebusites and the Hittites and the Jacqueminots!

No one was ever more devoted to her home, yet witness her unsentimental account of the move in 1855 back to the Dickinson homestead
where she had been born, the mansion on Main Street that was to be a
center of village and family hospitality for another twenty years:

> I cannot tell you how we moved. . . . I am out with lanterns, looking
> for myself. . . . I supposed we were going to make a 'transit,' as heav-
> enly bodies did— but we came budget by budget, as our fellows do,
> till we fulfilled the pantomime contained in the word 'moved.' It is a
> kind of *gone-to-Kansas* feeling, and if I sat in a long wagon, with my
> family tied behind, I should suppose without doubt I was a party of

emigrants! They say that 'home is where the heart is.' I think it is where the *house* is, and the adjacent buildings.

Her pen-portraits of the intimate family circle fill out the poetic auto-biography: 'I have a Brother and Sister,' she replied to Higginson's inquiry. 'My Mother does not care for thought— and Father, too busy with his Briefs— to notice what we do— He buys me many Books— but begs me not to read them— because he fears they joggle the Mind.' When Higginson came to see her she startled him with a query, 'Could you tell me what home is,' adding, 'I never had a mother. I suppose a mother is one to whom you hurry when you are troubled.' She followed the idea up in a letter several years later: 'I always ran Home to Awe when a child, if anything befell me. He was an awful Mother, but I liked him better than none.' To her cousins she presented another facet, writing once in early spring: 'Mother went rambling, and came in with a burdock on her shawl, so we know that the snow has perished from the earth. Noah would have liked mother.' Lest the sentimental be disturbed by this seeming lack of filial piety, it should be recalled that she nursed her mother devotedly through seven years of complete invalidism. A comment at the time of her death puts a finishing touch on the picture: 'We were never intimate Mother and Children while she was our Mother— but . . . when she became our Child, the Affection came.'

The father image is more complex. The literal-minded Higginson, who once met Edward Dickinson, could only see his austerity. She emphasized this aspect to him, saying, 'My father only reads on Sunday— he reads *lonely* & *rigorous* books.' After his death she wrote: 'His Heart was pure and terrible and I think no other like it exists'; later, 'When I think of my Father's lonely life and his lonelier Death, there is this redress'—and she quoted three lines of poety concluding with 'Immortality.' But the other side of this severe and repressive figure appears in the many humorous vignettes she sent to members of the family circle. To her brother away at law school she described her father going into the village on an errand before breakfast: 'He wore a palm leaf hat, and his pantaloons tucked in his boots. . . . I don't think "neglige" quite becoming to so mighty a man.' Again, after his election to the House of Representatives when he refused to let the family use his franking privileges, she lamented: 'It isn't *every* day that we have a chance to sponge Congress— . . . but Caesar is such "an honorable man".'

To one whom she thought of as a sister she reported: 'Father called to say that our steelyard was fraudulent, exceeding by an ounce the rates of honest men. He had been selling oats. I cannot stop smiling, though it is hours since, that even our steelyard will not tell the truth.' And to the same friend she defined her own unregenerate character in terms of kinship with her four-year-old nephew: 'Ned tells that the Clock purrs and the kitten ticks. He inherits his Uncle Emily's ardor for the lie.'

In an early letter she had said to her absent brother, her chief companion in wit and books among members of the household: 'We don't *have* many jokes tho' *now,* it is pretty much all sobriety, and we do not have much poetry, father having made up his mind that its pretty much all *real life.* Father's real life and *mine* sometimes come into collision, but as yet, escape unhurt!' This was written almost a decade before her career as a writer began, yet she was already aware that wit and poetry comprised 'real life' for her, setting her apart from the others. Both the strength and the weakness of her father was his lack of imagination, as she confided to her cousins. Though it separated them she saw it with humor: 'Father steps like Cromwell when he gets the kindlings'; and with compassion: 'You know he never played, and the straightest engine has its leaning hour.' His death was perhaps the severest loss she had to suffer. Her final vignette, written six years afterwards, records her sense of his greatness in a deceptively trivial anecdote:

> The last April that father lived, lived I mean below, there were several snow-storms, and the birds were so frightened and cold they sat by the kitchen door. Father went to the barn in his slippers and came back with a breakfast of grain for each, and hid himself while he scattered it, lest it embarrass them. Ignorant of the name or fate of their benefactor, their descendants are singing this afternoon.

This tissue of paradox in her family portrait, though it has been misunderstood as a willful mingling of flippancy and piety, has very real significance for her poetry. She had to reduce sentiment to a minimum in order to give her wit free play. She needed perspective, distance from the personalities surrounding her, in order to find out who she was. Through these verbal explorations she was discovering the identity of ED *poeta,* not necessarily the same person as the Emily Dickinson known in Amherst. That more prosaic self is also present in the letters (and briefly sketched in an epilogue to this book), sharing with family and friends all the normal ups and downs of experience. But for understanding her poems the emergent fictive self is far more instructive. She even gave this self a new name, 'Dickinson,' when signing some of her letters to Higginson, evidence enough that she could think of herself impersonally as an artist. If this were adopted as her literary name, following the convention for all artists (except, curiously, women authors), it would avoid the indignity of 'Emily' and the awkwardness of either 'Miss Dickinson' or the constant repetition of her full name.

She had explicitly warned Higginson at the beginning of their correspondence, 'When I state myself, as the Representative of the Verse— it does not mean— me— but a supposed person.' The letters helped her to create the mask she perfected in her best poetry. In them one can see it in the process of being formed. There may seem a touch of coyness in her self-portrait as a small child, somewhat abashed by an indifferent and even menacing adult world. But this is not only wren against crow and hawk, it is David against Goliath, reduced modern man confronting an incomprehensible universe. Her 'ardor for the lie' is not whimsy, but a poet's dedication to the fictions of imagination rather than the truth of prose. Her separation of idea and fact from the sentiments attaching to them is not irresponsible capering, but the poet's imperviousness to normal feeling in order to make experience available for artistic use. So she not only withdrew herself from the village but secluded her poetic self even from her family. In her correspondence she found an instrument for defining that detachment, even for creating it. Because she persisted in going her private way she became far more keenly aware than her successful contemporaries of the modern artist's alienation from society. She mastered this outer world by renouncing it.

Yet from her vantage point of withdrawal it was possible for her to see more sharply than those who were involved in the conventions of the day. Her letters, when they take cognizance of that world, are seasoned with salty commentary on characters and events. 'Mrs. S. [Sweetser] gets bigger,' she once wrote of a local dowager, 'and rolls down the lane to church like a reverend marble.' And a few years later the same lady called forth this sally: 'There is that which is called an "awakening" in the church, and I know of no choicer ecstasy than to see Mrs. S. roll out in crape every morning, I suppose to intimidate antichrist; at least it would have that effect on me.' Congratulating a friend whose son had just passed his oral examinations at the Columbia University Law School, she said: 'I am glad if Theodore balked the Professors— Most such are Manikins, and a warm blow from a brave Anatomy hurls them into Wherefores.' Outmoded evangelists, pompous men of affairs, the financiers responsible for the panic of 1873, all were touched off wittily for her correspondents.

So with current happenings in the world around her. When several fires broke out in succession at Amherst she indulged in a fanciful description of one, and then remarked drily: 'The fire-bells are oftener now, almost, than the church-bells. Thoreau would wonder which did the most harm.' Her capacity for ruthless comedy was given play in a quip at sensational journalism sent to a friend on the editorial staff of a newspaper: 'Who writes those funny accidents, where railroads meet each other unexpectedly, and gentlemen in factories get their heads cut off quite informally? The author, too, relates them in such a sprightly way, that they are quite attractive.' The great American spectacle that entertains old and young was given a miniature immortality by her quick pen: 'Friday I tasted life. It was a vast morsel. A circus passed the house— still I feel the red in my mind though the drums are out.'

Some of this found its way into her poetry. Like the wits of an earlier age, Dickinson found amusement in the passing scene and recorded some of its follies and pretensions in sparkling light verse. This has been largely neglected because of a proper concern with her grander poems on universal themes and because of the assumption that a recluse could know but little of the life around her. When her satires on contemporary America are read as a group, however, they offer an unexpected variety of comment on society and form an entertaining part of her 'letter to the World.' Her portrait gallery of village and national types comprises a fairly wide range: hollow men and hedonists, lost drunkards who 'cannot meet a Cork/Without a Revery,' urbane but shallow bankers, gossips and genteel females, several types of preachers and that man of the 'Apalling Trade,' the undertaker. When she turned to the artificial lives of the fashionable ladies of the day, to take just one example, her satiric vision came into focus sharply:

> What Soft— Cherubic Creatures—
> These Gentlewomen are—
> One would as soon assault a Plush—
> Or violate a Star—

Such Dimity Convictions—
A Horror so refined
Of freckled Human Nature—
Of Deity— ashamed—

It's such a common— Glory—
A Fisherman's— Degree—
Redemption— Brittle Lady—
Be so— ashamed of Thee—

On the surface she praises her feminine contemporaries in the conventional vocabulary of gentility. They are angelic and chaste, refined and lady-like. But these are mere manikin words to be knocked down. Indeed the whole organization of the poem is one of words in conflict. Almost every phrase is a pairing of opposites, and the over-all structure is coiled like a snake with its tail in its mouth. As cherubs these creatures are so soft they fail in the primary function of their sex. Nothing could dull the edge of desire like encountering velvet upholstery instead of a woman's flesh, though there is irony in the fact that 'Plush' suggests something not only soft but yielding. One is reminded of the devastating criticism of W.D. Howells' novels, that none of his heroines had bodies and none of his heroes seemed to notice the lack. Here it is tauntingly noted that the lack is so apparent they will never attract a seducer. Even worse, though the lusts of an American Lovelace might be kindled by a charming innocence, they would be dissipated by the cold virginal remoteness of a 'Star.'

From the erotic overtones of the opening stanza there is an unexpected turn at the end to spiritual concerns. The soft cherubs who missed out on seduction are transformed into ladies so brittle they have lost their chance of redemption, with an amusing reversal from angels on earth to ladies in heaven. There is no real inconsistency in the shift of attributes, however, for 'Soft' was applied to their mortal part and 'Brittle' to their souls. Salvation is not an exclusive 'Glory' but a common one, she reminds them, not the inherited rank of the élite but the 'Degree' conferred upon the lowly. The first to attain it, under the Christian dispensation, were those apostles nearest to Christ, not gentlemen but 'Fishermen.' For it is clearly the incarnate deity, he who consorted with thieves and harlots, of whom these ladies are 'ashamed.' In consequence 'Redemption' is ashamed of them, that is, the union of human and divine in the person of the Redeemer condemns their pretensions. His words of censure reverberate through the poem, for those familiar with the Bible: 'Whosoever therefore shall be ashamed of me . . . , of him also shall the Son of man be ashamed, when he cometh in the glory of his Father.'

The root of their troubles, heavenly and earthly, is their artificiality, as the central stanza makes vividly clear. They are so 'refined' they have a 'Horror' of being human, for human nature is 'freckled,' both in the sense of those blemishes on the skin against which their elegant parasols are their only protection and in the sense of moral imperfections against which they are protected by a sheltered life. Under such a code how could their 'Convictions,' their deepest beliefs and their strongest opinions, be anything but 'Dimity'—that light and dainty cotton stuff which symbolizes the demure Victorian maiden. What makes this poem memorable is the dexterity with which the lack of fundamental values like earthly and heavenly love are symbolized in terms of the genteel female as portrayed in the fashion magazines of the day, the manikin of *Godey's Lady's Book.*

The America of her day with its naive idealisms and blind belief in materialism offered many targets for the social satirist, and some of her light verse was aimed at these—abolitionism, balloon ascensions, the proliferation of journalism, the triviality of most messages sent over the newly invented telegraph. Her cartoon of the railway train, the most spectacular symbol of progress in that age, will serve to illustrate her talents in this line. It was the one great enthusiasm in the life of Squire Dickinson. He was a leading spirit in founding the Amherst-Belchertown Railroad, and the success of his project filled the household with excitement. By April of 1852 gangs of Irish laborers had begun work and clusters of little 'shantees' had sprung up along the proposed route. About a year later the line was formally opened with a nineteen-gun salute from the Amherst Artillery, and a train of three cars drawn by 'a comical little engine' made the twenty-mile run in fifty-five minutes, 'glory enough for one day' as her father commented. But her tendency to withdraw from all such events was already marked. When a delegation of Connecticut citizens celebrated the establishment of the new road by coming up to pay a 'morning call' on Amherst the next month, she reported to her brother: 'Father was as usual, Chief Marshal of the day, and went marching around the town with New London at his heels like some old Roman General, upon a Triumph Day. . . . They all said t'was fine. I spose it was— I sat in Prof Tyler's woods and saw the train move off, and then ran home again for fear somebody would see me.'

Instead of participating in the gala occasion itself, she staged a private celebration in her mind, embodied ten years later in a bright piece of wit:

> I like to hear it lap the Miles—
> And lick the Valleys up—
> And stop to feed itself at Tanks—
> And then— prodigious step
>
> Around a Pile of Mountains—
> And supercilious peer
> In Shanties— by the sides of Roads—
> And then a Quarry pare
>
> To fit its Ribs—
> And crawl between
> Complaining all the while
> In horrid— hooting stanza—
> Then chase itself down Hill—
>
> And neigh like Boanerges—
> Then— punctual as a Star
> Stop— docile and omnipotent
> At its own stable door—

The comedy is achieved by levying on every known syntactical device for speed. There is only one predication, completed in the first five monosyllables: 'I like to hear it.' All the rest is a series of infinitives activating the unnamed object: lap-lick, stop-step, peer-pare, crawl-chase, neigh-stop—all alliterating humorously except the last two pairs, but even so the final 'stop' goes back to the first to complete the circle. In addition to the cumulative effect of seven *ands* and four *thens,* many of the lines are run-on, most striking being the enjambment of stanzas ('step/ Around a' and 'pare/To fit its') which interlaces the first twelve lines in one breathless chase. It rushes madly over the miles, across valleys, around mountains, and downhill to home, not a depot but a stable. (The terminal of the new railroad, incidentally, had been domesticated for her by being built on the Dickinson Meadow, land formerly owned by her grandfather.)

For this is not a locomotive but a fabulous horse, described as 'prodigious,' 'supercilious,' 'complaining,' 'horrid,' and finally by the paradoxical 'docile and omnipotent.' The epithet 'iron horse,' already too hackneyed for her fastidious pen, is given a new humorous twist by the simile that brings the wild ride to an end, setting the last stanza properly apart: 'And neigh like Boanerges.' Instead of one of the horses of mythology, she chooses the figurative name 'Son of Thunder' bestowed by Jesus on two of his apostles because of their fiery zeal. In connection with launching the Amherst and Belchertown Railroad, she had heard plenty of loud-mouthed vociferous orators (the derived meaning of 'Boanerges') with much talk of opening up the hinterland and tying the towns together in prosperous trade. To her father railroads symbolized the beginning of a new era, but in her poem there is no suggestion of the standard nineteenth-century praise of material progress. There are no passengers or freight on her train, and no meaningful route; it simply roars around its circuit and then comes docilely home. This is her ironic tribute to modern science, which invents machines of monstrous power yet firmly controlled, here serving no purpose but her own amusement. Even Thoreau, the age's sharpest critic of economic materialism, was more romantic when he described the iron horse in *Walden,* though some of his imagery may have caught her eye. But her Son of Thunder is purely humorous. It was probably inspired as much by a prank of her brother as by her father's darling project. In the family reminiscences one may read:

> Austin loved excitement, and liked to drive down the Main Street from his law office with his horse going at racing speed, reins lying loose, turning in on one wheel at the old gate, and never slackening the pace till the flaring nostrils of the proud animal hit the carriage-house door: a bit of domestic circus for Emily's especial benefit, should she chance to be near the window, where her hand seldom failed its flash of salute.

Speed for its own sake, whether in horse of flesh or iron, provoked her sense of comedy.

Emily Dickinson had far different journeys to make than trains could take her on. Her withdrawal was deliberate, because solitude was indispensable for a poet dedicated to the inner world. The world of men and affairs serves her serious poetry only as a source of metaphor. In her quest for complete detachment she discovered, one by one, that no institution could hold her. So it was that by very reason of her greatness as a spiritual pioneer she felt it necessary to unchurch herself, just as Blake had done in the preceding century. The state of organized religion in her time and place led her to carry on an old tradition and dissent from the dissenters, though as a lone striker she was unable to make common cause with the main line of religious revolt available to her, New England Transcendentalism.

Her own unique religion is worked out affirmatively in the best of her serious poems, as will be seen in the succeeding chapters. But her detachment from the current orthodoxy was accomplished by her wit, which only the literal-minded will find sacrilegious. The glib piety of conventional church members, for example, she gave as one of the reasons for her withdrawal from society: 'Of "shunning Men and Women"– they talk of Hallowed things, aloud– and embarrass my Dog.' For her such matters could never be encompassed by the formulas of prose, only by the indirection of poetry. Of her own family she wrote: 'They are religious– except me– and address an Eclipse, every morning– whom they call their "Father".' As with St. Paul who saw God as a blinding flash of light and Jonathan Edwards who delighted to lie low in the dust before the splendor of His majesty, the anthropomorphic conception of deity seemed inadequate, hilariously so to her. But her declaration ('They are religious– except me'), when applied to one who faced creation with a primal sense of awe, can only be taken as ironic inversion on the grand scale.

None of the creeds or churches of her day satisfied her. After pretending to be frightened by 'an awful sermon' on Doomsday and the fate of sinners, she commented flatly in an early letter: 'The subject of perdition seemed to please him, somehow.' To such a hellfire preacher she devoted a whole poem, some lines of which have the smell of brimstone about them still. 'He stuns you by degrees,' she wrote, and then working up to his climax hurls one 'Imperial' thunderbolt 'That scalps your naked Soul.' Though she nimbly eluded the lightning of these old-line Calvinists, she could give credit to the dramatic intensity of their faith. But this emphasis on the divine wrath of Jehovah is probably what she had in mind when she said, 'I believe the love of God may be taught not to seem like bears.' Nor was the solution to be found at the other extreme in the unctuous modern liberal who 'preached upon "Breadth" till it argued him narrow.' She etched him in acid—a 'liar' and 'counterfeit,' not true gold but 'Pyrites' or Fool's Gold, for he was merely a secular moralist and not religious at all.

She solved the problem in a highly personal way, according to a pair of gaily irreverent verses. The early one begins:

> Some keep the Sabbath going to Church—
> I keep it, staying at Home—
> With a Bobolink for a chorister—
> And an Orchard, for a Dome—...

Twenty years later she carried her schism of fowls further. This time the same chorister of her outdoor-church 'overturned the Decalogue' and wrecked the poem too, but from the unfinished manuscript one can salvage such phrases as, 'Gay from an unannointed Twig/He gurgled— Let us pray.' By such blasphemy he boldly interrupted the meeting of the 'Presbyterian Birds' who were just opening the Sabbath 'in their afflictive Way.' To take this as advocating a return to natural religion would certainly betray lack of a sense of humor. It was simply part of her playful satire on a church that needed revitalizing. By the end of her life she had come a long way from those Presbyterian (or, rather, Congregational) birds down at the First Parish Meeting House.

In similar fashion she poked the Scriptures to make them come alive. The Bible was one of her chief sources of imagery and of truth but, as with all original religious thinkers, only when she could test it against her own experience and rewrite it in her own language. One way of achieving a fresh approach was through wit, especially for the Old Testament, which even by her day was coming to be felt as dead weight by the modern Christian. Her excuse for a series of bantering poems on sacred themes was her desire to reinterpret them for youth. 'It is a criminal thing to be a boy in a godly village,' she once remarked. Her nephew Ned, who seems to have resented starchy piety as much as she, formed a symbolic audience for her most outrageously mocking verses.

On one occasion, when he was confined at home by illness, she sent him as a substitute for the College Chapel exercises he was missing her 'Diagnosis of the Bible, by a Boy':

The Bible is an antique Volume—
Written by faded Men
At the suggestion of Holy Spectres—
Subjects— Bethlehem—
Eden— the ancient Homestead—
Satan— the Brigadier—
Judas— the Great Defaulter—
David— the Troubadour—
Sin— a distinguished Precipice
Others must resist—
Boys that 'believe' are bastinadoed
Other Boys are 'lost'—
Had but the Tale a warbling Teller—
All the Boys would come—
Orpheus' Sermon captivated—
It did not condemn—

Near the end of her life she said: 'The Fiction of "Santa Claus" always reminds me of the reply to my early question of "Who made the Bible"— "Holy Men moved by the Holy Ghost," and though I have now ceased my investigations, the Solution is insufficient.' The point of her attack is not the Old Testament but its expounders. 'Had but the Tale a warbling Teller,' she wrote, the younger generation might be saved. In the rough draft she set down thirteen variants—'thrilling,' 'spacious,' 'breathless,' 'magic,' and so on—before she hit upon 'warbling.'

In her retelling of the old stories she would captivate like Orpheus. Of Eve in the Garden of Eden she wrote:

The Garment of Surprise
Was all our timid Mother wore
At Home— in Paradise

Like Milton she had to give Satan his due, 'Because he has ability'; if he could only give up perfidy he would be 'durably divine.' As if she were planning a complete new version of the Bible, she reworked the climactic dramas of many of the old heroes and villains to suit modern needs: Abraham, Moses, Belshazzar, Jacob, and others. Toward the whole problem of the supernatural she habitually took a shrewd stand, neither accepting nor rejecting. So with her rendering of the famous account in the second Book of Kings, 'And . . . behold, there appeared a chariot of fire, and horses of fire . . . ; and Elijah went up by a whirlwind into heaven':

> Elijah's Wagon knew no thill
> Was innocent of Wheel
> Elijah's horses as unique
> As was his vehicle—
>
> Elijah's journey to portray
> Expire with him the skill
> Who justified Elijah
> In feats inscrutable—

The substitution of a New England farm wagon for the fiery chariot intrudes a note of homely realism, in traditional Puritan style. That Elijah got to heaven in such a vehicle, deprived of both wheel and driving shaft ('thill'), calls forth the laconic comment that his horsepower must have been 'unique.' To portray such a marvelous journey the modern writer has no skill; only the ancient chronicler could justify such an 'inscrutable' feat. If you do not believe it, she says, there it is in the Bible, 'authorized' (her variant word for 'justified').

Once, referring to their mother's shock at some unorthodox conversation between herself and her brother, Emily Dickinson said: 'I don't know what she would think if she knew Austin told me confidentially "there was no such person as Elijah." . . . She forgets that we are past "Correction in Righteousness".' What gives the bite to her satire in the poem is the strong sense of a lost faith that lies behind the doubting. 'On subjects of which we know nothing,' she said near the end of her life, 'we both believe and disbelieve a hundred times an Hour, which keeps Believing nimble.' Lacking such a center of tension, Holmes could make of 'The Wonderful One Hoss Shay' only a light piece of entertainment for the sophisticated. Dickinson's verse satires on the Bible were also *jeux d'esprit,* but they served a significant purpose as methods of detaching herself from a literal reading of the authorized text so as to make its truth and its poetry available to her as an artist. It would be a mistake, however, to give them undue weight as positive components of her religious belief. Her poems on themes of universal import—love and death, despair and immortality, nature and art—were to be her new scriptures.

Yet even on these 'flood subjects' she, saw the value of sharpening her perceptions by means of wit. Her lighter exercises on these themes are scattered among the serious in the following chapters, even as they were among her manuscript fascicles, to leaven the whole. Here it will suffice to glance at one that satirizes conventional prosody, the last institution of the contemporary world from which she felt it necessary to detach herself. Her early letters to Higginson, a fusillade of double-edged queries and comments on esthetic theory, form a prelude to her poem. She had been led to seek him out as a preceptor by reading his 'Letter to a Young Contributor' in the *Atlantic Monthly,* where he offered advice on such matters as the need to achieve correct form and 'to cut and contrive a decent *clothing of style.*' His criticisms of her first batch of poems can be inferred from her reply:

> Thank you for the surgery— it was not so painful as I supposed. . . .
> While my thought is undressed— I can make the distinction, but
> when I put them in the Gown— they look alike, and numb.

Higginson's taste in prosodic gowns was clearly old-fashioned, and her experimental creations apparently shocked him. He could only instruct her on how to cut them to fit the decent and correct.

After a. few exchanges, realizing she already had a fully formed esthetic mode that gave life and originality to her thought, she thanked him for his lessons and went her own way. What had begun as a sincere request for counsel soon turned to a game of wits. In her fifth letter saying meekly, 'Are these more orderly?' she enclosed a poem that scored her point:

> I cannot dance upon my Toes—
> No Man instructed me—
> But oftentimes, among my mind,
> A Glee possesseth me,
>
> That had I Ballet knowledge—
> Would put itself abroad
> In Pirouette to blanch a Troupe—
> Or lay a Prima, mad,

And though I had no Gown of Gauze—
No Ringlet, to my Hair,
Nor hopped for Audiences— like Birds,
One Claw upon the Air,

Nor tossed my shape in Eider Balls,
Nor rolled on wheels of snow
Till I was out of sight, in sound,
The House encore me so—

Nor any know I know the Art
I mention— easy— Here—
Nor any Placard boast me—
It's full as Opera—

By using the artifice of the classical ballet as a figure for the artificiality of conventional verse, she could make her point without being unkind to her pretended tutor. The surface comedy is one of logic, by setting the grammar at war with the meaning. The first stanza is a flat statement of the novice's ignorance, filled with inspiration but lacking any formal instruction. The rest of the poem is a maze of conditions and concessions contrary to fact, illustrating what she would do if she had 'Ballet knowledge.' But in the very act of making these denials she proves herself highly conversant with all the basic devices and techniques of the ballet. She begins with the initial stance *au point* ('upon my Toes'), followed by the familiar turn or 'Pirouette,' the only technical term actually used. Then comes the *extension* ('One Claw upon the Air,' grotesque yet graceful 'like Birds'), the leap or *entrechat* ('tossed my shape in Eider Balls'), and finally the whipped turn or *fouetté* ('rolled on wheels of snow') that carries her off the stage to deafening shouts of 'encore.' Such expert ballet knowledge seems almost incredible for one who had apparently never seen even an interlude at the Opera, the strokes also pictorial enough to conjure up the whole portfolio of Degas' sketches. And the milieu of the performance is vividly rendered too: the theater with its applauding audience, the stylized coiffure and *tutu* ('Ringlets' and 'Gown of Gauze'), the *corps de ballet* supporting the *première danseuse,* not forgetting the all-important billing ('Placard boast me').

What transpires, with fine irony, is that she does know 'the Art' she refers to so glibly here, though no one is aware because she is a private artist performing for herself and because even when she invites an audience of one, like Higginson, he is incapable of recognizing her radical new departure as art. She could easily perform the classical ballet that would bring applause from him and the public, but her compelling urge to dance springs from her discontent with this style that has become lifeless after a century of ritual repetition. What form of modern ballet she will have to create in order to express it is not the subject of this poem, rather the conventional form she is rejecting as inadequate. But there is more here than meets the superficial eye.

The key word to the submerged meaning, proving that her wit is directed at poetic instead of dance techniques, is 'Glee.' In Anglo-Saxon times the glee-man was the bard, chanting his poems to the accompaniment of a harp. Today 'glee,' when used at all, refers chiefly to merriment or to collegiate singing groups whose purpose is entertainment. But her dictionary still preserved the distinction between old and new meanings, specifying: '*Anciently*, music or minstrelsy generally.' Though something of the connotation of merry jesting is appropriate to her satiric intent, her emphasis is on the ancient concept of bardic inspiration as indicated by her old-fashioned verb form, 'A Glee possesseth me.' As such a possessed artist, she need only find the adequate techniques of rendering in order 'to blanch a Troupe– /Or lay a Prima, mad,' and to startle the audience out of its complacency till their encores transport her 'out of sight, in sound.' Meantime *among* my mind'—the bizarre idiom suggesting the completeness with which she is possessed—'It's full as Opera.' This concluding line is in apposition with the only other independent predication in the poem (the opening one, 'A Glee possesseth me'), making a kind of frame around the dance stanzas. So one is even tempted to the extravagance of finding in it a Latin pun, the *opera* being her own 'works' she is filled with, the poems she would send abroad if she only had the technical knowledge. The final jest is that her lament of ignorance is itself a highly skilled performance in her own unique idiom.

In prosodic form, as in all else, she had a compulsion to make it new. None of the contemporary molds were fit containers. The patterns elaborated by the Romantic poets were too ornate for her, and by the middle of the century they had lost the impulse that had given them validity in the first place, the need to break from the formal limitations of the heroic couplet. Her need was just as great to break with this rich profusion which had become an end in itself. She and Whitman and Hopkins were the three great experimenters of the age, searching for new forms, or mutations of old ones, in order to discover the meanings of their visions. Unknown to each other, they were kindred spirits only in the radicalism of their experiments. By common agreement today, it is unthinkable to separate form from content in Whitman and Hopkins. So it should be with Dickinson, her poetic mode being one with her meanings.

Perhaps the finest stroke of her wit was the choice of Common Hymn Meter as her basic pattern, a point of departure and return. She had heard hundreds in church like the familiar:

> God moves in a mysterious way,
> His wonders to perform;
> He plants his footsteps in the sea,
> And rides upon the storm.

Though the form went back at least three hundred years before her day as the standard in English hymnology, it offered the immediate advantage of novelty, since no poet had ever exploited it fully as a serious verse form. Even its rude simplicity could be turned into a vehicle of surprise by making it carry the burden of novel and intricate ideas instead of the platitudes of faith. Choosing such a primitive lute for her sophisticated devotionals was characteristic of her strategy. For most of her poems, too, were hymns in their own special way. Not traditional anthems swelling the cathedral vault nor pious psalms entuned in a Puritan nose, but the thin pipings of praise that were still possible for an estranged modern religious sensibility, diminished, tangential, sometimes actually canceled by doubt. That she consciously chose poetry as her medium of religious expression seems sufficiently indicated by the sentence introducing some consolatory verses, far from orthodox, sent to her Norcross cousins on the death of their father in 1863: 'Let Emily sing for you because she cannot pray.'

Though her structure was that of the Protestant hymn, she apparently knew also of the antiphonal form used in the medieval hymn and in Catholic and High Church services today, often putting it to work in special ways. In some of her poems affirmations by a sort of 'choir' are achieved in passages that echo the language of the Psalms or of Isaac

Watts' spiritual songs; these are then followed by the 'responses' of the poet, like a heretical priest or apostate believer, questioning, commenting ironically on, even denying, the affirmations. Knowing her natural motion towards unorthodoxy and alienation, she adopted the standard form of devotional music as a constant check and balance to her searching mind. Though she transmutes it from the ritual hymn in celebration of an accepted creed, it is always there in the background of the reader's consciousness as a point from which to measure the spiritual adventures of a schismatic soul.

The same stanza, of course, had another sub-literary history even older than the hymn, emerging from obscurity in the late Middle Ages as the popular ballad of England and Scotland.

> Alake and alas now, good master,
> For I fear a deidly storm;
> For I saw the new moon late yestreen,
> And the auld moon in her arms.

Here again this narrow vessel had been made the container of elemental human emotions, brusquely tragic or comic. Though rarely adopting the ballad's narrative structure, she took advantage of some of its qualities: the strong colloquial idioms, the roughened meters and proximate rhymes, and especially the swift climactic movement that overleaped sequences in its passion for conciseness. She eschewed the imitative 'literary ballad,' so attractive to poets during the past hundred years, but the spirit of early balladry is often present as an effective referent in her poems. Finally, there was a third sub-literary use of this stanza that may have had implications for her, the Mother Goose Rhymes popular since the seventeenth and eighteenth centuries.

> Sing a Song of Six-pence,
> A pocket full of Rye;
> Four and twenty Blackbirds
> Baked in a Pie.

Under their guise of nonsense lurked the suggestion of long-buried folk wisdom, irrecoverable by the modern mind. Her humorous poems frequently adopt a similar air of droll fable, throwing the reader off-guard with their nursery style, then offer the pleasant surprise of real meanings rising from their nonsensical meters.

The immediate analogue for her chosen prosodic form, however, was the Common Hymn Meter familiar to her from childhood. This rudimentary quatrain consisted of iambic lines, of four and three stresses alternately, with only the second and fourth rhyming. As worked out in the measures of Watts, a copy of whose *Christian Psalmody* was readily available in her father's library, there were other stanza forms with richer rhyme schemes, as in the Common Particular (*aabccb*), and numerous variations on these, by dropping syllables at the line ends or by reversing the accentual pattern so as to change iambic feet into trochaic. Her bold experimentations out from this center would have dismayed the formal precisionists from whose pious hymns she took her start. She avoided monotony by playing every conceivable change on these basic tunes, breaking and reshaping foot, line, and stanza until she could escape at will from her self-imposed strait jacket. More importantly, she achieved endless effects of high significance by her radical innovations, substituting silences for sounds, crowding emphatic monosyllables together, setting meaning-accents against metric-accents with subtle accommodations between the two, and so on. She created 'a counterpoint or descant on Watts,' as one recent critic has summed it up.

In her best poems she made the form so completely her own that the singsong of the traditional hymn has been absorbed into a flexible modern instrument of infinite skills. The reader, having been reminded of the origins of her prosody, should keep them subliminal and not prejudge her form by them nor pretend to admire her poetry while deploring the stiff limitations of her models. For a poet's uniqueness can only discover itself in techniques as original as the thoughts and feelings seeking embodiment. Her epigram on the oneness of form and content is another example of her skill in transmuting the basic quatrain, as well as a shining illustration of its own proposition:

> The pattern of the sun
> Can fit but him alone
> For sheen must have a Disk
> To be a sun—

She had found the disk to fit her sheen. It is true that Herbert and Marvell had occasionally redeemed the hymnology of Sternhold and Hopkins into true spiritual songs, Coleridge had made a startling success of the literary ballad, Lear and Carroll among her contemporaries were turning the nonsense rhyme into classics. But only Emily Dickinson transformed the primitive quatrain into a new mode of poetry, making it wholly her own as others had done with blank verse and the couplet.

Just as she opened out the manifold metric possibilities of this sup-posedly limited form, so she explored ways to vary and supplement its simple music. To the exact rhyming decreed by her heritage she added assonance, consonance, identical and suspended rhymes. These sound effects had been occasionally used in the sub-literary verse from which she derived her prosody, but they had never before been brought into orthodox English poetry as a principal mode of rhyming. Higginson was simply responding conventionally when he advised her to drop rhymes altogether if she could not make them perfect. In her reply she thanked him for his 'justice' but added, 'I . . . could not drop the Bells whose jingling cooled my Tramp.' Her phrasing is unnecessarily cryptic, but it at least reveals that her peculiar music was a deliberate device, rather than the failure of a bad ear, and that she was determined to con-tinue her pioneering with verbal 'Bells.' Exact correspondences of sound could not convey the dissonances that reached her ears from a fractured universe, though she could use them in moments of renewed faith or as ironic musical symbols of a world whose orderliness was illusory. The partial or tangential echo more nearly fit the steady tensions of her doubts and beliefs. Nor was there any pre-emptive sanction for her in limiting the music of verse to end sounds, or even to supplement these by internal exact rhymes and conventional alliteration, the standard sound effects available to her. Instead she experimented with initial reiteration, par-allelism, and the mingling of prose rhythms with poetic, like Whitman; and especially with complex alliteration, those intricate patterns of vowel and consonant tones strewn through the line that Hopkins is famous for and that another contemporary experimenter, Sidney Lanier, tried to find a technical name for, 'phonetic syzygy.'

A final analysis of Dickinson's poetry in terms of the sense of sound, or the 'sound of sense' as Frost has phrased it, will have to await the formulation of a more precise esthetics of verse music. But just how con-scious she was of its importance and the need for a new phonetics can be shown in a final example of her wit. Obviously in parody of that use of mellifluousness for its own sake which oversweetens much Victorian verse, she wrote her tribute to the starry heavens in the form of a musical joke:

> Lightly stepped a yellow star
> To its lofty place
> Loosed the Moon her silver hat
> From her lustral Face
> All of Evening softly lit
> As an Astral Hall
> Father I observed to Heaven
> You are punctual—

All the contrived sound effects of such poems as Tennyson's 'Lotos-Eaters' and lines like 'The moan of doves in immemorial elms' are levied upon to build up an aura of romantic loveliness. The first six lines form an intricate sequence of sibilants and liquids culminating in two highly poetic words, 'lustral' and 'astral.' But the latter is merely pretentious for 'starry' and the former is actually meaningless as applied to the moon's 'Face,' for what has it or this poem to do with ceremonial purification? (And what is its 'silver hat'?—the nimbus resulting from the diffraction of its light through vapor, held by farmers to be a sign of rain on the morrow?) Altogether they accomplish nothing but an elaboration of the pictorial, something quite foreign to her concise idiom.

Instead these lines, comprising nearly the entire poem, are simply foils for her strategy of wit. At the highest reach of her construct of artful loveliness, she topples the whole with a bald observation in prose, using the technique of incongruity she probably learned from the frontier tall tale. She congratulates the heavenly lamplighter for being on time, as though He were Squire Dickinson illuminating the parlor at the end of the day or the village lamplighter going his menial rounds. 'Punctual' not only describes the most trivial of human virtues but goes back to echo the resonance of her euphemism for heaven, 'Astral Hall,' the forced accent on its last syllable ('punctuál') only adding to the comedy.

This word, incidentally, is the only one in the poem that has significance in the way she normally employs verbal meaning, to complicate the issues. All the rest are either sham sonorities or simple denotations of the obvious. But 'punctual' explodes the poem with its connotations, applied as they are with a deliberate confounding of scale. For this is necessarily an earthly rather than a celestial word, meaningful only within the limitations of mortal time. In the heavenly halls the stars always shine; only for man can they appear to be alternately lit and extinguished. Punctual cannot apply to God, existing in eternity. Yet the rotating earth, like the circular motions of this poem from *l* to *s* and back again, creates the illusion that He punctures the black canopy of night with points of light according to a clock schedule. Her satire is aimed not at God, but at man's imperfect view of Him and the folly of trying to reach heaven through pretentious sounds. The ingenuity of her wit is demonstrated by making this point largely through the music of her words rather than their meaning. Her cosmic dislocation of values is rendered by her abrupt change of key from the sonorous to the flat and back to the sonorous again in her final comic word, which composes the whole into a musical joke.

All these maneuverings of sound and meter, of words and ideas and attitudes, were devices of the wit by which she created her poetic self. By means of them she also fashioned the unique idiom for her finest work, though the specimens so far considered were simply finger exercises for the developing poet. She well knew the difference between light verse and the higher uses of wit. She put this in a pair of quatrains, themselves boldly experimental, that bring this introduction to a fitting close and lead directly into a reading of her serious poems:

> We play at Paste—
> Till qualified, for Pearl—
> Then, drop the Paste—
> And deem ourself a fool—
>
> The Shapes— though— were similar—
> And our new Hands
> Learned *Gem*-Tactics—
> Practicing *Sands*—

2

WORDS

'For several years,' wrote Emily Dickinson of the period just prior to her first great outburst of poetic creation, 'my Lexicon– was my only companion.' This ambiguous reply to Higginson's query about her friends led him to emphasize the wrong half of her meaning. He could only be touched by the pathos of her lonely life. The possibility would not have occurred to him that for the poet, as distinguished from the person, a dictionary could be far more valuable than society. As a woman she was well aware that deprivation in life might be one of the pressures that produced art. Referring to some crisis, either a loss through death or the denial of love's feast, she could describe the verbal substitute as a dry wine: 'Easing my famine/At my Lexicon.' But as a poet she knew that words were the only medium of her art, like colors to the painter and notes to the composer. They are the molds which give form to the thoughts and things of experience. Indeed, experience is without meaning until it finds its identity in words. She would have applauded Auden's quip: 'How can I know what I think till I see what I say?' The reason we can never learn on earth to know each other, she wrote, is that only heaven can provide the vocabulary for that most buried secret, which puzzles us here 'Without the lexicon.' With it, words can become instruments of knowledge. A number of her poems are explicitly concerned with the power and the problems of language.

The declaration that during the crucial years her 'Lexicon' was her only companion occurs in the context of a letter exclusively concerned with her intellectual and poetic development. Looked at from the stand-point of art rather than biography it takes on an importance that cannot be treated lightly, even though it should not be interpreted too literally. She thumbed unweariedly her great copy of Webster's *American Dictionary of the English Language* in the enlarged edition of 1847, referred to hereafter as her Lexicon. But she had other sources of language. One was the vocabulary in action she absorbed from her reading. She ranged widely among books but selected with fine discrimination, as shown by her characterization of those most useful to her.

Of some book, presumably the Bible, she said: 'Should you ask me my comprehension of a starlight Night, Awe were my only reply, and so of the mighty Book— It stills, incites, infatuates— blesses and blames in one. . . . A Word is inundation, when it comes from the Sea.' Of the dramatic poet whom she knew by heart: 'While Shakespeare remains Literature is firm.' These were parts of the great lexicon from which she learned the way of words. The former was one of her chief sources of imagery, the latter her chief model in revitalizing language through new strategies. But her style was never Biblical or Shakespearean, as with writers like Melville. Instead of surface borrowings she plundered them outright, stealing the secrets by which they gave life and power to words, but transvaluating them so as to create an idiom all her own.

From the Bible she learned, among other things, the mode of juxta-posing elemental concrete things with equally fundamental ideas and feelings—grass, stone, heart, majesty, despair. But this method of achieving universality is given novelty by reducing the Bible's expansive narra-tive to startlingly compact lyrics. She rarely alludes to its stories and characters, except in the humorous poems, employing instead a subtler technique. Her stolen images, though sometimes overtly used, are nor-mally assimilated to her own style by being wrenched into unexpected contexts (as when the cross becomes the block on which the 'Auctioneer of Parting' brings his hammer down), or so submerged in her poems that only long peering below the surface reveals their allusive richness (as in two poems on the finding and losing of love, 'Mine by the Royal *Seal*' and 'Faith *bleats* to understand'). When she actually borrows any of its phrasings they are used as counters to be played against the rational terminology of science, just as she maneuvered the trite and sentimental against the iconoclastic. In fact, her battling with language is quite simi-lar to her skirmishes with the Bible, The Word, poking them both to make them come alive. She had heard enough sermons and hymns to know how inert these once great Scriptures could become in the hands of imitators, *The Bay Psalm Book* being a grim reminder. Perhaps these were the principal words on which she had been fed from childhood, and her revolt against them as theology was paralleled by her revolt against the language in which their doctrines were cast. In a sense, the Bible was the divine adversary she must overcome by assimilation in order to utter her own scriptures.

Her debt to Shakespeare was just as pervasive and even less visible. Poetic language in mid-nineteenth-century America had been reduced to a relatively flat and nerveless state, but he furnished her with clues for its resurrection. The major writers of the preceding generation had not only finished their careers but had brought the older way to a dead end. For a poet to come of age at such a time, as she did, may have been a handicap in that it deprived her of a living tradition within which or against which to work. But it also lessened the danger of derivativeness, such as had weighed so heavily on the writers following Milton, for example, and offered the advantage of challenge to original spirits. It would be interesting to inquire concerning such a bold experimenter with words whether her distinction does not derive from the very *élan* with which she drove forward out of the verbal doldrums in which she found herself. Shakespeare and the metaphysical poets wrought such miracles with language in the Renaissance, and Eliot and Pound took up a similar task in the twentieth century.

The devices all of them used to achieve 'semantic rejuvenation,' as pointed out recently by a distinguished linguist, sound like a summary of the techniques employed by a private New England poet in the 1860's. Etymology was one of them, sending the reader back to root meanings in order to force his participation in the esthetic experience. Here Dickinson is actually cited as a forerunner of modern poetic usage, but the other devices were part of her practice as well. Substitution of simple concrete terms for the abstract ones actually intended was her strategy for achieving vivid immediacy, and the opposite for giving transcendent value to the homely. Juxtaposition of words out of different connotative spheres she employed for ironic contrast, as with the legal and the amorous, and abrupt changes from one level of discourse to another for rhetorical shock, as from the serious to the comic, from eloquence to bald statement. Close kin to these are her rearrangements of word order

to secure emphasis and surprise, deliberately rather than through inept-
ness, often merely by exaggerating a familiar colloquial usage.

All these she probably learned from her great master. Two final devices are more recognizably Shakespearean. One is the shifting of grammatical categories (for example, 'pomp' as an adjective, 'create' as a
participle), by which she discovered forms that were both shortened and
novel. This gives a slightly archaic flavor to her verse that has been
objected to as affectation, but she would have justified her sparing use
of it, like Hopkins, as one of the admissible special 'graces' of the boldly
original poet. The other is her exploitation of punning, after centuries
of disrepute, not in a frivolous context but as the legitimate adjunct of
a superbly serious style. In thanking a friend for a happy pun she once
commented: 'How lovely are the wiles of Words.' No weighty pronouncement could express her kinship with the Elizabethans more effectively than this apparently casual remark.

When paying her ultimate tribute to Shakespeare she had asked, 'Why
is any other book needed?' but she did not mean this as abject surrender
to the great figure that loomed for her out of the literary past. For her
there was another book needed, one she was compelled to write, the
volume of her own poems. To do this she felt she had to vanquish another giant by trying to draw the strength of his mighty sword to her
pebble-sling. In suggesting how much she learned from this unequal
battle, there is no intention of setting up false comparisons. It is enough
to claim that her talent came to life by absorbing the revolutionary quality of her tradition in its most vital expression, without losing her indi-
viduality. So with the other books available to her. She searched them
for what they had to offer and absorbed their lessons, but was never
bookish. As a result, literary sources and analogues are the least fruitful
approaches to her poetry. She simply acted on Emerson's maxim, 'Imitation is suicide,' without any theorizing about artistic integrity other than
the quiet remark, 'I . . . never consciously touch a paint, mixed by another person.' If she ever went through any period of real apprenticeship
to any of her masters, no compositions indicating it have survived.

Another source of her poetic language was the particular idiom of
her heritage in the living speech of the Connecticut Valley. Some of her
special linguistic techniques sprang from native roots, and she under-
scored the importance of this by making it the conscious theme of several
poems. One of her devices for putting new life in the literary vocabulary

was to employ a fair sprinkling of homely and dialectal expressions. Though deplored by earlier editors who tried to purge her text of them (changing 'heft' to 'weight,' for example), it was deliberate, as proved by her defense of regionalism on general grounds as the truest mode of perception. So robin, nut, and winter in her poetry, 'Because I see— New Englandly,' she said, coining a wry adverb; had she been cuckoo born, she would sing like the British, for they too in their own way see 'provincially.' With none of the fanfare of professional literary nationalists like Whitman, she quietly set about exploring the poetic resources of the American language, including New England localisms, though she never limited herself to one vocabulary.

In Amherst she breathed an academic air as naturally as a rural one, and she adroitly played off the learned word against the simple Saxon for special effects in many poems. One illustration will make this clear. In contrasting the old-fashioned religious view with the newer one of science, she takes advantage of the historical composition of the English language, which has chiefly drawn from the classical tongues its speculative and technological words. The wit and irony of the following quatrain is wholly the result of this linguistic maneuvering:

> 'Faith' is a fine invention
> When Gentlemen can *see*—
> But *Microscopes* are prudent
> In an Emergency.

The faith of the fathers is rendered in the native language, the modern doubt in foreign borrowings.

The deliberateness of this contrast is shown in the skill with which she complicates the issues by throwing one unexpected Latinate word into the first line, so that faith becomes a mechanical thing; New Englanders, she is aware, had won fame as inventors, not only of things but of the Puritan theocracy. More subtly, she chooses as the defining word for microscopes that they are 'prudent.' This word means worldly wise, and is associated in American history with Benjamin Franklin, the great advocate of rational utility. But it also carried with it the medieval religious meaning of *prudens,* endowed with the capacity of perceiving divine truth. One of the best of the early Christian poets took the pen name of 'Prudentius,' and Puritan parents as well as clergy had kept the idea alive by christening their daughters Prudence. Science, then, furnishes the instrument for seeing.God? The final irony is in the use of 'Gentlemen,' deriving from both Latin and Saxon sources, hardly the word Cotton Mather would have used for the faithful. Does this suggest the decay of religion in her own day to a social propriety? We are not told what they see, nor what the 'Emergency' is when they must resort to microscopes. Any need for really seeing is an emergency, and in spiritual matters the crisis was particularly acute during the last half of the nineteenth century. The linguistic web is drawn tight, and the ambiguity heightened by deftly compressing the whole conflict between religion and science into sixteen words. But this is a word game, not a poem.

No child of the region ever exploited the laconic temperament so successfully in poetry. In striking contrast with the practice of her contemporaries is the brevity of her own forms, which she celebrated in an aphorism:

> Capacity to Terminate
> Is a Specific Grace—

This gift she developed into a highly elliptical style, pruning away all excess in her passion to get down to the clean bones of language. In a poem about writing a love letter the urgency of the message makes her impatient of verbosity and even the standard rules of construction:

> Tell Him— I only said the Syntax—
> And left the Verb and the pronoun out—

The lines also describe her own poetic way.

Another technique, thought of as peculiarly Dickinsonian, is of course the way of all poetry—by indirection. But the oblique approach, the sudden and unexpected turn, becomes such a pervasive habit as to constitute her unique mode of expression. 'Tell all the Truth but tell it slant,' she says, for it must be perceived and revealed gradually or it will dazzle into blindness. A passage in Emerson's 'Uriel' may have suggested the metaphor by which she justifies the circuitous approach:

> Too bright for our infirm Delight
> The Truth's superb surprise.

Slant and surprise, the distinctive marks of her best poetry, are the result of her brilliant verbal strategy. A kinship, rather than an influence, is revealed by the analogies that can be drawn from Emerson's *Poems,* one of her most cherished possessions being the copy given her in 1850 by the friend who first awakened her mind and creative powers. There she could have read, in 'Merlin' the archetypal poet, the best possible epigraph for her own poetic achievement:

> He shall aye climb
> For his rhyme....
> But mount to paradise
> By the stairway of surprise.

Concerned with expression from her earliest years, she is clearly referring to her need for freedom in finding her own voice when she complains in one of her poems: 'They shut me up in Prose.' 'They' were all the forces that militated against her being a poet. Living in a family of practical people and in an isolated community, she had little encouragement to leave the common-sense ways of prose. What she said of her father in a letter of 1851 could be applied to her environment as a whole, that he was too intent on 'real life' to have any interest in poetry. Similarly, at about the same time, she wrote to one of her few companions in wit and literature: '[We] please ourselves with the fancy that we are the only poets, and everyone else is *prose.*' Prose to her was limited, as the similes in the poem put it, like being shut up in a closet when a girl so she would be 'still,' or like putting a bird in prison. If they had only peeped and seen her 'brain go round,' she says, they would have known she had the madness of a poet who would not stay shut up in convention. The true singer breaks out of any prison, as the bird by an effort of will abolishes his captivity and sings. So she too, even in the letters which were virtually her only medium of expression until about the age of twenty-eight, broke out of the narrow limits of prose into poetic freedoms that make it hard to draw a line between her use of the two modes. 'They shut me up in Prose' may also refer to the conventional kind of verse her mentors urged upon her when she finally did venture into poetry. For this poem was written at the very end of 1862, after that first remarkable exchange with Higginson, the only letters in which they seriously discussed artistic problems. She soon put him down as another of those who would shut her up in prose, whom she must escape if she wanted to mount the stairway of surprise.

She extends the metaphor in another poem written the same month:

> I dwell in Possibility—
> A fairer House than Prose—
> More numerous of Windows—
> Superior— for Doors—

The house of poetry offers even more freedom for flights outward and upward than this; for the following stanzas add that its roof is the sky, its visitors 'the fairest' (the muses?), and the occupation of the one who dwells there: 'The spreading wide my narrow Hands/To gather Paradise.' This was somewhat less extravagant than her claim for the bird-poet in the preceding poem, who mounts up 'easy as a star' and laughs down upon the captivity of the prison house of prose. In a sequel, written two years later, she is concerned with pushing on beyond 'possibility' to 'impossibility,' which exhilarates like wine. Though the meaning is somewhat obscure, she seems to be saying that the 'faintest tincture' of impossibility put in a dram of possibility adds the ingredient of enchantment to the drink. These two poems go beyond mortal limits to supernal regions in the kind of too-easy flight she always at bottom distrusted. Yet even here, in the extravagance of her revolt against convention, this flight into ideal freedom is qualified by being frankly labeled 'impossibility.' Suppose, then, the poet is content to dwell in 'possibility'? When the hands reach out, not up, for Paradise they are described as 'narrow,' and the possibilities are limited by using the prospective form of an infinitive, 'to gather,' without expressing confidence that she will succeed.

The actual composition of poems, wrestling with the Angel of Philology, brought the proper sobering up. Her letters and verse make frequent reference to the inadequacies of language. Merely feeling gratitude too deep she writes: 'I can't thank you any more— . . . The old words are *numb*— and there *an't* any *new* ones.' Again, 'I . . . never try to lift the words which I cannot hold.' When the emotion is both overwhelming and too close, as after the death of her father, she can only say to those who venture consolation, 'it was too soon for language.' Distance and perspective can solve the problem sometimes, but there are emotions that defy communication: 'Speech is one symptom of Affection/And Silence one.' Again, there is a peak of ecstasy which, when she finds she cannot 'mould it into Word,' presents her with an insoluble dilemma; the furthest reach of beauty is 'a syllable-less Sea,' and when she tries to state its spell, 'My will endeavors for its word/And fails.' She consoles herself by observing that God himself has no tongue, 'His lisp– is Lightning– and the Sun–/His Conversation– with the Sea.' So with men, mightiest things assert themselves 'by intuitions, . . . not by terms.' These are the modest disclaimers of one who had remarkable success in finding words for almost all the subtle motions of the heart. More serious is the limitation implied in:

> I found the words to every thought
> I ever had– but One–

Though she does not name it, the simile employed suggests that it is heaven. It defies her, she says, as painting the sun would defy a race nurtured in the dark. So it is not just one thought that eludes words, but all mortal attempts to capture celestial truth.

Her own struggles in this direction are the subject of the following humorous verses:

> Shall I take thee, the Poet said
> To the propounded word?
> Be stationed with the Candidates
> Till I have further tried–
>
> The Poet probed Philology
> And when about to ring
> For the suspended Candidate
> There came unsummoned in–
>
> That portion of the Vision
> The Word applied to fill
> Not unto nomination
> The Cherubim reveal–

The special charm of this is that it re-enacts as a little comedy her own abandonment of numerous poems in the worksheet stage. The actors here are The Poet, The Words, The Muses (who fail her), and A Ghost (the original poetic vision). The stage props are a judge's bench, a lexicon, a summons bell, and the seats for the contending parties. The final touch is that this poem itself is unfinished, written in pencil, and with several unsummoned candidates at the bottom of the page, one of which would make line 4 read: 'Till I have *vainer* tried.' This reading implies that there are some visions beyond any poet's grasp: not even the angels can help the mortal name immortality. In any event, she relies upon 'Philology' rather than the 'Cherubim' when nominating words for election to her poems. This is at the opposite pole from Emerson's easy dismissal of the difficulties of poetic composition: 'When the soul of the poet has come to ripeness of thought, she detaches and sends away ... poems or songs.' Dickinson had more respect for the problems of technique.

The power of speech to move men's hearts both fascinated and appalled her:

> Could mortal lip divine
> The undeveloped Freight
> Of a delivered syllable
> 'Twould crumble with the weight.

She had heard some of the most effective evangelists of the day and some of its finest pulpit orators. There are many kinds of eloquence. Some words have special power through richness of connotation, and she sought them out for her poems: snow, Eden, circumference. 'Many a phrase has the English language,' she begins in a prosaic voice, but one is for her almost magical:

> Breaking in bright Orthography
> On my simple sleep—
> Thundering its Prospective—
> Till I stir, and weep—

The unspecified phrase, 'I love you,' is too filled with the power of life and death for her to name, but she cannot help crying, 'Say it again, Saxon! ... Only to me!'

The very potential of language, however, brings with it the danger of ambiguity, especially when written: 'a Pen has so many inflections and a Voice but one.' The great problem is to get the sound of sense into words that must live alone. Her special use of punctuation marks in the manuscripts, it has been pointed out, was probably an attempt to indicate the proper inflections. Certainly one must make every effort to read her poems with the right tune. Solemn critics have belabored some of them as mannered, through failure to realize how they should sound. For example, if one begins at a fairly high pitch and then descends chromatically, with a slight lift on the last word, 'I'll tell you how the Sun rose' becomes a deliberate fable, a fairy tale told to children about the wonder of daybreak. Fantasy of this sort is perfectly appropriate to light verse and is only infantile when it mars serious work. The sound is sometimes a key to the sense.

There is also the danger of over-saying or under-saying. Charging the frail vessels of written symbols exactly with their intended freight of meaning made composition, even in prose, seem little short of a miracle to her. 'A Letter always feels to me like immortality,' she declared, 'because it is the mind alone without corporeal friend. Indebted in our talk to attitude and accent, there seems a spectral power in thought that walks alone.' And again:

> What is it that instructs a hand lightly created, to impel shapes to eyes at a distance, which for them have the whole area of life or of death? Yet not a pencil in the street but has this awful power, though nobody arrests it. An earnest letter is or should be life-warrant or death-warrant, for what is each instant but a gun, harmless because 'unloaded,' but that touched 'goes off'?

A similar comment has survived in her rough drafts for two letters, each with variant phrasings, so that one can watch her touching the words to make them 'go off' with her exact meaning. On a scrap of paper there is a trial flight: 'What a Hazard a Letter is! When I think of the Hearts it has Cleft or healed I almost wince to lift my Hand to so much as a Superscription.' A few days later she revised this observation when writing the first draft of a letter to another correspondent: 'What a hazard an Accent is! When I think of the Hearts it has scuttled or sunk, I Hardly dare to raise my voice to so much as a Salutation > I almost fear to lift my Hand to so much as a punctuation.' Her letters were often as carefully wrought compositions as her poems.

These statements of belief in the power of language, made late in life, reveal the urgency of her queries to Higginson when she first sent him some of her poetry for criticism. Is it 'alive'? she asked. 'Should you think it breathed, . . . I should feel quick gratitude.' The point is expanded to form part of an unusually interesting poem:

A Word that breathes distinctly
Has not the power to die
Cohesive as the Spirit
It may expire if He—

The kind of life true poetry has is emphasized by the play on 'Spirit'
and 'expire,' as well as by the immortality implied in the understatement: the poem is no more subject to death than the soul is. The idea is
taken one step further in a verse aphorism incorporated in one of her
letters:

A word is dead, when it is said
Some say—
I say it just begins to live
That day.

Utterance does not kill words by using them up. On the contrary, they
are dead only when they lie inert, as in a dictionary. Giving expression
to words, then, actually 'creates' them, endows them with life.

It only remains to say that the living word has re-creative power. In
her search for some way to express her conviction about this, she finally
hit upon the perfect metaphor, drawn from the novel doctrine of 'The
Word' in the gospel according to St. John and from the symbols of the
Eucharist. It was a bold stroke, and her extension of its meaning from
religion to poetry was made in language that is deliberately extravagant.
Only so could she render her full belief in poetry's magical power.
Though she halts carefully this side of a supernatural thesis, the creation
of poetry and its re-creative power was, for her, the nearest approach to
miracle vouchsafed to mortals. The metaphor, and it remains just that,
is worked out strikingly in a series of poems.

Her first experiment with this cluster of ideas is tentative. This poem
is concerned with the rather worn subject of inspiration, its great worth
and its infrequency. She avoids the vague supernaturalism prevalent in
contemporary poetic theory about the divine afflatus by beginning with
the flat statement: 'Your thoughts dont have words every day.' Writing
in 1878 when her creative powers have long been on the wane, she is
probably looking back with wistful amazement to the years of her
frenzied production (for example 1862, when she averaged a poem a
day, more in that one year than in the last twelve). The moments of
poetic perception were then so 'native' she lists nine variants in the

manuscript to describe how easy creation had seemed. Now, she has to resort to a simile drawn from the Eucharist to express her wonder about the rare moments when thoughts do find their words. They come, she says,

> Like signal esoteric sips
> Of sacramental wine.

The miracle whereby thoughts are created into words she likens to this ritual as developed by the Church Fathers, who came to regard it as an initiation into knowledge of the divine essence. Christ's very discourses are his flesh and blood; eating and drinking the divine Word brings immortality. Just as He once dwelt in the body, so the bread and wine by consecration have become tenements in which the Word is reincarnated, and by swallowing them mortal souls partake of immortality. But she did not have to go the whole way with the dogma of Transubstantiation. The opposing theory would serve her metaphorical purposes just as well. Though the bread and wine remain physically what they were, they are spiritually raised to a higher power; the elements become a new vehicle of the spirit's influence, 'a fresh sojourning among us of the Word,' as one medieval monk, Ratramnus, put it.

The gospel of St. John, one of the books she pored over, was the chief basis for uniting the symbolic meaning of the Eucharistic elements and the doctrine of the Word. She makes startling use of this double image in a poem illustrating the miraculous power of language in the few great authors of her election:

> A Word made Flesh is seldom
> And tremblingly partook
> Nor then perhaps reported
> But have I not mistook
> Each one of us has tasted
> With ecstasies of stealth
> The very food debated
> To our specific strength— ...
>
> 'Made Flesh and dwelt among us'
> Could condescension be
> Like this consent of Language
> This loved Philology

She found an obvious parallel for the relationship between the word and the uncreated thought in the distinction between the manifested and the hidden deity, God as revelation and as essence, a subject familiar to her from the Old Testament.

The wholly new conception of the Being that had become incarnate in Christ was rendered most poetically by her favorite New Testament author. St. John, turning to the most useful term in the religious thought of his day, had announced his doctrine of the Word as lying at the foundation of the great story he was about to tell. He also took advantage of the significance of *Logos* ('the word') in philosophy, as the revelation of thought, and its usage in everyday life, as the medium of communication. Since 'No man hath seen God at any time,' how could He be 'made manifest' to men? The paradoxical distinction existing in the divine nature he put in his introductory verse: 'In the beginning was the Word, and the Word was with God, and the Word was God.' Thus it was possible for the Word to become the agency through which the world was created and God's life was declared. The advent of Christ, in all the fullness of its meaning for St. John, was rendered in his famous metaphor: 'And the Word was made flesh, and dwelt among us.' For him, through this miracle God's glory was first made visible; the purpose of the ensuing gospel was to show how mortal men can partake of this new life.

Emily Dickinson saw the dramatic force of his figure and seized upon it for her own purposes, to suggest the miracle by which uncreated thought is bodied forth in language. A surviving manuscript fragment shows her toying with the famous phrases in her search for new meaning: 'The import of that Paragraph "The Word made Flesh" Had he the faintest intimation Who broached it Yesterday! "Made Flesh and dwelt among us".' One result of her search was the poem quoted above, which renders the import this Biblical figure finally came to have for her. Rare indeed, she says there, when the truth is revealed in words, when a book is discovered to be the very food needed for nourishment of the spirit. One tastes such words with awe but with ecstasy, like the initiate into esoteric rites. The opening lines, by linking the 'Word made Flesh' with the Eucharistic term 'partook,' carry her poem from the advent, the first incarnation of the spirit, to the ritual by which it is shared, the 'fresh sojourning' of the Word among us. But both are accomplished, in her version, through the 'consent of Language.' The priest is now a poet, his elements nouns and verbs.

When Christ's earthly career had run its course new symbols were needed to perpetuate the incarnation. Again it was St. John who made possible the spiritual interpretation of the Last Supper. Her most successful poem on this theme develops the metaphor fully, pushing St. John's language to its extreme limits:

> He ate and drank the precious Words—
> His Spirit grew robust—
> He knew no more that he was poor,
> Nor that his frame was Dust—
>
> He danced along the dingy Days
> And this Bequest of Wings
> Was but a Book— What Liberty
> A loosened spirit brings—

'Precious' is balanced against 'poor,' 'Spirit' against 'Dust.' The divine words are physically digested, and the soul grows muscular. In these contrasts the image of immortality is built up to a climax in the winged dance down the prosaic ways of normal existence. The drama is tightened by the intricate alliteration, and emphasized by the caesura in the next to last line. But the Eucharist has served as a likeness only, an extended metaphor, as proved by the sharp breaking of the image in the concluding lines. The resonant scriptural language of the first stanza has gradually been replaced by the secular, even the final link of 'spirit' being deliberately not capitalized. The poem ends with a strictly esthetic proposition, pertaining to this world. Her bequest of wings is just a 'Book' and it brings the eater 'Liberty,' not eternal life. So with her imagery in the other poems. The sacramental wine is a simile for thoughts poured into words; the spiritual Word is embodied in the fleshly word, for the poet, merely by the grace of philology.

As worked out in all three poems her concern is clearly with the life-giving potential of ideas and the carrying power of words as vessels, the fusion of the two when they are brought alive in poems. The symbols of the Eucharist and the doctrine of the Word were simply metaphors to express her passionate conviction about the power of poetry. Even her most extravagant figure, of herself as word-eater and maker of edible words, is probably drawn from that other John, author of the Book of Revelation. In an apocalyptic vision he recorded that, just as he was about to write, a heavenly messenger descended and commanded him: 'And I took the little book out of the angel's hand, and ate it up; and it was in my mouth sweet as honey .... And he said unto me, Thou must prophesy again before many peoples, and nations, and tongues.' It would be a mistake to try to build out of these poems a theology or even to insist on the religious aspect of the idea of immortality in them. She is talking about the 'immortality' of art, but its mortal dimensions are also present.

A fourth poem, written much earlier, shows she could find an equally suitable metaphor in the pagan philosopher Hermes Trismegistus:

> Strong Draughts of Their Refreshing Minds
> To drink— enables Mine
> Through Desert or the Wilderness
> As bore it Sealed Wine—
>
> To go elastic— Or as One
> The Camel's trait— attained—
> How powerful the Stimulus
> Of an Hermetic Mind—

Here the setting is not the Holy Land but Egypt, with desert, camel, and the key word 'Hermetic,' for which her Lexicon furnished most of the needed connotations. The more common meaning from alchemy, of airtight sealing, fits throughout: the allusion to the camel's capacity for storing water, the simile of 'Sealed Wine,' the implication of the poem itself as a vessel for preserving a rare elixir. Webster also gave her the richer meaning of 'Hermetic' as referring to the 'Books of the Egyptians' which treat of universal principles. These were chiefly the writings of Hermes (Lord of the Divine Words), attempting to explain all the phenomena of nature, and the philosophy of Neo-Platonists like Philo Judaeus (who called *Logos* the heavenly bread, the cup of God, in metaphors similar to those used by St. John)—authors she was acquainted with through reading the works of Sir Thomas Browne. Such was 'an Hermetic Mind,' and he who drank these stimulating words would acquire the elastic step of the camel to take him on strange journeys. A very earthly substitute for wings, but it was the special kind of immortality poetry is capable of achieving and imparting.

Dickinson drew her metaphors from whatever source suited her needs, from Neo-Platonists and New Testament visionaries as readily as from law and agriculture and science. But she never confused the poetic way of thinking with the philosophic, and readers should not take her figurative expressions as literal statements of belief. It would be folly to try to make her into a Transcendentalist or any other kind of mystic on the evidence of such poems as these. Her concern here was not merger with God through intuition or ritual, but discovery of the inner paradise of art by the language of surprise. Startling imagery and unexpected verbal arrangements were simply her strategy for rejuvenating poetry, by projecting her thoughts into things through the medium of words, with the utmost of novelty and wit. To avoid any possible misunderstanding it seems wise to conclude this account of her belief in the power of language by coming down from the high extravagance of her doctrine of the Word to a soberer illustration. Significance can be measured in great literature, Henry James once ventured in an essay on Flaubert, by 'the quantity of metaphor thrown up.' She would have agreed and would have gone all the way with him in his formulation of the writer's creed. 'If you pushed far enough into language,' he concluded, 'you found yourself in the embrace of thought.' This was her belief, too, about the creative power of words.

3

CIRCUMFERENCE

If the poet is conceived as a 'maker' he tends to be thought of as godlike, unless two different kinds of creative power are discriminated. The early nineteenth century had seen a resurgent discontent with human limitations, a renewed hope that the poet had at least glimpses of divine truth and beauty. In America Poe held up the angel Israfel as his ideal, Emerson the sun-god Uriel, Whitman boldly proclaimed himself a demiurge. More than most of her contemporaries, Emily Dickinson held in firm control the temptation to storm heaven's gate and insisted on making the distinction between heavenly beauty and that which the poet can create. Her finest poem on this theme is achieved by a striking contrast between the splendor of the aurora borealis and the lowly 'menagerie' to which the mortal poet is limited:

> Of Bronze– and Blaze–
> The North– Tonight–
> So adequate– it forms–
> So preconcerted with itself–
> So distant– to alarms–
> An Unconcern so sovereign
> To Universe, or me–
> Infects my simple spirit
> With Taints of Majesty–

47

Till I take vaster attitudes—
And strut upon my stem—
Disdaining Men, and Oxygen,
For Arrogance of them—

My Splendors, are Menagerie—
But their Competeless Show
Will entertain the Centuries
When I, am long ago,
An Island in dishonored Grass—
Whom none but Beetles, know.

The northern lights, one of the grandest spectacles of the natural world, can fill the sky with shimmering color in multiform bands and curtains, arches, and rays streaming out from a central corona. Amherst is far enough north for auroral displays, and she apparently even saw one with the unusual predominance of violet, as witnessed in two poems. Nature has 'an awe' of the royal purple, she says, saving it for sunsets and for the 'Auroran widths' that are flung suddenly on men out of the night; again, the North erects its 'blazing Sign . . . in Iodine.' The part of the spectrum more normally displayed is from blood red through gold to chartreuse, as in the present poem. Since the purpose here is not pictorial the color suggestion is reduced to one word, 'Bronze.' By alliterating this with 'Blaze,' to bring out the constituent reds and yellows, and by breaking her first line into halves for emphasis, she opens her poem with the full brilliance of the phenomenon: 'Of Bronze— and Blaze—/The North— Tonight.'

The unusual splendor of an aurora could make it a notable occasion even in Amherst. She records one vividly in a letter written to her brother in 1851, ten years before the poem:

There was quite an excitement in the village Monday evening. We were all startled by a violent churchbell ringing, and thinking of nothing but fire, rushed out in the street to see. The sky was a beautiful red, bordering on a crimson, and rays of a gold pink color were constantly shooting off from a kind of sun in the center. People were alarmed at this beautiful Phenomenon, supposing that fires somewhere were *coloring the sky*. The exhibition lasted for nearly 15 minutes, and the streets were full of people wondering and admiring.

Father happened to see it among the very first and rang the bell *himself* to call attention to it.

Such a spectacular display of northern lights invariably fills the beholder with a kind of religious awe. After a similar description of the aurora in his Journal, September 24, 1870, the poet Hopkins declared:

> This busy working of nature wholly independent of the earth and seeming to go on in a strain of time not reckoned by our reckoning of days and years but simpler and as if correcting the preoccupation of the world by being preoccupied with and appealing to and dated to the day of judgment was like a new witness to God and filled me with delightful fear. . . .

The religious attitude, in her New England village version, is implied by the pious Squire Dickinson ringing the church bell. There is some detached amusement on her part, for she had studied enough astronomy to be abreast of current scientific speculations about the aurora borealis. But the glory and mystery were not dispelled for her by contemporary explanations that it was caused by some kind of electrical discharge in the rarefied upper atmosphere, any more than it would have been by the modern theory attributing it to cosmic rays. The mystery is simply translated into new terms for the poet who is still capable of feeling awe. In a later quatrain, awkward as poetry but useful as a gloss, she too used a purely religious interpretation, that the aurora is an image of the 'Celestial Face.'

In her poem 'Of Bronze— and Blaze' there can be no doubt that the first section is a celebration of divine beauty, made even more effective by being couched in terms of a cosmic esthetic. It is doubly appropriate for her theme by being apparently created right before her eyes. The unfolding pattern of rays and corona, mentioned in the letter, is rendered organically in the second line, 'So adequate it forms.' In her Lexicon 'adequately' had not acquired the diminished connotation of today, but retained the full root meaning of 'in exact proportion,' an attribute that can only attach to God. In contrast with such infinite fullness of expansion and infinite simplicity of principle she, in her human incompleteness and fragmentation, is by implication in-adequate. When she adds that it is 'preconcerted with itself' she is Latinist enough to know that this means a pre-established harmony and accord. The poet, on the other hand, is dis-concerted both with herself and with the heavenly beauty she sees.

The fourth line, 'So distant to alarms,' needs some elucidation. Elsewhere she speaks of the moon as untroubled by the problems that harass men—life, death, and the concern over immortality—but instead 'engrossed to Absolute/With shining'; and of birds singing at dawn not for applause but for an ecstasy 'independent . . . Of Deity and Men.' If this is true of the more commonplace manifestations of natural beauty, it is even more so of the aurora which displays itself with a sovereign 'unconcern' towards the universe as well as towards her. Its apparent motion outward from irradiating center to full circumference is only illusion, the symbol of unity-in-multiplicity taking form before mortal eyes. For it is actually motionless in time and space, the parts and the whole existing from eternity to eternity in equal correspondence ('adequate' from *adaequatus*), at peace in its self-sufficiency. 'Alarms' and fretful motions belong to the human not the celestial sphere, especially as she reaches up towards the divine circle she feels desperately concerned to imitate:

> Of Bronze— and Blaze—
> The North— Tonight—
> So adequate— it forms—
> So preconcerted with itself—
> So distant— to alarms—
> An Unconcern so sovereign
> To Universe, or me— . . .

This is the face of God shining through, the perfection of beauty unconscious of itself. This would be a model for the ideal organic art of the poet dreamed of by the Transcendentalists.

The second section of the poem comes to grips with this very possibility: Can man create such beauty? It is included as part of the same stanza because it is an answering half of the same theme and is even linked syntactically, being a predication of which the first six lines are a loosely formed but complex subject—the sheer substantive Being of heavenly beauty. Another device heightens the contrast between the two sections. In the line expressing the aurora's unconcern "To Universe, or me" the unorthodox comma makes the addition of herself seem like an afterthought, so insignificant is she by comparison. But this comes exactly at the point where the focus of interest shifts from the heavenly to the earthly creator of beauty. The humbly added 'or me' is gradually replaced with 'Till I take vaster attitudes—/And strut. . . .' The poet, and her poems, becomes the real subject throughout the rest of the poem.

As the human creator is tempted to rival the divine, even the grand scale diction is echoed. For 'adequate,' 'preconcerted,' 'sovereign,' in the first half there are 'spirit,' 'vaster,' and 'majesty' in the second, but the latter are always used in a shrunken or mocking context. Though the errors of previous editions no longer obscure her meanings, two alterations of the text in lines 7-8 deserve attention because they underscore her break with tradition at this point. Her early editors, partial to the romantic notion that contemplation of heavenly beauty exalts the poet to godlike power, changed these lines to read: 'It paints my simple spirit/ With tints of majesty.' But the manuscript makes it clear that instead of 'paints' and 'tints' she wrote *infects* and *taints*. The changes may seem small to the surface reader but they throw her into an opposite esthetic school. Her use of scientific terms, her usual strategy when opposing doubt to faith, is significant; and since she is concerned here with the very life of poetry, they were drawn appropriately from medical science. .

The mortal poet corrupts his true nature if he attempts to be divine, and the infection may prove fatal if it leads him to disdain 'Oxygen.' He may indeed have a 'spirit' but it is a simple one that should not aspire to 'majesty,' at least in the heavenly sense; and 'simple' suggests not only humility but naïveté, to the point of becoming a foolish poseur. It is not the gods but pretentious mortals who strike 'attitudes' and 'strut.' Both are theatrical words, and the latter has the added fault of pride. 'I can't *stop* to strut,' she once said, 'in a world where bells toll.' Controlled by the context of 'simple' and 'stem' in the present poem, 'strut' dramatizes the absurdity of such posturing. It is meant in the etymological sense, to project upward, but as she stretches her neck towards the circumference she loses contact with the center. 'Disdain' and 'arrogance' have been applied to those at the top of the hierarchy, but they are appellations of snobbery rather than nobility. The poet must remain earth-bound. He is tied to his fellow men by the bonds of humanity, to the air which he breathes for his very life, and by his stem to the earth where his roots are. He cannot be 'a Stemless Flower' like the moon. To ape the divine power that creates the aurora borealis is to lose his proper status and function:

> Infects my simple spirit
> With Taints of Majesty—
> Till I take vaster attitudes—
> And strut upon my stem—
> Disdaining Men, and Oxygen,
> For Arrogance of them—

These earthly clues form the structural links with the third section of her poem and prepare for the surprising announcement of the poet's true province: 'My Splendors are Menagerie.' In this context 'menagerie' is bizarre to say the least, and her meaning is somewhat enigmatic. Her only other use of the word is ambiguous ('Menagerie to me/ My Neighbor be'), but it seems there to mean society in the sense of its being a 'show.' Though she was amused by the spectacle of the social world, however, this was no more the province she chose for her poetry than was the aurora. 'Menagerie' was also the current term for the small traveling circus of her day, usually consisting chiefly of animals, hence a carnival. Perhaps the Bible will lead closer to her intention for Noah's Ark, the first menagerie, included not only animals and plants but the human species, everything indeed but spiritual entities. This emphasizes the meanings of variety and multiplicity as opposed to the simple splendor of the aurora, whose forms and colors though multiple are unified in a preconcerted harmony. 'Menagerie' was a grotesque word, deliberately chosen for dramatic contrast with the celestial world beyond her reach. It was her all-inclusive word for the things and thoughts of this earth, the proper subject matter of the poet.

Even so, she boasts that such poems are in their own way 'Splendors,' and they will 'entertain the Centuries.' It is notable that their function is beauty and pleasure, not moral instruction. These lines reach back to the beginning of the poem for final parallels and differences. 'Splendors,' from the Latin *splendere* meaning to shine, keeps up the image of the aurora's 'Blaze.' Further, she must have read in her Lexicon of the northern lights: 'They . . . serve to illuminate the earth and cheer the gloom of long winter nights,' especially in the higher latitudes where they are called the 'merry dancers.' These auroral splendors, she infers, will entertain eternity. Her own are not in competition with them, nor even with other mortal creators of beauty since she was a private poet. Her bid for the immortality of her 'Competeless Show' is not immodest by comparison, for she measures it by calendar time, 'Centuries.' 'After a hundred years,' she once wrote of a deserted graveyard, 'Nobody knows the Place'; strangers listlessly spell out the 'lone Orthography' of the forgotten dead. Similarly with her in the present poem, when she has been for a century or so 'An Island in dishonored Grass,' a neglected mound with its unremembered marker. But the poet in this last stanza, as opposed to the person, is taken out of time (and so saved from death) by the shock use of the universal present, 'am' instead of the expected 'have been,' followed by 'long ago' which refers to time long past. The ungrammatical comma between subject and predicate emphasizes this by forcing the accent on 'am' ('When I, am long ago'). She lives on for a few centuries through her poems, for which she claims the kind of immortality possible to art:

> My Splendors, are Menagerie—
> But their Competeless Show
> Will entertain the Centuries
> When I, am long ago,
> An Island in dishonored Grass—
> Whom none but Beetles, know.

The logical form of this poem, in its threefold contrast, reveals only part of its meaning. Its poetic structure is not linear but circular, the expansions and contractions of the two concepts of creative power taking place simultaneously. The drama is enacted in brief compass, the poet standing on the earth's surface, glancing up, then down, then within to measure her creative potential. As she contemplates the illimitable beauty of the heavens she makes the false attempt to lose herself by reaching out to the full circumference of the divine, but her mortal limitations immediately assert themselves and make this effort mere strutting. So she is drawn back to the earth as her proper center. It is only there that she can both lose herself and find herself in her poems. As long as the first person 'My' is insisted on, they are described by the limited earthly word 'Menagerie.' But with the true losing of the self at the center, sinking into the island of the grave, 'their Competeless Show' expands outward again to escape the limits of mortality. The poems become splendors, like the aurora.

The mortal who created them, on the other hand, becomes part of the menagerie, dies into the earth to be known only by the 'Daisies'—so the first version has it. But this choice was quickly recognized as conventional, endangering the poem with a weak ending, and it yielded to the alternate reading 'Beetles,' which retains the specific quality of earthiness and fits better with the idea of a menagerie. As the next to last word, it creates with shattering effect the contrast intended. For 'Beetles,' replacing the sentimental atmosphere with the grim, also takes the mind back through grass to stem, oxygen, and men—all perishable and of this earth, though when transformed in her gala show, a sort of perennial circus, they will outlast the centuries. This is the true province of the poet. 'Beetles' may also take the attentive ear back to 'Bronze and Blaze,' alliterating with these symbols of eternal beauty, towards which she can only feel awe. Such is the poet's legitimate goal. Her poems also may achieve circumference if she experiences the full meaning of her earthbound life. This poem does so itself by its awful comprehension of man's transitoriness and the limited immortality of his creations, set against the perturbless blaze of celestial beauty. The assurance with which she moves towards this knowledge seems to be echoed in the progress from the suspended rhymes of the opening quatrain to the threefold exact rhyming of the concluding lines.

'Of Bronze— and Blaze,' written at the end of 1861, would seem to have settled once and for all the problem of the poet's true province and function. But recognition of mortal limitations and the yearning to escape from them are not so easily reconciled, and the conflict continued to loom for several years. Dickinson's esthetic theory was fully established before she opened her correspondence with Higginson in the spring of 1862. Yet she continually asked him for precepts, at first seeking confirmation, later merely an exchange of views to help her measure the distance between her private theories and those of the conventional critic of the day. In answer to her requests for aid he had given technical criticism only, and she had thanked him for his 'surgery.'

In her fourth letter she broached the problem of her central concern as if it were new: 'Will you tell me my fault, frankly as to yourself, for I had rather wince, than die. Men do not call the surgeon, to commend—the Bone, but to set it, Sir, and fracture within, is more critical.' When she attempted to define this internal flaw, she had to fall back on metaphor: 'An ignorance, not of Customs, but if caught with the Dawn— or the Sunset see me— Myself the only Kangaroo among the Beauty, Sir, if you please, it afflicts me, and I thought that instruction would take it away.' There is some hoaxing of her preceptor in this pretended concern over the awkwardness of her verse as compared with the conventional smoothness of the day. But her deeper meaning is revealed in the irony of comparing herself to the kangaroo, whose leaping towards the sky only emphasizes his earth-bound nature. This is similar to the elastic step of the camel in a previously discussed poem, both deliberately grotesque images of the poet. She is really asking, Is it inescapable that the poet's 'Splendors are *Menagerie*,' or is this an affliction that can be overcome by learning? In the middle of this context she answered her own question by stating the essential doctrine of her poetics: 'My *Business* is Circumference.' The verbal displacement in these two statements, indicated by the supplied italics, sets up the tension of her paradox.

'Circumference' is a word that she returns to again and again. It is a pervasive image in her religious thinking and in her theory of art, though the meanings it carries are not always consistent. An exploration of its ambiguities seems in order. Significantly, she rarely used the kindred word 'circle' with its suggestion of a bounded inclosure. Her term was usually 'circumference,' occasionally its synonym 'circuit,' both compounded from Latin roots meaning to carry or go around. The emphasis is on the motion of encompassing, suggesting an extension outward to include something larger than can be found at a particular static point. It is close to the meaning now rare but copiously illustrated in the *Religio Medici* of Sir Thomas Browne, an author she specifically named as a favorite. In his effort to define it as a sense of boundlessness radiating out from a center, opposite to the normal sense of a limiting circle, he cited the formulation of Hermes: The sphere of which the center is everywhere, the circumference nowhere (*Sphæra cujus centrum ubique, circumferentia nullibi*). Though Browne frequently limited 'circumference' to the immediately surrounding environment, she began with this rare use and expanded it into a symbol for all that is outside. Her center is the inquiring mind whose business is circumference, intent upon exploring the whole infinity of the universe that lies before her.

At times 'circumference' seems associated with the idea of cosmic expanse, as opposed to the limited life centered on earth. 'A Coffin— is a small Domain,' she says, yet it contains 'A Citizen of Paradise'; and realization of this larger meaning of mortality can become the rudiment of a new apprehension, ampler than the sun's, 'Circumference without Relief—/Or Estimate— or End.' Again, expansion outward from the narrow center of death, the coming full circle of the individual spirit, will occur at the Resurrection, when the fragmented earthly life is made whole at last and 'Circumference be full.' Even in life, according to another poem, she could sometimes have a vision of touching the Universe and see herself as a lone 'Speck upon a Ball' going out to 'Circumference,' but the vision was a transient one and quickly receded. These certainly suggest the meaning of circumference as attainment of the divine reality.

Ultimate circumference may well be the extension of understanding from mortal limits to absolute fulfillment in immortality. But the image is more complex for her, even involute, and there are circumferences short of the celestial one that are not beyond the poet's reach. There are endless expansions for the spirit, opening out from the smallest center of consciousness to the fullest comprehension. But this growth cannot be attained too easily; it is more likely to be achieved through the vision and discipline of art than in the experience of life. The ecstasy of perfect love, she says in one poem, is a 'new Circumference' too exalted for mortals, conditioned as they are by the 'little Circuit' of ordinary life. Starting from these two concentric images, she goes on to develop her theme that the human way must go through pain and suffering to a fuller understanding of what heaven can be. It is only by encompassing the full circle of human possibilities that one is made ready to expand towards the divine circle. How grand the expansion can be even within limits of the mortal calendar leads her to exclaim in another poem: 'Time feels so vast', her finite self tends to become engrossed in 'this Circumference' to the exclusion of God. The poem concludes that this life is only a preface to eternity, preparing her by stages of growth 'For the Stupendous Vision/Of His Diameters.'

To couch her theory of art in religious terms was natural for one formed by such an environment. In her thinking the Creator became a model for the poet. The circumference of divine reality perceived through awe was at least a useful metaphor for the heaven-on-earth of his art achieved through the imagination. This linkage is made explicit in a quatrain written near the end of her life. Unsuccessful as a poem, its meaning is obscure without the accompanying letter, sent to the sculptor Daniel Chester French. She was writing to congratulate him for winning his fame (his momentary achievement of Circumference) 'reverently,' and since success is dust she begged God to keep him 'fundamental' so he could achieve it again. The verses themselves are addressed to 'Circumference,' who is properly the 'Bride of Awe' and so can be possessed only by the truly 'hallowed Knight.' Even then, possessed just momentarily in his art, she apparently means, since all is a metaphor for the artist's dedicated love of his Muse. Only so does he achieve occasionally the revelation of full meaning.

The most startling use of the term occurs in a late letter: 'The Bible dealt with the Centre, not with the Circumference.' This pronouncement is not so much baffling as unexpectedly bold. Set beside her own boast, 'My Business is Circumference,' it seems little short of blasphemous. Her poems are to accomplish something the Bible does not? Is she saying it is just a human record, the history of a religious people and a rule book for conduct, whereas her poetry will encompass revelation? She certainly searched the Bible for meaning, but though she found it a primary source for her imagery—most significantly in its most poetic books, the Psalms, the Revelation, and the Gospel of St. John—she did not find in it the divine reality.

Through Emerson she was well aware of the Transcendentalists' doctrine that all books, including The Book, are secondary to the fountain of truth within, and she could go so far with them as to affirm 'By intuition Mightiest Things/Assert themselves— and not by terms.' But her kinship with her predecessors is more tenuous than with her successors, especially some of the esthetic philosophers today. At any rate, like many modern poets she found art the substitute for her inherited religion, the only instrument of revelation left to her. Does she come then at last to contradict her poem 'Of Bronze— and Blaze,' which says it is spiritual pride to aim at celestial beauty since the poet's mortal lot is to make splendors out of menagerie? Perhaps all can be reconciled in a sort of dialectical sequence. The immediate leap into God is impossible, the poet cannot be like the aurora. He must go back to the earth, the human experience of pain and suffering, and work out from there towards the divine reality. She, also, may have to *deal* with the center, as the Bible does, though her ultimate *business* is to explore out to the circumference.

A final poem, successfully using this term by embodying it in a controlled metaphor, may help to clarify her meaning:

> The Poets light but Lamps—
> Themselves— go out—
> The Wicks they stimulate—
> If vital Light
>
> Inhere as do the Suns—
> Each Age a Lens
> Disseminating their
> Circumference—

The disjunctive 'but' in the first line emphasizes the homely implement of the lamp by which poets light the earthly way in contrast with the celestial light of the suns in the second stanza (and the aurora in 'Of Bronze— and Blaze'), which remains a simile. This light is not made by touching the words with a magical taper, but is kindled by a generative power within the artifact, as in the case of the lamps of heaven. Each of the key words that open out this meaning is of Latin origin, the only six in the poem. 'Stimulate,' *to animate* according to her Lexicon, leads into the life-giving idea of 'vital.' This is the necessary condition to be fulfilled in order that the wicks may 'inhere' in the poets' lamps, just as the heavenly wicks do in the suns, making them shine with a kind of immortality of their own. This comparison with the sun, center of her planetary universe, places the poetic lamps at the center of her private universe.

At this point a new element enters, germane to the principal image, which links this poem with those she wrote on fame. The 'Lens' is the glass of posterity through which the light is not only seen but magnified. The central meaning of a poem, its light, remains constant; succeeding ages merely interpret and reinterpret, broadening its effect. This is happily rendered by 'disseminating,' carrying both the idea of scattering abroad and the seminal nature of the poems as seeds. Such a connotation makes no break in the figurative language, however, for common usage has long abstracted the meaning of this word from its agricultural origins, as in the phrase 'disseminating truth.' The literal meaning of 'Circumference' as the boundary of a circle (like the disks of the lamps) has been expanded by her special meaning into a sphere like the sun, radiating its light outward to infinity. If poets can light such lamps they are content to 'go out' themselves, for death then becomes a means of going outward to illuminate the darkness surrounding the generations of man. The mortal life has been transfigured into the enduring life of their poems.

The normal human concern with fame is greatly increased for the private poet, since his is necessarily a posthumous one. Emily Dickinson's shy venture towards an audience, her rebuff by conventional forces of the day, and her decision not to publish during her lifetime, all occurred during the first few months of her correspondence with Higginson in 1862. But her poignant sense of loss lingered and erupted in more than a dozen poems, mostly written during the next two years. There are sharp lines, 'Fame is a fickle food/ . . . Men eat of it and die.' One quatrain adroitly takes the measure of worldly repute:

> Fame is a bee.
> It has a song—
> It has a sting—
> Ah, too, it has a wing.

Poetic obscurity, before she realized it was to be her estate, could be treated humorously, as in the light verse written in 1861 satirizing the desire for communication and applause:

> I'm Nobody! Who are you? ...
> How public— like a Frog—
> To tell your name— the livelong June—
> To an admiring Bog!

As permanent isolation from an audience came to be recognized as her lot, smoldering resentment warped her view of the artist's unavoidable relations with society. Once, the intensity of her feeling was almost fused into form by the metaphor of 'price,' not the small pay offered to the poet by his publisher but the cost entailed on the spirit by meeting the demands of the market place:

> Publication— is the Auction
> Of the Mind of Man—
> Poverty— be justifying
> For so foul a thing

Possibly— but We— would rather
From Our Garret go
White— Unto the White Creator—
Than invest— Our Snow—

Thought belong to Him who gave it—
Then— to Him Who bear
Its Corporeal illustration— Sell
The Royal Air—

In the Parcel— Be the Merchant
Of the Heavenly Grace—
But reduce no Human Spirit
To Disgrace of Price—

The heavy accents of the trochaic meter, rare in her poetry, echo the submerged vehemence. The commercial words ring through the stanzas with something of the invective of those modern critics who declare that the greatest enemy of literature today is the very prosperity of the book trade. Put the mind up for auction? reduce the spirit to marketable size? The beginning and end of the poem round out its unity by identifying the artist's inner essence as both his mind and spirit, which must not be violated in order to make them salable to the public.

The center of the poem, however, contains elements imperfectly assimilated to the structure and the dominant imagery. In her exacerbation at the Philistinism of the day she lashes out directly at the enemy and breaks the syntax by shifting to the imperative mode, though the lines gain uncommon strength from the heretical nature of her alternative. Sell over the counter the very air vital to life, she taunts, even 'Be the Merchant/ Of the Heavenly Grace' (since the pulpit has already reduced religion to a moral commodity)—but never barter the poet's soul. Even more tangential to the main theme of the poem are its most striking lines, in stanza three, one of her subtler renderings of the doctrine of the Word made Flesh. In its uncreated state thought belongs to God; it is made incarnate by the poet who gives it 'corporeal illustration,' and then it belongs to him. The conclusion is left to implication: in neither case is it for sale. She prefers the poverty of the artist in his garret, not only unsold but uncreating, pure perception returning to the Great Perceiver, rather than to invest her immortal spirit (rendered by her favorite private symbol, 'snow') in a marketable product. The violence and complexity of her emotional reactions to publishing shatter the controls of the metaphor, and what remains is a series of brilliant fragments instead of a poem. Her resentment against such an 'auction of the mind' is vividly there in its intensity, but not in its resolution.

Unfortunate in her literary advisers and severely limited in her experience of getting printed, she became convinced that the choice of remaining a private poet was forced upon her. Two of her poems printed in the Springfield *Daily Republican* in 1861-62, altered editorially to suit the popular conventions as to rhyme and imagery, made her conclude somewhat hastily that publication inevitably entails compromise. How jealously she guarded her artistic integrity is proved by her complaint against the editorial insertion of a single comma in another poem that found its way into print, without her permission: 'it was robbed of me—defeated too of the third line by the punctuation.' But her complaint was just rather than finical, for this change resulted in a distortion of her meaning that it has taken nearly a century to correct. Such experiences probably account for the archness of her report in an early letter to Higginson: 'Two Editors of Journals came to my Father's House, this winter— and asked me for my Mind— and when I asked them "Why," they said I was penurious - and they, would use it for the World.' Yet she had opened correspondence with her new mentor for the very purpose of seeking publication, provided she could at the same time preserve her integrity. When his conventional tastes made him unable to accept her work as art, she replied with another reversal: 'I smile when you suggest that I delay "to publish"— that being foreign to my thought, as Firmament to Fin.' She concluded with a paradox: 'If fame belonged to me, I could not escape her— if she did not, the longest day would pass me on the chase— and the approbation of my Dog, would forsake me— then— My Barefoot-Rank is better.'

This vacillating attitude toward literary renown has been deplored as a mark of her immaturity, a misplaced coquetry, taking 'five steps forward and two steps back.' She derided fame, according to this critic, yet carefully preserved nearly two thousand poems; but they were kept in a deliberately chaotic state, many of the manuscripts 'ostentatiously unfinished.' She often wrote cryptically in order to repudiate any earthly audience, he concludes, since only Eternity could understand her. Her attitude towards fame has been staunchly defended by another as proof of her deep-seated integrity and self-knowledge, leading her to sacrifice recognition during her lifetime for the judgment of posterity. There is some truth in both views. It is noteworthy that Hopkins, her only contemporary peer in originality, elected to be a private poet under not dissimilar circumstances. He also refused to fight for fame, even while he recognized that an audience might have made his work 'more intelligible, smoother, and less singular.' Perhaps the careers of both are prescient of the twentieth-century poet's concern over alienation from his public, the increasing eccentricity, the contentment with a minimum reception today while remaining confident he is creating enduring art.

The biographical relevance of her poems on fame, their chief interest, has been treated adequately by others. Since none of them are entirely successful as poems, they need no further mention here except in so far as they bear upon her esthetic theory. The feeling of deprivation that haunts the private poet, cut off from communion with any but posterity, accounts for her overemphasis on the 'immortality' of art. Compensation for the poet's failure to create an aurora is found in the assurance that her splendors will entertain the centuries long after she is dead. Her poems will arrive at the full circumference of their meaning only through the lens of succeeding ages. She could console herself by a feeling of superiority over those who are paid in the 'Bullion of Today' by boasting 'Some– Work for Immortality–/The Chiefer part, for Time.' One pardons the arrogance of ranging herself with the former, who are rewarded by 'checks' drawn on the bank of Fame. But one needs to understand her sense of loss in being deprived of an audience, so deeply felt as to make her insist that the survival value of art is the only true measure of its greatness. The theme runs like a thread through some of her finer poems, a minor flaw in that it is too idiosyncratic to have universal validity as an esthetic criterion. The matter was brought to rest most satisfyingly in the quiet lines that form a sort of epigraph for her life's work, like Chaucer's 'Go, little book,' posting her poems to her unknown readers of the future:

> This is my letter to the World
> That never wrote to Me.

She had made her peace with fame, and surely that which endures is preferable.

4

CENTER

Emily Dickinson was reasonably clear in her conception of the artist's proper goals and explicit about the integrity of her vision. Instead of trying to leap into the divine 'circumference' he must explore outward from the center of experience, content if his meanings reach their full expansion only with posterity. But how does he create, what goes on at the 'center'? This is the unanswerable question, yet one that neither poet nor critic can let alone. The ultimate mystery of poetic creation she confessed was beyond her grasp:

> This is a Blossom of the Brain—
> A small—italic Seed
> Lodged by Design or Happening
> The Spirit fructified—
>
> Shy as the Wind of his Lodgings
> Swift as a Freshet's Tongue
> So of the Flower of the Soul
> Its process is unknown....

The subject of her poem is the fully formed work of art, but the process of its flowering can only be expressed metaphorically. Its germ was a 'Seed,' so different from the garden variety she describes it as 'italic,' the type used for foreign borrowings. The novelty of this adjective redeems the triteness of the seed-flower metaphor. Whether it was dropped according to some inspired design or by accident can never be known, nor whether it grew in the mind or the spirit, for what is first called a 'Blossom of the Brain' becomes in the end a 'Flower of the Soul.' So the old dilemma of the respective roles played by the intuition and the shaping power of reason is left unsolved. Its motions upward into final form are elusive as the wind and swift as floods in spring, and 'Its process is unknown.'

On one aspect of the mystery of composition she is confidently articulate, however: the psychic pressures that compelled her to expression. Through an apt metaphor she rendered her conviction in remarkably compact form:

> Essential Oils are wrung—
> The Attar from the Rose
> Is not expressed by Suns— alone—
> It is the gift of Screws—
> The General Rose decay—
> While this— in Lady's Drawer
> Make Summer, when the Lady lie
> In Spiceless Sepulchre.

The flower image buried at the heart of this poem was valuable to her because of the tradition she could count on to enrich her meaning without employing it derivatively. The rose as symbol for the transiency of life, a favorite of poets because of its obvious beauty and fragility, had filled the preceding century with popular lyrics like Richard Henry Wilde's 'My life is like the summer rose.' She was skillful in evading the hackneyed, even while exploiting it as part of her poetic strategy. The whole convention of mutability is brought into play with a single line, 'The General Rose decay,' but this is not her theme. Instead, what can be salvaged from death's decay and how it is transmuted into a new life.

Flowers are everywhere in her poetry and letters, representing life at its fullest glory. For her the perfection of flowers was the damask rose, but in spite of several attempts she could not embody her favorite in a successful poem as the direct theme. Yet the essence of this perfection furnished her a striking metaphor of the perfume of life, so adequately sustained throughout the present poem that she did not need to violate the unity of her conceit by explicit reference to her real subject, how poetry is extracted from experience. The modern Webster defines 'essence,' in its philosophical sense, as the inward nature of anything, underlying its manifestations. The edition of a century ago carried this one step further by citing Locke's distinction between nominal and real essence, the latter being 'that which makes anything to be what it is' though unknowable to the senses. And as applied to perfumes, those qualities or virtues refined from grosser matter, her Lexicon was even more helpful by calling them 'essential oils.' This provided the opening words of her poem, a sensuous image embodying the Platonic idea of essence in the rich condensation suggested by oil—superimposed on the common meaning of 'essential' as indispensable.

The second line goes on to specify this as attar of roses, one of the most costly ingredients of perfume, described in her Webster in terms of its exotic origin: 'A highly fragrant concrete obtained in India from the petals of roses.' India was a loaded word for her, typifying opulence in awesome degree, and this is certainly included in her meaning here. To a young friend getting married she sent her congratulations 'that the shortest route to India has been supremely found,' and in a poem on her own moment of love she defines it in the concluding line as 'My drop of India.' These refer to the ecstasy of love, but since she frequently equates love with poetry it becomes clear that for her India, brought into this poem by 'Attar from the Rose,' is symbolic of the heaven-on-earth that includes them both.

That perfume is merely her metaphor for poetry, rather than her real subject, seems corroborated by her apostrophe to an unnamed genius written the year before:

> This was a Poet— It is That
> Distills amazing sense
> From ordinary Meanings—
> And Attar so immense
>
> From the familiar species
> That perished by the Door—
> We wonder it was not Ourselves
> Arrested it— before—...

The rude accents of the first line make emphatic her equation of poetry with perfume. There are some interesting points in this poem, chiefly that although the poet's materials are 'ordinary' and 'familiar,' what he distills from them is 'amazing' and 'immense.' But this is a less effective use of the perfume metaphor, since it is limited to a statement of resemblances with only a vague suggestion of the process in the word 'distills.' The importance of the poem under consideration is that the conceit is expanded there to include her theory of how poetry comes into being. Like all essential oils, it is hard to come by. Just as attar of roses is a fragrant concrete extracted from the petals of the flower, so poetry is condensed from experience, hers being notably compact.

It takes so much of the one to make so little of the other and there is only one way, it must be 'wrung.' The process of making perfume is rendered with precision in twenty words, several of which work equally well both ways, illustrating the process of creating poetry by subtle indirection:

> Essentials Oils are wrung—
> The Attar from the Rose
> Is not expressed by Suns alone—
> It is the gift of Screws—

Poetry and perfume are not natural products 'expressed by Suns alone.' They are manufactured by man's cunning artifice. This is at the opposite pole from the theory of composition of the Transcendentalists. Emerson epitomized this concept of organicism by declaring that poems should grow like corn or melons in the sun, and Whitman boasted that he put the theory into practice. Dickinson was nearer to Poe in her emphasis on craftsmanship, but nearer to the moderns in her theory of language as the instrument by which the essential oils of poetry are 'ex-pressed.'

This word fits perfume-making exactly in its root meaning and poetry in its derived sense, to represent in words or symbolize in art. Just as the presses used on flower petals are operated by 'screws,' so the powerful forces that produce the extract called poetry are those that operate on the poet to turn the stuff of life into enduring art. There is a fine irony in her use of the word 'gift.' It functions not only in its simple sense of a present, but in its figurative meaning of 'an endowment conferred by the Author of our nature,' according to her Lexicon. Taken straight this would support the loose romanticism of her predecessors in applying the term 'gifted' to poets, but she gives it an unexpected turn. By the shock of juxtaposition, 'It is the *gift* of *Screws*,' she adds to the requirement of innate genius the felt pressures of experience and the technical disciplines self-imposed by the artist.

The second half of the poem seems to veer off on a new theme, the re-creative power possessed by the thing thus created, the life of art that goes on beyond the death of the artist. But with her the immortality of poetry is frequently a complementary idea to the process of creation, and in this poem the two parts are firmly knit by the perfume metaphor which is dominant to the end:

> The General Rose decay—
> While this— in Lady's Drawer
> Make Summer, when the Lady lie
> In Spiceless Sepulchre.

Perhaps it was her desire to emphasize the absolute truth of what she was saying that led her to the puzzling verb forms employed here, 'decay,' 'make,' 'lie.' Her usage is certainly idiosyncratic, but one may conjecture a purpose that fits with the general intention of this poem. By omitting the final *s* she was trying to get down to the basic stem of the verbs, their pure uninflected verbal quality, paring away number, mood, and even the partial limitation in time implied by the present tense. By this ruse she was seeking to escape from all particularity—of quantity, quality, even calendar—into the Absolute: rose decay, just as poet die, but perfume make summer.

One other personal reference need not remain conjectural. The attar of roses, appropriately laid away in the lady's drawer, refers to the manuscripts of this private poet preserved in a similar way. Taken out by her, both perfume and poems, their fragrance can recall the life that has been compressed into them, odor being the psychological key to remembrance. Even when poet and rose are long dead this fragrance remains with power to 'make summer' again, and summer for her is emblematic of life. 'It is art that *makes* life.' This was the passionate statement of belief by Henry James at the height of his career, and she shared with him this belief in its creative power. Once, thanking a friend for a painting of flowers, she wrote: 'Your Hollyhocks endow the House, making Art's inner Summer, never Treason to Nature's.'

The perfume of poetry recreates the calendar summer, which itself has created the rose of life, out of which perfume and poetry were first expressed. By contrast the rose-life, now decayed, lies in 'Spiceless Sepul-chre,' not being an essential oil. The final line is especially felicitous and saves the poem from the near-disaster of a variant conclusion, 'In Cease-less Rosemary,' which would have introduced a sentimental note and an alien theme, distracting attention from the immortality of poetry to that of the poet. Much more appropriately, the fragrance has left the body to be transmuted into spirit, and the process has been brought full circle. By implication one more unifying structure can be adduced. As mor-tality is enclosed in the tomb and perfume in its phial, so the poet's meaning is contained in the form of the poem. Because of the particular perfume chosen, this can be pushed one step further. Attar of roses, as a 'fragrant concrete,' needs no outside container. Content and form are one and the same, inseparable as in the perfect poem.

The dual theme so successfully fused here makes a link backward to all those poems concerned with the recreative power of art and forward to those concerned with the particular pressures that compelled her to create. These rather than specific events of her life were the wellsprings of her poetry, as she herself testified many times. 'You told me Mrs. Lowell was Mr. Lowell's "inspiration," ' she once wrote Higginson, for example, adding: 'What is inspiration?' The main categories of her sub-ject matter, tallying the main divisions of this book, illustrate clearly enough what were the 'screws' that ex-pressed her poetry: an almost unbearable sensitiveness to natural beauty, the ecstasy and despair of earthly and heavenly love, a compulsion to break through appearances to ultimate realities on both sides of the grave. Fortunately there are also explicit comments on how they operate, which will be helpful in formu-lating her theory of the creative process.

The kind of poetry she aspired to write was the lyric of passionate intensity and intellectual power. This even led her to be attracted to inferior models at times. In the decade before her active career began, for example, she found herself much pleased with a volume of poems by Alexander Smith sent by her brother. 'They are not very coherent,' she commented, 'but there's a good deal of exquisite frensy, and some wonderful figures, as ever I met in my life.' Smith was one of the 'Spas-modic School' of poets, who created a small sensation in the 1850's but were quickly satirized for their extravagance, overwrought metaphors, lavish emotion and disjointed thought. She outgrew this taste, just as she escaped any serious influence from Elizabeth Barrett, whose passionate utterance she once admired as the very type of 'Divine Insanity,' the witchcraft that can make days step to 'Mighty Metres' and turn noon into heaven through 'very Lunacy of Light.'

Her mature aspiration was towards controlled power, violence surprised by the mind and snared in a net of words, such as she could have learned from the religious poets of the seventeenth century. Their special qualities as defined by Eliot, who rediscovered them for twentieth-century readers, sound like the qualities of her poetry as emphasized in these pages. In spite of striking parallels between her work and theirs, however, there is only slight evidence of any acquaintance with Donne, Herbert, and Vaughan, her only known favorite among the 'metaphysicals' being Sir Thomas Browne. Yet, with some possible suggestions from them she managed to recapture a similar mode largely by her own efforts. Emerson was a kindred spirit in some ways, as in his description of the ideal poet. 'Merlin's blows are strokes of fate,' he said; freeing himself from conventions, such a bard can mount to paradise by the 'stairway of surprise.' But the search for influences yields little in the case of such a burry original. A native intensity of mind and heart gave her all the power she could manage. Her chief problem was control, and what she learned of it she learned mostly in her own way.

Her awareness of the problem is revealed in the correspondence with Higginson. Even when the relation of pupil to preceptor becomes a game, one must give due weight to her reiterated concern over lack of control. There is some seriousness beneath the surface wit when she writes, 'You think my gait "spasmodic—" I am in danger— Sir— You think me "uncontrolled—" I have no Tribunal.' She is obviously spoofing when, with a new batch of poems, she asks in mock humility: 'Are these more orderly? . . . I think you called me "Wayward." Will you help me improve?' But the statement tucked in between these petitions reveals clear-sighted self-criticism: 'I had no Monarch in my life, and cannot rule myself, and when I try to organize— my little Force explodes— and leaves me bare and charred.' This important pronouncement the critic would do well to bear in mind as he surveys the shelf of her writings.

One can evaluate more justly her real successes if he faces candidly the possibility that on the whole hers was a poetry of fragments. This holds not merely for the five hundred poems abandoned before reaching the stage of final drafts, but for many of the presumably finished ones.

The flash of inspiration almost always ignited her poetic materials but all too frequently burned itself out before she could temper and mold them into form. A remarkable experience is afforded by merely scanning the Index of First Lines in the complete edition of her 1775 poems. A sample, with very little selection, will illustrate:

> Back from the cordial grave I drag thee ...
> Baffled for just a day or two ...
> Banish air from air ...
> Be mine the doom ...
> Beauty be not caused—it is ...
> Beauty crowds me till I die ...
> Because I could not stop for death ...
> Before I got my eye put out ...
> Behind me dips eternity ...
> Belshazzar had a letter ...

Almost without exception the reader is drawn to seek out the texts referred to by these provocative first lines, but not one in ten fulfills the brilliant promise of the opening words. It would be a mistake to discard the rest as failures. Some of the purest art has been caught in fragments, it could be argued by those who admire the notebooks of Leonardo and the sketches of Goya over their finished paintings. The student of poetry can find much that is rewarding in these notations recorded by the sensitive pencil of Emily Dickinson, even when her craft failed to match her powerful perceptions. But the critic concerned with close readings may properly adhere to the fiat placing a higher value on poems that have achieved final form.

One reason so many of her thoughts exploded before they found words lies in the very intensities she was bold enough to try to capture. The extravagance of the metaphors she used in describing her preference for the poetry of power is meaningful. 'If I read a book [and] it makes my whole body so cold no fire can ever warm me I know *that* is poetry,' she told Higginson at the time of his first visit. 'If I feel physically as if the top of my head were taken off, I know *that* is poetry. These are the only ways I know it. Is there any other way.' She knew the other ways, but the kinds of poetry they defined did not interest her. Her conventional literary friend was clearly shocked to find what an eruptive force lay beneath the quiet surface of this secluded life. It was with such as him in mind that she wrote: 'On my volcano grows the Grass,' but if one could see the fire below, it would fill him with awe. Equally baffled her young cousins must have been to receive this account of a concert by Rubinstein: 'He makes me think of polar nights Captain Hall could tell! Going from ice to ice! What an exchange of awe!' If ordinary life and discourse could be represented by the temperate zone, only fire and ice could symbolize the higher reaches of artistic expression. 'My own Words chill and burn me,' she confessed.

This concept of violence as the only mode for giving utterance to the poet's experience of awe is rendered with some effectiveness in a poem that illuminates the problem of controlling power with form:

> To pile like Thunder to its close
> Then crumble grand away
> While Everything created hid
> This— would be Poetry—...

This is certainly the kind of poetry she tried to write. This is close to Emerson's ideal of the 'artful thunder' that 'makes the wild blood start.' There is even some hint of his theory of imitating natural forms in the thunder-clap simile. But she knew it took the control of art to keep such powerful perceptions from crumbling into fragments in the act of expression. The vast endowments needed by the artist led her, according to an earlier poem, to despair of ever being one. She could not be a painter, she says, but merely wonder how it would feel to have fingers whose celestial skill evokes 'Such sumptuous— Despair.' Not a musician, for marveling at the power of the cornet to float her off to the horizons, upborne as a balloon 'By but a lip of Metal.' Even more unattainable seemed the awful privilege of being a poet, at least the kind she aspired to in the concluding lines:

> Had I the Art to stun myself
> With Bolts of Melody!

All too frequently her force does explode, as in the poem under consideration. To express oneself like a thunderbolt, 'This— would be Poetry' she had begun. But in the end this powerful figure is replaced by that of fire, the burning bush; such a poet would 'consume' himself, 'For None see God and live.' Elsewhere, in reworking the Biblical account of God's apparition on Mount Sinai, she scouts Moses' boast as an improbable fable, declaring 'No man saw awe.' Out of the fragments of these poems some interesting links can be made. The poetic experience is equated with religious awe, so that ultimate perception would be like seeing God. But this is impossible, and the poet can only hope to catch a glimpse and record it in earthly forms before he is consumed. Fire and ice, volcanoes, thunder and lightning—only the most violent images drawn from nature seemed adequate for the intensities that compelled her to expression. She had moved a long way in both theory and practice from the ideal of emotion recollected in tranquility.

The central lines of the thunderbolt poem veer off on a tangential theme, equating poetry with love. As with other lyric poets, the impulse to creation came to her 'coeval' with the experience of love, she says. In a letter of 1862 she had joined them in close sequence: '*My* business is to love. . . . *My* business is to *sing.*' Sometimes it was the surge of ecstasy, though usually with the implication of fulfillment denied. More often it was the pain of love that wrung the poem from her, if she could find adequate controls. Once she explicitly relates the inadequacy of her form to the overmastering power of such emotions:

> Sang from the Heart, Sire,
> Dipped my Beak in it,
> If the Tune drip too much...
> Bear with the Ballad—
> Awkward— faltering—
> Death twists the strings—

She found encouragement from identifying herself with the 'Martyr Poets' who 'wrought their Pang in syllable.' And she knew that suffering and despair were the mainsprings of her art. There must be a loss or woe 'To bend the eye/Best Beauty's way.' This is also the only path to the house of awe. The contentment of a happy life is like a 'quiet Suburb,' she says; it is only through affliction that she can 'range Boundlessness,' through agony achieve 'A nearness to Tremendousness.'

Two passages in the letters, convincingly related by her biographers to the experience of love and loss, specifically name these as psychic pressures responsible for her poetry. During her first great creative outburst in the spring of 1862, she described in stricken terms what is now generally accepted as the departure out of her life of one whom she had chosen as her muse and the object of an intense spiritual adoration: 'I had a terror— since September— I could tell to none— and so I sing, as the Boy does by the Burying Ground— because I am afraid.' And referring to a much earlier friend, who had died in 1853 just after expressing belief in her poetic genius, she said: 'Death was much of Mob as I could master— then.' This seems to explain the lapse of her creativity during the next five or six years, just as the sentence following suggests in its poignant nature referents that a dawning new love was what brought her back to poetic life: 'And when far afterward— a sudden light on Orchards, or a new fashion in the wind troubled my attention— I felt a palsy, here— the Verses just relieve.' What counts for the student of her poetry is not the identification of the autobiographical experiences but the language in which these powerful emotions found expression.

The conjoining of love and death held a particular fascination for her. Despite her wavering attitude towards immortality, she was teased with the hope that fulfillment denied here might be achieved in heaven. Then there was the dark obsession with the grave itself, situated at the center and looking both ways: 'That *Bareheaded life*— under the grass,' she wrote, 'worries one like a Wasp.' This is no exploitation of horror in the manner of the Graveyard School, but a concern with death as the extinguisher of vitality. For pain and loss were not the only springs of her poetry. The intensity of her response to life was another of the compulsions that made creation necessary for her. 'I find ecstasy in living,' she told Higginson, 'the mere sense of living is joy enough.' Lest this be taken as mere sensuous rapture, she adds in a poem that this is what enables finite man to be a creator like 'The Maker of Ourselves':

> To be alive— is Power— ...
> To be alive— and Will!
> 'Tis able as a God—

So the sequence runs from awe to love and pain, from loss to despair and death, and back again to love and the ecstasy inspired by natural beauty.

In an early poem, drunk with the joy of living, she expresses her transport in terms of a cosmic spree. Borrowing from the humorous tall tale its hyperbolic fantasy and other extravagant techniques, she writes:

> I taste a liquor never brewed—
> From tankards scooped in Pearl—
> Not all the Vats upon the Rhine
> Yield such an Alcohol!

The temptation can hardly be resisted to read this as a parody of Emerson's transcendental rendering of poetic inspiration in 'Bacchus,' which begins:

> Bring me wine, but wine which never grew
> In the belly of the grape ...

It adds to the burlesque that hers is a malty brew instead of the traditional Dionysiac wine. Having repudiated the false, she proceeds to extol the true in soaring imagery:

> Inebriate of Air– am I–
> And Debauchee of Dew–
> Reeling– thro endless summer days–
> From inns of Molten Blue–

Even so Emerson describes as nourished by the 'dews of heaven' the true vines which produce the archetypal

> Wine that is shed
> Like the torrents of the sun
> Up the horizon walls ...

All nature participates in her bacchanal:

> When 'Landlords' turn the drunken Bee
> Out of the Foxglove's door–
> When Butterflies– renounce their 'drams'–
> I shall but drink the more!

At this point the poems diverge widely. Nature is brought into Emerson's revel too but in a very different way:

> That I intoxicated,
> And by the draught assimilated,
> May float at pleasure through all natures;
> The bird-language rightly spell,
> And that which roses say so well.

His wine is the Plotinian 'flowing' of divine spirit. Drunk with it, the poet merges with nature, breaks through convention, annihilates time and space, and recovers his lost heaven. The 'remembering wine,' by analogy with the Platonic doctrine of 'reminiscence,' enables him once again to draw on the blue tablets 'The dancing Pleiads and eternal men,' as on the first day of creation. Dickinson declines to participate in any such inebriate visions. Her beery spree lands her in heaven too, but in a different condition. She continues to drink

> Till Seraphs swing their snowy Hats–
> And Saints– to windows run–
> To see the little Tippler
> Leaning against the– Sun–

This unorthodox scene of hurrahing in heaven, with its bold metaphor converting the sun into a celestial lamp-post, may well be a comic version of spiritual intoxication as set forth in the Book of Revelation, as has been noted. But the parallels with 'Bacchus' are even more striking. The close echoes of its language up to a climactic point and the sudden turn to an opposite conclusion seem to suggest a conscious parody of its doctrines. At any rate, neither here nor elsewhere is there any evidence that she accepted the mystical bases of Emerson's transcendental esthetic: that the poet can absorb the spirit that energizes nature and so achieve merger with the Oversoul. Parody or not, this is simply a humorous fable of the poet's inspiration, drunk with the joy of life and elevated into a very sensuous heaven.

Yet there is significant meaning to be drawn from it too. Cosmic inebriation is another deliberately extravagant metaphor to go along with thunder, fires, and volcanoes. For hypersensitivity to natural beauty was another of the pressures that produced her poetry. In a late poem she wrote:

> So gay a Flower
> Bereaves the Mind
> As if it were a Woe–
> Is Beauty an Affliction– then?
> Tradition ought to know–

And in two letters near the end of her life she said, first that she lived 'In a World too full of Beauty for Peace,' and again: 'How vast is the chastisement of Beauty, given us by our Maker!' At times her reaction to beauty in nature sounds like the lyric cry of pain that had become a convention since the early nineteenth century:

> Beauty crowds me till I die
> Beauty mercy have on me
> But if I expire today
> Let it be in sight of thee—

But this has less kinship with her romantic predecessors than with Jonathan Edwards, who held that the visible universe is 'an emanation of God for the pure joy of creation, in which the creatures find their justification by yielding consent to the beauty of the whole even though it slay them.' She rejected the theological dogma implied in this thesis, for she kept God and nature sharply differentiated, even while she seized for her own purposes its esthetic doctrine.

Beauty is her name for the ecstasy with which we perceive that nature is the process of dying into immortality. She also kept man and nature separate, but as a sensitive and perceptive poet she was constantly drawn to speculate on its possible meanings for her, a subject that must be explored further in order to define how the poet makes use of nature. She herself has left a subtle aphorism defining its relation to her poetry: 'Nature is a Haunted House— but Art— a House that tries to be haunted.' This is her cryptic explanation. It can only be solved after a thorough analysis of her theory of perception, the last step in a complete formulation of her esthetics and the necessary prelude to an understanding of her nature poetry.

Two:

THE OUTER WORLD

'This Whole Experiment of Green'

5
PERCEPTION

'This whole Experiment of Green.' Emily Dickinson never contrived a better phrase to express her general view of nature. It came to her late, in 1875, after considerable travail. The surviving rough draft of the poem containing it shows all her complex revisions aimed solely at giving this important line the final expression she feels it deserves. She first writes: 'This sudden legacy of Green.' But the idea of the world being man's chief material inheritance must have seemed too utilitarian, because she immediately substitutes for 'legacy' the term for prophetic disclosure, 'Apocalypse.' Both words may imply religious conceptions of nature, as that which is either handed down or revealed to man by God. In the former, she recognizes the act of the first and true owner bequeathing his wealth to his inheritors; in the latter, the manifestation of his glory in the very object of his legacy. But the shift from legal to visionary language makes for a vast difference in spiritual meaning: 'This fair Apocalypse of Green.' If the world is truly the revelation of God, the characterizing adjective must be adequate. So 'fair' at once yields to a long string of substitutes: gay, bright, fleet, sweet, quick, swift. In the end she gives up the effort to characterize such a marvel, rewriting the line with the neutral adjective she had put down first and then canceled: 'This whole Apocalypse of Green.'

However ingrained in her may have been the Christian conception of nature as the visible manifestation of God, she shies away from such a positive commitment to the orthodox view, and 'Apocalypse' is the next word to go. The list of alternate 'candidates' on the manuscript page brings to mind her humorous poem on the poet's probing of philology for true expression rather than depending on divine inspiration. 'There came unsummoned in–/That portion of the Vision/The Word applied to fill,' she had said. Legacy and Apocalypse having been struck from the slate, there remain in the running 'Experience,' 'Astonishment,' 'Periphery,' 'wild experiment,' and *'Experiment,'* likely candidates all. Her final election is indicated by underscoring, and two fair copies she made of the poem retain this reading, that nature is 'This whole Experiment of Green.' (The manuscript is reproduced on Plate IV, p. 312, below.)

So the traditional doctrine of nature as a finished creation, whether bequeathed or revealed to man, is replaced by a word with scientific overtones, suggesting that nature is a process by which essential truths are searched out and proved in particular experiments. In creating the world God was conducting a trial operation to see if he himself could 'discover' these truths for man by laboratory methods. Her Lexicon informed her that the purpose of an experiment in science was an attempt to 'disclose the *qualities* in natural bodies' as opposed to merely observing things 'as they exist in nature.' This first great 'Experiment' suggests not only the empirical method by which truth is disclosed in the external world, but the hypothetical character of that truth and its tentativeness— note the trial adjectives 'sudden' and 'fleet.' In her choice of this phrase she seems clearly in line with such a philosopher as Royce, who a generation later pointed the way to modern theory by holding that the supposedly precise statements by which scientists describe the universe are not literally and verifiably true, but are instead 'only extremely ideal ways in which science finds it convenient to conceive facts for the purpose of a brief theoretical description.' The confidence of science in her own day that the true meaning of nature would at last be disclosed through laboratory analysis has yielded a century later to the theory that it provides instead a highly abstract system of symbols which do not show forth this reality but merely constitute the most convenient method of keeping the books of science at the moment. This is close to Dickinson's concept of the symbolic understanding of external reality to which man is limited. 'This whole Experiment of Green' poses her philosophical dilemma.

The brief poem embodying this controversial line leads directly into the difficulty she finds in grasping the meaning of nature:

> A little Madness in the Spring
> Is wholesome even for the King,
> But God be with the Clown—
> Who ponders this tremendous scene—
> This whole Experiment of Green—
> As if it were his own!

She knew the ecstasy that makes the heart leap with the upsurge of the year, and she found it salutary; but any temptation to transcendental union with nature she punctured with irony or humor. (Intoxicated by the elixirs of nature she wound up in Heaven dead drunk—according to her poem previously discussed as a possible parody of Emerson—not a 'transparent eyeball' through which the currents of Universal Being flow.) The poet's spring 'Madness,' in fancying for a moment that he can perceive from his limited center the true reality of nature, is even 'wholesome,' provided he does not take his kingship literally and assume he is its owner. If he thinks nature is *his* he is worse than mad; he is the King's jester, a fool. For he cannot own it unless he can possess it and express it. So simple mimesis, literal imitation of the thing itself, is a miracle beyond mortal powers, as an early group of poems demonstrates.

She begins on the elementary level of pictorial representation. After struggling through six stanzas attempting to describe a day in midsummer, she confesses her defeat and seeks consolation in the similar failure of 'Vandykes Delineation' of a summer day. In an earlier poem she fails equally in her effort to catch the flowing colors of sunset, only to conclude:

> These are the Visions baffled Guido—
> Titian— never told—
> Domenichino dropped his pencil—
> Paralyzed, with Gold—

A variant last line carries the finality of her conclusion one step further by specifying the results of this paralysis, 'Powerless to unfold.' These same two illustrations are combined in another poem to form an explicit statement on the limits of art:

> The One who could repeat the Summer day—
> Were greater than itself—...
> And He— could reproduce the Sun—
> At period of going down—...
> His Name— remain—

The contexts of all three poems indicate the difficulty as partly the inadequacy of the artist's mimetic powers, partly that her desire was to go beyond mere photographic realism and record 'The Lingering— and the Stain' of sunset, the 'Far Psalteries of Summer.' Though she attempted many poems on these and other aspects of the natural scene, the only successful ones are those that aimed not at literal representation but at the creation of poetic fictions showing forth the significance of nature to the human spirit.

The problem of the perception of reality in the external world, and its expression, is set forth in a cluster of poems that clarify her theory of nature as possible material for the artist. Attempting to define it in terms of pure sensation, the common-sense materialist in her is immediately answered by the poet:

> 'Nature' is what We see—
> The Hill— the Afternoon—
> Squirrel— Eclipse— the Bumblebee—
> Nay— Nature is Heaven—
>
> 'Nature' is what We hear—
> The Bobolink— the Sea—
> Thunder— the Cricket—
> Nay— Nature is Harmony—
>
> 'Nature' is what We know—
> But have no Art to say—
> So impotent Our Wisdom is
> To Her Sincerity—

The whole range of the world of eye and ear is brought to mind by the novel juxtaposition of things in her skillful playing with magnitudes, from 'Cricket' to 'Eclipse.' The negating last lines of the first two stanzas do not deny the existence of this objective reality reported by the senses, but suggest that it is false if taken as the whole truth. This is probably why she consistently places external 'Nature' in quotation marks. It is the outer shell that contains the essence.

The inner truth of nature she can only define as 'Heaven' and 'Harmony,' not actually seen and heard but presumably intuited in the mind. The manuscript variant for the latter, 'Melody,' indicates that she is not necessarily implying here the harmonious coexistence of all things in nature or the Platonic world of ideal forms. Her poetic definitions are simply insisting on the reality of essential qualities that are being demonstrated by this experiment of green. The poet dimly perceives their existence through intuition and this, together with what is observed by the sense impressions, constitutes the whole of what we know about nature. But the tenor of all her poetry is against the possibility of such knowledge. She once stated categorically: 'Nature and God– I neither knew,' and the concluding lines of the present poem place ironic limitations on her ability to 'know' that set her apart from the Transcendentalists. Unlike them, she is powerless in her limited 'Wisdom' to understand the inner truth of nature, because of its remoteness. Nor can she express it by the effortless process of 'vent,' as Emerson called it, because its very transcendence places it beyond her 'Art.' This transcendence, which she defined as 'Heaven' and 'Harmony,' is finally described as 'Sincerity,' presumably as opposed to the deceptive appearances of the objective world of squirrels, ocean, and the like. Another version of the poem substitutes 'Simplicity' as the final attribute of inner nature, in contrast to the multiplicity of its outer manifestations reported by the senses. Faced with this dual aspect of nature, the poet's ability to 'know' and 'say' is limited by impotence and inadequacy. This poem, cast in the form of an argument between poet and naturalist, gives only a negative statement of her theory.

Alienated man is left on the outside of nature, she says in another poem. Her metaphor is probably borrowed from the traveling circuses which periodically came to Amherst:

> We spy the Forests, and the Hills,
> The Tents to Nature's Show,
> Mistake the Outside for the in–
> And mention what We saw–
>
> Could Commentators on the Sign
> Of Nature's Caravan
> Obtain 'Admission' as a Child
> Some Wednesday– Afternoon–

'Spy' suggests her eager curiosity, trying to slip up on this fascinating 'Show,' but she can only be a 'Commentator' on the sign and 'mention' the outside attractions, the flatness of both words revealing the keen disappointment. For the very young the carnival's colorful vans and tents are spectacle enough, but with the dawning suspicion that there is something inside the wonder arises, Can the child ever gain 'Admission'? Her diminutive stance in this case is appropriate to both image and idea. In his ignorance of the mystery that lies behind the bright facade, man must remain forever a child incapable of growing up to true knowledge. There is no hint here of Emerson's doctrine that man can live *in* the forms of nature and so achieve union with its informing spirit. This may account for the large number of her poems limiting the natural scene to a kind of theatrical entertainment with no attempt at interpretation. The image of a circus doubles this implication. For even if one gets 'inside,' all he sees is a painted spectacle whose meaning, if any, is still hidden from the spectator. Maybe there is none, the show's function being purely to entertain. Though the second stanza is cast in the form of an inquiry, the omission of the interrogation point reduces it to the level of a rhetorical question, more like a sigh of resignation to man's irreparable estrangement from nature's essential meaning.

A group of early poems, written about 1860, shows her playing with the idea that nature has an inner secret. The bee's song has a witchcraft, she says, daybreak exalts the soul and autumn colors fill her with awe; but why or how, 'Artist— who drew me so—/Must tell!' In a fanciful moment she suspects that nature is privy to divine truth and all parts communicate with each other—sky, hill, tree, flower, bird. All but man. She accepts this exclusion as the mortal lot: 'If nature will not tell the tale/Jehovah told to her,' then man must needs be 'Admonished by her buckled lips.' She concludes with sharp impertinence: 'So keep your secret— Father! . . . In your new-fashioned world!' There may be some verbal play here to the effect that, in contrast with the old-fashioned world in which natural fact revealed spiritual truth by divine analogy, the Great Experimenter has fashioned a new world, like that conceived by the modern physicists, whose 'reality' is strictly unknowable, even unimaginable. At any rate, taking the pose of a child who prefers black magic to dogma, whether scientific or theological, she goes so far as to imply her preference for ignorance: 'If Summer were an *Axiom*—/What sorcery had *Snow*?' Though these early explorations are more coy than profound, she was moving towards the final formulation of her theory of reality.

As a poet she continued to be teased by the mystery that eluded her. Her religious training taught humble resignation since all would be made clear in heaven, but the ambiguity of the grave's meaning to her set up an ironic discontent with mortal limitations. The resulting tensions produced one of her most interesting poems on nature's secret:

> The Tint I cannot take— is best—
> The Color too remote
> That I could show it in Bazaar—
> A Guinea at a sight—
>
> The fine— impalpable Array—
> That swaggers on the eye
> Like Cleopatra's Company—
> Repeated— in the sky—
>
> The Moments of Dominion
> That happen on the Soul
> And leave it with a Discontent
> Too exquisite— to tell—
>
> The eager look— on Landscapes—
> As if they just repressed
> Some Secret— that was pushing
> Like Columns— in the Breast—
>
> The pleading of the Summer—
> That other Prank— of Snow—
> That covers mystery with Blonde—
> For fear the Squirrels— know.
>
> Their Graspless manners— mock us—
> Until the Cheated Eye
> Shuts arrogantly— in the Grave—
> Another way— to see—

The secret that baffles her in the procession of nature is strongly hinted in this succession of flashing but unfused images: colors more gorgeous than those displayed in an oriental fair, a vision of the starry host out-shining the legendary splendor of Cleopatra's court, the pressure of pain from too much beauty, the plaintive cry of summer, and the white miming of winter.

In these images nature seems on the verge of revealing a secret. There are even moments of brief ecstasy, according to the central stanza, when 'Dominion' seems actually to have happened, but it is impossible to maintain one's self in possession of that knowledge long enough to 'tell' it. The opening door closes, leaving the soul in an exquisite 'Discontent' because of the tints she 'cannot take.' Such are the 'graspless' beauties the mortal poet will never be able to express. The final stanza raises another question: Is death the meaning she intuits from nature, or immortality? Elsewhere she says that in the 'Soul's Superior instants' what is disclosed is the 'Colossal substance' of immortality. Here her pursuit of the secret ends, ambiguously, in the grave. The eye, cheated by the inscrutable forms of nature during life, will see at last the meaning of its process as ending in the extinction of death or the vision of immortality. It is notable that some of her most effective nature imagery occurs in poems on these two entwined themes.

In spite of the obsessive pull of what lay beyond the grave, however, Dickinson was not one to renounce this world altogether. As a practicing poet she is concerned also with the tints she can take, and there are several further texts that advance our understanding of her theory of perception and expression. In one late mature poem the awe she felt when confronted and excluded by nature's inner secret is rendered with haunting effectiveness. A single object is selected from the external world, 'a well,' to embody her dilemma. This magical image conjures up a whole realm of supernatural lore: healing waters, oracles for revealing the will of the gods, the wishing-well for divining the future or making dreams come true, the dark hole down which a child peers to see China or eternity in the reflected stars. The first two stanzas bring all this into play without having to specify what everyone knows, then multiply the awe by shutting the poet out from any of these beliefs:

> What mystery pervades a well!
> The water lives so far—
> A neighbor from another world
> Residing in a jar

Whose limit none have ever seen,
But just his lid of glass—
Like looking every time you please
In an abyss's face!

The well serves as the perfect image of the paradox of external nature.
So near and yet 'so far' from man's comprehension, uncomplicatedly
simple yet an insoluble 'mystery,' contained in 'a jar' yet a fluid that
eludes his grasp. And when he tries to probe its depths he is stopped by
the surface which either reflects his own face or opens up that of 'an
abyss.'

The central stanzas suggest that there may be some affinity between
other objects in nature and even such a mystery, for the grass grows
right up to its edge apparently unafraid of 'what is awe to me.' The
poem is then brought to a conclusion with an unforgettable metaphor
that leads to her final definition of the poet's relation to external nature:

But nature is a stranger yet;
The ones that cite her most
Have never passed her haunted house,
Nor simplified her ghost.

To pity those that know her not
Is helped by the regret
That those who know her, know her less
The nearer her they get.

The involute ambiguity of these closing lines can be partly clarified by
reference to poems already analyzed in this chapter. There are some,
presumably many, who do not know nature; yet they are the ones, she
says, who 'cite her most.' They are the pragmatists who simply accept
it, but 'mistake the Outside for the in.' They are also the orthodox Christians who take for granted that nature is the handiwork of God, but
make no further effort to give 'corporeal illustration' to her ghost. They
are, finally, those poets and scientists who have assumed that literal
representation of nature is possible. On the other hand, we are told that
there are 'those who know her,' though they are presumably few and
undoubtedly poets of a very special sort. At the moment all that is clear
is that their knowledge does not come from empirical analysis, but is

predicated on a recognition that nature is a 'haunted house.' What is meant by this phrase, what approach is possible, and what can be known —all this must wait until her theory of perception has been more fully explored.

The question remains as to how the poet can make use of this world if he cannot get 'inside' nature by the Transcendentalist's easy assumption of merger, the one approach she has definitely discarded. There are two possible answers left: that the only meaning is the objective reality itself, which can be grasped; or that the true meaning lies inside the perceiver. These alternatives are debated by a poet and a skeptic in a pair of poems, written in 1862 and 1864, both using the same image of a bird and its song. In the first, the poet's view triumphs:

> To hear an Oriole sing ·
> May be a common thing—
> Or only a divine.
>
> It is not of the Bird
> Who sings the same, unheard,
> As unto Crowd—
>
> The Fashion of the Ear
> Attireth that it hear
> In Dun, or fair—
>
> So whether it be Rune,
> Or whether it be none
> Is of within.
>
> The 'Tune is in the Tree—'
> The Skeptic— showeth me—
> 'No Sir! In Thee!'

There is a certain irony in the insertion of 'only,' line three, emphasized by the necessity of an extra foot. It would normally attach to 'a common thing,' and the displacement that attaches it to 'divine' makes this a sort of pyrrhic victory for the skeptic, who is scornful of Ideal reality. Again, a word of comment seems needed for the last words used to characterize the tune, whether it be Rune or none. 'Rune' means not only a mysterious or magical symbol, but also any poem or song; and the manuscript offers 'din' as a variant for 'none.' This brings them in

line with the paired adjectives in the first and third stanzas. So whether
it be song or mere sound, 'fair' or 'dun,' 'divine' or 'common,' depends
entirely on the ear that hears it. She refuses the gambit that pragmatists
have shown to be a contrived dilemma by adroitly dodging the strict
argument of idealism versus materialism. That is, she does not deny
that the bird is in the tree, nor does she say that the sound waves have
to be heard in order to exist; these are simply objective things that go on
out there, separated from man and graspless by him. Her subject is not
the singing but the hearing, '*To hear* an Oriole sing.' It is perception
that makes it a 'Tune,' gives it meaning, and this is wholly subjective.
So the skeptical ornithologist is out on a limb when he insists that the
tune is in the tree.

'Skeptic' is used here, not in the philosophical sense of one who doubts
the real existence of the objective world, but in the opposite common-
sense meaning of one who does not believe without proof of the senses.
This is made clear in the companion poem, where he is identified as
doubting Thomas. This time the empiricist is given a free hand to prove
that the 'Tune is in the Tree' by vivisecting the bird, and his experiment
seems on the surface to contradict the poet above:

> Split the Lark— and you'll find the Music—
> Bulb after Bulb, in Silver rolled—
> Scantily dealt to the Summer Morning
> Saved for your Ear when Lutes be old.
>
> Loose the Flood— you shall find it patent—
> Gush after Gush, reserved for you—
> Scarlet Experiment! Sceptic Thomas!
> Now, do you doubt that your Bird was true?

Again she employs a rhetorical structure to give the impression of a
demonstration in logic. But the scientist's success is rendered in images
that can only be read as irony, so that the poem's real meaning is inverted. In his zeal to get at the 'Music' as an objective material thing
that can be analyzed, he pulls out the inmost 'Bulb' and peels off layer
after layer. But as the botanical image implies his search for the essence
brings him down to nothing, for the life of it is *in* the layers, not contained by them.

In the living lark these living tissues would have been unrolled in one silver song after another, and their music stored up imperishably in the spiritual ear. The surgical image of the second stanza turns on the ambiguity of *it* in the promise 'you shall find it patent.' The essence he is seeking, the music, disappears under his scalpel and the only thing 'patent' is a gush of blood. 'Thomas's faith in Anatomy was stronger than his faith in faith,' she wrote in a late letter. His insistent demand for proof in this poem results in a 'Scarlet Experiment.' Her reference in poem and letter may be to Biblical Thomas, who doubted the risen Christ until he had proof of the senses; but it seems also an allusion to the skeptical Sir Thomas Browne, one of her acknowledged masters. A passage in *Religio Medici*, beginning 'In our study of anatomy there is a mass of mysterious philosophy,' tells of his carving up a corpse to find the seat of the soul. His experiment resulted in discovering 'no organ or instrument for the rational soul,' and this he concluded was a strong argument for the existence of 'something in us that can be without us, and will be after us.' Even as dissection convinced Sir Thomas of the reality of spirit, so her poetic experiment effectively disposes of the empirical approach to nature's secret for her, as suggested by the withering irony of the final question, 'Now, do you doubt that your Bird was true?' The limits she set to discovery of meaning through the analysis of objective reality, contrasted with the perceptive power of the imagination, make explicit her break with the literary and scientific naturalism that dominated the last half of the nineteenth century.

The final formulation of her theory shows her kinship with the poets and philosophers of today, as well as with Coleridge half a century before:

> Perception of an Object costs
> Precise the Object's loss—
> Perception in itself a Gain
> Replying to its price—
>
> The Object Absolute, is nought—
> Perception sets it fair
> And then upbraids a Perfectness
> That situates so far—

Her dialectic begins with a utilitarian metaphor, congenial to the New England mind, by adopting the bookkeeper's method of balancing profits and costs. What is lost is external reality, the 'Object'; what is gained is a mental equivalent, the 'Perception.' But this apparently simple mercantile transaction is complicated by the ambivalence of the 'Object Absolute' introduced in the second stanza. Her meaning presumably takes off from Locke's distinction between the primary qualities of objects, which are absolute in the sense that they exist whether perceived or not (such as bulk, extension, and motion), and their secondary qualities, which depend on the perceiver for their existence (such as taste and color). But by adding that the Absolute Object 'is nought' she embraces the modern extension of this concept, namely, that since these absolute qualities lie beyond the bounds of human perception they are as nothing to her. This central negation, then, is not so much a denial of the existence of the material world from the standpoint of traditional Idealism as it is a recognition that in a strict sense it is unknowable by the consciousness, as in the terms of the new theoretical physics, and hence has no graspable meaning for man. He is left in the end with his perceptions. He can only know what he perceives, what he himself 'creates.' This alone has value or meaning.

The poet's consciousness can only sense dimly this ultimate reality that exists independently outside his reach, the 'Perfectness/That situates so far,' or as the variant last line puts it 'so Heavenly far.' This is what she meant in the poem on the mystery of the well when, standing near and peering in, she said: 'The water lives so far.' Perception gives man human reactions to things, but never the thing-as-such. It abstracts one or more of the infinity of possible impressions of the object and then presents them as a pseudo-object, whether poem or scientific formula. This is the mode of Dickinson's best nature poems, in which these philosophical problems are not argued out, as here, but are so implicit that they reverberate in the background of the reader's awareness. Such fictions make up the world of her perceptions, the only one in which she can live since they have annihilated the external world as something directly knowable. This is perception's 'Gain,' compensating for the 'loss' of the object. When she describes the former as 'fair' it must be remembered that this is a shining word for her, matched in the poem on the oriole by 'Runic' and 'divine.' Finally, these perceptions are given expression by her novel use of language, which she is convinced has a creative power, like God's. Thus she anticipates the belief of twentieth-century poets in the magical transformation which the consciousness can make out of the world by a new union of word, thing, and thought.

Her essential kinship lies not with literary realism but with that development of poetry *From Baudelaire to Surrealism* so persuasively set forth by Marcel Raymond. Although she had no knowledge of the French symbolists and their successors, nor they of her, the literary historian will enrich our understanding of this great modern tradition by finding her proper place in it.

It is possible now to return to her cryptic statement that nature is a 'haunted house' and seek a clearer understanding of its meaning. Thing and thought are already united in the external world, but since man can neither grasp the thing nor get inside the Platonic idea of it, nature remains a haunted house to him. Though he can never hope to 'simplify her ghost,' this does not mean that nature is utterly useless to him if he is a perceptive poet. The skeleton key is found in the extension of this statement made in a letter written in 1876, about the same date as the poem: 'Nature is a Haunted House— but Art— a House that tries to be haunted.' Undue emphasis on the word 'tries' would imply that art should try literally to imitate nature. Intuition may convince the artist that an inner significance inheres in the forms of nature, but its meanings are not really accessible to him though he may be tempted to guess them in general terms of life, death, and immortality. Thus a literal imitation of nature is impossible. To return to the other key poem written in 1875, defining nature as 'This whole Experiment of Green,' it is now apparent why she abandoned the alternate definitions: 'Legacy,' as a possession too readily available, and 'Apocalypse,' as a revelation too comprehensible. Nature to her is graspless and its meaning unmanifest. God has simply made his experiment and she must make hers. It is the poet's task to create in a similar way, so that his poem also will contain the kind of dual significance he has discovered in nature by coercing the flux of experience into intelligible forms. Since his poems are artifacts rather than natural facts, he must 'try,' as nature does not need to, in order to make them haunted. Nature best serves him, then, not as a source of subject matter nor as a key to meaning but as exemplar. Also as a reservoir of imagery, since through perception he can select certain aspects of nature, or rather define his impressions of them, and give them a quasi-symbolic value that helps him create his own world.

The sharp distinction she kept between the inner and outer worlds is reflected even in her light verse. Witness one presumably composed immediately following the serious poem awarding immortal fame to any poet who could reproduce the sun in the glory of its setting. In the lighter piece, which was sent as a letter, she says that she has been running a competition with the day and boasts that she has finished two sunsets while he was making one. 'His own was ampler,' she admits, but 'Mine— is the more convenient/To Carry in the Hand.' Art is a very different thing from nature. Indeed, from the standpoint of the creative perceiver the latter may even owe its continuing existence to his consciousness. If perception and expression are constituent parts of her 'Faith' in the following poem, it becomes clear that she is referring to this demiurgic power of the artist when she writes:

> My Faith is larger than the Hills—
> So when the Hills decay—
> My Faith must take the Purple Wheel
> To show the Sun the way—...
>
> How dare I, therefore, stint a faith
> On which so vast depends—
> Lest Firmament should fail for me—
> The Rivet in the Bands

The manuscript offers two variants for 'Firmament,' 'Universe' and 'Deity,' so that the poet's powers create and sustain all—heaven, earth, the Creator himself.

In exploring the relations of man, nature, and God, she emphasizes their separateness as entities that cannot be merged, except metaphorically. And it is notable that in setting up her hierarchy of values it is man, as poet, who is supreme:

> I reckon— when I count at all—
> First— Poets— Then the Sun—
> Then Summer— Then the Heaven of God—
> And then— the List is done—
>
> But, looking back— the First so seems
> To Comprehend the Whole—
> The Others look a needless Show—
> So I write— Poets— All—

Their Summer— lasts a Solid Year—
They can afford a Sun
The East— would deem extravagant—
And if the final Heaven—

Be Beautiful as they disclose
To those who Trust in Them—
It is too difficult a Grace—
To justify the Dream—

This poem throws light on the earlier chapters setting forth her esthetic theory. The poet cannot expand to the divine circumference, but he does not need to for he can create his own. His true center is not even the outside world but his consciousness of it, and this inner world is a fiction made with words. She ranked poets first and chose to be one herself because they can create both heaven and earth, a heaven more attainable and a nature more satisfying than any the real world can offer. In this sense only is the poet 'able as a God.' This is why she elected to live in the world of perceptions, where she too could be a maker and achieve immortality in her art.

As with most poets of the nineteenth century nature plays a large part in her writings, but with radical differences. She delights in its forms and renders her perception of them with unrivaled precision. But few were as aware as she of the rigorous techniques needed for this, and of the impossibility of possessing and expressing nature by literal reproduction. For her the artist's limitation defined his proper concern: to imitate not the thing itself but its significance to the human spirit. Her break with tradition was sharp, and her foreshadowing of modern attitudes striking. She was unequaled by any of her contemporaries in preserving towards nature the approach of the artist rather than of the philosopher. Though the formulation of her highly original theory of perception came late, it is implicit in all of her best poems. It would be foolish, however, to expect consistency in one who was not promulgating a doctrine. She also experimented in several lesser modes—fantasy, light verse, even the sentimental. These comprise the great majority of her five hundred or more nature poems, and are probably responsible in large measure for her wide popular appeal. But only occasionally do any of them engage the talents of the critic.

There remains a sizable body of her poetry dealing wholly or largely with nature that deserves serious consideration, some twenty-five to fifty poems, and in some cases they yield their full meaning only after close reading. They are grouped for convenience by themes: those on the variety of natural forms, especially the odd and neglected, and their evanescence; those on nature as process, going down to death yet raising the question of immortality. In the chapters that follow they are examined in some detail.

6

FORMS

For the poet beginning a career about 1860 there was no subject so used up as nature. After more than a hundred years of drawing from it, her predecessors had almost exhausted the possibilities of an original approach. Nature as divine analogy, as escape from the evils of civilization, as healer and moral teacher, as the garment that veils indwelling spirit— all had run their course, from Thomson to Bryant to Emerson. The decade of the 1850's filled the void with a flood of sentimental nature pieces in prose and verse. Few writers of the period were wholly immune to the new fashion, even major poets like Tennyson. The Amherst circle of young people, in which Emily Dickinson and her brother and his fiancée were leading wits, was also touched by this popular sentimentalism, one of their favorite books being D. G. Mitchell's *Reveries of a Bachelor* (1850). Two references by her explicitly connect him with their nature cult. In 1852 she wrote to her brother, calling their author by his pen name: 'It's a glorious afternoon. . . . It seems to me "Ik Marvel" was born on such a day'; and to her future sister-in-law, looking forward to their customary evening walk: 'Perhaps we would have a "Reverie" after the form of "Ik Marvel". . . . We will be willing to die Susie— when such as *he* have gone, for there will be none to interpret these lives of our's.' One of the charms he held for them was his dreamy treatment of nature.

A few more samples from the letters will show how pervasive was this influence from the sentimentalists of the Fifties, and how long it lasted. Typical of her correspondence as a young lady is the message in 1854 to a former schoolmate, who has now married and left town, telling her that the bees and flowers miss her: 'in their little faces is sadness, and in their mild eyes, tears.' It may be pleaded in extenuation that a sheltered life had delayed her maturing; also, that one test of a good letter writer is that she uses the language desired by the recipient. But why did she write in 1877 to her chosen literary adviser what must have embarrassed him, conventional journalist though he was: 'Day is tired, and lays her antediluvian cheek to the Hill like a child. Nature confides now.' This sentimentalism, so disturbing to a modern reader of her personal correspondence, occasionally suffuses an entire poem as well. An early example pictures winter in terms of the flowers sleeping in their cradles, while nature hums her 'quaintest lullaby' till the bumble bees wake them in the spring. So lasting was this influence, she could be guilty of a variation on the same theme ('Nature– the Gentlest Mother') even after the full height of her poetic powers had been reached. Such mawkishness is atypical of her poetry as a whole, but the tendency was so persistent that most of her best nature poems do not come until quite late, in the 1870's.

Another manifestation of the cult of sentiment was the loose indulgence in fantasy, also characteristic of Ik Marvel's *Reveries*. It was often used by her in poems written expressly for her nephews, young cousins, and others of her small private circle who had retained something of a child's attitude towards the world. Some of them are redeemed by humor into classics of light verse; some elevate fantasy into fable and are related to her serious theory in that they present the world as a spectacle of wonder beyond the powers of interpretation. They are examples of what has been labeled not inappropriately her 'Christopher Robin' mode, and will continue to entertain their proper audience. But the fanciful for its own sake remained a troublesome aspect of her own temperament throughout maturity, as witnessed by the game of playing 'little girl' that she indulged in to the very end of her life. In the winter of 1861, for example, she wrote: 'The hills take off their purple frocks, and dress in long white nightgowns'; in the spring of 1870: 'It is lonely without the birds today, for it rains badly, and the little poets have no umbrellas'; even as late as 1881: 'We have had two Hurricanes ... and one of them came near enough to untie My Apron.' How could this childish habit be overcome, or turned to poetic advantage?

These traits would be irrelevant to the study of her poetry except that they sometimes mar her serious efforts. Many of her poems use imagery that seems uncomfortably similar to that of the letters. What has been overlooked by her critics, however, is that even sentimentalism can be one of the resources of language for the mature artist. When she detached herself from it she could employ it effectively as a foil for her wit. For example, 'Babbles the Bee in a stolid Ear,' a fusion of the trite and the unexpected, is her ironic thrust at those sleeping in confidence of the Resurrection yet in deprivation of the sights and sounds of this world. Similarly, in the best poems, her apparently undisciplined flights of fancy are caught in images of surprise. Such are the bat's wing, 'His small Umbrella quaintly halved,' and her reassuring symbol that the temporal process has resumed after the threatened 'Eclipse' of a thunderstorm: 'Nature was in an Opal Apron,/Mixing fresher Air.' As will be shown in subsequent discussions of these poems, such fanciful and sentimental tendencies were brought under control by being incorporated in her verbal strategy; instead of a flaw in her writing, they were turned into one of her special techniques for giving novelty to the poet's perceptions. Another discipline against the sentimental and the didactic was her strict adherence to the artist's approach. If she did not pretend to understand nature's meanings, as many of her predecessors did, she could at least be entertained by its show. While she rejected the Transcendentalist's search for its ideal inside, she eagerly explored its motley exterior as a source of metaphor. Having no fully articulated philosophy of nature she made few attempts to generalize about it, but chose instead for most of her successful poems some single facet to light up a truth of the inner life.

With traditional subjects drawn from nature, like flowers, she never escaped entirely from the sentimental and the fanciful. In spite of all her efforts to capture her favorite, the rose, it comes out 'a damask maid,' a 'pigmy seraph' gone astray. Her poem on the arbutus makes a fine beginning, with its precise notations:

> Pink— small— and punctual—
> Aromatic— low—
> Covert— in April—
> Candid— in May—

But her sentimental response to this early bloomer breaks the poem down in the middle with 'Dear to the Moss . . . Next to the Robin/In every human Soul.' Arbutus had been emblematic of the flower cult of the young Amherst circle. A pressed sprig of it is pinned to the manuscript of the earliest surviving note from her brother to his future fiancée, in 1850, and the stylized sentimentalism of his letter calls forth the following comment by the editor, Mrs. Bianchi: 'And it is with a bunch of arbutus hung as a May basket upon her door after dusk with all secrecy, in the pretty romantic fashion of their youth, that these letters of Austin to Sue Gilbert begin.' That Emily Dickinson shared this youthful cult is evident from a letter of about the same date naming the trailing arbutus at the head of her list of 'beautiful children of spring.' A quarter century later it intruded on this promising poem, and she only partially recovered her balance in her concluding salute to the harbinger of the new year:

> Bold little Beauty—
> Bedecked with thee
> Nature forswears
> Antiquity—

It was only by going outside the charmed circle of Flora that she achieved distinction in this area of nature.

Some of the romantics, notably Wordsworth and Whitman, had already turned to the homely aspects of the natural scene, but it was either to find God in a blackberry vine or to preach the democracy of all created things. Finding both these philosophies alien, she sought new approaches, as in a group of poems celebrating the aristocracy of leisure in nature's humbler forms. In one of them she went to the extreme of praising a weed for being unconscious of its ignominious station, at summer's close sweeping 'as lightly from disdain/As Lady from her Bower.' More successfully, she praised the clover as a 'Purple Democrat,' resolving that paradox by underscoring the royal connotation she always attached to purple; the clover's 'progress' through the summer, she said, is proclaimed by the bee. 'In sovreign— Swerveless Tune.' Perhaps the choice of weed was too perverse, and clover too closely allied with the utilitarian bee, despite her play on the word 'progress.'

In her search for the perfect symbol of the beauty and glory of mere being, she might well have fallen back on one of the flowers traditionally associated with this idea. The famous New Testament parable on the lily was certainly a favorite of hers, echoed several times in her letters, once most pertinently: 'the only Commandment I ever obeyed—

"Consider the Lilies." ' But she read the Bible more closely than most, at least as a treasure-house for poetic imagery. She did not stop with: 'Consider the lilies of the field, how they grow; they toil not, neither do they spin: And yet I say unto you, That even Solomon in all his glory was not arrayed like one of these.' She went on to the next verse where she found: 'Wherefore, if God so clothe the grass of the field. . . .' This was her avenue of escape from the trap of convention. Her poem on grass that sprang from this beloved parable, usually considered just an amusing tour de force, is an integral part of her esthetics, a celebration of the majestic leisure of nature:

> The Grass so little has to do—
> A Sphere of simple Green—
> With only Butterflies to brood
> And Bees to entertain—
>
> And stir all day to pretty Tunes
> The Breezes fetch along—
> And hold the Sunshine in its lap
> And bow to everything—
>
> And thread the Dews, all night, like Pearls—
> And make itself so fine
> A Duchess were too common
> For such a noticing—
>
> And even when it dies— to pass
> In Odors so divine—
> Like Lowly spices, lain to sleep—
> Or Spikenards, perishing—
>
> And then, in Sovreign Barns to dwell—
> And dream the Days away,
> The Grass so little has to do
> I wish I were a Hay—

The equation of grass with universal nature is achieved in one line: 'A Sphere of simple Green.' Its beauty is celebrated in appeals to the eye, the ear, and the sense of smell, but chiefly in the idyll of its happy life and death. This beauty is enhanced by the glorious leisure of nature: the grass merely sits, lies in sleep, and dreams. Its nearest approach to activity is that it dances to the wind's music, does fancy work, and bows to all the world—very queenly behavior, at least in fiction. The over-all image is a regal one. The grass is sovereign in this fable, the dew furnishing a chaplet of pearls, the barn serving as a palace, or rather a mausoleum. One is tempted to go so far as to invoke the dogma of royal divinity from the euphemism of its death: 'to pass/In Odors so divine'; and to suggest that Solomon enters the poem in the guise of a duchess, beneath the notice of this queen and scarcely recognizable to the reader without the aid of an ingenious cicerone. The grandeur of the East is conjured up more directly by the choice of 'Spikenards, perishing' (to replace the earlier variant 'Amulets of Pine,' which has no proper connection with grass). The Bible frequently uses this rare and costly ointment as a symbol of sovereignty, once specifically of the resplendent Solomon. But spikenard also brings the poem back to a simple green meadow in New England, where it is found in abundance, an aromatic field herb whose fragrance would be inevitably mixed with the 'lowly spices' of grass during fall mowing. And this circular pattern is reinforced by the repetition of the first line in the conclusion: 'The Grass so little has to do.' This brings up again the paradox of nature's leisure. Considering the numerous tasks the grass performs, 'so little' seems an ironical way of describing all this doing, an antiphrasis. But 'little' refers to the simplicity rather than to the small number of its activities. Like those of a queen they make up a single 'Sphere' of activity, all the manifold aspects of its life and death forming a 'simple' circle around a regal center of being. In contrast to the frenetic business of normal existence, this is indeed leisure.

'Loafe with me on the grass' had been the theme song in a volume of poetry published a few years before, and already famous, but she was not acquainted with *Leaves of Grass.* Just a month or so after composing her own poem on grass, she answered a query of Higginson's (April 25, 1862): 'You speak of Mr Whitman. I never read his Book— but was told that he was disgraceful.' This is not the word she would have used had she actually read him, unless to express esthetic disapproval. But they were poles apart in all ways, as the contrast in their treatment of grass illustrates. His is a democratic symbol, hers aristocratic. His is based on a pantheistic merger of God, nature, and man; hers, at least by implication, keeps the three quite separate. Though both include the idea of leisure, Whitman's point, seriously driven home as a basic philosophy, is that if man will loaf with him at ease 'observing a spear of summer grass' he will find kinship with nature and the Oversoul. God does not figure at all in Dickinson's poem, either as creator or indwelling spirit. And, significantly, in her celebration of the leisure of nature man is left out altogether too.

It is true the poet enters in her last line, but only as an excluded spectator. 'The Grass so little has to do,' she says, 'I wish I were a Hay'—ending appropriately on a comic note. The grammatical joke, which disturbed one of her literal-minded early editors just as it has solemn critics ever since, was clearly deliberate. To relate herself to grass or hay posed a problem, since both words had lost their singular reference and become collective. But the idea of such a relation was sufficiently eccentric to justify breaking through the convention of number and using an obsolete form, 'a Hay.' She had made use of the same heresy before in a letter of 1856 that has an interesting connection with this poem. After a beginning in the mode of high comedy, she suddenly changed key: 'I have another story, and lay my laughter all away, so that I can sigh. Mother has been an invalid since we came *home*. . . . I don't know what her sickness is, for I am but a simple child, and frightened at myself. I often wish I was a grass, or a toddling daisy, whom all these problems of the dust might not terrify.'

In the poem, just as she dodges the preachment against mammonism which had motivated the parable of the lilies of the field, so she wisely omits the didactic theme of nature-as-healer which had grown hackneyed in the poetry of her century, and which is at least incipient in this letter. As she matured she learned to accept the loneliness of the human condition. 'I wish I *was* a grass,' the lightly expressed volition in the letter, became 'I wish I *were* a Hay.' Man only enters the poem through the subjunctive mood, his desire to escape into nature being contrary to the scheme of things. 'Hay' implies, if possible, an even greater simplicity and leisure than 'grass.' Having lost all motion and color, it no longer exists except as an anonymous center of radiating odors and dreams. Similarly, at death she might hope to 'pass' into her poems. But the majestic leisure of nature is foreign to the living poet, who stands outside the show. And, it may be added, the 'Christopher Robin' attitude could produce some of her best humorous poems.

A companion piece, her seemingly trivial poem on the pebble, supplements her tribute to grass by emphasizing more insistently nature's separateness from man:

> How happy is the little Stone
> That rambles in the Road alone,
> And doesn't care about Careers
> And Exigencies never fears—
> Whose Coat of elemental Brown
> A passing Universe put on,
> And independent as the Sun
> Associates or glows alone,
> Fulfilling absolute Decree
> In casual simplicity—

There are a few effective strokes, as when she centers attention on her symbol with the shock of inverted logic, by having the universe borrow its color from the 'elemental Brown' of the little stone, which is thus placed at the heart of nature. But the expository purpose intrudes on the poetic possibilities of the subject, so that the result is chiefly a statement of philosophic position. This is of extreme interest, however, as is the argument by which it is reached. The stone is carefree because it fulfills 'absolute Decree,' that is, not merely the law of its own nature but the universal laws that manifest themselves in suns as well. Finding its own color reflected in the universe, it 'associates' or enjoys its individual existence with equal casualness. By calling it 'independent as the Sun,' she brings to mind her praise of the moon for being untouched by mortal harassments—life, death, immortality—but instead 'engrossed to Absolute—/With shining.' Its perfect serenity results from its 'simplicity,' as with the grass. But this happy state of affairs is impossible for the human being, whose consciousness separates him from this harmony. The stone is utterly content, and incapable of feeling alone, because it is unconscious. Unlike man it is not concerned with 'Careers' and never fears 'Exigencies,' the two words that evoke the human contrast in a poem otherwise concerned solely with the absolute separateness of nature.

Butterflies and bees, along with flowers, figure prominently in her poems but with these traditional favorites too she had difficulty in avoiding fantasy and sentimentalism. The butterfly seemed the very embodiment of nature's mystery, but her pursuit of its magical flight never netted her a successful poem. A spectacular illustration of her failure is the effort beginning:

> Two Butterflies went out at Noon—
> And waltzed upon a Farm—
> Then stepped straight through the Firmament
> And rested, on a Beam—...

Completed in 1862, this poem never satisfied her. She went back to it for another try sixteen years later, broke down the fair copy into a worksheet draft, and finally abandoned it in a complicated tangle of phrases —'a fascinating document of poetic creativeness in travail,' according to her editor. Only when she turned to the image of the cocoon was she able to put this gaudy miracle to work significantly in her poems.

Similarly the bee usually led her into fantasy, as a lover ravishing a flower or as a knight errant. Once she transformed the latter into a buccaneer with some success, but what gives this poem its distinction is the dialectical twist in the second stanza:

> Bees are Black, with Gilt Surcingles—
> Buccaneers of Buzz.
> Ride abroad in ostentation
> And subsist on Fuzz.
>
> Fuzz ordained— not Fuzz contingent—
> Marrows of the Hill.
> Jugs— a Universe's fracture
> Could not jar or spill.

By calling the bees buccaneers she conjures up those free-booters, like Sir Francis Drake, who raided the Spanish Main in the sixteenth century. The term, from *boucan,* was originally applied to wild hunters in Haiti who lived on the country, independent of civilized markets. So her black knights are land-pirates, mounted on horses rather than ships, and ranging 'abroad' over the countryside. Her epithet combines the suggestions of looting and swaggering. 'Buccaneers' also fits the alliterative pattern which helps to puncture their pretentiousness, for 'Buzz' along with its rhyme word 'Fuzz' cuts them down to size. The horn they wind is that absurd hum-bum that has given the bumble-bee his name. The plunder they proudly carry off is just pollen. Though they seem free and self-sufficient, like Emerson's 'Humble-Bee,' they are dependent on the lowly fuzz if they are to 'subsist.' For all their 'ostentation' their panoply is 'gilt' not gold. Are these anthropomorphic bees? a sly comment on men as pretentious swaggerers who are in the end dependent on the very nature they loot?

The second half of the poem moves in another direction, with the theological overtones of 'ordained.' 'Surcingle' in stanza one, it may be noted, prepares for this since it can mean the girdle of a cassock as well as a saddle-girth. Has the bee-buccaneer become a priest, pollen and the nectar from his 'Jugs' now transformed into the elements of a miniature Eucharist? At any rate the bee's sustenance, actually a paste made of the two, is declared to be 'ordained.' This term suggests the stable order of creation as distinguished from what is accidental, what is appointed and decreed rather than merely 'contingent.' The bee's food is also described by a novel metaphor, 'Marrows of the Hill,' that innermost quintessence which contains the vital energy. Even if there are earthquakes or universe-quakes—if the bones of the hills or the honey-jugs of blossoms 'fracture,' if the flowers themselves fade away in their contingency and likewise the bees that subsist on them—still the essence of life will remain unspilled because it is necessary, that which we cannot conceive as non-existing. But it would be folly to push the theological import of this poem too far. The whole argument about 'ordained' and 'contingent,' it must be remembered, has been brought on by 'Fuzz.' This takes the reader back to the comic rhyming of the first stanza, and to the context of the letter in which the poem was sent: 'I must show you a Bee, that is eating a Lilac at the Window. There— there— he is gone!' Addressed to a gay-hearted friend who usually called out her lightest moods, these are scarcely the words to introduce a profound poem. It is an interesting one, but certainly not a serious statement of her philosophy.

Birds occur in her poems next to bees in frequency, but rarely with distinction. The perennial darlings of American poets like the robin and bluebird were hers too, but her many attempts to catch them, despite her adroit descriptive powers, tended towards fantasy with little meaning. The quarrelsome blue jay, seemingly at war with nature, produced a sharper poem. She commissioned him a 'Brigadier,' levying on the root meaning of strife and contention as well as on the current usage of this word as the designation of a commanding officer. The military terms set the tone, from 'warrior' in the opening lines to 'redoubt' at the end, with some highly effective passages such as:

> The Pillow of this daring Head
> Is pungent Evergreens—
> His Larder— terse and Militant—
> Unknown— refreshing things—

But the controls are not firm enough to bring off the symbol of one at war with all the world. The bobolink as the irreverent 'Rowdy of the Meadows' also appealed to her. His attire is impudent and defiant, his sentiments seditious, his song 'Heresies of Transport/Or Puck's Apostacy.' He pays his brief melodious compliments to creation, then suddenly the 'Sorcerer . . . is gone,' lured away on undisclosed business of his own. Some of the phrasing is striking but the sorcery is not sustained. This intended effect is more fully achieved in her poem on the oriole. His splendor is figured forth as that of Burmah, a flashing meteor, or the theatricality of pageant and oratorio; his dual nature in the riotous living of the yet beloved prodigal son and in the casuistry of a Jesuit. But the rush of details is overwhelming, and they fail to cohere in a convincing image of the 'Dissembler' with his golden magic.

As Dickinson had less success with flowers than with the lowly grass, so she wisely turned from the conventionally treated creatures in nature to the odd and neglected. Using the technique of scientists, who often make important discoveries by investigating apparent exceptions or 'freaks' in the natural order, she made some of her best guesses at nature's secrets by analyzing its 'eccentrics.' At the same time she discovered one of the novel approaches that made her nature poetry the beginning of a new mode rather than the end of an old one. One quatrain, that seems to begin on a sentimental note, will serve as a proem to her most original exploitation of nature's forms:

> If Nature smiles— the Mother must
> I'm sure, at many a whim
> Of Her eccentric Family—
> Is She so much to blame?

Nature is menagerie, but it is more than mere entertainment. In the side shows of its carnival she sought both amusement and instruction.

Poking around among the odds and ends of nature, she was alert to the possibility of finding flaws in the cosmic order, at least as established by orthodoxy. In her poem on the housefly, her initial metaphor is too fanciful to sustain but it does lead to an interesting conclusion. 'Those Cattle smaller than a Bee/That herd upon the eye,' she says, are the most domestic of animals but not happily domesticated. Having no barns of their own they take stalls in the house, but their activities are so 'odious' the only possible reaction of the human family is one of 'abhorrence.' Unable to see how they fit into the scheme of things, she rejects them:

> Of their peculiar calling
> Unqualified to judge
> To nature we remand them
> To justify or scourge—

The theological connotations of 'justify' do not serve her purposes here as well as the legal. She is certainly not asking nature to apply the doctrine of Atonement to the fly, though she may have in mind something of the Miltonic purpose of explaining the enigmas of God to man. Growing up in a household of lawyers, she probably meant chiefly that nature must vindicate the fly by proving him conformable to law, to show the justice in his existing at all, or else punish him as an offense against the natural order. Since he is outside her jurisdiction, she herself is 'Unqualified to judge.'

Another domestic animal, the rat in the wainscot, is subjected to the same test. She evokes the stock response without having to name it, that he is so inimical to man his presence in the house is denied as shameful or only admitted with a shriek of terror. Yet she accepts him as an integral part of nature:

> The Rat is the concisest Tenant.
> He pays no Rent.
> Repudiates the Obligation—
> On Schemes intent
>
> Balking our Wit
> To sound or circumvent—
> Hate cannot harm
> A Foe so reticent—
> Neither Decree prohibit him—
> Lawful as Equilibrium.

'Concisest' works several ways in this poem. It describes the rat's relationship with society as terse and succinct, typified in the laconic second line, 'He pays no Rent.' Reversing the plight of the fly who is repudiated by man, here she posits the rat as one who repudiates civilization, founded as it is on the laws of property. Yet though he lives in the midst of it, his difference is such that all our wisdom cannot fathom his activities nor can the decrees of society apply to him. The rat is not contingent on another's will but is necessary like any other part of the natural order: 'Lawful as Equilibrium.' 'Concisest' also in the sense that his story says so much in so little, a tight comprehensive summary of the whole issue of nature's separateness from man. And finally, because this word describes the form and style of her poem.

In general she suspected all the objects in nature of fitting into some harmonious scheme, or at least of having relations with each other, however obscure to man's understanding. The emphasis is usually less on this natural concord than on man's separation from it. But in her poem on the bat she chose one of the most shockingly different of the eccentrics as a signal for man's belief in and praise of an ordered creation:

The Bat is dun, with wrinkled Wings—
Like fallow Article—
And not a song pervade his Lips—
Or none perceptible.

His small Umbrella quaintly halved
Describing in the Air ·
An Arc alike inscrutable
Elate Philosopher.

Deputed from what Firmament—
Of what Astute Abode—
Empowered with what Malignity
Auspiciously withheld—

To his adroit Creator
Ascribe no less the praise—
Beneficent, believe me,
His Eccentricities—

The chief visual image, an 'Umbrella quaintly halved,' is memorable because of its novelty, but this is not just a whimsical figure. The bat is so 'unnatural' that its wings—its distinguishing feature—can only be described in artificial terms, as if they were contrived rather than created. Though true wings, they are not feathered but leathery membranes stretched taut. It flies but is not a bird; instead, a flying mammal, unique among its order in possessing such power. This is its spectacular eccentricity, rendered by the mechanical metaphor of the umbrella. (The disparity at all other points, as in the umbrella's utility, is negatived by cutting it in half.) Such an important point tempted her into the rare excess of describing it a second time, 'with wrinkled Wings,' a far less effective phrase but followed immediately by a striking simile, 'Like fallow Article.' This reinforces the idea of an artifact, and at the same time introduces another oddity: it is neglected, like an uncultivated field, somehow left out of the normal routine. 'Fallow' also adds the withered brown of fading autumn colors to the dull swarthiness of 'dun.' The cumulative effect of all this is that the bat is a crepuscular thing, taking on the obscurity of the twilight in which it wheels.

'And not a song pervade his Lips.' Several accurately noted details are here put to special use. A mammal with a mouth but with feebly developed vocal cords, in some species actually atrophied, this is a bird without a beak that cannot sing—its very silence contributing to the awe felt by the poet. 'Or none perceptible,' she adds significantly, implying that there may be things going on out there beyond man's powers of perception, here precisely the bat's 'song' at a pitch beyond the range of the human ear. Likewise the 'Arc' of its career is 'inscrutable,' its erratic flight being guided not by eyesight but by its preternaturally sensitive nose-leaf and wing membranes. Is the next line, 'Elate Philosopher,' a sly thrust at the all-seeing Emerson, who proclaimed the humble bee an exalted seer in exactly the same phrase? The whole passage, lines 6 to 8, tempts one to such a reading. 'Describing' suggests that the bat is writing on the air, his wings being really his hands, fingers with spread membranes. He is spelling out his philosophy, his arcs or bridges that span from nature to God to man, from the sensory world to the world of absolutes. These are the same kind of 'arcs' of meaning that the Transcendentalists tried to make when 'elated' by their vast intuitions of ultimate truth. But the bat's handwriting is 'inscrutable,' undecipherable hieroglyphs. At any rate, she confesses that she does not know whether the bat is a deputy from some subtle region above or from the powers of darkness. The surviving manuscripts indicate that she tried 'Malevolence' before deciding upon the more extreme degree of evil expressed by 'Malignity,' which calls up all the traditional lore of the vampire. For her the final meaning is 'auspiciously withheld.' But, though man can no more truly see the bat than he can hear it, he can at least praise the ingenuity of a creator whose ways are past understanding.

'Beneficent' because it clears the air of insects, of course, but what about the species that lives by sucking the blood of other animals? The most casuistical defense of the Great Chain of Being, as it became more and more temporalized, argued that gradation implies difference and extreme degrees of difference beget conflict, so that 'nature red in tooth and claw' is a sign that all is well. She seems to be justifying the bat by this argument. Even more so the worm, in an otherwise trivial poem. Until she saw it furnishing breakfast for a bird, she says, it seemed 'a needless life.' This function gave it a place in the chain, or as she puts it 'left the little Angle Worm/With Modesties enlarged.' But the structure of this poem throws the meaning in another direction, for she begins by calling the 'Pink and Pulpy multitude' that appears on the ground after rain 'Our little Kinsmen.' Puritan divines in exalting the sovereignty of God had compared man to a worm so many countless times as to make the identification almost automatic. The inference seems inescapable here, especially since at the end she wonders if God may have judged her as she had judged the worm, 'a needless life,' before discovering her place in the scheme. Does man gain status only because he is eaten by the Great Bird, or swallowed in the maw of death? Rather, by shifting the emphasis from worm to man, she seems to concern herself less with expounding doctrine than with finding amusement in the Christian insistence on humility. 'Our Pastor says we are a "Worm",' she commented in a letter. 'Do you think we shall "see God"?'

Indeed, it is quite impossible to demonstrate any consistent theological or philosophical system as forming the basis of these poems on nature's eccentrics. They are not written to support Calvinism, the doctrine of Plenitude, or any other established convention. 'Nature is "old-fashioned",' she said late in life, 'perhaps a Puritan.' But there she is merely defining one way of looking at its forms, as literal manifestations of God's power. By contrast her own poems seem strikingly new-fashioned. In them the worm is accepted as a kinsman, but the fly is rejected; the bat is praised for beneficence and the rat justified as integral with nature, while the mushroom is cast out as an apostate (as will be seen). Each poem is simply its own exploration of truth. These do not add up to a Great Chain of Being. This idea, to be sure, was familiar to her from childhood in old-fashioned Amherst, where James Thomson remained after more than a century the favorite poet of external nature. Her acquaintance with the autumn section of *The Seasons* is indicated by her casual allusion to 'Mr. Thomson's "sheaves"' in an early poem. But though this furnished her a ready source of the doctrine, there is little evidence that she subscribed to it. When she did attempt a full-scale celebration of Plenitude (as in a lyric written the same year, 1859, 'Bring me the sunset in a cup'), she fell into rhetoric. As with many of her thoughtful contemporaries, all 'the traditional systems of belief had broken down for her so that she could only use them as part of her strategy of paradox. She had to create her own structures of belief at the same time that she illustrated them in her poems. Those on nature's forms exemplify a theory of separateness that is entirely her own. Even if there is a 'chain' in nature, man is excluded from it.

In her passion for originality Dickinson managed on the whole to avoid the dangers of derivativeness in her nature poetry, partly by choosing novel forms to 'imitate.' But having rejected the conventional approaches of the past hundred years, she found nature an increasingly difficult and baffling subject. When she treated it as mere spectacle her poems tended to run off into fantasy, though she achieved some real successes in this genre, as in her tribute to the grass. When she attempted to capture it directly they tended, in spite of her acute descriptive powers, to shatter themselves in a cataract of images, except for her poems on eccentrics like the bat. Her best efforts grew more directly out of her theory of perception—that which is gained by the mind in compensation for the loss of the object. The former is the only reality the poet can know, and it defines the kind of beauty he can create. Emphasis on the latter produced a corollary to her general rule limiting the mimetic powers: her theory of the evanescence of objective beauty before the poet's very eyes. It is the explicit subject of a brief poem:

> Beauty— be not caused— It is—
> Chase it, and it ceases—
> Chase it not, and it abides—
> Overtake the Creases
>
> In the Meadow— when the Wind
> Runs his fingers thro' it—
> Deity will see to it
> That You never do it—

She begins with the general Platonic notion of beauty as an essence belonging to a realm higher than the sense world of cause and effect. But since she is not a philosopher she does not concern herself with the problem of whether ideal forms can actually be embraced by men's minds.

Instead, the problem of the poem is that the *where* of beauty can never be pin-pointed. The senses create the illusion that it 'abides' in certain objects or places, but it does not reside there and hence cannot be pursued. It is not a thing that can be caught, but is intangible like the wind. How then express it in words? 'The Creases in the Meadow' is her apt metaphor for it, not an entity but a nothingness, the spaces where the grass was until the wind 'Runs his fingers thro' it.' If one tries to 'overtake' them they vanish and others appear further on. The image works both visually and as an exemplification of her esthetic theory. But the triple rhyming in the last lines gives humor to her conclusion: 'Deity will see to it/That you never do it.' She avoids the solemnity of arguing propositions in philosophic idealism by simply saying that the poet's attempts to capture objective beauty end in failure. As to the possibility of embracing it as an essence, she says elsewhere, 'The Definition of Beauty is/That Definition is none.' The pain caused by her inability to analyze it is eased by recognizing that it is an Absolute. It manifests itself only evanescently and so cannot be grasped. The beauty of nature, whether as external object or ideal form, is only a quasi-legacy to man, according to still another poem: 'a syllable-less Sea' that cannot be possessed or told in words. But the perception of its evanescence can be expressed, as the poems in the next chapter will show.

7

EVANESCENCE

Of all Emily Dickinson's bird poems there is only one that realizes the full potential magic in flash of color and whir of wing, and it does so paradoxically by concentrating on their disappearance rather than their appearance. This is her famous eight-line snare for the hummingbird, set late in life. Deservedly admired as a flawless lyric, it is also significant in relation to her theory of perception, being her most vivid rendering of the elusive, even perhaps illusory, quality of objects in nature. She made two attempts to catch this bird, nearly twenty years apart, and a comparison of the early with the late will show her progress from an attempt at literal description of an object to the discovery of a perfect image for its evanescence. The beginning of her poem in 1862 was particularly discursive:

> Within my Garden, rides a Bird
> Upon a single Wheel—
> Whose spokes a dizzy Music make
> As 'twere a travelling Mill—
>
> He never stops, but slackens
> Above the Ripest Rose—
> Partakes without alighting
> And praises as he goes,

> Till every spice is tasted—
> And then his Fairy Gig
> Reels in remoter atmospheres—
> And I rejoin my dog—...

The rape of the rose was too long drawn out, the speed of flight blurred by conflicting images, and for the bird's magical disappearance she fell back on a fanciful cliché from fairy tales. More significantly, very little of the hummingbird was there in fact or in effect, as none of the special techniques by which she finally caught him were employed.

When she returns to the theme in 1880 all this sprawling first half of the poem is reduced to a single stanza, which approaches a Japanese *haiku* in the conciseness of its notation and in its reduction of a natural phenomenon to a mental image:

> A Route of Evanescence
> With a revolving Wheel—
> A Resonance of Emerald—
> A Rush of Cochineal—...

The esthetic problem of imitation is raised at the outset by 'Evanescence,' a word that in her day had not yet acquired the modern abstracted sense of fleeting or transitory, but held strictly to the root meaning of 'vanishing.' How can the artist represent a hummingbird if its flight is a 'disappearance from sight,' as her Lexicon defines it, 'by removal to a distance'? She undoubtedly chose such an extreme example of elusive form in nature because of its dramatic value. But for her it also represented a general truth, as she phrased it in a letter of the same period: 'All we secure of Beauty is its Evanescences.' This miracle is then rendered in terms of motion, sound, and color intricately woven into an image pattern by synaesthesia. To begin with, the outline of the bird's figure is replaced by its disappearing path across the field of vision. The visual effect is the converse of the photographic one of multiple rapid exposures of a moving object on a single plate. Her first line records not the simultaneous presence but the simultaneous vanishing of the bird at every point. The second, even in the phrasing given above, 'With a revolving wheel,' helps to complicate this effect because it does not describe the actuality of vibrating wings so much as the optical illusion created by them. Better still, a rough pencil draft offers a fascinating series of variants: 'With a delusive, dissolving, dissembling, renewing wheel.'

Almost any of these would have been more pertinent to her purpose, especially 'dissolving' which would have turned the motion of the whirling wheel into a trick of prestidigitation, the bird vanishing before astonished eyes.

'A Resonance of Emerald' transmutes the humming sound by sympathetic vibration into iridescent color. Lest this be thought extravagant, one can quote from the normally sober *Encyclopaedia Britannica* in the edition available to her. There the great zoologist Alfred Newton, in his article on the hummingbird, declared that 'ornithologists have been compelled to adopt the vocabulary of the jeweller in order to give an idea of the indescribable radiance' of its plumage. Dickinson's ecstasy was shared by contemporary scientists, though the use of synaesthesia to make the music become visible in the emerald sheen of wings and back is her own effective contribution. Again she showed her originality by avoiding such a hackneyed image as 'ruby throat' and writing instead, 'A Rush of Cochineal.' No jewel offered quite the brilliance of this rare pigment used since ancient times to make especially vivid reds, like crimson and scarlet. To see this spot on the hummingbird's throat, the poet-spectator-reader must take the stance of the flowers themselves. Then, as color is transformed into a rushing assault, the miracle of the hummingbird vanishes in a blinding flash of cochineal. The regius professor of zoology at Cambridge was not far behind her in expressing his wonder. As he enumerated the dazzling splendors of this tiny bird, he confessed that for him each newly discovered modulation of its beauty 'excites fresh surprise and exemplifies the ancient adage—*maxime miranda in minimis Natura.*' But the marvel the poet is seeking to evoke is of a more philosophical order.

In her earlier attempt to explain this, it was the discursive method she employed that broke down the poem as a poem. Returning now to the conclusion of this 1862 version, one finds after the bird's sudden departure an unexpected shift to exposition, 'And I rejoin my dog.' These two intruders then proceeded to argue the problem of appearance versus reality, and the positivist won out over the idealist in a logical Q.E.D.

> And He and I, perplex us
> If positive, 'twere we—
> Or bore the Garden in the Brain
> This Curiosity—

> But He, the best Logician,
> Refers my clumsy eye—
> To just vibrating Blossoms!
> An Exquisite Reply!

She was caught in a double trap of mode and meaning. In her final triumph two decades later she escapes from the artificial dilemma (is Reality 'out there' or 'in here'?) by making a structure of images instead of logic. Here, after the mounting tension of her brilliant notations of color, sound, and motion in the first stanza, she relaxes for two lines, in which the hummingbird is conspicuous by his absence, in order to catch her breath before launching the daring image of her conclusion:

> And every Blossom on the Bush
> Adjusts its tumbled Head—
> The mail from Tunis, probably,
> An easy Morning's Ride—

That jet planes can actually accomplish this today is not a sign of her prophetic powers, but a reminder of the modern reader's need to understand her metaphor in its own terms if he is to feel the full effect of her bird's flight beyond the barriers of space and time. 'The mail from Tunis,' when connected with the idea of 'resonance' and 'revolving' wheels, may suggest the speed with which sound and light are dispersed through space. 'Tunis' was infinitely remote to her, and an 'easy Morning's Ride' from there could only have been achieved on a magic carpet. Yet from this exotic place at such incredible speed comes the commonplace daily 'mail,' the familiar figure of the postman on his 'Route' jostling the wonder of it all.

She may well have found the suggestion for her image in a passage from *The Tempest*: The Queen of Tunis, who dwelt 'Ten leagues beyond man's life,' could not possibly get letters from Naples 'unless the sun were post.' For the reader intimate with Shakespeare, as she assuredly was, this sidelong allusion may extend the poem's meaning far beyond the specific lines of the source. It brings to mind the figure of Prospero gazing in wonder at the elusive beauty of this green earth, and the even more shimmering beauty of the unseen world within which the poet can create by invoking his muse Ariel. As she developed her theory of perception, she gradually came to believe, as the twentieth-century scientist does also, that objects in nature cannot be literally grasped by the senses or reproduced by mimetic skill. She does not pretend to offer a real hummingbird snared from the external world but a poetic hummingbird, the perception of one in the garden of the brain. 'All we secure of Beauty is its Evanescences.' Bird or poem? Her own flights from Tunis, the packets of extraordinary poems left in manuscript, she described elsewhere as her 'Letter to the World.'

A passage in her correspondence during the same period clarifies the significance of all this for her esthetic theory and relates it specifically to this poem. Thanking a friend for painting her a small panel representing a group of Indian Pipes, she first referred to her life-long preference for this weird flower, saying that 'when a wondering Child [it seemed] an unearthly booty, and maturity only enhances mystery, never decreases it.' Then, turning to the painting itself, she made a cryptic comment on the temerity of man's attempts at representing nature: 'To duplicate the Vision is even more amazing, for God's unique capacity is too surprising to surprise.' A few days later she wrote to the same friend, 'I cannot make an Indian Pipe but please accept a Humming Bird':

> A Route of Evanescence
> With a revolving Wheel—
> A Resonance of Emerald—
> A Rush of Cochineal—
> And every Blossom on the Bush
> Adjusts its tumbled Head—
> The mail from Tunis probably,
> An easy Morning's Ride—

The only change she made in the draft of the poem included in her letter was to omit the comma before 'probably,' making the modifier restrictive. This removes any doubt that it is all a metaphor.

The elusiveness of natural forms can be shown most vividly when they are in rapid motion. If this is pre-eminently true of the hummingbird it is nonetheless true of all winged things. Once she dramatized the idea of evanescence for birds in general, using the domestic setting of a garden to suggest the possibility of rapprochement, then touching the spring of difference to separate the two worlds suddenly and irrevocably:

A Bird came down the Walk—
He did not know I saw—
He bit an Angleworm in halves
And ate the fellow, raw,

And then he drank a Dew
From a convenient Glass—
And then hopped sidewise to the Wall
To let a Beetle pass—

He glanced with rapid eyes
That hurried all around—
They looked like frightened Beads, I thought—
He stirred his Velvet Head

Like one in danger, Cautious,
I offered him a Crumb
And he unrolled his feathers
And rowed him softer home—

Than Oars divide the Ocean,
Too silver for a seam—
Or Butterflies, off Banks of Noon
Leap, plashless as they swim.

What undercuts the make-believe of friendliness in the first part of the poem is the casually dropped second line, 'He did not know I saw.' As long as the poet is unobserved, the life of nature goes on with such spontaneous informality as to give her some hope of participating in it. But the clues showing this to be an alien world are planted thick.

The bird's dinner is a worm, eaten 'raw,' an attribute set off in commas for emphasis; the human being cooks his meat and sticks to vertebrates, in general. Stanza two excludes her from the scene more effectually still by introducing an ingenious bit of grammatical magic. 'Dew' and 'grass' are too small for man to take cognizance of except in the plural sense; but by the unorthodox addition of an article to make the collective nouns singular she keeps the whole garden world reduced to the bird's size. The poet is left towering above and outside, having no magical elixir like Alice in Wonderland to shrink her to a level where communication is possible. So after washing down his repast with 'a

Dew' the bird continues his 'walk,' recognizing his fellow the beetle with a show of courtesy, still unaware of the human intruder. As she stoops to join in, the bird's eyes become 'frightened Beads.' According to folk wisdom the surest sign of recognition between human beings, when speech and gesture are withheld, is the expressiveness of the eyes; only in death or a state of extreme fright would they be described as glassy. But those of the bird are always beady, and now as he senses danger they glaze with fear.

'I offered him a Crumb.' With this first movement on the part of the spectator the game of friendly relations is up. The fantasy of the last six lines is in striking contrast to the miniature scene and slow action of the first three stanzas. Only by extravagant language could she render the speed and distance of his removal. The wing motion is that of oars rowing through the seamless ether, to take him 'home.' How remote that is from the home of the poet, to which she now presumably returns with her unpartaken crumb, she illustrates by the even more fanciful figure of butterflies swimming 'off Banks of Noon.' All winged things seemed to her to live in another world, as she said elsewhere of the butterfly, who vanishes 'To Nowhere . . . in purposeless Circumference.' Again she wrote: 'High from the earth I heard a bird'; baffled in her attempt to follow his flight or understand his behavior, she could only come up with the prosaic conclusion: 'How different we are!' Her failure to establish relations with the one in her garden dramatizes this difference.

A companion piece to the bird who disappears in the air is her poem on the frog who disappears in his watery home. This April orator rises from his 'Mansion in the Pool' and sits on a log to make a statement. His auditors were two worlds, she says, not counting herself; but though the poet knows she is excluded from both spheres of this amphibian's life, she tries to establish relations by applauding. To her chagrin

> Demosthenes has vanished
> In Forums Green.

Such exercises in light humor or simple wonder do not often lead to good poems, but they fill out her picture of nature as irrevocably separated from man, the belief underlying her best work. One final comment, from the letters, carries this a step further: nature is indifferent to man's feelings. Writing in the summer after her father's death she complained that the birds were 'trifling in his trees, . . . even frolicking at his grave.' The inference she draws is in sharp contrast to the nature poetry of her heritage, 'Nature must be too young to feel, or many years too old.' Finding some support in the Puritan separation of nature, man, and God, her typical attitude looks forward to the modern one, that nature is alien to man because the external world is ultimately unknowable by the mind. Even its forms vanish before his eyes.

Only once does she treat nature as actively hostile and this is in a poem on the snake, the traditional embodiment of the Great Adversary. Even here just the concluding stanzas, a kind of epilogue, are concerned with this hostility:

> Several of Nature's People
> I know and they know me
> I feel for them a transport
> Of Cordiality
>
> But never met this Fellow
> Attended or alone
> Without a tighter Breathing
> And Zero at the Bone.

The final line creates the shock of sheer terror. Her reaction to the venous-blooded snake goes deeper than mere freezing of the heart. Is this the Eden Serpent, the terror that of confronting cold live evil? In another poem this ancient symbol with all its erotic overtones seems undeniably conjured up. In her room one winter, she relates in nightmarish terms, there suddenly appeared 'A snake with mottles rare' and 'ringed with power.' Her reaction, like that of Eve before her, was compounded of fear and fascination. Shrinking, she tried to propitiate him by praising his beauty. 'Afraid . . . of me? No cordiality'—he hissed, and 'fathomed' her. Then she fled beyond the horizon, only to conclude abruptly: 'This was a dream.' Unsuccessful as a poem, this curious recording of unconscious symbolism must be left to the psychoanalytic biographer. But it may serve as a gloss on the intensity of 'Zero at the Bone,' the nadir of human warmth and feeling.

In this her best poem on the snake, he seems hostile only because of the instinctive emotional reaction of terror that needs no explanation, at least in the convention of the Christian world. For the rest, the first

four stanzas that are centered on the snake himself, he is merely alien—
and elusive:

A narrow Fellow in the Grass
Occasionally rides—
You may have met him? Did you not
His notice instant is—

The Grass divides as with a Comb—
A spotted shaft is seen,
And then it closes at your Feet
And opens further on—

He likes a Boggy Acre—
A Floor too cool for Corn—
But when a Boy and Barefoot
I more than once at Noon

Have passed I thought a Whip Lash
Unbraiding in the Sun
When stooping to secure it
It wrinkled and was gone—...

Like the hummingbird, his route is one of instantaneous appearings
and disappearings. And his home, like that of the bird and frog, is
remote from man. Instead of using the conventional swamp for habitat,
she enhances the quality of separateness by juxtaposing 'boggy' with
'acre' and then saying it is 'too cool for corn'—acre being the standard
measure of agricultural land, and corn the basis of civilization. But the
characteristic that makes him most alien to man is the suddenness of
the apparition and the vanishing. This pervades the whole poem, but
only as a generalized atmosphere until the farm boy is introduced. Then
she gets in her most effective stroke by dramatizing the evanescence. As
he stooped to pick up the lash of an abandoned whip, 'It wrinkled and
was gone'—the speed of these six lines being emphasized by the omission of all marks of punctuation. The elusive and slithering motion,
recalling the Biblical curse 'upon thy belly thou shalt go,' is enough in
itself to make the snake startlingly alien, and a valid cause of the terror
that stops her breath in the end.

A short undated poem, representing another trial at the same theme, survives only in an unfinished draft with two conflicting endings that illustrate the ambiguity of her reaction. Here again is the secret swamp, the encounter, the yearning to get back to civilization. As first written, the conclusion names evil as the cause of her 'enthralling' flight:

> A snake is summer's treason,
> And guile is where it goes.

But at the bottom of the manuscript there is a set of variants that completely shifts the meaning, when substituted:

> A snake is nature's drama,
> And awe is where it goes.

Here the quality of illusion is paramount, with a kind of religious wonder in the eyes of the beholder. This is her more usual response. The same attitude colors her general statement about wild nature in a letter to Higginson (1862): 'When much in the Woods, as a little Girl, I was told that the Snake would bite me, that I might pick a poisonous flower, or Goblins kidnap me, but I went along and met no one but Angels, who were far shyer of me, than I could be of them.' Even in the traditional symbol of the archenemy, then, nature is not really hostile. It is merely elusive, not 'Goblins' but 'Angels,' the latter word not implying a Christian view so much as an order remote from man and ungraspable by him.

One of Dickinson's key words for nature is *juggler*. She ransacked the vocabulary of the theatre and magic to underscore her conviction of the illusory quality of objects in the external world, and once made a succinct general pronouncement on the subject:

> Nature affects to be sedate
> Upon occasion, grand
> But let our observation shut
> Her practices extend
>
> To Necromancy and the Trades
> Remote to understand
> Behold our spacious Citizen
> Unto a Juggler turned—

Nature as a serene and settled order is mere pretense that deceives only those who do not look close. She herself was rarely attracted by the 'sedate' and 'grand,' and usually failed when she did attempt them. Let us but turn our backs, she says, and this tranquil composition begins to waver and shift. Indeed one who looks out of the side of the eye, painter or poet, can catch the juggler at her tricks. Conjuration is specified, and blacker arts yet are suggested in the 'Trades remote to understand.' But there is nothing evil or injurious in any of this 'Necromancy.' It is merely that the most seemingly solid 'Citizen' of the universe is a sleight-of-hand artist, entertaining the spectators with a show.

To illustrate this with a bird on the wing or a snake in the grass was easy, with a plant rooted in the earth harder but more effective. The excitement of her discovery of the mushroom as an exemplar of sorcery is revealed in the state of the manuscripts. Half-a-dozen versions have survived, and most of the variants are aimed at pin-pointing its unreality and its eccentricity:

> The Mushroom is the Elf of Plants—
> At Evening, it is not—
> At Morning, in a Truffled Hut
> It stop up on a Spot
>
> As if it tarried always
> And yet its whole Career
> Is shorter than a Snake's Delay
> And fleeter than a Tare—
>
> 'Tis Vegetation's Juggler—
> And Germ of Alibi—
> Doth like a Bubble antedate
> And like a Bubble, hie—
>
> I feel as if the Grass was pleased
> To have it intermit—
> This surreptitious scion
> Of Summer's circumspect.
>
> Had Nature any supple Face
> Or could she one contemn—
> Had Nature an Apostate—
> That Mushroom— it is Him!

It is noteworthy that only one phrase is pictorial, 'a truffled Hut.' She herself coined the participial form from the name of the mushroom's underground cousin, the truffle, probably being attracted by the derivation her Lexicon gave from the Spanish *trufa,* meaning deceit or imposition (an etymology since abandoned).

For the rest she depends on an intricate web of images of evanescence. The mushroom is the 'Juggler' par excellence in the vegetable world, a wandering hobgoblin ('Elf') that inhabits unfrequented places. It is also a mere 'Bubble' or an 'Alibi,' that last plea of the accused, 'Not me, I was elsewhere.' These images, concentrated in the center of the poem, are supported by the verbal structure that runs from beginning to end. It is, it is not; it anticipates itself, then speeds away. The Biblical overtones of the alliterating 'tarried' and 'tare' enlarge the idea of the transcience of all life on this earth, the parable of the tares of the field which spring up suddenly among the wheat, even the Son of God who tarries but a night. The last action of disappearance, 'Intermit,' introduces an unexpected corollary: the mushroom is a pariah. The summer, for all its prudent watchfulness, has let this clandestine sprout slip into the picture and would be better pleased to have it go away. Precisely at this juncture the process of personification sets in. Though an elf living in a hut, the mushroom up until this point has been referred to as 'it.' Now it is called a 'scion,' a term that was just beginning to develop from the horticultural meaning of 'shoot' to the genealogical one of 'off-shoot.' In the last stanza the transfer from 'it' to 'Him' is explicit.

On the supposition that nature could reject one of its own—another version reads, 'Could she a *Son* contemn'—she piles on the attributes that brand him as eccentric, even more in the variants than in the final text. She tried 'plated' and 'outcast' to qualify his face before settling on 'supple,' apparently intending the derived meanings of unstable and hypocritical. She had already compared him to a snake and a weed earlier in the poem. Now she calls him an 'Apostate,' and in another version she changes this to the archetypal traitor 'Iscariot.' Why all this opprobrium heaped on the humble mushroom? (If she had meant to emphasize the poisonous rather than the esculent variety she would have specified toadstool.) Perhaps she was taken by the figurative usage of mushroom as an 'upstart,' a low fellow who presumes to a sudden rise in life, cited in her Lexicon with a reference to Bacon. Even more pregnant of meaning was the quotation from Timothy Dwight which followed: 'The origin of man, in the view of the atheist, is the same with that of the mushroom.' She would not have shared the atheist's view that man is purely of the earth, that he grows out of and returns to a dunghill. But the human analogy with a mushroom offered other implications. In the long perspective that geology and other sciences had just opened up, man seemed one of the most recent and fleeting forms of life on this planet. In the new direction that philosophy was beginning to take, only man, separated from his green home, seemed to be a real pariah. Is this overnight fungus in her poem anthropomorphic? Is she saying that man is the rejected Iscariot?

As an object in the natural world, the mushroom is a striking example of evanescence; as a symbol of man, an equally striking illustration of his transitoriness and his alienation from nature. Whichever way one reads it, he should remember that her conclusion is cast in a strictly suppositional form:

> *Had* Nature an Apostate—
> That Mushroom— it is Him!

The colloquial idiom at the end breaks down into humor any serious suggestion that something has gone awry with the Great Chain of Being. The mushroom only seems like nature's apostate because of man's eccentric point of view.

All things counter and strange, 'Whatever is fickle, freckled,' fascinated Emily Dickinson just as they did Gerard Manley Hopkins, but for different reasons. For him they were evidence of the Plenitude of God's creative power. For her they offered novel forms, like the bat and grass, by which she might avoid the hackneyed in previous nature poetry, and at the same time facilitated her shift from the imitation of things to imitating their significance. They also provided several dramatic examples of vanishing forms, like the snake and mushroom, that lead directly to her concern with activity in the natural scene as opposed to static objects. Of all the eccentrics in her limited world of nature the spider drew out her talents oftenest. Though she held out a friendly hand to this 'Neglected Son of Genius,' as she called him in a lesser poem, it was the web rather than the weaver that caught her fancy best:

> A Spider sewed at Night
> Without a Light
> Upon an Arc of White.

If Ruff it was of Dame
Or Shroud of Gnome
Himself himself inform.

Of Immortality
His Strategy
Was Physiognomy.

All here is deftly contrived for evoking the magic of the verse-riddle.
The triple rhyme-scheme, the pointedly brief lines of 3-2-3 accents, the
homely vocabulary suddenly turned philosophical, the compact capsule
of three three-line stanzas—these set the tone of deliberate artifice. This
is her incantation to cast a spell on the spider and make him yield up
the secret of his web.

The riddle is put succinctly in the second stanza. Has he woven a fine
muslin collar for a lady, or grave clothes that veil a very earthy sprite?
Read me this, the old riddles would say. But these are false leads. Instead, the design he makes is a sort of ritualistic expression of himself.
She was apparently aware of the modern scientific concept that his web-
building is an instinctive dance. For she says in another poem, 'The
Spider . . . — dancing softly to Himself/His Coil of Pearl— unwinds.'
As such an unconscious artist, the spider in the present poem instinctively swings his 'Arc of White' from pillar to post and goes to work
on his tapestry, orbicular in shape with radial lines and concentric circles
going out to circumference. The folklore that he is a nocturnal weaver,
spinning 'at Night/Without a Light,' is given a new twist: he makes
his design out of the dark secret of himself. He is the source of his own
form, 'Himself himself inform,' creating out of his inner self the web
that becomes his exterior symbol. Moreover, this involute line involves
a double word-play: he can also read the meaning of his pattern, but he
does not 'inform' anyone except himself as to what it is.

The questioner is left on the outside. She can only guess at the meaning, so the answer is rendered in cryptic terms which the literal-minded
may shrug off as sheer obscurantism. But the last stanza is the real point
of the poem, her oracular answer to the riddle:

Of Immortality
His Strategy
Was Physiognomy.

The simple domestic language of the first six lines ('sewed,' 'Ruff,' 'Shroud') veers subtly into the erudite—polysyllabic abstractions suggesting both the religious and the scientific, but coming to rest in the ambiguous term 'Physiognomy.' By 1869, the date of her poem, whatever was salvageable from this pseudo-science had been taken over by the physiologists like Darwin and Spencer, who were merely concerned with reducing to a system the muscular manifestations of the emotions. The unscientific aspects of physiognomy, including its lesser claim that individual character could be determined from facial features, had fallen into disrepute. Even the wide influence of Lavater on literary men was on the wane, though he had some appeal for the Transcendentalists as a fellow antagonist of rationalism, and occasional articles on him still appeared in New England magazines after mid-century. She had registered her attitude towards this aspect of physiognomy some years earlier. The 'Picture' one sees painted on a face—'On fine— Arterial Canvas—/ A Cheek— perchance a Brow'—is undoubtedly a precise representation of the inner spirit, according to a poem written in 1862. But she concludes, in very un-Emersonian terms, man cannot fathom this 'Secret' that 'Eyes were not meant to know.'

How much less credible to her the strictly mystical claim that outward appearances furnish a true means of divination. Her Lexicon, after defining physiognomy in the usual sense, has a bracketed note: 'This word formerly comprehended the art of foretelling the future fortunes of persons by indications of the countenance.' Yet it is clearly this obsolete sense, connected with astrology and magic, that she has resurrected for her poem on the spider. He spins out his inner self into his web, a figurative extension of his face. If his design corresponds to his soul then this is his 'Strategy' for comprehending 'Immortality,' but not revealing it. If spiritual meanings can be induced from external patterns, then temporal as well as spatial barriers fall, for the soul belongs to the immortal world, not this one. To discover these meanings has been the ultimate goal of all religious seekers, and one may choose to read into her poem a commentary on the Puritan theology so pervasive in her heritage. She certainly shared the view of her enlightened contemporaries that it was a thing of cobwebs. Yet she may have taken one cue for her poem from Jonathan Edwards, the subtlest weaver of them all, who had vividly used the image of the spider and his net in one of his most famous sermons on man's slim chances of heaven.

Artists likewise, though in a somewhat different sense, seek to reflect inner and eternal values in their outward designs. Her other two poems on the spider praise him as an artist of 'surpassing Merit' whose tapestries, wrought in an hour, are 'Continents of Light' (variant: 'Theories of Light'); but they are ephemeral, 'He plies from Nought to Nought/In unsubstantial Trade.' Both versions end tragi-comically, as spider and web dangle from the housewife's broom. Her own poems were her strategy of immortality, more lasting designs of the soul than his, she fervently hoped. In the best of them, like the one under consideration on the spider, she does not fall back on easy mystical solutions. Her riddle ends in the paradox of whatever may be one's attitude towards such a mode of cognition as the pseudo-science of 'Physiognomy.' One can learn immortality from the spider's art just as surely as one can read a person's destiny from his face—and no more so. Her web is taut, the seeker caught.

Another silken web containing a secret gave occasion to a kindred group of poems, on the cocoon. The earliest invokes it as a symbol of the heavenly secret as well as the earthly one, 'Cocoon above! Cocoon below!'; but in spite of a promising beginning this is on the whole a conventional effort. The one closest to the spider poem is quite literally a verse-riddle, written in a spirit of comedy for her three-year-old nephew and sent to him with a cocoon:

> Drab Habitation of Whom?
> Tabernacle or Tomb—
> Or Dome of Worm—
> Or Porch of Gnome—
> Or some Elf's Catacomb?

The worm-chrysalis-butterfly sequence makes an obvious symbol, of course, and the poet must be dexterous if he would avoid the hackneyed. The riddle was one way out. Here again is the stylized structure of unconventionally short lines and an intricate quintuple rhyme-scheme, ringing several changes on a suspended sound but with the first two lines and the last two making exact pairs. All is in the form of questions, compact and adroitly phrased to pose the alternatives: Is it tomb of the dead or portal from which the soul takes flight? A similar dual image occurs in another poem:

> A Sepulchre of quaintest Floss—
> An Abbey— a Cocoon—

Though the dilemma is not solved by direct answer in either poem, one is all too well aware that the butterfly does emerge eventually, and that it is the traditional symbol of the soul. There was little new that could be said about this. Besides, such positive faith was not shared by Emily Dickinson.

Silk threads, gossamer, spider webs, down, all things white and filmy are her recurring symbols of heaven. In one more poem she seeks such a divine clue in nature:

> Its little Ether Hood
> Doth sit upon its Head—
> The millinery supple
> Of the sagacious God—
>
> Till when it slip away
> A nothing at a time—
> And Dandelion's Drama
> Expires in a stem.

The winged seeds of the dying dandelion seem to form a halo made by the Great Milliner. Although he is a sagacious God, or perhaps because he is sagacious, the heavenly hat he bestows on it is 'supple,' a word that usually implies for Dickinson *duplicity,* as in the poem on the mushroom. In his wisdom he conceals from mortals his great secret, decks out his meanings in evanescent forms. As this ethereal hood disappears, 'A nothing at a time,' the scattered seeds bear witness to only one possible conclusion, diametrically opposite to that of the cocoon. But again she refuses to make an explicit analogy. Her word is not death but 'Drama.' The show is over and the curtain is down, at least on this small stage. Nature is elusive, perhaps even illusory, and no ultimate truths relevant to man can be drawn from it, only metaphors.

Yet the odd and the ethereal in nature continued to fascinate her. Writing in 1876 to thank her childlike Norcross cousins for a gift from the woods, she exclaimed: 'Oh that beloved witch-hazel ..., witch and witching too, to my joyful mind.' Rare at least to her was this late blooming New England shrub, whose lacy fringed flowers only appear in autumn when its leaves are falling:

> I never had seen it but once before, and it haunted me like childhood's Indian pipe, or ecstatic puff-balls, or that mysterious apple that sometimes comes on river-pinks; and is there not a dim sugges-

tion of a dandelion, if her hair were ravelled and she grew on a twig
instead of a tube,— though this is timidly submitted. For taking
Nature's hand to lead her to me, I am softly grateful— was she willing
to come? Though her reluctances are sweeter than other ones' avowals.

If she could not understand nature, at least she could enjoy it.

But matter always interested her less than energy. The meaning of
nature's forms eluded her grasp, because they vanished before her eyes.
With nature as process she sometimes felt she was on the brink of discovery, though meaning was elusive here too. If she could only be alert
enough to fix for the purposes of analysis its daily motions and seasonal
changes, then perhaps she could read its paradoxes: symbols of immortality in its autumnal decline, omens of death in the year's upsurge. 'You
mentioned spring's delaying—' she once wrote, 'I blamed her for the
opposite. I would eat evanescence slowly.' Man's relation to objects in
space might be less significant than his relationship to the illusions of
time.

8

PROCESS

The sun is at once the most familiar and the most spectacular object in the physical universe. As the source of light and heat and also the measure of human time, it is the inevitable symbol of nature, even life itself. From the beginning of history poets and priests have seized upon it as a central image. Its glory and power have been so exhaustively celebrated that by the latter half of the nineteenth century only a poet of distinguished mind could hope to write of it with novelty. Like other moths, Emily Dickinson was lured by this celestial candle. She returned to it again and again, as the subject of more than twenty-five poems, and finally succeeded in embodying the new thing she had to say.

Direct representation she knew was impossible, as pointed out in the chapter on 'Perception.' The artist who could reproduce a summer day or a sunset, she said, must needs be 'greater than itself.' But as the colors teased and the magic called, she tried the oblique approach of fable. Her successes in this minor genre have been widely popular—'I'll tell you how the Sun rose,' 'She sweeps with many-colored Brooms,' 'Will there really be a "Morning"?' They record with naive wonder the advent of a new day or the spectacle of its decline, but it would be an impertinence to intrude critical commentary on what anyone can enjoy who has not lost the heart of a child.

One rendering of sunrise comes close to transmuting this mode into poetry of a high order:

The Day came slow— till Five o'clock—
Then sprang before the Hills
Like Hindered Rubies— or the Light
A Sudden Musket— spills—

The Purple could not keep the East—
The Sunrise shook abroad
Like Breadths of Topaz— packed a Night—
The Lady just unrolled—

The Happy Winds— their Timbrels took—
The Birds— in docile Rows
Arranged themselves around their Prince
The Wind— is Prince of Those—

The Orchard sparkled like a Jew—
How mighty 'twas— to be
A Guest in this stupendous place—
The Parlor— of the Day—

The jewel imagery carries the color sequence from dawn to full day with flashing speed—'sprang,' 'sudden,' 'shook abroad,' 'sparkled.' More importantly it creates an aura of oriental splendor. Rubies, folds of purple and topaz-colored brocade, and the diamonds of dew, evoked as a submerged rhyme to make the orchard glitter 'like a Jew.' With these strokes she renders nature as magnificent artifice and recalls all the richness imported from the East during the Italian Renaissance, as invoked by Shakespeare in *The Merchant of Venice*.

Then by an unexpected reduction of magnitudes this marvel is domesticated in 'The Parlor— of the Day.' That tidy little room, always kept ready to receive a visitor, is transformed into a stupendous place because of the grandeur of some one who has come to call. But who is this guest? The 'Lady' of the second stanza is clearly Aurora, and the 'Prince' of the third is specified as the wind. The guest seems to be the poet, who is curiously enough a visitor in his own house, recording the advent of the sun. But the monarch of the orient never arrives in person. The expectation raised by the magian figure of the Prince, acclaimed by Biblical 'Timbrels,' falls off into the confusion of a rival celebration.

So the chorus of birds is as distracting here as the initial simile, 'Like . . .
the Light/A Sudden Musket spills,' striking though that may be in itself.
To bring wonders down to homely credibility, according to Coleridge,
is a poet's proper business, but when so many details misfire the miracle
does not quite come off.

To lift the commonplace to supernatural significance has the sanction
of Christian tradition as well as of Wordsworth's dictum. Two generations of poets since the *Lyrical Ballads* had hardened this revolutionary
idea into a new convention. But Dickinson managed to give it novelty
by out-maneuvering both the old and the new orthodoxies, in a poem
describing the sunset as heavenly beauty beyond the reach of time-
trapped man:

> The Lilac is an ancient shrub
> But ancienter than that
> The Firmamental Lilac
> Upon the Hill tonight—
> The Sun subsiding on his Course
> Bequeathes this final Plant
> To Contemplation— not to Touch—
> The Flower of Occident.
> Of one Corolla is the West—
> The Calyx is the Earth—
> The Capsules burnished Seeds the Stars—
> The Scientist of Faith
> His research has but just begun—
> Above his synthesis
> The Flora unimpeachable
> To Time's Analysis—
> 'Eye hath not seen' may possibly
> Be current with the Blind
> But let not Revelation
> By theses be detained—

One of the oldest and commonest of flowers, the lilac, is the conceit
happily chosen for the efflorescence of sunset, the bloom flung back on
the sky by the sun going down to death. It is an image bequeathed 'to
Contemplation,' however, not an object 'to Touch.' So the natural scien-

tist, merely glimpsed askance through the parade of botanical terms (corolla, calyx, capsule), cannot test it empirically. Likewise it floats above the synthetic dogmas of the 'Scientist of Faith,' whether an exponent of rational Unitarianism or of the new Higher Criticism of the Bible.

Her own position went beyond all these as well as beyond the logical structures of Calvinist theology. With irony she invokes one of the cornerstones of commonsense Protestantism—that miracles are not vouchsafed to mortals ('Eye hath not seen . . . the things which God hath prepared for them that love him')—only to say that this is the failure of belief among the blind. But for her metaphor she goes behind the 'theses' of Paul's epistles to the vision of John on the Isle of Patmos: the firmamental lilac is 'Revelation' for those who can see. Ten years earlier she had put this more explicitly in a letter:

> I was thinking, today– as I noticed, that the 'Supernatural,' was only the Natural, disclosed–
>> Not 'Revelation'– 'tis– that waits,
>> But our unfurnished eyes.

The later poem shows how her eyes have been furnished, not with telescopes or exegesis but a new vision of the poetic imagination. The heavenly flower, she says, cannot be discredited by 'Time's Analysis.' This is the phrase that lifts her poem above conventional treatments of natural beauty as manifestations of God, and takes her view beyond contemporary science to the mathematical philosophers of today. The rationalist, whether theologian or scientist, is limited by being caught in the trap of time. The sun, the point from which time is measured, is paradoxically free of this limitation and exists in the eternal world. Its floral shadow cast on the earthly sky is merely an illusion of time, an image offered to the poet's contemplation. And it is offered with the injunction that his vision of heaven be not 'detained' (a variant uses the stronger word 'profaned') by the postulates of logic, the 'theses' which are invariably assumed by the reasoning mind.

The limitations of *'Time's* Analysis'! This was her little ontological discovery: that man's inability to grasp supernal beauty and truth is the result of his mind's imprisonment in time rather than the imprisonment of his spirit in a body. In the external world, what seem like objects to the limited mortal view are really aspects of nature as process, nature going down to the 'death' of eternity. And conversely, what man sees as process and change are the illusory pictures cast by the immutable on his time-trapped senses. It is man who moves, in his fretful living and the endless circling of his planet. If he were not earth-bound, that is, time-bound, he could see that motion and fixity in nature are relative to his eccentric point of view. Because of the grand-scale optical illusion involved, the sun offered her a dramatic symbol for making all this concrete. Its brilliant diurnal life from sunrise to sunset is but a trick of our planetary motion. Seen from the vast reaches of interstellar space it would not be a leaping flame but a 'fixed' point of light, or eclipse. The manipulation of this reversible paradox furnished a new strategy for her poems on immortality, and a new way of writing about the grand processionals of nature. It is notable that most of the time-imagery scattered through her works is found in poems on one or the other of these themes.

To write about the sun within time the poet is limited to appearances, and so to observations that have become hackneyed. Could he escape from time, he could see the sun as it really is. For if time is an illusion, the sun is the conjurer that creates it. Although the poet cannot literally escape out of time, he can recreate the magician by seeing through his sleights with the aid of the imagination. The language of the stage was one resource for rendering this. Once it controlled a whole poem: the sunset seen through the trees beyond her house became a consciously contrived illusion, 'The far Theatricals of Day.' Again, drawing on a kindred mimetic art, she showed the 'Wizard Sun' at work with his magic palette. Called to the window by a rationalist to witness what he insisted was a 'Sunset,' all she saw was a herd of 'Opal Cattle' feeding on a 'Sapphire Farm.' Even as she looked, this 'dissolved' and in its place was displayed a vast sea and mountainous ships. But this too 'the Showman rubbed away,' leaving nothing at last save a blank canvas where the phantom pictures had been. Knowing she was looking at the illusions of time, she sometimes fell back in a kind of desperation on the language of fantasy. But as fancy is no substitute for the imagination, so experiment after experiment failed to bring off her vision of the sun's legerdemain.

When she shifted her emphasis from the gaudy spectacle of the tricks to the process of conjuring itself, she wrote her most successful poem on the sun:

> Blazing in Gold and quenching in Purple
> Leaping like Leopards to the Sky
> Then at the feet of the old Horizon
> Laying its spotted Face to die
> Stooping as low as the Otter's Window
> Touching the Roof and tinting the Barn
> Kissing its Bonnet to the Meadow
> And the Juggler of Day is gone

The daily life and death of the sun is rendered in terms of heat and light by a single line. As a ball of fire it blazes across the sky and quenches in the night, the full spectrum of diffracted sunlight being covered by the range from red-gold dawn to purple sunset. This concise handling of color is proof that for once in these poems on sunset she has her tendency to fantasy in control.

Giving short shrift to the literal image of the sun, she springs her surprise conceit in the second line. It is not a ball of fire but a leopard, leaping from the east up to the zenith and then falling to death on the western horizon. The subtle ferocity and arching leaps of this wildcat from the orient make it a flashing simile for the sun's career across man's field of vision. The colors of its fur, the rufous-buff ground and nearly black spots, echo in subdued tones the brighter colors of the opening line. And in the Near East the leopard's skin is a symbol of royalty, like purple and gold in Europe—both sets of attributes being linked to the monarch in this poem who makes his progress from orient to occident. Even the sudden taming of its wild power 'at the feet of the old Horizon' finds support in the domestication of the cheetah in India. But if there is any relation between its 'spotted Face' and the dark 'spots' sometimes visible on the sun's surface, it is too obscure for more than conjecture. One is tempted to suggest that she was looking back to the Biblical query, can the leopard-sun change his spots, or forward to the modern guess relating two cosmic phenomena: that the energy dying out in solar spots is reborn in the aurora borealis. But these are indeed conjectures.

The leopard, of course, is an illusion, another sleight of the old conjurer. But in making the transition to this disclosure the poem falters in direction for two lines, her uncertainty being shown in three variant versions. As the dying leopard-sun flings back his parti-colored wraith from the west, she fixed it once on the church across the road from her home:

> Bending low at the oriel window
> Flooding the steeple, and tinting the barn....

Again, looking out of her other bedroom window, she wrote what she saw there:

> Stooping as low as the kitchen window—
> Touching the Roof—
> And tinting the Barn....

Both of these fit the facts of her Amherst landscape well enough, but they do not fulfill any function in her poem other than a lame attempt to domesticate the wild creature. The former implies a religious meaning not relevant to her purpose. The latter merely raises the question, Why the kitchen?, until the private fact is adduced that it was on the western side of her house. The latest revision is something of an improvement, 'Stooping as low as the Otter's Window,' because it keeps to the natural setting. 'Civilization spurns the Leopard,' she wrote in another connection.

None of them is as effective as another example of the sun's legerdemain would have been, though she might reasonably have despaired finding one as striking as the leopard. The reader would have welcomed a series of dissolving shows before the juggler vanished, 'Kissing its Bonnet to the Meadow.' The jester's cap waved in farewell recalls the medieval connotation of juggler, including both impostor and magician, and its derivation from the Latin for jokester, amusing with his tricks. One of the standard feats of his skill, the one he is chiefly known by today, is tossing balls in the air and keeping them in continuous motion apparently in defiance of the laws of gravity. So here the sun's master trick, such a commonplace of science as to need no mention, is that it tosses the earth and the other planets into perpetual orbit; but by the power of its magic this appears in the poem as in nature only by inversion, creating the illusion that the juggler-sun itself is spinning through space.

Like a skilled prestidigitator herself, she knew that timing is essential to magic and achieved one of her best effects by a novel device. The first seven lines consist of an unbroken sequence of present participles rendering the speed of the sun's mutations syntactically. The only predication is in the last line, where the same point is made as an idea: 'The Juggler of Day is gone.' So the poem ends with her finest figure for the elusive reality of the sun. It is not fiery ball nor leopard nor sunset tint. These are the illusions of time created by the great conjurer, not only day's juggler but the juggler *of* the day. It appears only in illusory shows, even creating the screen of time on which they are projected, then disappears into eternity. The what and where of the sun itself eludes time's analysis and the comprehensions of the finite mind, as she put it succinctly in a quatrain:

> It rises– passes– on our South
> Inscribes a simple Noon–
> Cajoles a Moment with the Spires
> And infinite is gone–

To this poet, the postulated stable order of nature usually seemed precarious. Even the explosive colors of sunset could give her a vision of dissolution, inspiring awe. But there was another 'Caprice of the Atmosphere' more dramatically acceptable as a symbol of Doomsday, the midsummer electrical storm. Next to the sun it tempted her pen more than any other of the so-called sublime aspects of nature, prompting some fifteen poems throughout her career, though the best came late. The most successful of the early ones adopts the mode of fable, but this is only a cover for its serious meaning:

> The Wind begun to rock the Grass
> With threatening Tunes and low–
> He threw a Menace at the Earth–
> A Menace at the Sky.

> The Leaves unhooked themselves from Trees–
> And started all abroad
> The Dust did scoop itself like Hands
> And threw away the Road.

> The Wagons quickened on the Streets
> The Thunder hurried slow–
> The Lightening showed a Yellow Beak
> And then a livid Claw.

The Birds put up the Bars to Nests—
The Cattle fled to Barns—
There came one drop of Giant Rain
And then as if the Hands

That held the Dams had parted hold
The Waters Wrecked the Sky,
But overlooked my Father's House—
Just quartering a Tree—

The details are vividly precise yet suggestive of chaos unloosed. This nightmarish atmosphere is created partly by hyperbole and personification, but chiefly by surrealistic images that juxtapose the catastrophic and the domestic, making nature seem as shaky a contrivance as wagons, barns, and houses. 'The Leaves unhooked themselves from Trees,' 'The Dust . . . threw away the Road,' the celestial dams broke and 'Waters Wrecked the Sky.' In the face of such impending doom the Christian refuge would normally be faith in an overwatching Providence. But there is irony rather than coy piety in the concluding picture of the little girl safe in her 'Father's House.' Behind the overt thanksgiving that 'His eye' was on Squire Dickinson is the implied near-miss that makes the reader catch his breath.

What might happen another time is made clear in her more serious poems. Several of them threaten the earth's surface life, including man, but this is as nothing compared to the possibility that creation itself might vanish in a storm. Once when the wind brought a torrential rain, she used the language of cataclysm:

It pulled the spigot from the Hills
And let the Floods abroad—

Water is of this earth, however, and so a familiar destroyer. Winds, coming from the outer reaches of the universe, may be the agents of a more cosmic doom. In combination, and with the theatrical support of thunder and lightning, they might well bring on the poetic end of the world. By utilizing all of them to describe effects rather than events and to give a spectral cast to things, she very nearly achieves this:

There came a Wind like a Bugle—
It bubbled in the Grass

And a Green Chill upon the Heat
So ominous did pass
We barred the Windows and the Doors
As from an Emerald Ghost—
The Doom's electric Moccasin
That very instant passed—
On a strange Mob of panting Trees
And Fences fled away
And Rivers where the Houses ran
The Living looked that Day—
The Bell within the steeple wild
The flying tidings told—
How much can come
And much can go,
And yet abide the World!

Something is happening to reality here that has not been achieved by all the exaggerated language of the preceding poems. It has become fluid and illusory, on the point of disappearing, lured by an 'Emerald Ghost.' All the fixed objects like trees, fences, and houses 'fled,' while the violent forces of the storm loomed and 'bubbled.' The wind became Gabriel's trumpet and the church bell, set tolling by the swaying steeple, sounded like the last gong. Even the Biblical allusions, faint as they are, contribute to the sense of cosmic upheaval: these 'tidings' are the very opposite of peace on earth, yet in the end it is the unstable earth rather than man's more permanent home that 'abides.' For 'Doom's electric Moccasin' passed in an instant—with the stealth of an Indian and the speed of that 'subtile agent' which her Lexicon still defined as 'the electric fluid'—and reality came back to the world.

Her finest poem on the storm came when she applied her discovery of the temporal rather than the spatial conditioning of reality. The physical destruction of the world, to which the whole of the preceding poem was devoted, is here compressed into the first two lines:

It sounded as if the Streets were running
And then— the Streets stood still—
Eclipse— was all we could see at the Window
And Awe— was all we could feel.

By and by– the boldest stole out of his Covert
To see if Time was there–
Nature was in an Opal Apron,
Mixing fresher Air.

The few words allotted to the insubstantiality of spatial reality are enhanced by special effects that create the preliminary state of shock she desired. The optical illusion that confuses a moving with a stationary object under certain conditions here reverses wind and streets, so that the streets are 'running' and the wind need not even be named. Indeed, all the physical elements of the storm are dispensed with—wind, water, thunder, and lightning—yet they are all dramatically there. And by synaesthesia the illusory quality is taken one step further: what should have made a visual image merely made a 'sound,' the familiar street transformed into the bodiless wind. This clears the slate for the one thing she really could see at the window—'Eclipse.'

By turning to the temporal aspect of this phenomenon, she gave a new twist to the primitive belief that blotting out the sun would signalize the end of the world. She was not one to invoke mystery by subscribing to folk superstition, but neither was she limited by the old-fashioned astronomer's time-bound calculations. An early poem shows her working towards her own theory. Eclipses are usually predicted by science, she says, but if one comes without warning 'Jehovah's Watch– is wrong.' And once in a letter, reporting a thunder storm 'so terrible that we locked the doors,' she used a similar cosmic simile to account for a domestic coincidence: 'and the clock stopped—which made it like Judgment day.' This concept is worked out in its final form in the present poem. When the storm's menace suddenly withdrew, 'the boldest stole out of his Covert' not to see if the physical world still existed but 'To see if *Time* was there.' (Is this a submerged reference to Noah peering out of his Ark, after storm and flood have subsided, to see if the face of God is still in eclipse or if time, in the sense of a new dispensation, has begun again?)

She is seeking a far more fundamental reassurance than merely that the material processes of earthly life have resumed. 'Again the smoke from Dwellings curled,' she concluded another poem on a summer storm. But how could she make dramatically concrete the resumption of the temporal process? One attempt in a letter is interesting by way of analogy:

> We have had two hurricanes within as many hours, one of which came near enough to untie my apron— but this moment the sun shines, Maggie's [the cook's] hens are warbling, and a man of anonymous wits is making a garden in the lane to set out slips of bluebird. The moon grows from the seed.

The variants in several drafts of her best storm poem show her struggling to overcome this tendency to fantasy: 'Nature was in the best of humors,' then 'Nature was in her Beryl Apron,' and finally

> Nature was in an Opal Apron
> Mixing fresher Air.

'Apron' and mixing bowl replace the menace of cosmic destruction with the reassuring ritual of the kitchen, and 'Opal' gives a theatrical iridescence (Noah's rainbow?) to the vision of a restored world that is superior to the merely pictorial yellow-green of 'Beryl.' But in spite of the ethereal effect of 'fresher Air,' which is also meteorologically precise, the emphasis is on the resumption of material rather than temporal process; and the conclusion is something of a letdown from the brilliant image of 'Eclipse' that forms the central conception of the poem.

To return to this idea, if 'Nature's Sterling Watch' should stop (her epithet in another poem) man would be transported out of time into eternity. To earth-clinging mortals such a threat to existence could only inspire terror, but to a poet concerned with Revelation the reaction was more profound: 'Awe— was all we could feel.' 'Awe' and 'Eclipse' clearly have spiritual implications in her poem. This interpretation is borne out by the well-known description of her family sent in an early letter to Higginson: 'They are religious— except me— and address an Eclipse, every morning— whom they call their "Father".' As for what her own revelation would be, should a cataclysm of nature free her from the prison of time, she remains ambiguous. The comforting orthodoxy of God manifest in all His works was too simple a faith for her. When a 'Cap of Lead' was drawn 'tight and surly' across the sky, as one storm poem puts it, she could not find the 'mighty Face'; instead, she experienced an unearthly chill that seemed to come from Hell. She did not, like Cotton Mather, pretend to read the wonders of the invisible world in the phenomena of nature.

Her storms, it should be remembered, are all metaphorical. She knew well enough that if the constricting walls of time could be rent it would be by poetic lightning, by her own 'Bolts of Melody.' Then indeed there might be revelation:

> To pile like Thunder to its close
> Then crumble grand away
> While everything created hid
> This— would be Poetry— ...

The subjunctive mood, the emphatic 'would be,' poses this as an ideal unattainable by mortal poets, and the concluding line tells why: 'For None see God and live.' But this poem seems to bring her close to the modern position, as formulated by Whitehead: that if man is to break out of the bondage of time into eternity, it will be through the imagination of the artist rather than through philosophical thought or religious faith. The poet's partaking of the creative process is his immortality, the poem his revelation.

The seasonal processes of nature fascinated Dickinson even more than its daily motions, being a subtler demonstration of time running down— either to death or to immortality. Storms may threaten creation with violent dissolution, the sun's legerdemain explode reality by proving that the mortal show is mere illusion. In the cycle of the seasons there is a slower but surer dirge, the inescapable paradox that nature is a process of dying out of time as well as living in it. In turning to the themes of transience and renewal, she knew she ran the risk of triteness. Playing the game of pupil and preceptor in her letters to Higginson, she could pretend to the naive view as late as 1877: 'When flowers annually died and I was a child, I used to read Dr. Hitchcock's Book on the Flowers of North America. This comforted their Absence— assuring me they lived.' But normally, even in prose, she at least sought freshness of phrasing: 'We go to sleep with the Peach in our Hands and wake with the Stone, but the Stone is the pledge of Summers to come.'

In an occasional poem on spring's rebirth she eludes conventionality by the novelty of her language. 'The Dandelion's pallid tube,' she once wrote, 'Astonishes the Grass'; and its signal bud, followed by a 'shouting Flower,' is the sun's proclamation 'That sepulture is o'er.' But the best of these lack originality of conception, the poorest fall into the sentimental tradition. Even Hitchcock's handbook made it clear that 'perennial' is man's pathetic boast for flowers with a mere life-cycle of more than two years. When alert she was not trapped by the sophism of immortality in nature's process. Instead she gave a new twist to the evidence: 'Conclusion' is the goal of all living things, according to one poem; they can only hope 'At *most* to be perennial.' Escape from death through seasonal renewal is merely temporary, and it does not save the individual. At most it can serve as a symbol, recalling that larger escape from time into immortality man yearns for.

'Changelessness is Nature's change,' she wrote a friend late in life, reducing the paradox to an aphorism. Twenty years earlier she had given point to a simple poem by holding in delicate balance these equal and opposite certainties, the endlessness of the ritual cycle and the finality to which the process leads:

> It will be Summer— eventually.
> Ladies— with parasols—
> Sauntering Gentlemen— with canes
> And little Girls— with Dolls—
>
> Will tint the pallid landscape—
> As 'twere a bright Boquet—
> Tho' drifted deep, in Parian—
> The Village lies— today—
>
> The Lilacs— bending many a year—
> Will sway with purple load—
> The Bees— will not despise the tune—
> Their Forefathers— have hummed—
>
> The Wild Rose— redden in the Bog—
> The Aster— on the Hill
> Her everlasting fashion— set—
> And Covenant Gentians— frill—
>
> Till Summer folds her miracle—
> As Women— do— their Gown—
> Or Priests— adjust the Symbols—
> When Sacrament— is done—

The vantage point from dead of winter gives a particularly vivid life to her projected spring and summer. But the pictorial effects of the first stanza, so like a painting by Renoir, quickly fade in the second into a phantom landscape on a blank canvas, an illusion carved on the snow's marble. For her dissolving panorama is prophetic as well as ancestral. 'Many a year,' 'Forefathers,' 'Covenant'—these give assurance of the changelessness of the seasonal round, the 'everlasting fashion' of the flowers contrasting ironically with the impermanent ones of ladies and gentlemen.

For, when the 'miracle' of nature's life is over once more, the change of death will follow just as surely as with human beings, its bright body put away like a castoff 'Gown.' But it is transmuted by another miracle: autumn is the Eucharistic season of the year. The symbol of the sacrament substitutes one paradox for another and rescues her from the necessity of a logical decision as to nature's meaning. Changelessness or change? Mortality or immortality? The terms shift places and the meanings dissolve into one another. Religious overtones are associated with images of autumn throughout her writings. 'These Indian-Summer days with their peculiar Peace remind me,' she began a letter of consolation to her cousin, the Reverend Mr. Cowan, on the death of his sister, and then went on to say: 'I suppose we are all thinking of Immortality, at times so stimulatedly that we cannot sleep. Secrets are interesting, but they are also solemn— and speculate with all our might, we cannot ascertain.... Dying is a wild Night and a new Road.'

The ambiguousness of the transitional season between the life and death of the year made it the inevitable locus for her many efforts to give final expression to this paradox. Simple response to its beauty would have produced merely another conventional autumn-piece, like her description in a schoolgirlish letter: 'We are having such lovely weather— the air is as sweet and still, now and then a gay leaf falling— the crickets sing all day long— high in a crimson tree a belated bird is singing— a thousand little painters are tingeing hill and dale.' But recognition of the ambiguities covert in the season gave her a new way of maneuvering just such obvious components of its beauty as these, and her first successful poem on this theme came quite early. The title it has long been known by, 'Indian Summer,' was editorially supplied but it has pertinence, since the epithet 'Indian' was adopted into the American language to connote whatever in the New World looked like the real thing but was not. This illusory season is one of the glories of New England's climate, coming as it does between a brief but brilliant summer and the long snowbound winter.

> These are the days when Birds come back—
> A very few—a Bird or two—
> To take a backward look.
>
> These are the days when skies resume
> The old—old sophistries of June—
> A blue and gold mistake.
>
> Oh fraud that cannot cheat the Bee—
> Almost thy plausibility
> Induces my belief.
>
> Till ranks of seeds their witness bear—
> And softly through the altered air
> Hurries a timid leaf.
>
> Oh Sacrament of summer days,
> Oh Last Communion in the Haze—
> Permit a child to join.
>
> Thy sacred emblems to partake—
> Thy consecrated bread to take
> And thine immortal wine!

Woven in with her probing of the season's ambiguous appearance is the allied query: Does it symbolize death or immortality? The structure is indicated by the balanced exclamations, 'Oh fraud,' 'Oh Sacrament.' Which it is she never says. Instead of diverting poetry to the solution of problems in philosophy or religious belief, she uses their dilemmas to shape her poems, the warring images poised in ironic tension. The first half of this poem displays the fraud, the second half celebrates the sacrament. The central lines look both ways: the illusion is almost plausible enough for belief, the sure signs of death are transfigured by language that looks forward to the Eucharist.

This structure of ambiguities is supported by the carefully controlled sound pattern throughout. The parallel phrasing of the first and fourth lines, 'These are the days,' opens the poem on a note of confidence. But this is sharply in conflict with the rhyming, which goes against the stanzaic pattern rather than with it. ('This is the rhyme scheme of the most lyrical of hymn meters, *aabccb*, the so-called Common Particular; both the movement and the meaning of the poem call for a division into three double stanzas instead of the six as printed.) Instead of the expected initial couplet there is only the internal rhyme 'few-two,' and in the second couplet there is merely the assonance of 'resume-June.' The ear is further shocked by the suspended rhyme, 'mistake' answering 'look,' but picks up the buried sound 'take' and the sequence 'back-backward' to make an intricate pattern of sounds, both rhyming and half-rhyming, all of which echoes the uncertainty and the desire for certainty that lend ambiguity to the first double stanza.

It is only in the second, where the balance between belief and doubt is perfectly maintained, that the rhyme scheme is entirely regular. In the last, though the couplets rhyme perfectly, the sounds that should bind the whole in a unit, 'join-wine,' only rhyme if the old-fashioned pronunciation, still common in hymnals, is used. Absolute faith is possible only for the old-fashioned? All three divisions are linked by the rhetorical device of anaphora (repetition of identical opening words). It is used in the first to suggest confident affirmation, as already pointed out. This becomes so overwrought in the third as almost to submerge conscious belief in the incantation of ritual ('Oh . . . Oh . . . Thy . . . Thy'). In the middle stanza itself there is none, but the opening words 'Oh fraud' leap across to clash with the benedictory 'Oh Sacrament' and thus establish the ambiguous poles of the poem's total structure.

She plays the same kind of changes on traditional subject matter that she had rung on conventional form. Knowing that atmosphere is a prime creator of illusion, she punctures the sentimentalism of predecessors like Longfellow by announcing that October's bright blue weather is a 'mistake.' Then she scores her point by reminding that these skies are just a resumption of the 'sophistries' of June. The hope of unending summer was just as plausibly misleading then, when life was at full tide, as it is now in Indian Summer. The birds are deceived, at least a few of them, but the bees are not. Science does not confirm her returning bird and uncheated bee, but folklore provides a sufficient basis for her poetic whims. Birds are not earth-bound, and by association with the soul they may be predisposed to believe in immortality. But even they are not sure. They merely come back to 'take a look,' as rural lore has it. On the other hand, they are one of the 'major nations' living on the surface of the earth and so are not deep in the secret of nature as 'minor nations' are, like the crickets in a companion poem. Bees are such insects, however, one of the oldest and wisest of species according to popular belief. In her poems they are always sharp-eyed realists, unsentimental and unromantic, a quality rendered here by the skeptic's words 'fraud' and 'cheat.'

With the seed and leaf we are somewhere in between. They are non-sentient 'automatic' nature, and express themselves not in knowing but in doing. They do only what they have to do, but its meaning is ambiguous, suggesting both the ancient sacrificial ritual of the dying year and the Christian sacrifice of Communion. So the seeds 'bear witness'— to the death of the particular plant but also the promise of rebirth in the immortality of the species. And though the leaf hurries down to death, the pun on 'altered'—the elements of the Eucharist as well as the air of Indian Summer—implies its transubstantiation into eternal life. All of this, inclosed by 'softly' and 'timid,' looks forward to the professing child of the last stanza.

Such is the poet's dilemma. She has been reasoning empirically, like an adult, from the evidence of nature. Following this is the sudden reversal invoked by the scriptural allusion, 'Except ye be converted, and become as little children, ye shall not enter into the kingdom of heaven.' Only if she can become as 'a child' will she understand the emblematic meaning. Then the sacramental view will be possible; the body and blood of this autumnal death, flaming leaf and decaying stalk, will become symbols for immortality. But irony pervades the conclusion too. This Communion is 'in the Haze,' both the atmosphere of Indian Summer, the sophistry of its blue and gold skies, and the veil covering eyes that would see and believe. The 'immortal wine' is the same nectar that could not cheat the bee, a natural rather than a miraculous one, since like 'bread' it is a product of the autumn harvest. 'Child' may suggest a first communion, an initial act of faith by her or any child that wishes to 'join.' But as a mass for the dying year these are last rites.

To recapitulate: In the first stanza the surface of things in Indian Summer suggests that life is everlasting, but this is an illusion of the 'Indian giver.' In the second the inner secret, first intuited and then explicitly revealed, is that the year is really dying; but immediately the paradox is reversed and the underside of death bears witness of rebirth, of altered elements, at least to one who wants to believe. Finally, this desire for belief becomes plaintive; with all the evidence against her the poet can only say, Permit me to become a child and partake, sacramentally, of immortality! The poem itself is a kind of 'last Communion' between her critical mind and her yearning heart.

There are subtler ways of snaring the life-death mystery in nature than by juggling paradoxes. Turning from the long-drawn-out illusion of Indian Summer, Dickinson sought to surprise the ambiguity of nature's process by pin-pointing the very moment of transition, convinced like Thoreau that summer passes to autumn in an instant:

> As imperceptibly as Grief
> The Summer lapsed away—
> Too imperceptible at last
> To seem like Perfidy—
> A Quietness distilled
> As Twilight long begun,
> Or Nature spending with herself
> Sequestered Afternoon—
> The Dusk drew earlier in—
> The Morning foreign shone—
> A courteous, yet harrowing Grace,
> As Guest, that would be gone—
> And thus, without a Wing
> Or service of a Keel
> Our Summer made her light escape
> Into the Beautiful.

The strangeness of its evanescence is her overt theme and many details contribute to this effect. The summer 'lapsed'—all the connotations of this word seem pertinent—then 'escaped.' Its last hours were 'sequestered,' distilling a twilight quietness or shining with a 'foreign' light; its departure 'harrowing,' as if a cherished friend insisted on leaving without reason. Yet she knew there was no justification in being wounded, since the summer had never been anything but a 'Guest' and parting was inevitable. On this occasion, by a unique kind of courtesy, the leave-taking was effected 'Too imperceptible . . . To seem like Perfidy.' The near-betrayal attributed to summer's going here makes a curious reverse echo of the 'fraud' of its pretending to stay in the preceding poem. Time is treacherous in both its illusions, whether of lingering or fleeing.

A more complex meaning, the poet's ambivalent reaction to this strange evanescence, is set in motion by the opening simile: the summer passed away 'As imperceptibly as Grief.' The manifest comparison is apt. Nothing lapses so imperceptibly as grief, for one never feels, or at least admits, any diminishing of it until the sudden realization that it has already gone. But the latent meanings should fit too, because the similarity of their vanishings implies some likeness in their essences. How then is summer a grief? Only for those whose eyes are set on autumn. There is indeed a recurrent note in her poetry that life is mostly pain, and death a release into some kind of eternal peace. She could find plenty of Christian precept for this, her hymnal being filled with references to 'this vale of tears' and a yearning for deliverance into Jerusalem 'the Beautiful.' So the closing figure may be read that 'Summer made her light escape' into heaven—though without benefit of 'a Wing.' This may be another way of saying that the grief of human experience has been transformed into the beauty of her poem. Yet the lapsing of life into art (summer into autumn), like the escape through death into immortality, would seem like 'Perfidy' to the living if it did not come about so imperceptibly. Even so, it is a 'harrowing Grace,' a blessing and a beauty lacerating to the human spirit. The poet allows her reaction to come to rest in an ambivalence that carries over to her most cryptic rendering of the seasonal process of nature, 'Further in Summer than the Birds.'

One more link between the two poems may be pointed out. An early version of the one just discussed contains, in some discarded lines beginning 'The Cricket spoke so clear,' a reference to the insect whose chirruping came to symbolize for her this mysterious moment in the year's transition. The initial obscurity in the poem that follows is clarified by the title she herself supplied when inclosing a copy of it in a letter, 'My Cricket':

> Further in Summer than the Birds—
> Pathetic from the Grass
> A minor Nation celebrates
> Its unobtrusive Mass—
> No Ordinance be seen—
> So gradual the Grace
> A gentle Custom it becomes—
> Enlarging loneliness.

Antiquest felt at Noon
When August burning low
Arise this Spectral Canticle
Repose to typify—
Remit as yet no Grace—
No furrow on the Glow—
But a Druidic Difference
Enhances Nature now—

This is her finest poem on the theme of the year going down to death and the relation of this to a belief in immortality. It is also the climactic poem in a series dealing with the relationship of man and nature, ranging from cordiality to alienation. Though it will never have the wide appeal of her more spontaneous lyrics, its difficulty is not that of an intellectual game. The obscurity is justified because it inheres in the poetic idea, and the poem deserves serious study as one central to her vision. This is a deeper probing into the secret meaning of nature than any yet, and the discrimination of a more complex reaction to nature by the poet-observer. Because of all this and because of the poem's intense strangeness, there will probably be no end to the readings of its riddle.

The moment of seasonal transition, as the surface theme, links this with the preceding poem in several ways. There the summer lapsed away 'imperceptibly,' here the cricket's warning signal is 'unobstrusive' and its ritual not actually seen but felt. The 'sequestered afternoon' of the former is echoed in the 'repose' typified by late August. 'The Morning foreign shone' is answered by 'Antiquest,' 'Spectral,' 'Druidic' in the second stanza; and 'A courteous, yet harrowing Grace' by the loneliness and 'gradual Grace' of the first stanza. Though the previous poem ends on a clearer note of triumph, with the summer escaping into heaven, there seem good grounds for a religious interpretation of this one too.

The dominant metaphor of the mass in the opening lines, sustained by a pervasive liturgical language throughout, sets up an unmistakable frame of reference. In addition to the suggestive language of 'celebrates,' 'burning low,' 'typify,' and 'remit' there are several specific terms. 'Ordinance' is an established ceremony of the church such as the Lord's Supper, 'Canticle' a sacred song sung at solemn vespers in honor of the mystery of the Incarnation; and one is tempted to add 'the Gradual,' the oldest and most important chant by the choir during the Proper of the Mass, though it appears in the poem as an adjective rather than a noun. Since the mass is both a memorial ritual of the sacrificial death of Christ and a sacrament promising his resurrection, it might well symbolize the transitional moment of the year, looking back on the lost life of summer and forward to the cyclical renewal after the year's death. In this sense the mass is a '*pensive* Custom' (as a variant reads) in memory of the former divine presence, 'enlarging [man's] loneliness' through awareness of Christ's absence now. On the other hand the promise of 'Grace' in its sacramental aspect 'enhances' nature, however 'gradual' man's realization of the second coming may be. Since the final grace comes only in the life-after-death, the cricket's canticle does not yet 'remit' this future promise, the 'furrows' that forecast the fruitfulness of recurrent spring have not yet appeared. The grace that emerges now is primarily one of 'repose,' but in the context of the whole poem it is just possible to read this as the pledge of immortality that death bestows.

Here, however, the old ambiguity raises its head again, as always when one seeks to force a dogmatic answer from her profoundest poems. Is this 'repose' the changelessness of eternity or the long sleep of winter? The latter seems indicated by her characterization of this poem in an accompanying letter as 'a chill Gift.' It all depends on how one interprets the 'Difference' that heightens nature at this moment of transition. The Christian ceremony of the mass when carried through to completion produces a change, it is true, the reincarnation in which mortals symbolically share. But this is after all a ritual of crickets, not men; their canticle is a 'Spectral' one, producing a 'Druidic Difference'—all suggestive of a pre-Christian nature rite whose meaning is lost in the dim past ('Antiquest'). Perhaps they are celebrating, not the promise of immortality man yearns for, but the principle of mortality in nature, the process of the year going down to death.

Another version of this poem, previously unknown, supports this view. It is more discursive and inferior as a poem, but illuminating. The first eight lines, setting up the image of the mass, are identical. From that point it veers off in a different direction, dropping the figure and pursuing the crickets' song as a natural phenomenon for twelve lines. It is more audible at dusk, when nature is merely waiting to 'terminate in tune,' she says; it continues without change of cadence and apparently without cessation, except that it ends some time at night when the poet is asleep. Then follows her comment on its meaning:

> The earth has many keys—
> Where melody is not
> Is the unknown peninsula.
> Beauty is nature's fact.
>
> But witness for her land,
> And witness for her sea,
> The cricket is her utmost
> Of elegy to me.

There seems little ambiguity here. When earth's song is finished, she arrives at the 'unknown peninsula,' her recurrent image for the incomprehensible. The poet, as singer, must seek beauty not in the hope of heaven but in 'nature's fact.' One of the finest witnesses for that is the song of the cricket, and its meaning for her is explicit: it is the 'utmost of elegy,' she says, using the classic term for a lament in praise of the dead.

It may be objected that this is really a different poem, but reading it sends one back to the shorter and finer version alert to new meanings. Both versions begin with the same ambiguous metaphor of the Sacrament:

> Further in Summer than the Birds—
> Pathetic from the Grass
> A minor Nation celebrates
> Its unobtrusive Mass—
> No Ordinance be seen—
> So gradual the Grace
> A gentle Custom it becomes—
> Enlarging loneliness.

Listening with ear close to the ground, the poet hears the earth-song of the insects, unspecified except as a 'minor Nation.' They are minor both in the scale of creation, as compared to the major nations more visibly dominating the life of the earth (*birds* are mentioned, *man* is implied in the poet's presence), and in the fact that they chirp in a diminished key, as compared with those who are still singing buoyantly as though summer will·never cease. Thus their song does not obtrude on the surface life of nature but comes up 'pathetic' from the grass, moving the tender emotions of sorrow and grief in the poet rather than her pity for them, so that she gradually becomes aware of them celebrating their mass for the dying year. For they are 'Further in Summer' than the birds, not only symbolic of a later phase in the calendar year and so able to prophesy like Druids the coming seasonal change, but deeper into the secret meaning of nature and so not deceived by the surface illusion of eternal summer.

The poet, belonging likewise to one of the major nations, stands aloof above the grass, unable to participate in the phantom ceremony that comes up to her. She is so far removed it is not visible, scarcely even audible; she can only feel it, 'pathetic' being used in its root sense. The sixth line, 'So gradual the Grace,' is clearly central to her meaning, but it is also one of the most cryptic passages in the poem. 'Grace' can have the mere generalized meaning of reconciliation to God's ways, instead of the more specific Christian promise of eternal life. It can also mean simply beauty, as deified in pagan mythology. Whatever the message it reaches her only gradually, inspiring a sad meditative mood, 'pensive' (variant for 'gentle') at the end of the stanza echoing 'pathetic' at the beginning. Since the antecedent of 'it' in line 7 remains ambiguous, one may hazard the guess that both the ancient ritual itself and the poet's fascination by it have become 'a pensive Custom,' brooding on a meaning lost to the insects through habitual repetition and not yet found by the poet through intuition. Perhaps this is just what the poem does mean: that nature's meaning in her secret processes has come to be hidden from man as he developed consciousness, and the most he can know is this sense of loss. In another poem on the transitional season she said similarly that the vanishing summer put up 'both her Hands of Haze . . . to hide her parting Grace/From our unfitted eyes.' ('Oh Last Communion *in the Haze*' was her most confident attempt to find meaning in Indian Summer through Christian symbolism.) Such a discovery of her alienation from nature's secret could only increase her sense of 'loneliness.'

If the first stanza can be read plausibly as the plight of man in a natural universe where he is a foreigner, feeling nostalgia for a mode of being which he perceives imperfectly and in which he cannot share, the second may be her impressionistic attempt to record the quality of that 'Difference':

> Antiquest felt at Noon
> When August burning low
> Arise this Spectral Canticle
> Repose to typify—
> Remit as yet no Grace—
> No furrow on the Glow—
> But a Druidic Difference
> Enhances Nature now—

The collapse of syntax in these lines makes everything dreamlike and unreal, a confession that cryptic notations are all she can offer by way of interpretation. One can merely conjecture how to clear up the obscurities and fill in the ellipses. From its use in numerous other poems the meaning of 'Noon' can be fixed with reasonable certainty as that moment between the completion of one clock-cycle and the beginning of another when time escapes out of numerals into timelessness—the beginning of eternity, or merely the death of human time. In pagan myth it was the hour of Pan's sleep. But does 'Antiquest' modify her loneliness, which is felt to be most primeval during the hot hum and stillness of late August, when life seems at its peak but is actually beginning to decline, at the very moment of noon? Or should it attach to the mass, which though celebrated continuously is felt to be most archetypal when it is the last communion for the dying year? Possibly both. At any rate, as summer burns low the insects' song rises, sacred but ghostly, the very emblem of that ambiguous state called 'Repose.' (To secure the emphatic meaning of *typifying*, rather than *in order to typify*, she resorted to the apparently awkward inversion 'Repose to typify.')

The concluding lines picture the poet looking back to the earth's surface, still at summer's full. The whole tone of the poem being elegiac rather than hortatory, 'remit' should not be read as an imperative but as an elliptical form of the participle 'remitted.' For similar reasons, 'Grace' here seems to have an esthetic rather than a theological emphasis. Hence the fifth line in this stanza probably means: There is as yet no diminution of the beauty. This finds its natural complement in the next: No mark of change on the brightness, no 'furrow' on the golden glow of Indian Summer which has not yet been plowed under. A similar phrase occurs in one of her letters, 'no film on noon,' and again in another poem, 'no goblin on the bloom.' But the beauty of this transitional moment was always a torment to her by reason of its ominous strangeness. As she put it in yet another poem:

> There seemed to rise a Tune
> From Miniature Creatures
> Accompanying the Sun—
>
> Far Psalteries of Summer—
> Enamoring the Ear
> They never yet did satisfy—
> Remotest— when most fair ...

In her finest poem on the theme this strangeness is rendered most hauntingly. From the insects' secret ritual, faint though her intuition may be, she feels a 'Druidic Difference' that changes the meaning of nature now, intensifies it and lifts it up to a new key. What this difference is, both in the appearance of nature and in the feeling of the observer, she despairs of defining explicitly. It is a prophecy that something will happen, but that something lies beyond the poem. Perhaps some wisdom out of the dim past, only half guessed at by the alienated mind of man but fully and automatically participated in by the unconscious life of minor nations, has hinted to her that there is an essential cleavage between nature and man. Imprisoned in time he cannot see through the illusions of the old conjurer to whatever meaning lies beyond. Nature's processes are inscrutable, just as its forms are evanescent.

This mystery was best symbolized for her in the transition from summer to winter, through that phantom season called Indian Summer that inspired so many of her poems. Looking back over them one finds a constant theme and a consistent language of ambiguity. If summer lingers beyond its time it is a fraud and a cheat; when it really goes it shines with a foreign and harrowing grace; the cricket who signalizes its departure sings a spectral canticle that puts a druidic difference on the face of things. A similar note recurs in a dozen other poems. In one she guesses that October may be 'The Revelations of the Book/Whose Genesis was June.' But elsewhere, when summer departs 'Forever— until May,' she concludes paradoxically: 'Forever is deciduous—/Except to those who die.' The variant for 'deciduous' ('recurrent') makes clear her meaning that nature falls only to spring again, but this does not imply that immortality is the destiny of man, for he is one of 'those who die.'

Again, the season of crickets and retrospects is characterized by 'a dissembling Breeze' and a 'sear Innuendo'

> That makes the Heart put up its Fun—
> And turn Philosopher.

In another, with birds returning when nuts are ripe, she can only respond to the query, Fall or Spring? by confessing 'My wisdom loses way.' The same baffled inquiry pervades her letters. In an early one she turned it into fantasy:

> *Summer?* My memory flutters— had I— was there a summer? You should have seen the fields go— gay little entomology! Swift little ornithology! Dancer, and floor, and cadence quite gathered away, and I a phantom, to you a phantom, rehearse the story! An orator of feather unto an audience of fuzz,— and pantomimic plaudits. 'Quite as good as a play,' indeed!

Shortly before her death, convalescing from nervous prostration, she put the mystery in occult phrase: 'The Summer has been wide and deep, and a deeper Autumn is but the Gleam concomitant of that waylaying Light.'

A final poem on the transitional season in nature hints at the reason why this paradox lies in ambush to take the mortal mind by surprise:

> 'Twas later when the summer went
> Than when the Cricket came—
> And yet we knew that gentle Clock
> Meant nought but Going Home—
> 'Twas sooner when the Cricket went
> Than when the Winter came
> Yet that pathetic Pendulum
> Keeps esoteric Time

The summer is simply 'Going Home,' but where is that? The cricket strikes the hour for its departure, but man is not enough of an initiate to tell time by that 'pathetic Pendulum,' for it bears only an 'esoteric' relationship to the larger seasonal clock of dissolving days, months, and years that he pretends to understand. As a mortal he is trapped in the illusion of calendar time and so cannot comprehend the inner processes of nature, which follow a secret schedule to an obscure end.

Sometimes she is even haunted by the suspicion that at its center nature is only automatic process, without any meaning of a sort that the conscious mind can recognize. As the year dies, there are further shows for her baffled entertainment:

> Apparently with no surprise
> To any happy Flower
> The Frost beheads it at its play—
> In accidental power—
> The blonde Assassin passes on—
> The Sun proceeds unmoved
> To measure off another Day
> For an Approving God.

'Apparently' not only modifies the opening words but controls the whole poem. This is not necessarily the way things are, merely the way they appear to the mortal view. Flowers are happy in life, but are not surprised when frost kills them; frost has this power not by desire or design but accidentally; the sun goes about its business unmoved, and God approves all. Man, nature, and God are three entirely separate entities, moving in this poem like figures in a dream. The parts of nature seem to have some relation with one another—flowers succumb to frost and this in turn must go when the sun comes out again—but the relation is unmotivated and unconscious. It is simply the automatic function of frost to freeze, of flowers to die when cold, of the sun to measure time. There is not even any indication of an ordered plan. For frost can come prematurely, as here, killing flowers before the seed stage has been reached and a cyclical purpose served. The smiling face of the sun next day, recalling the happy life that could have gone on but for this 'freak' of nature, mocks the human cry of Why?

The poem's irony is centered in the triple punning on 'unmoved.' The sun 'proceeds' in its function as juggler of the day, but without moving; its sympathies are not touched by the death of flowers it could have saved by shining; finally, God does not 'move' the sun (or rather the earth) but merely 'approves' all these motions as part of the proper processes of nature. By implication, the flowers themselves are 'unmoved.' Unconscious that they are dying, they simply go without 'surprise.' Only man is inclined to protest. Though this is not stated it is

implied by the sly intrusion of the pathetic fallacy that assumes the
flowers are 'happy' while growing, and that protests the seasonal action
of frost by personifying it too. ('At its play' refers ambiguously to both
frost and flower, suggesting that the former is only playing 'Assassin.')
A didactic poet would have used such untimely death in nature solely
for its human analogy, the sentimental shock when a person is cut off
in the full flower of his days. This attitude is incipient in her letter to
a friend whose child had suffered a crippling blow: 'To assault so minute a creature seems to me malign, unworthy of Nature—but the frost
is no respecter of persons.' Even there she modified her emotional reaction by 'seems' and by the frost image, which translate nature's apparent
cruelty into indifference: it is hostile to man and flower only in not
being designed wholly to accommodate their flourishing.

In the poem she achieves absolute detachment, the protest being submerged in a striking epithet, the single metaphor that gives life to what
might otherwise have been a barren aphorism. The frost comes stealth-
ily in the night to behead its victim. But instead of conjuring up the
swarthy image suggested by the word's etymology, the Moslem drugged
with hasheesh falling upon the unsuspecting Christian, hers is a 'blonde
Assassin,' the adjective being used only in the sense of light as opposed
to dark. All the ambiguity of whiteness, even as Melville's famous chapter in *Moby-Dick* explores it, is here invoked to symbolize the mystery
of death. Frost is not the hired agent of God, who has no hand in this
murder except as an approving spectator, but is agent and principal in
one. And what seems to man like a tragic event in time is but another
aspect of nature's automatic process—'apparently.'

A final example of the illusions flung back on the screen of time by
nature's seasonal procession is her poem on the snowstorm. In an early
version she confined herself to the pictorial aspects of this wintry
pantomime:

> It sifts from Leaden Sieves—
> It powders all the Wood.
> It fills with Alabaster Wool
> The Wrinkles of the Road—
>
> It makes an Even Face
> Of Mountain, and of Plain—
> Unbroken Forehead from the East
> Unto the East again—

It reaches to the Fence—
It wraps it Rail by Rail
Till it is lost in Fleeces—
It deals Celestial Vail

To Stump, and Stack— and Stem—
A Summer's empty Room—
Acres of Joints, where Harvests were,
Recordless, but for them—

It Ruffles Wrists of Posts
As Ankles of a Queen—
Then stills its Artisans— like Ghosts—
Denying they have been—

(In another manuscript the next to last line reads: 'Then stills its Artisans— like Swans.') Many of the details here call to mind Emerson's
poem 'The Snow-Storm' in which the north wind, 'the fierce artificer, . . .
myriad-handed,'

Curves his white bastions with projected roof
Round every windward stake, or tree, or door. . . .
On coop or kennel he hangs Parian wreaths;
A swan-like form invests the hidden thorn;
Fills up the farmer's lane from wall to wall,
Maugre the farmer's sighs; and at the gate
A tapering turret overtops the work.

That this fine lyric did not escape her eye as she thumbed her cherished
copy of his *Poems* is proved by a surviving manuscript fragment with
one of its best phrases, 'Tumultuous privacy of storm,' transcribed in
her handwriting. Her details in the early version were less effective than
Emerson's, fused as his were by the controlling image of 'The frolic
architecture of the snow.' But there was also a Transcendental meaning
implicit in his poem, the world-spirit delighting to manifest itself in
forms, that was foreign to her thinking; by-passing this she limited herself to the purely pictorial.

Perhaps it was this likeness and this difference that made her rework
the poem two years later into an entirely new one, both to avoid imitation and to embody more positively her own angle of vision. Whatever
the impulse, the final version is far more characteristic of her best work

than the earlier one, substituting the temporal for the spatial aspects of the snowstorm. When she had occasion to send a copy to a friend late in life, this concise text is the one she chose:

> It sifts from Leaden Sieves—
> It powders all the Wood—
> It fills with Alabaster Wool
> The wrinkles of the Road—
>
> It scatters like the Birds—
> Condenses like a Flock—
> Like Juggler's Figures situates
> Upon a baseless Arc—
>
> It traverses yet halts—
> Disperses as it stays—
> Then curls itself in Capricorn,
> Denying that it was—

All the pictorial effects to her present purpose are taken care of in four lines, identical with the first stanza of the early version. The earth's luxuriant head of hair, the vegetation of the woods, is powdered with white wool, 'Alabaster' being a favorite symbol of death. The ruts in the road are the 'wrinkles' of time now smoothed out by the obliterating snow, like those on the face of plain and mountain which she had elaborated in the second stanza of her initial effort to render the snowstorm. Fascination with this pantomimic aspect had then led her to an involvement in the picturesque that continued throughout the rest of the poem, circumscribing its potential meaning.

The new version parts company with the old after the opening stanza, which here serves to establish the first illusion of the snowstorm as the death of the year. For nature is also a 'Juggler,' and next its snowflakes become flocks of birds scattered in the air then condensing on the earth, till the base of the sky's leaden arc is shrouded in a ghostly veil. The snowflakes are now the objects which the prestidigitator's magic keeps suspended in the air without visible support. (She first wrote 'Flowers,' then the more geometric 'Figures,' suggesting the intricate crystalline forms.) This sets the stage for the last act. The third stanza identifies the juggler, as might be expected, with the sun. The first two lines apply equally to snowstorm and sun: both are unmoved movers and entities capable of being broken up into their myriad components. But when the show is over, whether sun or snow, it 'curls itself in Capricorn/ Denying that it was.' Capricorn is the zodiacal sign for the winter solstice; when the sun enters it at the end of December, it is said in folklore to stand still, a belief embodied in the Latin root *sol-sistere*. This is another and more complete kind of eclipse.

In nature's cyclical process the year goes down to death. If this were also the end of time, as the snowstorm's illusion and the sun's eclipse suggest, then man would escape into eternity. What seems like process within the limits of the temporal scheme, according to her system of images, may well turn out to be something quite different in the limit- lessness of eternity. There motion may become inseparably fused with motionlessness, in what she called nature's 'changeless change,' but this is beyond the mortal poet's grasp. Dickinson did not pretend to read ultimate meanings in nature, human or divine, either in terms of Butler's *Analogy* or Emerson's 'Correspondences.' For her it was an endless carnival of entertainment. It was also a source of metaphor to illustrate the truths of her interior world, the one she created and the only one she could understand. Her truth in these poems on nature's process was the life-death paradox itself, in man as well as in nature. It cannot be resolved by scientists, philosophers, or theologians, who can only give a name to what is essentially nameless. But the poet can hope to encom- pass it, by making its ambiguity concrete and hence acceptable as part of man's inescapable 'reality.'

So from the supposed tangibles of the external world she turned to the intangibles of the spirit, hoping to find in them something more accessible to human understanding. When this led her in the end to speculations on the meaning of the grave and man's dream of surviving it, she encountered a mystery that drew out her talents more powerfully than the mysteries of nature had done—as will be seen in the concluding section of this book. In between there was always the inner world of feeling to be explored. When she tried to define this self in relation to the inscrutable world outside and also to the unknown one beyond, to analyze all the stages of consciousness from ecstasy to despair, she found the themes for some of her most original poems. These are the subject of the chapters immediately following.

Three:

THE INNER WORLD

'Within a Magic Prison'

9

ECSTASY

'I find ecstasy in living– the mere sense of living is joy enough.' This was one of the barrage of exclamations Emily Dickinson fired at Higginson during his first visit to her in 1870. These were clearly her most cherished principles, but so phrased that they struck him as 'the very wantonness of overstatement.' The context in which she spoke of her ecstasy, according to his notes on this remarkable and largely one-sided conversation, should have given him the direction of her meaning. She had just delivered her explosive definition of poetry as that which 'makes my whole body so cold no fire ever can warm me' or makes me 'feel physically as if the top of my head were taken off.' Then she announced her dedication to the 'few real books' that have ever been written. Next came salvos like 'Truth is such a *rare* thing it is delightful to tell it,' and 'Enough is so vast a sweetness, I suppose it never occurs, only pathetic counterfeits.'

When she followed all this by affirming her 'ecstasy in living,' the gregarious Higginson was only baffled by what the joys of a recluse's life could be. For he responded by asking if she did not feel lonely in her solitude, and was not enlightened by her deliberately extravagant reply spelling out for him how utterly inconceivable this was. Yet the second half of her declaration alone: 'The mere *sense* of living is joy enough,' should have made it clear that she found her joy in the life of the mind and the emotions. The sources of his fulfillment, as a disciple of two older nineteenth-century traditions, were not hers. Mankind may have been the proper study of the humanitarians, but as a poet she felt no urge to expound social truths. Nature may have seemed to be an open book to the Transcendentalists, but it was a closed one to her.

Finding the natural world impenetrable, and withdrawing from society as alien to her special talents, she sought her meanings in her own interior world. 'Soto! Explore thyself!' she admonished in a pithy quatrain; there alone will be found the 'Undiscovered Continent.' This may be taken as her resolve to explore a poetic New World untried by her timid contemporaries. The language does not suggest a return to the subjective lyricism of the past hundred years so much as a looking forward to the exploratory drives of Existentialism or backward to the techniques of psychic discovery employed by the Metaphysical poets. But she was enough a child of her own century to challenge the arrogant claim that intellect is all, by giving a new twist to that boast, 'My mind to me a kingdom is,' which had served as a sort of theme-song for the Renaissance. For her the mind is indeed the 'State' but the heart is its 'Capital,' as she put it in a minor but interesting poem; the two together make 'A Single Continent':

> This ecstatic Nation
> Seek— it is Yourself.

Her absolute loyalty to mind, governed as she knew it was by the heart, is her distinguishing trait as a poet. In her religious poetry she does not hesitate to name the sovereign of this kingdom, sitting enthroned though unseen, as the soul. But while it is 'Immured the whole of life' within the 'magic Prison' of the flesh, she is content with a simple division of the mortal world into feeling and thought, fused as they are into 'One Population,' the self.

Philosophical poetry she eschewed, but much of her best work, exploring various aspects of consciousness, is a subtle poetry of ideas. Since she was also a lyric poet, her aim was to achieve a true fusion of thought and feeling. She did so in a series of remarkably precise analyses of intense pleasure and intense pain. A concordance to her poems confirms the casual reader's impressions by revealing extraordinarily large word clusters around these two poles. There are nearly three hundred poems with key words ranging from the worldly 'gay' to the celestial 'bliss,' more than two hundred covering every shade from 'ache' to 'woe.' For one who is aware of her preference for the poetry of power, and one who remembers the extremes of her nature poetry leaping from spiders to the aurora, it is not surprising to find that the strongly charged emotions drew her most: rapture and transport, anguish and misery. The chapter titles of the third section of this book follow these divisions, 'Ecstasy' and 'Despair.'

From the evidence of the letters Emily Dickinson found her personal pleasure like other mortals in home and friends, nature and books. But the ecstasy of her lyric poems springs from a more compulsive source. 'Sang from the Heart, Sire,' one begins, 'Dipped my Beak in it.' In another avowing 'Bind me— I still can sing,' she says that banished or slain she will remain 'Still thine.' Some deep personal experience of love seems behind these poems, and some emotional crisis related to it may have precipitated her poetic career, shortly before the age of thirty. It was in later life, presumably, that she summed up more calmly:

> That Love is all there is,
> Is all we know of Love.

This all-encompassing word is as elusive in her poetry as in any of the other great explorations of it, whether by artist, philosopher, or poet. It is not always possible to tell in a given context whether she is delineating both sacred and profane love like Titian, embodying a spiritual essence in sensual metaphor as in the Song of Songs, or climbing the ladder from initial to celestial love with Plato. The fusion of the two is man's oldest experiment in paradox. The spirit meshed in the body, the other world mirrored in this, passion that is most divine when most human.

The range of this poetry, covering all the motions of the heart in its progress through the profoundest of human experiences, has tempted biographers to seek a parallel love affair in her actual life. In addition to absurd guesses, there have been plausible theories linking her romantic attachment to two men, both of whom were already married and only dimly aware, if at all, of her hopeless adoration. But the external evidence remains fragmentary in the extreme, and the dilemma is only increased by the recent discovery and publication of three unsent love letters in her handwriting, echoing the phraseology of the poems and addressed to an unidentified 'Master.' Whether the problem is ever solved or not, it remains a strictly biographical one. It is precarious enough to use creative writings to reconstruct a love affair in the artist's life. It is even more dangerous to reverse the process and use the conjecture as a guide to the poems, for this tends to divert attention from their intrinsic value to their usefulness in filling out a supposed pattern. The reader with this interest uppermost is frequently attracted to inferior poems because he is moved by the 'autobiographical crisis' he thinks he can piece out from the fragmentarily sketched narrative, rather than by the poem as a work of art.

The reader who chooses to avoid the autobiographical issue and concentrate on the poems as poems has warrant for so doing in her own words. Near the beginning of her correspondence with Higginson she warned him, in a letter of July 1862: 'When I state myself, as the Representative of the Verse— it does not mean— me— but a supposed person.' Of the half-dozen poems she had sent him by this date, the one whose fictive 'I' she most wanted to dissociate herself from was in all likelihood 'There came a day at summer's full,' recounting a momentous interview between star-crossed lovers doomed to renunciation. In turning for advice to a literary critic for the first time in her life, she was simply asking him to read her poems as art rather than as personal history. Yet this one has been used as a cornerstone in reconstructing an actual love affair.

If the biographers are right, this may be one explanation why it is unsuccessful as a poem: the poet has been moved to take 'events' rather than feelings as her facts. Feelings must be detached from literal experience, reshaped by a sensitive and controlled language, and transmuted into symbols that contain their own meaning, in order to create a successful poem. In 'There came a day at summer's full' the images (mostly similes) seem contrived, and because of their disparity they tend to make the poem fly apart rather than cohere in a structural whole. The situation involving the renunciation is so obscure the reader is not able to share in the anguish, nor for that matter are the lovers. As a final clue to its failure the very conventionality of the language, its lack of the characteristic Dickinsonian novelty and surprise, suggests a literary inspiration. Convincing evidence has in fact been adduced that its source, at least in part, was Tennyson's 'Love and Duty.' The student intent upon her best love poems should be wary of those that seem to derive too closely from either her life or her reading. And following the spirit of her injunction, that her 'I' is a 'supposed person,' he would seem justified in taking both lover and beloved as poetic figures, and in reading the individual poems as images of love rather than as aspects of a narrative.

Effort after effort, in more than thirty poems, was squandered in a vain attempt to measure the worth of love. 'What would I give to see his face?'—she answers without hesitation, 'I'd give my life— of course.' She will use all her wealth to buy one smile; she will banquet sumptuously if her table 'Is laden with a single Crumb/The Consciousness of Thee.' When the sensual note enters, 'He touched me,' her song rises to new heights: 'My Gipsy face— transfigured now . . . As if I breathed superior air.' No extravagance is too great to measure the fullness of her ecstasy: 'Unable are the Loved to die,' she says, because love is a god who immortalizes the beloved. But the mortal allotment is just 'A single Dram of Heaven,' and for this she must pay the market price, 'Precisely an existence.' In spite of some freshness of phrasing and an occasional haunting image, these poems tend to fritter themselves away in a series of exclamations. One suspects that most of them failed because their inspiration was literary. When she begins one with the query, ' "Why do I love" You, Sir,' setting the opening words in quotation marks, there seems little doubt that its source was Elizabeth Barrett's well-known 'How do I love thee? Let me count the ways,' and many others echo the general tenor of her *Sonnets from the Portuguese*. The Brownings were favorite poets, and perhaps their romance was the parallel in real life that troubles her here.

Spontaneity as well as control is essential to the pure lyric cry, as her rare success in this genre illustrates:

> Wild Nights— Wild Nights!
> Were I with thee
> Wild Nights should be
> Our Luxury!
>
> Futile— the Winds—
> To a Heart in port—
> Done with the Compass—
> Done with the Chart!
>
> Rowing in Eden—
> Ah, the Sea!
> Might I but moor— Tonight—
> In Thee!

The frank eroticism of this poem might puzzle the biographer of a spinster, but the critic can only be concerned with its effectiveness as a poem. Unless one insists on taking the 'I' to mean Emily Dickinson, there is not even any reversal of the lovers' roles (which has been charged, curiously enough, as a fault in this poem). The opening declaration—'Wild Nights should be/Our Luxury!'—sets the key of her song, for *luxuria* included the meaning of lust as well as lavishness of sensuous enjoyment, as she was Latinist enough to know. This is echoed at the end in 'Eden,' her recurring image, in letters and poems, for the paradise of earthly love. The theme here is that of sexual passion which is lawless, outside the rule of 'Chart' and 'Compass.' But it lives by a law of its own, the law of Eden, which protects it from mundane wind and wave.

This is what gives the magic to her climactic vision, 'Rowing in Eden,' sheltered luxuriously in those paradisiac waters while the wild storms of this world break about them. Such love was only possible before the Fall. Since then the bower of bliss is frugal of her leases, limiting each occupant to 'an instant' she says in another poem, for 'Adam taught her Thrift/Bankrupt once through his excesses.' In the present poem she limits her yearning to the mortal term, just 'Tonight.' But this echoes the surge of ecstasy that initiated her song and gives the reiterated 'Wild Nights!' a double reference, to the passionate experience in Eden as well as to the tumult of the world shut out by it. So she avoids the chief pitfall of the love lyric, the tendency to exploit emotion for its own sake. Instead she generates out of the conflicting aspects of love, its ecstasy and its brevity, the symbol that contains the poem's meaning.

However fleeting love's glory or precarious its earthly fulfillment, she announces her dedication in terms of unalterable finality:

> The Soul selects her own Society—
> Then— shuts the Door—
> On her divine Majority
> Obtrude no more—
>
> Unmoved— she notes the Chariots— pausing—
> At her low Gate—
> Unmoved— an Emperor be kneeling
> On her Rush mat—
>
> I've known her— from an ample nation—
> Choose One—
> Then— close the Valves of her attention—
> Like Stone—

It is possible that this poem (written in 1862) has some relation to her choice of a life of seclusion made about this time, preferring her own small circle and closing the door on the general world, as the opening lines suggest. But the select 'Society' of the first stanza seems specifically limited to the chosen 'One' of the third. It is also possible to identify this One as muse rather than lover. In the poems of this period there is certainly some fusion of three great events in her life that seem to have taken place almost simultaneously: withdrawal into solitude and dedication both to poetry and to the image of a beloved.

A surface reading of the present poem seems to make this quite simply an affair of the heart. The central stanza weights the meaning in that direction, for the pausing 'Chariots' and kneeling 'Emperor' certainly suggest future suitors being rejected because of the chosen One, rather than the lures of society that might distract her from her art. On the other hand this 'One' may be God, as suggested by the capitalization and by the fact that her choice is possible only at spiritual maturity ('divine Majority'); finally, there is the hint of a nunnery ('Rush mat') where she waits for Him alone, the king of Heaven surely taking precedence over mere mortal emperors. Whether her devotion is to an earthly or a heavenly lover, she is 'unmoved' by the petitions of all others, closing the 'Valves of her attention' to them. The organic 'Valves' in this climactic image make the exclusion more vital than the variant 'lids' in the manuscript, mechanical doors that shut out further vision by voluntary effort. With their anatomical reference, as in those arterial valves devoted to the single function of the heart, they suggest the instinctive closing off of communication in all directions except the life-giving one. To all others she turns a heart of 'Stone,' the shock word that makes her choice final.

One of her best poems of dedication pledges eternal fidelity in terms that give new meaning to the body-soul tug of war:

> Of all the Souls that stand create—
> I have elected— One—
> When Sense from Spirit— files away—
> And Subterfuge— is done—
> When that which is— and that which was—
> Apart— intrinsic— stand—
> And this brief Tragedy of Flesh—
> Is shifted— like a Sand—

> When Figures show their royal Front—
> And Mists— are carved away,
> Behold the Atom— I preferred—
> To all the lists of Clay!

The tension in this poem comes from the verbal play that meshes spirit and flesh even while she seeks to make them stand 'apart— intrinsic.' As in this life, so necessarily in any prevision of an after-life. Seen from the human side at death, the solid sense 'files away,' the 'lists of Clay' fall back as she salutes the invisible 'Spirit.' Then, with her eyes on eternity, the attributes of body and soul are reversed. This 'Tragedy of Flesh,' the mortal life, becomes 'Subterfuge,' shifting sands, 'Mists [that] are carved away,' so that the true reality of spirit can show its 'royal Front.'

Her choice of the beloved is made almost godlike by usurping the theological term of Election, then brought sharply back to earth by her surprise use of the scientific 'Atom' to designate her preferred soul. Throughout a lifetime of separation she vows her loyalty to the image of the incarnate soul she herself has 'elected.' But though this poem is addressed to a beloved she has only known in his earthly embodiment, it moves swiftly to her adoration of his spiritual essence. The celestial reunion lies just beyond the last line, but their imminent meeting is evoked by her daring salutation to his soul at the end: 'Behold the Atom— I preferred!' Were it not for one irreducible 'if' she could make her renunciation of mortal love sharply, as in another poem:

> If certain, when this life was out—
> That yours and mine, should be—
> I'd toss it yonder, like a Rind,
> And take Eternity— . . .

But worldly love has its own sources of ecstasy, and she was not content till she had tried to record them all. Time after time she sought to express her sense of the joys of fidelity and devotion, but the results are usually exclamatory or enumerative, more like love letters in verse than poems.

Love is doing as well as being, however, and this opened up new possibilities. Once she found an instrument adequate to render her need for fulfillment through absolute commitment to love's service:

> My Life had stood— a Loaded Gun—
> In Corners— till a Day
> The Owner passed— identified—
> And carried Me away—

And now We roam in Sovreign Woods–
And now We hunt the Doe–
And every time I speak for Him–
The Mountains straight reply–

And do I smile, such cordial light
Upon the Valley glow–
It is as a Vesuvian face
Had let its pleasure through–

And when at Night– Our good Day done–
I guard My Master's Head–
'Tis better than the Eider-Duck's
Deep Pillow– to have shared–

To foe of His– I'm deadly foe–
None stir the second time–
On whom I lay a Yellow Eye–
Or an emphatic Thumb–

Though I than He– may longer live
He longer must– than I–
For I have but the power to kill,
Without– the power to die–

The poem begins with a brilliant conceit. Fused from the ambiguous abstraction 'Life' and the explicit concretion 'Loaded Gun,' it expresses the charged potential of the human being who remains dormant until 'identified' into conscious vitality. 'At last, to be identified!' another poem began. And when she heard of a friend's engagement to be married she wrote: 'The most noble congratulation it ever befell me to offer– is that you are yourself. Till it has loved– no man or woman can become itself– Of our first Creation we are unconscious.'

The paradox of finding oneself through losing oneself in love is rendered in her poem by one word: she achieves *identity* when the lover claims her as his own. The ecstasy of being swept up into the possession of another led her once to an extravagant succession of similes. She was borne along 'With swiftness, as of Chariots,' then lifted up into the ether by a balloon, while 'This World did drop away.' In the gun poem she puts far more in a single line, 'And carried Me away,' the double meaning encompassing both the portage of the gun and the transport of the beloved. The first stanza presents a tightly knit unit:

> My Life had stood— a Loaded Gun—
> In Corners— till a Day
> The Owner passed— identified—
> And carried Me away—

Its shock value inheres in the extreme disparity between the two things compared, incongruous in all ways except the startling points of likeness that can be ferreted out. The trap lies in the great precision needed to avoid confusing them, the vital but subjective 'Life' and the objective but inanimate 'Gun.' If she had chosen to use the strict method of metaphysical poetry, the succeeding stanzas would have been devoted to complicating and reconciling these disparities until they coalesce violently in the end.

Instead, after a brief setting introducing her over-image, she proceeds to develop it by the ballad narrative, to which her chosen metrical pattern was so well suited. In another sense, her poem is a domestication on American soil of the tradition of courtly love. The knight has turned pioneer, his quest a hunting expedition in the wilderness, his bower a cabin with feather-pillow and trusty rifle at his head, his lady the frontier wife who shares his hardships and adventures. In such a folk version of the troubadour lyric, the ballad stanza properly replaces the intricate Provençal forms. In the special climate of frontier America, another turn is given to the convention. Since the male provider is unavoidably committed to the strenuous life, here it is the woman who celebrates the softer arts, pledging eternal fidelity and the rapture of love's service. So the courtly roles are reversed: he is only the adored 'Master' while she is the joyous servant, which accounts for her assuming the active role in the love-game.

The hunting action of the second and third stanzas is given over to its devotional aspects. As steadfast companion, her words of love ring out in the gun's explosion, echoed by the mountains; her looks of love are the 'cordial light' of its fire, like the glow of Vesuvius in eruption. The quarry they hunt, 'the Doe,' is appropriate to the romantic theme. But to counterbalance the danger of sentimentalism she makes a pervasive use of hyperbole, suggesting the tall-tale mode of western humor. The protective action of the next two stanzas portrays the service of love. To guard his sleep is better than to share his bed. This may only mean that she places a higher value on giving him peace than on enjoying connubial bliss, though there is a curious suggestion that the love is never fulfilled in physical union. To give him security also calls forth an unquestioning loyalty destructive of his enemies, the jealous anger of the flashing muzzle's 'Yellow Eye' being a particularly happy extension of the image with which she began, the 'Loaded Gun.' Standing for the amorous potential of a newly vitalized life, this has been sustained through all the narrative center, successfully taking the risks inherent in this anatomical-mechanical fusion of part to part—'speak,' 'smile,' 'face,' and 'eye' applying to the gun as well as to love's servant. With 'thumb' it seems to break down in a shift of agency. Only the 'Owner' has a thumb to raise the hammer, and a finger to fire the gun, but here it fires itself. Her gun-life has so usurped the initiative as to reduce his function to hunting while she herself does the shooting. One of the hazards of the private poet is that the self tends to become the only reality. The lover here certainly plays a negative role.

The final stanza presents a more serious problem to be resolved. A metaphysical poet would have brought his series of shocks to rest in some unexpected figure evolved out of the initial conceit, but her gun only survives in the teasing antithesis of 'kill' and 'die.' A balladist would have rung down the curtain with an ending in surprise comedy or stark tragedy. Instead, she makes a third switch in technique and concludes with an aphorism that seems to have little structural relation to the rest of the poem:

> Though I than He— may longer live
> He longer must— than I—
> For I have but the power to kill,
> Without— the power to die—

If this poem was a deliberate attempt to weld a new form from all these disparate ones—folk ballad, troubadour lyric, tall tale, metaphysical and aphoristic verse—it was a bold experiment even though it did not quite come off. But though the conclusion is a disturbing departure in mode, it may be ventured that its thematic relevance is such as to make it a resolution of all that has gone before. Perhaps this is a poem about the limitations of mortal love and a yearning for the superior glories of the immortal kind. If this is so, then the last stanza is not a moralistic commentary on the narrative but the very meaning which the elaborated image finally creates.

The clues for such an interpretation are not planted thick enough, but there are some. The joys of merely sheltering the beloved are preferred to sharing the marriage bed. And this is the kind of love that finds its expression not in an earthly paradise but in roaming woods that are described here as 'Sovreign,' one of a cluster of words running through her poems to evoke the celestial estate. Earthly love, in spite of the ecstasy of passion and the bliss of service, she was forced to conclude is mortal. Such is the inanimate but loaded gun, once it has been touched into life by being identified by the owner. The physical existence of the gun, her mortal love, may outlast the earthly life of her master, the 'Owner,' but in immortality he will outlive it. So she too must have the 'power to die' into heavenly love in order to become immortal. Limited by her gun-body she has only the 'power to kill,' including paradoxically the soul of the beloved, by making him too enamored of the Eden of this life. In the plaintive 'I have but the power to kill' there may even be the backfire of a suicidal wish, to free him from the encumbrance of her mortal love. It may be reasonably objected that this meaning is too fragmentarily embodied in the poem; and the breakdown of the conclusion into prose brands it, when judged by the highest poetic standards, as a failure. But it is a brilliant one, repaying close study. Moreover, the theme here suggested, though conjectural, is in keeping with the whole trend of her love poetry and will help to illuminate it.

Worldly love, whether fully realized or not, has been the paradoxical image and counter-image of all human aspiration towards spiritual union with God. The lure of the flesh must be overcome, yet mystics have found no language except that of sexual love to express the ineffable they were seeking. The painful transition from one to the other is the direct theme of a key poem:

> You constituted Time–
> I deemed Eternity
> A Revelation of Yourself–
> 'Twas therefore Deity
>
> The Absolute– removed
> The Relative away–
> That I unto Himself adjust
> My slow idolatry–

Once again, entrapment in time rather than in the body symbolizes the mortal conditioning. The earthly lover, in the first stanza, comprises the whole realm of temporal reality in which she has been a willing subject. So imprisoned, she could not even conceive of Eternity except as a projected image of the face of Now.

In a very different poem, wholly given over to idolizing a temporal lover, she elaborated the exclusiveness of this worship. I could not serve heaven, she said,

> Because You saturated Sight—
> And I had no more Eyes
> For sordid excellence
> As Paradise . . .

Her thralldom made her renounce even the hope of heaven with startling blasphemy:

> Because Your Face
> Would put out Jesus'. . . .

She made the same point more quietly in a letter to Samuel Bowles: 'My friends are my "estate." . . . God is not so wary as we, else he would give us no friends, lest we forget him! The Charms of the Heaven in the bush are superceded I fear, by the Heaven in the hand, occasionally.' When the 'friend' is the elected one, the bondage is infinitely harder to break out of.

To return to the poem 'You constituted Time,' the concluding stanza faces the exigency that the earthly lover must be 'removed' completely before she can give herself to God. The need to discipline her emotions for this is conveyed by the abstractions she has reduced the rivals to: 'Relative' and 'Absolute.' The difficulty of her renunciation is the burden of the whole poem, but what brings it home with a shock is the final word:

> That I unto Himself adjust
> My slow idolatry—

This term today is more commonly used for worship of a person or a worldly pursuit. Though the taint of paganism still clings to it, one must go back to her Lexicon to recover the full disapproval of contemporary New England theology. Idolatry, she knew, was 'The worship of idols, images, or any thing . . . which is not God.' Turning her adoration to Him, as a troubled worldling in this poem, she uses a word that orthodox Christians of her day would have found profane.

The largest successful group of her love poems centers around the ritual of marriage. These also move steadily away from the human institution, which was not a part of her experience, towards several versions of the betrothal in heaven that became an obsessive and perhaps compensatory image with her. The one that begins closest to the worldly ceremony of a wedding, though never worked out to its final form, makes an interesting bridge between the two kinds of love and has a special charm all its own:

> I'm ceded— I've stopped being Their's—
> The name They dropped upon my face
> With water, in the country church
> Is finished using, now,
> And They can put it with my Dolls,
> My Childhood, and the string of spools,
> I've finished threading— too—
>
> Baptized, before, without the choice,
> But this time, consciously, of Grace—
> Unto supremest name—
> Called to my Full— The Crescent dropped—
> Existence's whole Arc, filled up,
> With just one Diadem.
>
> My second Rank— too small the first—
> Crowned— Crowing— on my Father's breast—
> A half unconscious Queen—
> But this time— Adequate— Erect,
> With Will to choose, or to reject,
> And I choose, just a Throne—

Two sacraments, baptism and marriage, are set against one another and out of the comparison two kinds of status emerge. Both are name-giving ceremonies and the names are the signs by which she is identified, first in life then in love. In one it is dropped from the family tree upon the upturned face of an 'unconscious' life which is thus given identity, but only as one of 'theirs.' In the other a new name is 'consciously' chosen by an adult who is thus identified as the beloved—'Adequate— Erect' in contrast to the 'whimpering, dangling' babe on its father's breast (variants in the manuscript for 'Crowing,' in line 15).

In a companion poem she even fused the terms of the two sacraments: 'Baptized— this Day— A Bride.' In the one under consideration the water imagery of the baptismal drops in the 'country church,' with the surrounding aura of innocence, reappears in the later ceremony with submerged sexual implications in 'Existence's whole Arc, filled up.' The 'Crescent,' symbol of virginity, has been replaced by the full moon of a 'Diadem.' The final signs of her 'second Rank,' replacing the castoff 'Dolls' and 'spools' of childhood, are the crown and 'Throne' the mature queen freely chooses for herself. These royal terms, echoing the status words used in the Bible for heavenly rank, are further exalted by such a phrase as 'Baptized . . . of Grace—/Unto supremest name.' The redundant superlative 'supremest' and the doctrinal term 'Grace' suggest that her new name may be Bride-of-the-Lamb, her exchange of vows the promise of eternal life bestowed on the dedicated. But the poem concludes, 'With Will to choose, or to reject,/And I choose.' This is not the way mortals achieve God's grace. Though she began with orthodox humility, 'I'm ceded,' this transfer of title and ownership of herself turns out in the end to be an act of royal will. The ceremony hovers indecisively between heaven and earth.

Here as elsewhere in the marriage poems, one meaning merges into the other. If it is unwise to be dogmatic in reading particular poems of this group, it is more so to force consistency of meaning on her poetic vocabulary, even for words that are pervasive. There are certain features common to all, however, that make the cluster method of treatment illuminating. In all of the bridal poems, to cite the most revealing clue, the bridegroom is conspicuous by his absence. Since she was writing poems rather than a personal confession of faith, she could deal creatively with any version of the sacramental act. At least once she used language that is unambiguous, choosing the conventual terminology of Roman Catholicism:

> Given in Marriage unto Thee
> Oh thou Celestial Host—
> Bride of the Father and the Son
> Bride of the Holy Ghost.
>
> Other Bethrothal shall dissolve—
> Wedlock of Will, decay—
> Only the Keeper of this Ring
> Conquer Mortality—

On another occasion, using Catholic images of prayer such as 'Taper' and 'Shrine,' she prayed: 'Madonna dim, to whom all Feet may come,/ Regard a Nun.' From odd facts in her life, lit up by poems like these, some have been tempted to transform Emily Dickinson into the 'Nun of Amherst.' This is indeed her most explicit treatment of the marriage theme as a celestial sacrament, but the fictive license of the poet should be remembered. If *I*, 'the supposed person' of her verse, should take the veil it would be like this.

She could wear an opposing mask with equal ease, however, as in the poem which seems to begin in a similar vein: 'God is a distant— stately Lover,' who woos vicariously 'by His Son.' This solemn doctrine suddenly brings to her mind an unexpected parallel out of New England history, John Alden's absentee courtship of Priscilla. With no need to rehearse the anecdote made familiar in Longfellow's *Courtship of Miles Standish,* she plucks out its humor and gives it a new slant. Holding it up as a mirror to her poem, she brings the heavenly wooing to a most unorthodox conclusion. What if the soul, like fair Priscilla, should 'Choose the Envoy— and spurn the Groom'? But God circumvents this mishap with a paradox, vouching 'with hyperbolic archness' that they are 'Synonyme.' This is hardly the expectant rapture of the novitiate, nor even sound trinitarian doctrine.

The poet sings in many keys. The solemnity of one of these poems is balanced by the wry comedy of the other. Different as they may be in doctrinal formulation, both are exclusively concerned with the heavenly lover. The very fact that they are more like prose statements than poems emphasizes her thematic obsession with that image, rather than with one remembered from literal experience. Even the biographical assumption that the One Lover must necessarily be a compensation for loss of the other is no more warranted than the romantic notion that a nun always takes the veil to overcome a specific disappointment in human love. For both it may be merely the renunciation of the world in general as inadequate to the aspirant soul.

The struggle between earthly and heavenly love remains central to the most successful poems in the marriage group. More accurately it is the source of the tension she sets up by embodying the heavenly theme in earthly terms, then making these into images with celestial reference, even while the rapture descends to take on some coloring of the flesh. Two strategies of language are responsible for this success, the language of Status and the Signs which denote the elevation from one level to another. In Christian teaching rank is a basic concept, the spiritual estate usually rendered in the hierarchical terms of this world. In the hymns she sang, the sermons she heard, and the Bible she read, heaven is referred to as a kingdom, where all the inhabitants are crowned. More specifically, the Puritan doctrine of Election posits an aristocracy of grace revealed in advance only by signs, and her favorite New Testament book, The Revelation, is particularly rich in the panoply of royalty: 'Behold, a throne was set in heaven, and one sat on the throne . . . in sight like unto an emerald. And round about the throne were . . . elders sitting, clothed in white raiment; and they had on their heads crowns of gold.'

Regal terms not only give a concrete worldly splendor to the redeemed but, conversely, they are a means of exalting earthly lovers to high estate. Her capacity for worship took on such feudal coloring even in her letters, as witnessed by one that has clearly been established as a love letter, written late in life to Judge Otis Lord: 'The trespass of my rustic Love upon your Realms of Ermine, only a Sovereign could forgive— I never knelt to other.' A similar language permeates her love poetry, whether addressed to a human or divine image of adoration. So with the paraphernalia which become the signs of a change of status for her. The married woman has two obvious ones, the new name and the wedding ring. Both of these appear in several guises in her poems. The ring can become a diadem as in the poem 'I'm ceded,' in another the 'perfect pearl/The Man— upon the Woman— binds,' and again 'the Belt around my life' which when he snapped it on made her 'imperial.' The name may be 'Queen' or simply 'Wife'; or it may appear indirectly as 'Crests— . . . on my Buckles,' the noble arms standing for the family name, her new rank so signified entitling her to wear 'Ermine— my familiar Gown.' In one poem the language is particularly interesting. The sign she will take with her when she goes 'out of Time' to establish her 'Rank' by in heaven will be the face of her lover; and the angels will exchange this for a 'Crown,' recognizing her right to this new degree 'As one that bore her Master's name—/ Sufficient Royalty!' Once again the ambiguous term for the lover, 'Master'—human or divine?

In the last chapter of the Book of Revelation the heavenly reward of those who serve God is described in strikingly similar language: 'And they shall see his face; and his name shall be in their foreheads.' It is filled with such references to signs: 'To him that overcometh will I give ... a white stone, and in the stone a new name written,' and again, 'I will write upon him the name of my God.' Moreover, if the dominant image of this Book is royalty, the subordinate image is that of marriage. Even as in the traditional interpretation of the Song of Songs, making it an allegory of Christ's union with the church, the heavenly host in the New Jerusalem are transfigured as 'the bride, the Lamb's wife.'

With this word cluster from her poetry and the Bible in mind, her two finest poems on the earthly-heavenly marriage take on new meaning:

> Title divine— is mine!
> The Wife— without the Sign!
> Acute Degree— conferred on me—
> Empress of Calvary!
> Royal— all but the Crown!
> Betrothed— without the swoon
> God sends us Women—
> When you— hold— Garnet to Garnet—
> Gold— to Gold—
> Born— Bridalled— Shrouded—
> In a Day—
> 'My Husband'— women say—
> Stroking the Melody—
> Is *this*— the way?

The central figure is that of a royal marriage, but it is curiously incomplete. There has been a change of status, but the presence of the Sign is denied three times, 'without the Sign,' 'without the swoon,' 'all but the Crown!' This is not a worldly wedding, no ring in fact or in mutation. But the felt presence of one crowds painfully on the 'divine' invocation of the opening and dominates the language of the last half of the poem.

Perhaps it is the smothered emotion of this that breaks the otherwise perfectly rhymed couplets into irregular line lengths on her page, from this point to the end. There has been none of the 'swoon' of joy of the betrothed maiden, tremulous with anticipation, at that moment when the loss of virginity will become the gain of love's consummation. The double-ring ceremony, 'Garnet to Garnet—/Gold— to Gold,' conjures up all the rich sensuousness of the physical union denied to her. Instead, hers will be spiritual. Yet in looking forward to it she makes one final reference back to the normal fulfillment 'God sends us Women'—for that too is a sacrament—to ask out of her inexperience if the earthly marriage holds any clue for the heavenly. The poem ends with the young wife's song, saying for the first time 'My Husband'—

> Stroking the Melody—
> Is *this*— the way?

The spoken phrase, putting a catch in the voice of one who will never speak it in this sense, binds the conclusion back to the paradoxical 'Wife' of the beginning. Deprived of one status, she has not quite achieved the other and more glorious one. She has the divine title of 'Empress,' but it is so far only an 'Acute Degree,' suggesting the pain rather than the glory of her elevation. For hers as yet is only the empire of 'Calvary,' one of the most charged symbols in her vocabulary, filled with agony but with the promise of grace. The experience she is undergoing is the paradox of redemption, which involves a death to the world as well as birth to a higher spiritual life. Were she already enthroned, which she is not, her crown would appropriately be adorned with garnets, answering to the scarlet robe, the crown of thorns, and the imperial title mockingly bestowed on Christ at the Crucifixion. Her divine title is chiefly painful now, because the Sign that will give her full rights to it has yet to come. The normal woman is 'Born— Bridalled— Shrouded—/In a Day,' the bride's whole existence being her wedding day, which brings death to the virgin and birth to the wife. Hers is the long day of this life, though it will at last culminate in her elevation to a new 'Degree'— christening clothes, bridal gown, winding sheet all to be exchanged for a spotless white robe. Then she will be truly an empress, with the crown and without the Calvary, but also still without the swoon that is the glory of the mortal wife. The absent Sign for her now is death, which when it does come will confirm her in full possession of the state of grace.

In a companion poem the hold of the heart is reduced to the vanishing point while the soul rises to a state of supreme ecstasy, though it can attain in this life only to heavenly betrothal, not marriage:

> Mine— by the Right of the White Election!
> Mine— by the Royal Seal!
> Mine— by the Sign in the Scarlet prison—
> Bars— cannot conceal!

> Mine– here– in Vision– and in Veto!
> Mine– by the Grave's Repeal–
> Titled– Confirmed–
> Delirious Charter!
> Mine– long as Ages steal!

The exclamatory style and the repetition of the rapturous 'Mine' at the beginning of six lines seem to cast this in the mold of rhetoric, the rhetoric of the hymns celebrating heavenly love. This is only a façade, however, behind which she maneuvers an intricate web of language. The words fall into several separate but overlapping categories, with distinct but interrelated meanings. All are controlled by her 'White Election' to the state of grace, and are multiple facets of the redemptive process.

The first is the legal group, including: 'Right,' 'Seal,' 'Bars,' 'Repeal,' 'Titled,' 'Confirmed,' and 'Charter.' The change of status set forth in these terms is achieved by the acquisition of a new property, its sign the Charter, a solemnly executed instrument suggesting exclusive rights and title in perpetuity. The devious ways of law courts will not obscure it, 'Bars– cannot conceal.' Nor can time steal it by 'the Grave's Repeal,' for though ownership is normally repealed by death, the Royal Signatory of this document has himself repeated the power of the grave. The second or prison group uses several of these words in a similar sense ('Seal' and 'Charter'), some greatly changed ('Repeal' and 'Bars'), and adds to them 'Vision,' 'Veto,' and 'Scarlet prison.' The new estate this time is freedom, for the Charter is a pardon signed and sealed by the King. Though still behind the bars she is delirious with joy that her sentence has been repealed and she will be recalled from exile, from the prison's burial in anonymity, and given again a name or title. But this is only a vision of celestial justice, vetoed of necessity here and now since she is inexorably a prisoner for life.

Another pair of meanings for some of these words arises from the addition of 'White Election' and 'Confirmed.' The obvious one is that of a wedding, the bride entitled with her new name, the 'Seal' (ring) the sign of her wedded state, the Charter her certificate of marriage. The other is a faint suggestion of the ritual of confirmation, an initiation into the spiritual life by accepting the sign of the cross, after which this candidate too is given a certificate of status. In both sacramental images the 'Scarlet prison' could stand for a dimly lit cathedral with the leaded bars and stained glass of its windows. For a final transformation of the Charter, the word 'Titled' may suggest a patent of nobility. The sign and bars could then be the heraldic devices acquired by the new nobleman, the royal seal entitling him to wear the ermine of exalted rank. The multivalence of all this language sends the mind on far journeys.

Whatever levels of meaning the ingenious reader may be tempted to find above and below the literal text, it will undoubtedly be enriched by the very boldness of these excursions. One can return now in confidence to the basic pattern of a hymn in praise of heavenly love. The lure of the world has been completely overcome. The pain of such renunciation had been the burden of many other poems. 'To put this World down, like a Bundle,' she said in one of them, is to take up the pilgrim's road of agony: ' 'Tis the Scarlet Way.' Now it is reduced to a pigment and the body to a temporary house of bondage, 'the Scarlet prison'—more exactly the heart, as the seat of worldly attachment. Though immured behind these bars, the dedicated soul may yet perceive the sign of its Election to future bliss, or such was the belief of her heritage.

To pin down the exact significance of 'White' for Dickinson is impossible. It permeates her writings, with many shades of meaning. She used it for example as the characteristic color of death, 'the White Exploit,' and of God, 'the White Creator.' That she chose to dress in white exclusively for the last fifteen or twenty years of her life, probably beginning about the time she composed her poem on the 'White Election,' offers a fascinating field for conjecture. But she never gave an explanation for it. (It may even have been an obscure whim, as with Mark Twain.) At any rate it does not serve the critic, for the meaning of the act in life is more obscure than the meaning of the word in a particular poem. For this one, the scriptural usage seems most helpful. In the Bible it is most often the symbolic color not of innocence and purity but of the regenerate: 'wash me, and I shall be whiter than snow,' and 'though your sins be as scarlet, they shall be as white as snow.' The contrasting scarlet of her prison, incidentally, stands presumably for sin only in the generic or theological sense, the way of all flesh since the Fall, rather than a confession of specific moral sins.

Her Election is in white chiefly as symbolizing her assumption of the heavenly bridal gown, as she could read in The Revelation: 'Let us be glad and rejoice, . . . for the marriage of the Lamb is come, and his wife hath made herself ready . . . arrayed in fine linen, clean and white.' Her second wedded sign is better than a ring, or even the ring metamorphosed into the crown common to the regenerate. It is a 'Seal.' In the poem most clearly couched in terms of divine marriage ('Given in Marriage unto Thee/Oh thou Celestial Host'), she put down as a variant for the 'Ring' of God 'the Seal.' The same sign for the Elect appears in The Revelation, 'we have sealed the servants of our God in their foreheads.' The heavenly bridegroom claims personal possession, and the bestowal of his signet gives ring and name in one token, 'the Royal Seal.'

Reading Election as a strictly doctrinal term one still remembers that orthodox Puritans, even when sure they had been given the Sign, knew that for mortals it is only a 'Vision' of a state of grace to come. The mystical tendency deeply buried in Puritanism, implying the possibility of union now with God, she would have rejected as she did the mystical basis of Transcendentalism. Her intuitive 'Vision' is nearer to the simple yearning for a glimpse of the supernal common to many poets. This is why she introduces the 'Veto' in the second stanza. As it is necessary to renounce this world in order to enter heaven, so during the prison term of life heavenly grace exists only 'in Veto.' But the great 'Charter' of redemption, signed by Christ at the time of the crucifixion, has repealed the grave's sentence of mortality with the guarantee of eternal life for all who will simply take his name. 'Confirmed' by this solemn pledge, 'Titled' Bride-of-the-Lamb-to-be, she is lifted temporarily out of the scarlet prison. 'Delirious' signifies that this 'Wife' has achieved something far surpassing the swoon of ordinary women, a state of pure ecstasy. It is all things—an initiation into the spiritual life, a royal estate, a promise of return from exile and earthly imprisonment to the heavenly home in the language of her hymnal. It is also, at least in prospect, an entry into the aristocracy of grace, a spiritual union, a joy-bringing perpetual gift sealed by God that will release her from the bondage of time, 'Mine— while the Ages steal!'

It would be unwise to jump at biographical conclusions from a poem like this, as evidence that she finally attained pure spiritual dedication, for in the whole body of her work it is the exception rather than the rule. There is no more consistent record of such ecstasy than of the more earthly sort. After the death of Judge Lord, for example, she wrote: 'Till the first friend dies, we think ecstasy impersonal, but then discover that he was the cup from which we drank it, itself as yet unknown.'

Each rare experience of ecstasy must be taken on its own terms, 'itself
... unknown.' So the student of her poetry as well as of her life would
do well to avoid generalizing about the terminology of love in her writings. 'Mine— by the right of the White Election!' is simply a poem, a
rare one out of many, an imaginative projection of what it would be
like to be betrothed to God.

In contrast to the sure rhapsody with which she there claims the illumination of heavenly love as her own possession, she could construct another ecstatic poem solely on the multiple aspects of its elusiveness:

> The Love a Life can show Below
> Is but a filament, I know,
> Of that diviner thing
> That faints upon the face of Noon—
> And smites the Tinder in the Sun—
> And hinders Gabriel's Wing—
>
> 'Tis this— in Music— hints and sways—
> And far abroad on Summer days—
> Distills uncertain pain—
> 'Tis this enamors in the East—
> And tints the Transit in the West
> With harrowing Iodine—
>
> 'Tis this— invites— appalls— endows—
> Flits— glimmers— proves— dissolves—
> Returns— suggests— convicts— enchants—
> Then— flings in Paradise—

Instead of trying to define this indefinable essence, she piles verb on verb
to tell what it does to her, in its evanescence and ambiguity. The paradoxical nature of its effect gives the poem its structure and some of its
finest phrases, as in the sunset coloring of 'harrowing Iodine.' Its irreducible ambivalence is indicated in the variant suggested for one line on
the beauty of sunrise, ' 'Tis this enamors>afflicts us in the East.' The
climax is reached in the last stanza, where twelve alternative predicates
intervene before she can conclude, ' 'Tis this . . . flings in Paradise'—an
experiment in catalogue syntax that outdoes Whitman.

Since her chase leads her through the maze of nature's most ethereal
illuminations rather than through the mazes of the heart, one might
say that this is the poet's effort to catch a glimpse of supernal beauty,
not love. Since it hinders the wings of the archangel whose special func-

tion is to bring news of the farther heaven, perhaps it is simply her vision of that beauty which flings her in the paradise of art. But the equation of love and poetry is pervasive in her writing, and the opening lines clearly define her subject here as the contrast between human and divine love. Her poem is concerned with the vastly superior glory of the divine, but the poet can only describe it in terms taken from 'Below.' The symbolic relation is that of 'filament' to fullness, her Lexicon defining the former as 'the fine thread, of which flesh, nerves, skin, etc. . . . are composed.' A modern extension of filament applies it to the nearly invisible wires of the light bulb which become incandescent when brought to intense heat by electricity. Whether she was aware of the experiments leading up to Edison's invention in 1878 is not known, but she would have embraced this meaning with joy if it had been available to her. 'Electricity' is one of her most extraordinary epithets for the heavenly lover, as will be seen in the following poem. Earthly love, and beauty, are the only threads from which she could weave her web of heaven, however gossamer they may be. Without doing violence to her expressed creed, one can expand it to read: All we know of beauty and love, human or divine, is their evanescence.

A final effort to catch the heavenly gleam and fix it in her verse was made near the end of her life:

> The farthest Thunder that I heard
> Was nearer than the Sky
> And rumbles still— though Torrid Noons
> Have lain their Missiles by—
>
> The Lightning that preceded it
> Struck no one but myself
> And I would not exchange the Flash
> For all the rest of Life—
>
> Indebtedness to Oxygen
> A Lover may repay—
> But not the obligation
> To Electricity—
>
> It founds the Homes
> And decks the Days
> And every clamor bright
> Is but the gleam concomitant
> Of that waylaying Light—

The Scene was quiet as a Flake—
A Crash without a sound—
How Life's reverberation
Its explanation found—

The most famous 'waylaying Light' in the annals of the western world was the one that blinded St. Paul on the road to Damascus: 'And it came to pass, that . . . suddenly there shone from heaven a great light round about me. And I fell unto the ground. . . . I could not see for the glory of that light.' This was the initiation into spiritual life for Saul of Tarsus, and it is interesting to note that the first sign of his dedication to the light and love of Christ was his acquisition of a new name.

The parallel makes a religious interpretation of Dickinson's poem inescapable. First there was the unexpectedness of the experience: 'suddenly there shone,' he records; and she: 'The Scene was quiet,' then the 'Crash.' Again, the revelation was to one only: others 'saw indeed the light . . . but they heard not the voice,' according to the Biblical account; in the poem: 'A Crash without a sound . . . Struck no one but myself.' Finally, there is the complete and permanent change wrought in the lives of both, the abiding subject of his epistles and of her poems. For her as for St. Paul it meant love and joy and ultimate truth: 'It founds the Homes,' 'And decks the Days,' and reveals the meaning of 'Life's reverberation'—not its sights and sounds but its re-echoings and reflections.

She adapted the same key phrase to a context of nature, it is true, in a letter of about the same date: 'The Summer has been wide and deep, and a deeper Autumn is but the Gleam concomitant of that waylaying Light.' But even there the overtones are religious, as was pointed out in the last chapter, the faint intimations of immortality she catches in the ambiguous light of Indian Summer. There are important differences, however, between St. Paul's conversion and hers, if such it may be called. One is her emphasis on 'Gleam *concomitant*.' The poem, written in 1881-83, recounts the great event as having happened in the long ago past. When it struck it was indeed a 'Flash,' of such splendor that she would not exchange it 'For all the rest of Life.' Since then she has only known the 'Torrid Noons' of normal life, unilluminated by 'Missiles' of celestial fire though presumably by an occasional 'Gleam.' So with St. Paul too, perhaps, but the memory of his single experience burned with such a fierce light that it drove him across the known world on a proselytizing mission.

She, with the proper difference between a poet and an apostle, has been content to speculate on the meaning of what happened to her and how she can 'repay' the debt. Her method is suggested in the climactic stanza: to show how 'every clamor' of this world can be made bright only by the light of the next. Love of life, nature, art, people—all are parts of the ecstasy of one who has been struck by the love of God. This is the intent of many of her best poems, to find a 'Gleam' of spiritual meaning in beauty and love and death. The faith of the fathers was one way. But that light was dimmed for her, though her wide divergence from orthodoxy should not obscure the essentially religious cast of her mind. Instead, she turned to the *ignis fatuus* of art, which for her was not delusion but divine illusion. The worldly might turn to human love, but this she says can only repay 'Indebtedness to Oxygen,' mere physical life without its 'reverberations.'

Some twenty years earlier she had made the decision as to how she could repay her obligation to 'Electricity,' her new name for the blinding light of the heavenly lover. She dedicated her life to writing poems. In one sense, then, the flash of lightning symbolizing her moment of illumination is one of those 'Bolts of Melody' which, in another poem, she makes the distinguishing mark of the truly inspired poet, thus merging once again the images of lover and muse. In the present poem the dominant image is light. But two others, written about the same time, are couched in language that seems to bring it back again to love, or rather to the earthly lover transfigured. In one, dating from the year of Judge Lord's death, she says it is not the 'swaying frame' but the 'steadfast Heart' she misses; had it lived a thousand years it would have beat for love alone:

> Its fervor the electric Oar,
> That bore it through the Tomb....

The other, composed just after the Rev. Mr. Wadsworth died, begins:

> Image of Light, Adieu—
> Thanks for the interview—...

Whether love or light, human or divine, at least it can be said that in her poetry spiritual ecstasy burns with a purer incandescence than amorous joy, and it creates better poems.

I 0

DESPAIR

Emily Dickinson was no visionary intent on escaping the prison of this flesh. What gives weight to her poems that tug to be free and soar is her solid sense of reality, not just of scene and thing but of thought and feeling. More than most of her contemporaries she knew how to discriminate between vision and fact, and was aware how small a part ecstasy makes in the sum total that comprises life. Her normal impulse is to load the scales against it, as in this early poem:

> The Heart asks Pleasure– first–
> And then– Excuse from Pain–
> And then– those little Anodynes
> That deaden suffering–...

Then permission to sleep and finally, if the 'Inquisitor' wills it, 'The privilege to die.' With a different emphasis, reversing the compensatory doctrine of heavenly reward for a life of suffering, she says in a late letter: 'To have lived is a Bliss so powerful– we must die– to adjust it.'

Her effect of reality is achieved not by an accent on pleasure or pain but by her dramatic use of their interaction. As an artist she took full advantage of contrast as a mode of definition, making the pleasure-pain antithesis a running strategy in her poetry. As 'Water is taught by thirst,' so 'Transport– by throe.' Again:

> Delight– becomes pictorial–
> When viewed through Pain–...

191

> Transporting must the moment be—
> Brewed from decades of Agony! . . .

And finally, from among her earliest efforts, there is a poem constructed entirely of such contrasts, in terms of intensity and duration, beginning:

> For each extatic instant
> We must an anguish pay
> In keen and quivering ratio
> To the extasy. . . .

'Time is a pain lived piecemeal,' as one critic astutely epitomizes this poem, 'and the sum of the pieces equals a moment of joy.' But this is just an exercise in hedonistic calculus.

There is a wide range of pain explored in her poetry. She distinguishes misery, as a hurt that can be relieved, from suffering which stresses the act of enduring. But these milder aches and griefs did not challenge her powers of analysis like the extreme forms from affliction to woe that are recurrent in her poems. She discriminates among them somewhat as her copy of Webster did. He defines 'agony' as the pain so excruciating as to cause bodily contortions 'similar to . . . the sufferings of our Savior in the garden of Gethsemane'; 'anguish' as any keen distress of the mind 'from sorrow, remorse, despair, and the kindred passions'; and 'despair' itself as the extremest form of all, resulting in hopelessness, though with only subordinate theological connotations. But the purpose of her poems is something far other than the niceties of the lexicographer. She simply separates the lesser pains that will heal from the greater pains that will not and chooses the latter as her special concern, noting with precision their qualities and above all their effects.

If she had emphasized their causes, as from a loss of love or fame or religious faith, there would be more justification for biographical inquiry. Even so, her very obsession with the theme of extreme pain has made inevitable the conjecture that some experience of unusual intensity was the source of it. There is scattered evidence for this in the letters, but only one explicit statement. Written to Higginson in 1862, at the beginning of her creative flood tide, it has often been taken as explaining why she turned to poetry as a career: 'I had a terror— since September— I could tell to none— and so I sing, as the Boy does by the Burying Ground— because I am afraid.' It is doubtful that the nature of this 'terror' will ever be clarified by further.external data. But the poems of this period likewise seem to reflect an extreme emotional and psychological crisis that tempts speculation. Some fifty of them have been arranged recently by one of her biographers in an impressive display of the severity and many-sidedness of such a conjectured crisis.

A number of her poems, though not usually the best, seem to relate this extreme suffering to a loss in love. One of the quieter ones, written in 1864 on the theme of renunciation until 'He' and 'I' can be reunited, presumably in heaven, begins and ends with phraseology remarkably similar to her statement in the letter to Higginson just quoted: 'I sing to use the Waiting . . . To Keep the Dark away.' Another, ten years later, makes a memorable song out of pain as one of the pressures that wrings poetry from the heart, though declining to name the instrumentality as love:

> Not with a Club, the Heart is broken
> Nor with a Stone—
> A Whip so small you could not see it
> I've known
>
> To lash the Magic Creature
> Till it fell,
> Yet that Whip's Name
> Too noble then to tell.
>
> Magnanimous as Bird
> By Boy descried—
> Singing unto the Stone
> Of which it died— . . .

Singing to conquer pain is again the theme. The images are sharp— 'Club,' 'Stone,' 'Whip,' culminating in the evocative 'Magic Creature' that makes the heart a living person. Nor is the third stanza an extraneous prose trailer, but a flash that brings the whole into focus. The boy, Eros with a slingshot, kills the bird of his desire heedless of its song. But the very real stone here links back to the invisible one at the beginning, denied into a whip, which makes the smitten heart sing too, now that the oblivious lover-killer has faded out. The suffering has been mastered and the beauty remains.

Her most anguished record of a hopeless love, 'I cannot live with you,' never quite rises out of pain into poetry, though some of the lines sing. For the most part it is a discursive monologue (fifty lines, her longest single effort in verse), struggling vainly to resolve an impossible dilemma. I cannot live with you or without you; I cannot die, or go to heaven, or even desire heaven without you. Yet there is no hope of reunion in Paradise either, because of some obscure flaw in their love. The reader is shaken by an eruption of emotion that is threatening from somewhere behind the poem to break out into the text, but it is never sufficiently under control to be channeled into language except to a modest degree in the final stanza:

> So We must meet apart—
> You there— I— here
> With just the Door ajar
> That Oceans are— and Prayer—
> And that White Sustenance—
> Despair—

The prerequisite for mastery, as in all Dickinson's best poetry, was to abandon the cumulative and logical for the tight symbolic structure that was her forte. Closely connected with this was the narrowing of her concern to one emotion at a time. Two of her better poems on the pain of renunciation deal, respectively, with the acceptance of loss as an inescapable part of the human condition and with the sheer quality of the resulting agony. In both, the specific event of a love-parting is reduced to a generalized idea of deprivation. The first of these achieves conciseness of theme if not of form:

> I should have been too glad, I see—
> Too lifted— for the scant degree
> Of Life's penurious Round—
> My little Circuit would have shamed
> This new Circumference— have blamed—
> The homelier time behind.
>
> I should have been too saved— I see—
> Too rescued— Fear too dim to me
> That I could spell the Prayer
> I knew so perfect— yesterday—
> That Scalding One— Sabacthini—
> Recited fluent— here—

Earth would have been too much– I see–
And Heaven– not enough for me–
I should have had the Joy
Without the Fear– to justify–
The Palm– without the Calvary–
So Savior– Crucify–

Defeat whets Victory– they say–
The Reefs in Old Gethsemane
Endear the Shore beyond–
'Tis Beggars– Banquets best define–
'Tis Thirsting– vitalizes Wine–
Faith bleats to understand–

The search for peace begins creatively with two concentric symbols, one circle for the mortal lot and one for the heavenly expansion unattainable on earth. If they had been developed to control the whole poem, their interaction might have encompassed not only the fact and the vision but the adjustment between the two, in a more satisfying fusion of theme and form. Though this advantage is not followed through, the first stanza sets up the limits of the human condition as a realized center for measuring the pressure of pain to follow. Justifying to herself why she was deprived of ecstasy, the ecstasy of heavenly love presumably, she says that it would have made her unjustly disdainful of the 'penurious Round' of ordinary life. One cannot escape from the 'little Circuit' of petty realities by leaping directly into a 'new Circumference.' Had such heavenly bliss actually been bestowed on her she would have proved inadequate to it. Being still limited by the human capacity for expansion, she would have dishonored ('shamed') the potentialities of such love and could only have 'blamed' her failure on the deficient preparation of the 'homelier' life she had known before. The uplifting from a 'scant degree' to an exalted one is not so easily obtained. Mortal experience will never become a center from which the inner self can expand toward limitless joy. The geometry of earthly and heavenly circumference is drawn with inflexible and mutually exclusive precision.

Leaving these two encompassing images, the poem develops instead by linear argument to prove that the human way is not the easy but the hard one, the way that must go through pain to a fuller understanding of what heaven can be. Some sort of logical unity is preserved by the syntactical pattern. The conditional mood, 'I should . . . ,' is maintained throughout (except in the last stanza), giving the whole poem the quality of a hypothetical case history. Again, 'Too rescued . . . too saved' in the second stanza echoes 'Too lifted . . . too glad' in the first and is answered by 'too much' in the third. Once in a letter she used the syllogistic paradox with shock effect to argue: 'To be human is more than to be divine, for when Christ was divine, he was uncontented till he had been human.' Similarly here: as Jesus before reaching his divine expanse had to experience mortal suffering to the point of temporary despair and utter his *Sabachthani,* so must she in order to spell out the human prayer, 'My God, my God, why hast thou forsaken me.' She can say it fluently now because she has been forsaken, though 'Recited' gives it the air of ritualistic formula, as if she were rehearsing the words of Another to make them her own.

A more important kind of unity derives from thematic linkages. The 'little Circuit—new Circumference' antithesis reappears at the beginning of the third stanza in the exalted earthly life that would blot out the heavenly. At its close the 'Scalding' prayer that gives the poem its center is balanced by a daring redaction of the historic renunciation in Gethsemane ('Not my will, but thine, be done') in her startling plea: 'So Savior— Crucify.' The personal intensity ends with this climactic juxtaposition of opposites that began with Joy and Fear, Palm and Calvary. The last stanza seems on the surface like a mere appendix of aphorisms in further illustration of the pleasure-pain contrast. But this is the truth as 'they say' it, and two submerged metaphors identify 'them' as the authors of the Gospel story. 'Gethsemane' recalls the night before the crucifixion, 'Defeat-Victory' the agony of Golgotha that must follow the triumphal entry into Jerusalem, 'Banquets' and 'Wine' the spiritual feast of the Last Supper. That this was also the celebration of the Passover evokes the image of the Paschal lamb, slain and eaten at that time, which reappears indirectly in the final line: 'Faith bleats to understand.' This brings to mind many Biblical references to the Savior as the Good Shepherd, but also in its plaintiveness links back to the cry from the cross that forms the poem's passionate center. If glory must first be denied into despair for Christ, how much more so for mortals? Pain and loss, sharpened by a momentary vision of ecstasy, constitute the human condition she has been trying to adjust herself to throughout. For all her attempt to verbalize this, in the end she can only cry as a sheep.

The nature of despair itself, rather than the story of how she rebelled against it or finally accepted it, called out her finest talents:

> The Auctioneer of Parting
> His 'Going, going, gone'
> Shouts even from the Crucifix,
> And brings his Hammer down—
> He only sells the Wilderness,
> The prices of Despair
> Range from a single human Heart
> To Two— not any more—

This poem comprises the most remarkable pun in nineteenth-century Anglo-American literature, reviving that clowning Elizabethan device for the purposes of serious poetry long before Joyce and Pound rediscovered its efficacy. What is being sold, what is 'Going,' is gone-ness itself. What is being knocked down from the cross—and the verbal play makes that horrific extension inescapable—is death, the symbolic last 'Parting' of all. The wooden rap of the ordinary auctioneer's gavel makes all sales final, and this one transformed into a 'Hammer,' such as drove the nails into God's body, has the finality of Fate. The purchaser cannot back out, he must take possession of what he has bought.

He has bought the 'Wilderness,' not in the American sense of a primeval forest but as in Biblical references to those waste places where life cannot be supported. Her Lexicon, differing from modern dictionaries, gives prominence to this definition, 'a barren plain . . . , uncultivated and uninhabited by human beings,' citing by way of example the deserts of Arabia in which the Israelites wandered for forty years. The presence of 'Crucifix' in her poem makes her meaning unmistakable: a desert where the lost wander. 'Wilderness' is her new designation for 'that White Sustenance— Despair,' the utter desolation of the human heart. That any one should buy the wilderness voluntarily may seem strange. Yet parting short of death is an act of free will, however desperate the circumstances that force the choice. The price of this 'death' is a living heart, two if both make the renunciation, a single one if the other is unaware of love's commitment. (It is only in these last two lines that there is any suggestion of a love-parting; otherwise the theme seems to be separation from God, made doubly poignant by its unuttered cry from the cross.) So the figure of the auction carries through to the end. The movement of the poem is unavoidably downward, dictated by the hammer's stroke. The powerful conceit reaches its climax in the second line, the devastation spends itself in the center, and the force of both is dissipated in the cool air of calculation at the end. The violent emotion comes to rest here in quiet analysis, it is true, but this is the mood that creates her best poems on the extremity of pain.

Her justification for such bold adaptations of the great Christian symbol to human agony is made explicit in another poem. 'One Crucifixion is recorded— only,' she says, but there are as many unrecorded ones as there are people: 'Gethsemane–/Is but a Province– in the Being's Centre.' The theme of her own 'Calvary' in many poems is generally taken to be her suffering through the frustration of an earthly love. Yet this assumption must be balanced against references to herself as a creature 'Of Heavenly Love– forgot' and the general tenor of poems like the two just discussed. Her use of 'Despair' sometimes comes close to the traditional Christian definition, the last one cited in her Lexicon: 'Loss of hope in the mercy of God.' Such a suggested meaning in these poems is usually supported by a pervasive religious language– Sabachthani, Calvary, Crucifix. In others she uses despair simply as the extremest form of mortal suffering, 'the anguish of despair' as Webster phrased the secular illustration, which is similar to but not identical with the soul's helplessness of heaven. It seems wisest to read the whole range of her poems on pain, as in the case of those on ecstasy, simply as poems, free of entanglement in autobiographical conjecture or the formalism of theology. Let the 'I' be fictive, the 'supposed person' who stands for Everyman, and let the pain be secular unless the evidence of the whole poem makes it otherwise.

Anguish confined entirely to this world can be devastating enough, by reason of its very intensity. It is aggravated by the realization that man can find no help for it outside himself, as he can with spiritual despair through the hope of God's grace. Contrary to many of the romantic poets who preceded her, she found no healing balm in nature for human hurt. The absolute cleavage between man and the external world was one of her basic convictions, as previous chapters have demonstrated, and its indifference to his plight is the theme-song in many of her poems. Her best one on the theme of human suffering confronted by nature's gay parade seems on the surface to be in danger of a reverse use of the pathetic fallacy, for here the indifference is threatening at several points to break out into open hostility, but a close reading proves she has not lapsed into the error of making nature sentient. On the contrary, she has made deliberate use of emotional extravagance to create

a sense of nightmare, such as might result when anguish had reduced
its victim to irrational terror:

> I dreaded that first Robin, so,
> But He is mastered, now,
> I'm some accustomed to Him grown,
> He hurts a little, though—
>
> I thought if I could only live
> Till that first Shout got by—
> Not all Pianos in the Woods
> Had power to mangle me—
>
> I dared not meet the Daffodils—
> For fear their Yellow Gown
> Would pierce me with a fashion
> So foreign to my own—
>
> I wished the Grass would hurry
> So— when 'twas time to see—
> He'd be too tall, the tallest one
> Could stretch— to look at me—
>
> I could not bear the Bees should come,
> I wished they'd stay away
> In those dim countries where they go,
> What word had they, for me?
>
> They're here, though; not a creature failed—
> No Blossom stayed away
> In gentle deference to me—
> The Queen of Calvary—
>
> Each one salutes me, as he goes,
> And I, my childish Plumes,
> Lift, in bereaved acknowledgement
> Of their unthinking Drums—

She feared the sounds of spring would 'mangle' her, its colors 'pierce'
her, and so on. Nature is not only personified but on the warpath, the
poet's soul so hypersensitive it can be wounded by anything, her emotions exaggerated to the point of being ludicrous. These certainly seem

like the signposts of sentimentalism, and the casual reader may easily misinterpret them. Aware she was using a precarious technique, she matched her skill to the risk. The overwrought center is deftly set apart by being related in the past tense and is provided with a frame of irony by the opening and closing stanzas, which enable her and the reader to view it objectively from the calmer present. The nightmare is confined to stanzas two through five. They record not what actually happened but what she 'dreaded' would happen. The past tense, and the subjunctive mood, shows that for this part of the story's enactment spring had not yet come; the section opens with the clue 'I *thought* if I could only live/Till. . . .' The events that follow never existed anywhere except in her deluded imagination, but in that interior world they constituted the whole of reality and they function with terrifying precision. For an adult to hide behind grass blades for protection against the spears of attacking daffodils would indeed be insane, but that is just the point. This and the other imagined events are paranoid images skillfully objectifying the hallucinatory world of her fears.

The initial image sets the tone by evoking the exact sense of unreality desired: 'Not all Pianos in the Woods/Had power to mangle me.' In one sense 'Pianos' is a metaphor for the treble of birds, the bass of frogs, and all the range of natural sounds in between, with their wild harmony and counterpoint. In a letter to Higginson she once said, 'the noise in the Pool, at Noon— excels my Piano.' In a lesser poem on the same theme she uses a similar figure, the black birds' 'Banjo,' accurate enough for their twanging monotone and with the added humor of an oblique reference to the Negro minstrels popular in that day. But the humor appropriate to anguish is macabre, not grotesque, and the 'Pianos' here give just that touch. For in another sense they are not metaphorical but real, or rather surrealistic, like the objects in a painting by Dali. Placed in the woods instead of in the parlor, by the distortion of terror, they could become instruments of torture. Caught behind the keyboard of a gigantic piano she would be 'mangled' by its hammers even as she was driven mad by the booming strings, helplessly dodging blows whose source, timing, and spacing she could not guess. This is indeed the world of nightmare, induced by dread when unbearable pain has unhinged the reason.

The framing stanzas are not for the purpose of ridiculing this terror or repudiating it as mere insanity. Their relation to the center of pain is much more intricate. The opening one is mainly in the present tense, after spring has come, but it begins with a throwback to the fear that had gripped her earlier, 'I dreaded that first Robin, so.' The following lines appear to modify the excess of terror by saying calmly, 'He is mastered, now,' all the more reassuring by being couched in homely idiom ('I'm some accustomed to Him grown'). But the reader is the one who is actually reassured, knowing that the creator of the poem has mastered herself rather than the robin, though the experience lingers vividly in her memory and still 'hurts a little.' He is now prepared to accept as true her account in the succeeding stanzas of the dread produced by coming spring, in all the intensity of its psychic reality. As her mind reviews that past time of nightmare her language breaks into the turgid and improbable. One surrealistic scene after another flashes before her in a fantastic parade, the shouting mob of birds, daffodils, grass, and bees she 'could not bear ... should come.'

The conclusion returns to the quiet mood of adjustment, in the present tense, with which the poem began: 'They're here, though; not a creature failed.' Arrogating to herself the title 'Queen of Calvary' might seem to indicate that some of the distorted vision still remains, but this is undercut by irony. Her imagined subjects do not obey her wish by staying away 'In gentle deference' to her grief. Instead, they file past her with gay sounds and colors quite as 'foreign' to her present state as she had feared in the nightmare. This, of course, is not the parade conjured up by her terrified imagination. It is the orderly procession of spring, which follows winter just as a resurrection should follow her 'Calvary.'

Whether she desires it or not spring brings renewal of life to nature, taunting the stricken soul with its signs of health. It is only in this root sense that it 'salutes' her, the assumed deference of subject to sovereign being part of the calculated mockery. She can do nothing but accept this false promise of a return to well-being. Hence her 'bereaved acknowledgement' of spring's greeting by lifting her 'childish Plumes.' They are the insignia of her royalty and of her grief, as in the purple plumes of traditional monarchy and the black ones of hearse and horse in the funerals of her own day. Her recognition that both are childish is the mark of a certain stage of recovery, the awareness that at least her irrational terror is now dead. For all that she has outlived it, 'mastered' it, it was none the less real while it lasted. And the new wisdom she has gained from this adjustment is perhaps even more awesome. It is apparently the conviction that her anguish was not insane but the processes of nature are, in the sense that they have no relation to her interior world. Its loud and meaningless life continues to beat on her consciousness with 'unthinking Drums.' Any outward demonstrations of terror and grief in the face of nature's indifference are childish, just as man's claim of sovereignty over it would be. The anguish that remains, though not named, is her sense of the suffering mind's isolation in an alien Universe.

The pain that Dickinson explores in the major poems is of a sort the victim never fully recovers from. 'Split Lives– never "get well,"' she commented in a letter. 'It is simple, to ache in the Bone, or the Rind,' according to one of her poems, 'But Gimlets– among the nerve–/Mangle . . . terribler.' Such pain goes to the quick. It usually involves a 'death' to some part of the person's life and an awareness of change to a new dimension of being. There is nothing occult or morbid about all this. Certain basic human experiences are universally recognized as answering exactly to this description, though the resulting anguish is usually glossed by wit or otherwise played down in popular speech, probably because of its very intensity. The more obvious ones may be readily agreed upon: the struggle out of adolescence into maturity, with its loss of freedom; the breaking of the dream, whether of glory or love or joy; the benumbing discovery that the grave is not just for others, with the consequent first experience of 'dying.' The vocabulary of utility desperately applied to them (growing pains, disillusionment, common sense) stresses the gain in wisdom, but it cannot conceal the loss to the spirit. This kind of anguish, the distinguishing mark of the human consciousness as opposed to animal and vegetable being, is valid subject matter for the artist and she made it one of her special provinces. Though she rarely makes the experience specific, it may be indicated in a general way as that whole area of crisis, looming behind the record of the years 1859-1866, which transformed her from an obscure woman into a great poet.

Her best poetry is not concerned with the causes but with the qualities of pain, an emphasis that removes it effectively from the category of the sentimental. She even takes care to differentiate between the kind manufactured by poetasters and that which engages her attention: 'Safe Despair it is that raves–/Agony is frugal.' Her own approach at times seems almost clinical, but this is simply the mode she adopted to gain the proper distance between her personal emotions and her art. It separates her sharply from the subjective lyricism of an older tradition and reveals her kinship with the twentieth century. The qualities she sought to fix with greatest precision are its intensity, its duration, and the change it brings about. In several minor poems she used time as a measure of degree in defining that extremity of pain that was her real concern. To the readiest cliché of both the sentimentalist and the pragmatist, that 'Time assuages,' she replied, not when it is 'Malady'; and in a letter: 'to all except anguish, the mind soon adjusts.' Extreme suffering even changes the very nature of time, she demonstrated in a pair of dialectical quatrains: 'Pain– expands the Time– ... Pain contracts– the Time.' It makes clock and calendar meaningless and annihilates the very idea of eternity; the true center of pain exists in a temporal vacuum, containing its own past and future. Spatially it is equally limitless and without definable locality: it 'ranges Boundlessness.' Unlike contentment, which resides lawfully in a 'quiet Suburb,' agony cannot stay 'In Acre– Or Location–/It rents Immensity.' It absorbs the whole of consciousness, condensed to a measureless, momentless point.

Pain is thus a quality of being that exists outside time and space, the only two terms in which it can possibly be externalized. Her dilemma in describing this formless psychic entity was how to contrive outward symbols that would make the internal condition manifest. In solving this difficulty she borrowed from the techniques of the theatre, man's supreme contrivance for presenting illusion by making scene and action a set of appearances through which the spectator must penetrate to the reality beneath. With the aid of this device, supplemented by the rituals of formal ceremonies like trials and funerals, the effects of extreme pain are rendered by her in a series of unusually interesting poems.

In the most extraordinary of them, the abstract concept of 'death' as inflicted on the consciousness by despair is projected in one of those courtroom scenes of nightmare made vivid to modern readers by Kafka.

The victim is on trial for his life, though for some nameless crime, and the machinery of an inexorable justice grinds to its conclusion, without moving, in a kind of wordless horror:

> I read my sentence— steadily—
> Reviewed it with my eyes,
> To see that I made no mistake
> In its extremest clause—
> The Date, and manner, of the shame—
> And then the Pious Form
> That 'God have mercy' on the Soul
> The Jury voted Him—
> I made my soul familiar— with her extremity—
> That at the last, it should not be a novel Agony—
> But she, and Death, acquainted—
> Meet tranquilly, as friends—
> Salute, and pass, without a Hint—
> And there, the Matter ends—

The proliferation of pronouns here is not a sign of artistic confusion but a grammatical echo of the dream chaos, whose intricate meaning can be parsed readily enough if the analyst follows the mode of the subconscious drama. 'I,' 'Him,' and 'She' are all aspects of the persona of the poem, as in the dream all characters are projections of the dreamer.

The poem falls into two equal parts of eight lines each, though the climactic quatrain that introduces the second is written as an extended couplet, thus giving emphasis to the previously unnamed 'Agony.' This twofold division corresponds roughly to the duality of body and soul. The fictive 'I' stands for the whole of the mortal life that dominates the first half, as mind-heart-body react to the sentence of death. The extrapolated 'she,' the filmy protagonist of the second half, is the immortal part, this section being primarily concerned with the effect of the verdict on the soul. Yet both are spoken by 'I,' for Dickinson could not indulge in an outright *Debate between the Body and the Soul* as the medieval poet could, his belief in the absolute reality of both not being available to her. The law refuses to take any cognizance of such duality and addresses the reunited halves of the prisoner as 'Him,' though it does so at the very point where the jury in condemning his body to death makes use of a formula from traditional piety to recommend mercy on his soul. 'Him,' placed exactly at the juncture between the two halves of the poem, likewise unifies them and at the same time gives the persona wholeness of being for the duration of a single word, though even then only as the third person condemned in the nightmare, anonymous and detached from the agonized dreamer-narrator.

The legal language, concentrated in the first half, not only sets the scene but controls the meaning throughout. Brought up in a family of lawyers, she came by it naturally. But far more important than her precision in handling its terminology is the imaginative fitness with which she puts it to work. The dramatic appeal of a criminal trial comes from the contrast of the lawless emotions involved in the original actions and the ordered procedure by which the court re-enacts them, with the possibility that at any moment the violently human may erupt through the formalism of its jargon. From this situational irony she creates her strategy, giving it a unique twist by having one actor, the masking 'I,' slip successively into all the leading roles—prisoner-in-the-dock, defense counsel, judge, jury, and courtroom spectators.

The poem opens with the flat statement that the unidentified speaker, completely subdued to the mechanism of the ritual, has read his sentence 'steadily,' or as her Lexicon defines it 'without tottering, shaking,' such as might be expected of one condemned to die. This air of professional disinterestedness holds throughout the first eight lines, as the speaker performs both judicial and counselling functions. 'Reviewed it' suggests that this is a court of appeal, perhaps of last resort, reviewing the decision of a lower trial court; also that the defense, counsel and client, are going over a familiar document, not with the heart but 'with my eyes,' alert to any technicalities of 'date,' 'clause,' or 'manner' that might serve as a basis for requesting a reversal of the opinion; finally that the condemned is even looking for an extra-legal loophole in the one human phrase that has crept into this otherwise formally pronounced judgment, but the jury's vote of 'God have mercy' is just a 'Pious Form' without legal consequences. All the ingenuity of the profession and the meticulous care of the accused have revealed 'no mistake,' however, and the sentence stands in its 'extremest clause.' So ends the first scene.

The same elaborate device of a dream-trial is used in another poem in the form of a simile to stand explicitly for the 'death' that can come from 'Agony.' It crept nearer every day until the benumbed victim dropped 'lost [as] from a Dream.' Then, 'As if your Sentence stood—pronounced,' she says, and you were led from the luxurious doubts of the dungeon to the gibbet and sure death, suppose some creature should gasp 'Reprieve' at the last moment, would this lessen the anguish? Only temporary relief, not pardon and remission, is possible for the pain of the human condition, she is saying, and death itself might well be preferable. But in that poem the agony, being insufficiently controlled, shatters the form with fragmentary and conflicting images. The superior mastery of the one under consideration consists in the skill by which the metaphor of the legal nightmare becomes both cover and contents, so that the thematic meaning of pain can be gradually unfolded by what the poem enacts, clarified in the last part even as it is given a new direction.

Beneath the stylized language of this drama the speaker knows he is none of these other parties, judge or jury or attorney, not even the disinterested spectator, a role reserved for the reader. He is the one condemned to death. (The exigencies of discourse require the use of the third person throughout the rest of this discussion of what happens to the 'I' of the poem, but this must not be confused with her special use of 'Him' in line eight.) He is also aware that the whole ritual is simply a nightmarish image of another and worse kind of death, the dying of consciousness under the pressure of despair. But he has lost his sense of identity, and this is what accounts for his apparent apathy. His detachment is such that he can read his own death sentence as if it applied to someone else. As she put it elsewhere: 'A Doubt if it be Us' assists the mind, staggering under extreme anguish, until it finds a new footing.

To lose one's identity by such a living death is in a sense to be separated from one's soul, which justifies the colloquy in the second section. But the mortal part still does all the talking, 'I made my soul familiar' answering in uninterrupted sequence to the opening line, 'I read my sentence— steadily.' The continuity of speaker binds the two parts together, and this limited point of view provides a further irony by relating an immortal sequence in mortal terms. The soul, previously introduced only in the jury's callous formula, now becomes an entity, and the theme of death-dealing pain emerges with an effect of shock from the metaphor of a legal death-sentence. The scene has now dissolved from the courtroom to some shadowy anteroom, perhaps the death-cell or even the execution chamber itself, with that inconsequent shifting so familiar in dreams. Fearing that what killed his consciousness may also kill his soul, the speaker is solicitous that 'she' should be prepared for 'her extremity' so that in the end 'it should not be a novel Agony.' 'Novel' means not only unexpected, the final shock he wants to make her familiar with in advance, but also new, implying that she has gone through all his past agonies with him too.

In his ignorance of the nature of souls he apparently thinks they are subject to death as well as to suffering. So the last irony is that the 'novel Agony' is reserved for him, not her. 'She and Death' it turns out are old acquaintances, as symbols of mortality and immortality, but since they have no common ground save the moment of passing they simply 'Salute' courteously and go their respective ways, 'without a Hint' to him of what they are really like or where they have gone. His surprise discovery is that in this friendly meeting it is only he, 'the Matter,' which has been annihilated. His sentence has been executed not by legal but by verbal machinery. In the triple pun, 'And there, the *Matter* ends,' the fictive 'I' experiences a new death by losing his soul as well as his identity in the depths of despair, the curtain is rung down on the bad dream along with all the legal theatricalities that bodied it forth, and the poem destroys itself in a tour de force. The reader, if any one, suffers shock.

That Dickinson could make a macabre joke out of agony will offend only those who take poetry solemnly. Perhaps it was one mode of rescue, as literal death would have been another, from a pain that was unbearable. Still another kind of escape, into a state of trance, proved most fruitful of all to the maker of poems on pain. She put it succinctly once in prose: 'Anguish has but so many throes— then Unconsciousness seals it.' Again, as a compact metaphor:

> There is a pain— so utter—
> It swallows substance up—
> Then covers the Abyss with Trance—
> So Memory can step
> Around— across— upon it—
> As one within a Swoon—
> Goes safely— where an open eye—
> Would drop Him— Bone by Bone.

The alternations of substance and abstraction make an intricate structure here. The inner quality of suffering 'swallows up' the reality of self and world and turns them into a bottomless 'Abyss,' which her Lexicon illustrated by quoting the description of pre-Genesis chaos, 'Darkness was upon the face of the abyss.' To cover this nothingness, pain makes itself concrete in the insubstantiality of 'Trance,' so that consciousness can step upon it or around it and blot out the memory of it in a kind of living death. Otherwise, if the victim should materialize again, the intensity of the pain would drop him 'Bone by Bone.' This makes a striking definition of the mind's protection against its own suffering by falling into the blankness of 'Swoon,' but not a very memorable poem.

Her best poems on the extremity of pain, the kind producing a state of trance, make its quality of spiritual death concrete in terms of physical death and at the same time dramatize it in the ritual of burial. In the first of these, the levels of sinking down to unconsciousness follow step by step the ceremony so familiar in her village world:

> I felt a Funeral, in my Brain,
> And Mourners to and fro
> Kept treading– treading– till it seemed
> That Sense was breaking through–
>
> And when they all were seated,
> A Service, like a Drum–
> Kept beating– beating– till I thought
> My Mind was going numb–
>
> And then I heard them lift a Box
> And creak across my Soul
> With those same Boots of Lead, again,
> Then Space– began to toll,
>
> As all the Heavens were a Bell,
> And Being, but an Ear,
> And I, and Silence, some strange Race
> Wrecked, solitary, here–
>
> And then a Plank in Reason, broke,
> And I dropped down, and down–
> And hit a World, at every Crash,
> And Got through knowing– then–

The stage lies within the cortex of the brain, and the drama is rendered exclusively in terms of unarticulated sounds, transformed into motions which enact the pantomime through its inexorable progress to extinction.

The subdued step of mourners in the real world became in the first stanza a heavy relentless 'treading' to this tortured consciousness, until it feared that 'Sense was breaking through.' The twofold meanings here, of the mind giving way and of the sensations threatening to quicken again from their comfortable state of numbness, are picked up in the following stanza and the concluding one. When the funeral service began, its incessant droning made the mind at last actually begin 'going numb,' though with the disquieting echo of a pagan ritual in its beating 'Drum.' By the time the third stanza is reached, the mind is so dissociated it is now both the extinct life in the coffin and the agonized soul across which the pallbearers creak. 'With those same Boots of Lead, again' implies that the experience was re-enacted over and over yet simultaneously, with the lead of the coffin grotesquely transferred to the boot-soles of the attendants. This same duality of consciousness continues as the procession leaves the church and the funeral knell sounds, announcing the death of the body of agony and at the same time killing the listening spirit. This sound is so cosmic only the most extravagant simile will compass it: 'As all the Heavens were a Bell,/And Being, but an Ear.' Such a climax has an absolute rightness about it. For the poem has consisted exclusively of a succession of images all auditory and reiterated—treading, beating, creaking. And with this final tolling, the consciousness is 'Wrecked, solitary,' except for the companioning 'Silence,' more harrowing than any of the sounds had been.

For the mind to apprehend beyond the pale of death, even the hallucinatory death of obliterating pain, would be to go beyond the limits of judgment. To avoid this the poem ends with the mind simply giving way, but this too in terms of the last act of burial. Just as the coffin is about to be lowered into the grave, 'a Plank in Reason broke,' and the persona dropped down through level after level of unconsciousness, hitting a new 'World' of extinction 'at every Crash.' These were the last soundless sounds of agony, as the mind 'got through knowing.' Being has been swallowed up in trance. Perhaps the only flaw in this poem is that the metaphor of 'Funeral' comes near stealing the show. The powerfully dramatized ceremony, with all its ghastly detail, tends to draw the reader's attention away from the spiritual death it was intended to illuminate. That extreme form of mortal pain she likened to 'despair' did not need to be named as her theme, to be sure, but its qualities and effects should have been more vividly evoked as the final meaning of the whole sequence of images. Since this was not quite adequately done, there is some danger of the poem being misread as merely the fantasy of a morbid soul imaging its own death, which would certainly diminish its significance.

There are two kinds of death, however, not counting the death of the soul in the theological sense of 'despair.' One may literally die away from the world, but she never made the mistake of trying to embody her own decease in a serious poem. On the other hand, the world may die away from the perceiving consciousness under stress of pain, and the resulting death to the spirit can be experienced and rendered. Such pain overwhelmed Emily Dickinson during her last years, as death thinned the ranks of her intimate circle and all but extinguished her small world. The cumulative impact of all this brought on a nervous breakdown, which she recorded in almost clinical fashion:

> I saw a great darkness coming and knew no more until late at night. I woke to find Austin and Vinnie and a strange physician bending over me, and supposed I was dying, or had died, all was so kind and hallowed. I had fainted and lain unconscious for the first time in my life. . . . The doctor calls it 'revenge of the nerves'; but who but Death wronged them?

Such actual experiences do not produce poems but collapse, as she phrased it in another letter about the same time: 'Blow has followed blow, till the wondering terror of the Mind clutches what is left, helpless of an accent.' Twenty years earlier she projected her imagined spiritual death from excessive pain in 'I felt a Funeral, *in my Brain*.' No specific autobiographical source is needed to explain this poem, for its close similarity to the preceding and following ritual dramas makes its meaning unmistakable.

In her most remarkable poem rendering the extinction of consciousness by pain in terms of a funeral, the deftness of her strategy shows just what could be done with this technique. Its three stanzas faintly shadow forth three stages of a familiar ceremony: the formal service, the tread of pallbearers, and the final lowering into a grave. But metaphor is subdued to meaning by subtle controls:

> After great pain, a formal feeling comes–
> The Nerves sit ceremonious, like Tombs–
> The stiff Heart questions was it He, that bore,
> And Yesterday, or Centuries before?

The Feet, mechanical, go round—
A wooden way
Of Ground, or Air, or Ought—
Regardless grown,
A Quartz contentment, like a stone—

This is the Hour of Lead—
Remembered, if outlived,
As Freezing persons, recollect the Snow—
First— Chill— then Stupor— then the letting go—

This poem has recently received the explication it deserves, matching its excellence. But its pertinence to this whole group of poems is such as to justify a brief summary of the interpretation here.

'In a literal sense,' according to this critic, there is 'neither persona nor ritual, and since it describes a state of mind, neither would seem to be necessary.' Instead, as befits one who has lost all sense of identity, the various parts of the body are personified as autonomous entities (*the* nerves, *the* heart, *the* feet), belonging to no one and moving through the acts of a meaningless ceremony, lifeless forms enacted in a trance. As a result, attention is centered on the feeling itself and not on the pattern of figures that dramatize it. As the images of a funeral rite subside, two related ones emerge to body forth the victim who is at once a living organism and a frozen form. Both are symbols of crystallization: 'Freezing' in the snow, which is neither life nor death but both simultaneously; and 'A Quartz contentment, like a stone,' for the paradoxical serenity that follows intense suffering. This recalls her envy of the 'little Stone,' happy because unconscious of the exigencies that afflict mortals, and points forward to the paradox in another poem, 'Contented as despair.' Such is the 'formal feeling' that comes after great pain. It is, ironically, no feeling at all, only numb rigidity existing outside time and space.

In two final poems, her use of 'despair' seems to be unmistakably in the direction of the Christian meaning, though her treatment of this theological term is unorthodox to say the least. From the point of view of the poet, the chief problem is that despair is amorphous and needs to be bodied forth in some palpable form, such as the ritual drama she used so successfully, in order to be fully realized. But this may tend to restrict its meaning since, from another point of view, it is a protean condition. It feels somewhat like this and somewhat like that, like none and yet like all. To give shape to this quality she used the technique of throwing up a shower of varied images, the great feat of skill requisite being to make them at once discrete and sequential, capable of coalescing into an unexpected whole.

In one attempt the power of the separate images is undeniable, though the fusion is not quite made:

> It was not Death, for I stood up,
> And all the Dead, lie down—
> It was not Night, for all the Bells
> Put out their Tongues, for Noon.
>
> It was not Frost, for on my Knees
> I felt Siroccos— crawl—
> Not Fire— for just two Marble feet
> Could keep a Chancel, cool—
>
> And yet, it tasted, like them all,
> The Figures I have seen
> Set orderly, for Burial,
> Reminded me, of mine—
>
> As if my life were shaven,
> And fitted to a frame,
> And could not breathe without a key,
> And 'twas like Midnight, some—
>
> When everything that ticked— has stopped—
> And Space stares all around—
> Or Grisly frosts— first Autumn morns,
> Repeal the Beating Ground—
>
> But, most, like Chaos— Stopless— cool—
> Without a Chance, or Spar—
> Or even a Report of Land—
> To justify— Despair.

The opening and closing words, 'It was not Death' but it was 'Despair,' pose the problem and set up the surface dialectic. In between are a series of negations, or mere similes of possibility, each followed by an opposing statement or qualification. Occasionally they are interlocked in series by turning the affirmation of one pair into the thing denied in the next, notably in the second stanza. It becomes immediately apparent, however, that these are not statements at all but figures of speech, and the relations between them are far more poetic than their superficial resemblance to Hegelian logic indicates.

The first sequence begins with an image of the recumbent dead in contrast with her own erect figure, which rules out death as her status even while the quality of it is retained. This is picked up in the third stanza where her feeling of going through a living death recalls the figures of the dead she has seen 'Set orderly, for Burial.' Out of her local experience she undoubtedly knew about country funerals, where corpses were laid out in the parlor in unrelieved *rigor mortis,* but these are the dead that 'lie down.' This image is blended with one evoked out of her knowledge of old cathedrals, like Westminster Abbey, with their stone effigies raised up above the horizontal sarcophagi. These are the erect 'Figures' of the dead whose cold semblance of life 'Reminded me, of mine.' This carries back to her own 'Marble feet' in the preceding stanza, which are lifeless enough to 'keep a Chancel cool,' whether buried beneath its floor or standing in some niche nearby. The burial theme also follows over into the fourth stanza, without even a break in the syntax, 'As if my life were shaven,/And fitted to a frame.' In this image of death, seemingly nearer to the rural kind she was acquainted with, the body is not being placed in a box for burial, however. It is itself being carpentered into one, 'shaven and fitted,' and the new 'frame' into which the old one of bone and flesh is being transformed is a kind of humble wooden effigy answering to the marble ones of the great. The 'key' referred to in this passage may seem somewhat out of place since corpses are sealed in coffins rather than locked. But spirits are locked in bodies, and since coffin and corpse are one here, her vital life 'could not breathe without a key' to release it from the body of this despair.

Another set of relations works out from the second half of the opening stanza: 'It was not Night, for all the Bells/Put out their Tongues, for Noon.' The brilliance of midday, reinforced by the clangorous sound of bells and their swinging motion, seems the very image of life in contrast to the night of death, but there are overtones of irony in all this. 'Tongues,' borrowed directly from the folk metaphor for bell clappers, has the inevitable connotation of wagging, and the colloquial idiom 'put out' completes the suggestion of brazen mockery of her state. Bells also toll notably for death, which links this with the funeral imagery already pointed out. Though 'Noon' is the height of the day's life it is also the beginning of the sun's decline. For this reason it is a recurrent image for the escape out of time in her poetry, as in the conceit of the stopped clock which went out of decimals 'into degreeless Noon.'

In the present poem she also uses the other end of the clock's cycle for the moment of death and, after denying that her state was one of 'Night,' returns twelve lines later to admit that it was 'like Midnight, some.' This is the hour 'When everything that ticked– has stopped,' with no friendly reassurance from such commonplaces as the pendulum of measured time or the visible objects of a familiar room or landscape. Instead, 'Space stares all around' with the glazed eyes of death. Then the scene moves on from the midnight of black despair to the even more blank whiteness of an autumn morning when 'Grisly frosts . . . Repeal the Beating Ground.' The ticking life that had ceased in the silence of night is reinforced by more powerful phrasing, the pulsing life of earth abrogated by the coming death of winter. The sound effects from the verbal play of 'Beating' and 'Repeal' make this at last the actual funeral knell so long hinted at. There is also a final link back to the earlier 'Frost' that had been denied in line 5 as the true symbol of despair.

The obscurity of this second stanza is symptomatic of the risks inherent in the technique employed for this poem. The reader is left with more to explain than to experience in the unresolved disparity of its images: 'not Frost' but 'Siroccos,' not 'Fire' but—whatever it is that is going on in the 'Chancel.' She seems to have felt the need to clarify, for her only suggested revisions in the manuscript come exactly at this crucial point: 'on my Flesh>my Knees' . . . and 'just my>just two Marble feet'. . . . One can only clutch wildly at meaning. As the poet knelt at the chancel rail, beyond which sacrament and conviction are at white heat, did she feel first cold whiteness, then a hot oppressive wind off the desert, then fire that cooled her feet to marble? The functioning of the Eucharist in relation to 'Despair,' if such was her intention, never quite comes through. The very obscurity of the rite hinted at in this stanza suggests that she is trying to use despair here in the traditional Christian sense, for Holy Communion is exactly what would be beyond the reach of one who had lost hope in the mercy of God, and any attempt to partake of it would be baffled and confused. This theological doctrine was almost as unavailable to her as the sacrament would be to the lost, and they find only a dim embodiment in this poem.

The spate of images flows on, however, mostly similes. It was none of these—not death or night or noon, not stone effigies or flesh turned to wood, not blank silence whether black or white—'yet, it tasted like them all.' Is 'tasted' a final effort to bring off the communion metaphor: the sense organs must feed on and incorporate these sensations until substance and experience are one? The next to last image for despair is most harrowing of all, its effect increased by the insistent beat of four accented syllables in succession that fall like hammer blows: 'But, most, like Chaos— Stopless— cool— . . .' By extending measurable time into eternity and familiar locale into staring space, beyond the ordered universe, this image removes the last signs by which suffering man can identify himself as human. The cumulative effect of all this overwhelms the consciousness, but the images refuse to coalesce into a whole. The poem is as chaotic as despair itself, its only form being multiform formlessness. If the harried reader may be allowed one despairing quip, he may express his fear that the method itself as here employed is 'stopless.' For a final anticlimactic image of shipwreck is added ('Without a . . . Spar—/Or even a Report of Land'), which fails even more to 'justify,' in the Miltonic sense, all this suffering.

The ultimate problem, then, was not to master despair, which she presumably succeeded in doing as a woman when she took the artist's path to peace, but to manage the images evoked by her sensibility so as to transform the experience into great poetry. The same technique used in the preceding attempt was brought under perfect control in her finest poem on despair:

> There's a certain Slant of light,
> Winter Afternoons—
> That oppresses, like the Heft
> Of Cathedral Tunes—
>
> Heavenly Hurt, it gives us—
> We can find no scar,
> But internal difference,
> Where the Meanings, are—

> None may teach it– Any–
> 'Tis the Seal Despair–
> An imperial affliction
> Sent us of the Air–
>
> When it comes, the Landscape listens–
> Shadows– hold their breath–
> When it goes, 'tis like the Distance
> On the look of Death–

For more than half a century this poem was placed by her editors under the category of nature. But winter sunlight is simply the over-image of despair, inclosing the center of suffering that is her concern. Grammatically, the antecedent of the neutral 'it' whose transformations make up the action of the poem is this 'certain Slant' of light, but in figurative meaning 'it' is the 'Heavenly Hurt.' This is a true metaphor, sensation and abstraction fused into one, separable in logic but indistinguishable and even reversible in a poetic sense. The internal experience is not talked about but is realized in a web of images that constitutes the poem's statement, beginning with one drawn from nature, or rather from the firmament above it, and returning to it in the end with a significant change of meaning.

These multiple images exemplifying the protean condition of despair are vividly discrete, but they grow out of each other and into each other with a fitness that creates the intended meaning in shock after shock of recognition. Its amorphous quality is embodied at the outset in 'light,' a diffused substance that can be apprehended but not grasped. Further, this is a slanting light, as uncertain of source and indirect in impact as the feeling of despair often is. Finally, it is that pale light of 'Winter Afternoons,' when both the day and the year seem to be going down to death, the seasonal opposite of summer which symbolized for her the fullness and joy of living. It is when he feels winter in his soul, one remembers, that Melville's Ishmael begins his exploration of the meaning of despair. Next, by the shift of simile, this desolation becomes 'like the Heft/Of Cathedral Tunes.' The nebulous has now been made palble, by converting light waves into sound waves whose weight can be felt by the whole body. The strong provincialism, 'Heft' (smoothed away to 'Weight' by former editors), carries both the meaning of ponderousness and the great effort of heaving in order to test it, according to her Lexicon. This homely word also clashes effectively with the grand ring of 'Cathedral Tunes,' those produced by carillon offering the richest possibilities of meaning. Since this music 'oppresses,' the connotation of funereal is added to the heavy resonance of all pealing bells. And since the double meaning of 'Heft' carries through, despair is likened to both the weight of these sounds on the spirit and the straining to lift the imponderable tonnage of cast bronze.

The religious note on which the prelude ends, 'Cathedral Tunes,' is echoed in the language of the central stanzas. In its ambiguousness 'Heavenly Hurt' could refer to the pain of paradisiac ecstasy, but more immediately this seems to be an adjective of agency, from heaven, rather than an attributive one. The hurt is inflicted from above, 'Sent us of the Air,' like the 'Slant of light' that is its antecedent. In this context that natural image takes on a new meaning, again with the aid of her Lexicon which gives only one meaning for 'slant' as a noun, 'an oblique reflection or gibe.'. It is then a mocking light, like the heavenly hurt that comes from the sudden instinctive awareness of man's lot since the Fall, doomed to mortality and irremediable suffering. This is indeed despair, though not in the theological sense unless Redemption is denied also. As Gerard Manley Hopkins phrases it in 'Spring and Fall,' for the young life there coming to a similar realization, 'It is the blight man was born for.'

Because of this it is beyond human correction, 'None may teach it— Any.' Though it penetrates it leaves 'no scar,' as an outward sign of healing, nor any internal wound that can be located and alleviated. What it leaves is 'internal difference,' the mark of all significant 'Meanings.' When the psyche is once stricken with the pain of such knowledge it can never be the same again. The change is final and irrevocable, sealed. The Biblical sign by which God claims man for his own has been shown in the poems of heavenly bridal to be a 'Seal,' the ring by which the beloved is married into immortal life. But to be redeemed one must first be mortal, and be made conscious of one's mortality. The initial and overwhelming impact of this can lead to a state of hopelessness, unaware that the 'Seal Despair' might be the reverse side of the seal of ecstasy. So, when first stamped on the consciousness it is an 'affliction.' But it is also 'imperial . . . Sent us of the Air,' the heavenly kingdom where God sits enthroned, and from the same source can come Redemption, though not in this poem.

By an easy transition from one insubstantial image to another, 'Air' back to 'a certain Slant of light,' the concluding stanza returns to the surface level of the winter afternoon. As the sun drops toward the horizon just before setting, 'the Landscape listens' in apprehension that the very light which makes it exist as a landscape is about to be extinguished; 'Shadows,' which are about to run out to infinity in length and merge with each other in breadth until all is shadow, 'hold their breath.' This is the effect created by the slanting light 'When it comes.' Of course no such things happen in nature, and it would be pathetic fallacy to pretend they did. The light does not inflict this suffering nor is the landscape the victim. Instead, these are just images of despair.

Similar figures are used in two other poems. In one the declining motion of the sun seems just a symbol of the inexorability of death:

> Presentiment– is that long Shadow– on the Lawn–
> Indicative that Suns go down–
>
> The Notice to the startled Grass
> That Darkness– is about to pass–

But in relation to the whole body of her poetry such apprehensiveness of the coming of 'Darkness,' like a dreaded king whose approach has already been heralded, suggests that this 'Presentiment' is one of unbearable pain. In the other poem it is so named. When lives are assailed by little anguish they merely 'fret,' she says, but when threatened with 'Avalanches . . . they'll slant,'

> Straighten– look cautious for their Breath–
> But make no syllable– like Death–

So with the slant of light 'When it goes,' as the sun finally sets and darkness covers all, ''tis like the Distance/On the look of Death.' Such is the difference between the coming of despair and the aftermath of extinction. The latter calls up an image of the staring eyes of the dead, the awful 'Distance' between life and death, and, as the only relief in sight, the distance between the poet and her experience that has made this sure control of form and language possible. The final and complete desolation of the landscape is the precise equivalent of that 'internal difference' which the action of the poem has brought about.

Such is the mortal view of despair, the quality and effects of which are the exclusive theme of this poem. Yet certain ambivalent phrases in it, like 'Heavenly Hurt' and the great 'Seal' of God (which by implication, at least, has a reverse side), seem related to the curious conjoining of ecstasy and despair that pervades much of her writing. In one poem it is explicit. The moment of ecstasy, given then withdrawn, is rendered in a series of paradoxes culminating in the lines:

> A perfect— paralyzing Bliss—
> Contented as Despair—

This is strikingly similar to Andrew Marvell's conjunction of joy and pain in 'The Definition of Love.' Seeking to discriminate a love so rare that mortal hope could never reach it on 'tinsel wing,' he concludes:

> Magnanimous Despair alone
> Could show me so divine a thing.

Whether she was acquainted with this poem is not known but it is analogous to several of her own, in its shock imagery and the technique of juggled ambiguities more than in theme. For when she sought heavenly fulfillment for earthly denial it was directly through Biblical metaphor, without the mediating convention of the cult of Platonic love. Fortunately for her originality, she derives as an artist from the Calvinism of New England rather than from the tradition of metaphysical poetry.

For a final exploration of dual meaning, one may return to that ambiguous 'certain Slant of light' which pierced her from above with 'an imperial affliction.' It calls to mind the 'waylaying Light' that struck her once like lightning, and brought the heavenly 'gleam' with which the preceding chapter on 'Ecstasy' concluded. It is notable that she used exactly the same metaphor in another poem to describe a blistering pain, that came not once but continually and 'burned Me— in the Night':

> It struck me— every Day—
> The Lightning was as new
> As if the Cloud that instant slit
> And let the Fire through—...

By spiritual insight she had discovered the close relation between human despair and the yearning for heavenly ecstasy, just as a kind of primitive wisdom had led her back to the juncture of love and death in the instinctual world. But these were only motions of the heart, up and down.

Always thrusting itself between was the conscious mind, that flickering identity that tries to give meaning to the bafflingly familiar pilgrimage from cradle to grave by defining, discriminating, questioning. This is what saves her from the sentimentalism that would have resulted had she adopted either extreme of ecstasy or despair as her whole view. Instead, she created her poems out of the tensions that issue from the clash of such powerful opposites. Further, she declined the gambit of an easy escape into paradox, for she never made an exact equation between love and death, ecstasy and despair. In her poetry their relations are much more complex: they form interlocking and reversible sequences. What gives this especial novelty is the direction of her emphasis, which is the opposite of that taken by her New England predecessors in the orthodox handling of these ambiguities. For example, in place of the Puritan view that earthly suffering is the ordained path to a heavenly reward of bliss, she makes the momentary glimpse of ecstasy both measure and cause of the despair that is the essence of the human condition. As she wrote in a late stanza:

> The joy that has no stem nor core,
> Nor seed that we can sow,
> Is edible to longing,
> But ablative to show. . . .

To be human is to yearn for the heavenly ecstasy we are deprived of on earth, 'ablative' being the Latin term for the case of deprivation. And so with the subtle interrelations of love and death. When her friend Higginson lost his wife she said in her letter of consolation: 'Do not try to be saved– but let Redemption find you– as it certainly will– Love is its own rescue, for we– at our supremest, are but its trembling Emblems.' These themes, fused from polar opposites, permeate her writings in prose and verse.

Her absolute loyalty to mind was the instrument by which she achieved this balance and maneuvered her emotions into forms. But she rarely lost sight of the fact that it was merely a technique of control, not the source of her poems. It is true that in her later years she indulged her penchant for aphorism in a number of verses that tend to run off into sheer intellectualism, even as some of her earliest efforts had been pure expressions of personal sentiment. Her best poems, however, present their themes in the full context of intellect and feeling, concerned not with exploiting either as such but with rendering the experiences that fuse them both. An eminent critic has put this succinctly: 'Unlike her contemporaries, she never succumbed to her ideas, to easy solutions, to private desires . . . ; like Donne, she *perceives abstraction and thinks sensation.*' And he makes this the basis for a high claim to distinction, that she was probably the only Anglo-American poet of her century who achieved a fusion of sensibility and thought, attaining 'a mastery over experience by facing its utmost implications.'

Inevitably, her search for meaning within the self, as well as in the non-self outside, led to a search for rediscovery of the maker of these selves. A poem written in mid-career, of small intrinsic worth, has considerable interest as a statement of her progressive concern with nature, man, and God. At first she thought that 'nature' was a sufficient subject for her poetry, she says, until 'Human nature' came in and absorbed the other 'As Firmament a Flame'; then, when she had just begun her exploration of that, 'There added the Divine.' All of her major themes are listed here in order: the outer world and the inner, the other world and, by implication at least, the paradise of art as the nearest she could come to attaining the 'Divine.' As a schoolgirl she had explained her inability to make peace with God because 'the world holds a predominant place in my affections.' Her withdrawal from society after maturity merely changed the terms of her loyalty, first to external nature then to the interior world of the self. As a poet she concluded that this last was the only reality she could know. It was also, she discovered, her best instrument for perceiving the processes of time and for conceiving the stasis of eternity, so that the reader today sees the ultimate purpose of all her explorations as religious in the profoundest sense of that term. And she would have rejoiced in the confirmation of her world view by modern thinkers, as in the recent definition of religion by an eminent scientist as 'a search for the relation between human desire and purpose on the one hand and cosmic change and indifference on the other.'

In contrast with the orthodoxy of her own day this approach could only seem heretical, however, which explains her tendency to discountenance herself as a religious person, as in her terse self-portrait late in life, 'I am but a Pagan.' The letter containing this phrase encloses a poem which furnishes the title for this section and brings it to a fitting conclusion:

> Of God we ask one favor,
> That we may be forgiven—
> For what, he is presumed to know—
> The Crime, from us, is hidden—
> Immured the whole of Life
> Within a magic Prison
> We reprimand the Happiness
> That too competes with Heaven.

Her pained sense of estrangement from the religion of her fathers lingered to the end, but so did the integrity that gave her courage to go her own way, to continue her search for heaven through poetry rather than through a theology she could not accept. This debate frames her perfect image for the earthly paradise where she wrestled with her angel. The mind and heart, the consciousness, the self, the soul—whatever word one wishes—this was the 'Magic Prison' she always explored in her poetry. 'Immured the whole of Life' within its walls she accepted the mortal lot as inescapable, trapped in time and wavering perpetually between doubt and belief in another life beyond. There she dedicated herself to creating the one thing of absolute value that, in her view, the human being is capable of. It goes under the rather inadequate name of religion, or art, the vision that comes with man's utmost reach towards truth and beauty. Its essence is longing, with ecstasy at one end and pain at the other, the leap of the heart and the despair of the mind.

Four:

THE OTHER PARADISE

'The White Exploit'

I I

DEATH

The most vivid embodiment of life to Emily Dickinson in her later years was the cherished nephew next door. When he was suddenly ravished from life and from her love by an early death, the most poignant cry she ever uttered broke from her lips:

> 'Open the Door, open the Door, they are waiting for me,' was Gilbert's sweet command in delirium. *Who* were waiting for him, all we possess we would give to know— Anguish at last opened it, and he ran to the little Grave at his Grandparents' feet— All this and more, though *is* there more? More than Love and Death? Then tell me its name!

These questions she was never able to answer. Rather, she made many answers, in prose and verse, but for the most part they simply asked the same questions in other forms or resolved them in paradoxes. Love may be the crowning glory of life, but one becomes fully aware of such transcendent value only when confronted with its extinction in death. The conjoining of love and death, loss in the grave raising the hope of reunion in heaven, is probably the oldest motivation to a belief in immortality. Yet even when she felt the need of a traditional response, as in the verses sent to Gilbert's bereaved mother, the tension between mind and heart saved her from platitude:

> Pass to thy Rendezvous of Light,
> Pangless except for us—
> Who slowly ford the Mystery
> Which thou hast leaped across!

The soul is made to 'pass to' its dimly envisioned destination by an act of will on the part of those left behind. In between lies only 'Mystery.' That this was more a poem than a personal lament is suggested by her using the same elegy a year later on the death of a favorite author, to go with the gift of Cross's *Life of George Eliot,* introduced by the laconic comment: 'Biography first convinces us of the fleeing of the Biographied.'

Her correspondence is filled with such ambivalent responses to personal loss. At the time of her mother's death she wrote to her cousins: 'I believe we shall in some manner be cherished by our Maker— that the One who gave us this remarkable earth has the power still farther to surprise that which He has caused. Beyond that all is silence. . . . I cannot tell how Eternity seems. It sweeps around me like a sea.' Again to an acquaintance: 'Her dying feels to me like many kinds of Cold— at times electric, at times benumbing— then a trackless waste, Love has never trod.' And finally, to an intimate friend, the anguished query: 'Is God Love's Adversary?' This dilemma of the heart had been rendered more quietly in a poem many years before. It seems to have no autobiographical reference but instead a literary one, apparently taking off from a phrase ('a bustle in the house') in Dickens' *Dombey and Son*:

> The Bustle in a House
> The Morning after Death
> Is solemnest of industries
> Enacted upon Earth—
>
> The Sweeping up the Heart
> And putting Love away
> We shall not want to use again
> Until Eternity.

She could give new meaning to the most orthodox of sentiments by the freshness of her phrasing.

An extraordinary succession of blows shattered her hold on life during the last years, as one by one friends and kin dropped out of her beloved circle—not only nephew and mother but her father, her two closest intellectual friends (Bowles and Holland), and her two 'Masters' (the Reverend Mr. Wadsworth and Judge Lord). How deeply these losses were felt is reflected in the late letters: 'A friend is a solemnity and after the great intrusion of Death, each one that remains has a spectral pricelessness besides the mortal worth.' Likewise in her letters many years before, for hers was a small world that she felt closely bound to. For example, the great conflict of the Civil War enters her writings chiefly through this personal channel, as when she wrote of the Amherst friend killed in battle: 'Poor little widow's boy, riding tonight in the mad wind, back to the village burying-ground where he never dreamed of sleeping! Ah! the dreamless sleep!' And when Colonel Higginson was wounded, she followed her prayer for his recovery by saying: 'Perhaps Death— gave me awe for friends— striking sharp and early, for I held them since— in a brittle love— of more alarm, than peace.' That one could actually turn to writing poetry again after deep loss provoked her comment in 1864, after the death of Elizabeth Barrett: 'I noticed that Robert Browning had made another poem, and was astonished— till I remembered that I, myself, in my smaller way, sang off charnel steps.'

Her best poems on death were not inspired by personal experiences, however. They sprang instead from the inherent ambiguity of the grave, that obsessive image for poet and priest. 'Death,' according to one of her very earliest poems, is 'but our rapt attention/To Immortality.' What we experience at graves, 'Death's bold Exhibition,' she says in another, enables us to infer more precisely both what we are and what we may become. And again, nothing can reduce our 'Mortal Consequence' like knowing that soon we shall not exist, nothing can exalt it like the belief that we shall exist again. The experiences of this world, outer and inner, had furnished a center of gravity for the majority of her poems, but an opposite pull drew the rest like a lodestar:

> Death is the other way—...
> It is the White Exploit.

She never found a better image for its ambiguity than this, man's bold adventure into blankness. Death or Immortality? The separation of her poems on these entwined themes in the following chapters is made possible by her emphasis on the grave as Janus-faced, looking arrogantly back to one life and dimly forward to another.

The essence of the human condition, differentiating man from the other animals, is his ineluctable awareness that one day he will die. This is the focal point of religion since it raises the question of immortality, whether man has a soul and what its relation to God may be. It is also a point of measurement for the humanist seeking to evaluate the mortal span, which he is forced to recognize as neither an affair of the moment nor of eternity but of a limited duration. No wonder death has been a traditional theme for poetry. Obsessive concern with it is no more morbid than is a compulsion to escape from it. Attitudes toward death become valid when it is made the occasion of a search for meaning rather than an expression of emotion for its own sake. The natural complement to an intense love of life is an intense fear of death. Dickinson's poems are her triumph over this fear. She justified her own obsession in philosophical terms: 'Death being the first form of Life which we have had the power to Contemplate, our entrance here being an Exclusion from comprehension, it is amazing that the fascination of our predicament does not entice us more.' In a letter following up this idea she said: 'Of our first Creation we are unconscious' and of living, too, until death forces us to be conscious of it. A passage in another letter of the same period, prompted by the death of a fellow poet, Bryant, rounds out this sequence of her meditations: 'I suppose there are depths in every Consciousness, from which we cannot rescue ourselves— to which none can go with us— which represent to us Mortally— the Adventure of Death.'

In her poems these abstractions find concrete embodiment, because she saw 'New Englandly,' though with a difference. The stable society of a small town made death a more conspicuous part of daily life than is possible in the transient urban world. Modern man may seem more verbally realistic about it, because of his rejection of euphemisms, but the circumstances of his life tend to make dying remote and abstract. On the other hand, the pious language of a hundred years ago may seem evasive, but people then dealt with the fact of death at firsthand. Her only problem was to revitalize the language. Two light verses show her trying to achieve distance by wit. In one ('There's been a Death, in the Opposite House') she uses the mock-grotesque to paint a genre sketch of the whole sequence from death to burial in old-fashioned Amherst, 'just a Country Town,' made memorable by her figure for the undertaker as that man of the 'Appalling Trade.' In the other she satirizes the professional smoothness of modern funeral parlors with their satin-lined metal caskets ('Sweet— safe— Houses'), corpses turned into people of 'Pearl' by the embalmer's art, and 'Muffled Coaches' that cushion the anguish of the tomb. The undertaker has been transformed into the mortician, whose function is no longer to bury the dead but to obscure the fact of dying for a hedonistic society that has lost its belief in the soul; but by sealing out the reality of death it has cut itself off from immortality too. For her serious poems she found the rituals in the village world of her childhood more dramatic, as in her stark recital of the old custom of laying out the body at home for burial. Here she reunites the personal experience of death with its religious meaning, as the long wake concludes:

> And We— We placed the Hair—
> And drew the Head erect—
> And then an awful leisure was
> Our faith to regulate—

As a test case, to prove that she was not exploiting death for its own sake, one may choose an extreme example of what seems like excessive concern with mortuary detail, as she examines a corpse:

> How many times these low feet staggered—
> Only the soldered mouth can tell—
> Try— can you stir the awful rivet—
> Try— can you lift the hasps of steel!
>
> Stroke the cool forehead— hot so often—
> Lift— if you care— the listless hair—
> Handle the adamantine fingers
> Never a thimble— more— shall wear—
>
> Buzz the dull flies— on the chamber window—
> Brave— shines the sun through the freckled pane—
> Fearless— the cobweb swings from the ceiling—
> Indolent Housewife— in Daisies— lain!

The sense of touch is extinguished in the 'cool forehead' and 'listless hair,' the sense of hearing in the 'dull' buzzing of flies, the sense of sight as only a 'freckled' sunlight filters through the window of the death chamber. Corpse borrows the characteristics of coffin, riveted with steel, 'soldered mouth,' and 'adamantine fingers.' But these ghastly details are only means to an end, a vivid rendering of lifelessness as opposed to life. This implied contrast is brought out strikingly by one word in the climactic line: '*Indolent* Housewife– in Daisies– lain!' Though the root meaning is simply 'feeling no pain,' it has come to signify 'without energy.' The irony here dispels any possible judgment that this is a morbid poem, either in intent or effect. 'To be alive– is Power,' she says elsewhere, and from a purely secular point of view the tragedy of death is the extinction of that power.

'A woman died last week, young and in hope but a little while– at the end of our garden,' she reported in a letter, adding: 'I thought since of the power of death, not upon affection, but its mortal signal.' In the present poem her irreverent reprimand to the newly deceased for being 'Indolent' has the effect of shock, coming as the culmination of a death-bed scene where an atmosphere of awe has been built up by echoing the conventional language of solemnity in the presence of death. Living to the fullest means energy in its radical sense, 'Existence– in itself . . . Omnipotence– Enough,' as she once put it. The opposite of activity is that 'famous Sleep' which made her query in another poem, 'Was ever idleness like This?' For the grotesque extreme of idleness is *rigor mortis,* stiffening in death. In a third poem she takes her stance at the grave-stone of another indolent housewife. But this 'Carrara Guidepost,' instead of pointing the way to extinction or to the heavenly life, brings a flashback to the earthly life when, near its conclusion, 'Death lit all the shortness up' and she praises the 'Busy Darling' for her former indus-triousness. In a final one, contemplating her own death, she looks back to 'Busy needles, and spools of thread' as the symbols of her life, once 'so precious charged,' that has now reached the strange goal of the grave. This use of domestic imagery for the mighty theme of death was her means of making capital out of the narrow range of actual experience; and her economy became her unique strategy, rendering the cosmic in terms of the trivial. In the poem on the corpse chosen as a test case of morbidity, the abandoned thimble is implied by the 'adamantine fingers,' the dropped broom by the swinging 'cobweb' that will never again be swept down by this 'Indolent Housewife– in Daisies– lain.' The great eclipse of death has been made concrete in images of power laid low. To express the fullness of her love for life she frequently resorted to inversion. It was also her mode for avoiding triteness.

Several poems pivot on the exact moment of death, with a twofold advantage. First, when dying is juxtaposed with living the possibilities of contrast are heightened. This also poses the danger of falling into a hackneyed convention, it is true, but few things triggered her impulse to originality like platitude. The very atmosphere she breathed in Amherst was her second advantage. Christian belief in general made crucial the dividing line between mortality and immortality, and the emphasis was doubled by insatiable Puritan curiosity to know who are the Elect. In her old-fashioned village every death would still prompt the customary questions. Did the dying eye catch a glimpse of God, reflected in its final vision? Did the physical ear hear the choiring of angels? Did the last mortal words bring an echo from beyond? When death struck close she too could respond in the traditional pattern. Shortly after her first 'tutor' Ben Newton died, she inquired of his pastor 'If his last hours were cheerful, and if he was willing to die'; concerning a young friend she begged her cousins to 'tell us all you know about dear Myra's going.' On the occasion of a more intimate loss she reported: 'Mother was very beautiful when she had died. Seraphs are solemn artists. The illumination that comes but once paused upon her features, and it seemed like hiding a picture to lay her in the grave.' Even a few of her poems tend to fall into the trap of this convention.

In writing her best poems, however, she was never at the mercy of her emotions or of the official rhetoric. She mastered her themes by controlling her language. She could achieve a novel significance, for example, by starting with a death scene that implies the orthodox questions and then turning the meaning against itself by the strategy of surprise answers:

> I heard a Fly buzz– when I died–
> The Stillness in the Room
> Was like the Stillness in the Air–
> Between the Heaves of Storm–
>
> The Eyes around– had wrung them dry–
> And Breaths were gathering firm
> For that last Onset– when the King
> Be witnessed– in the Room–
>
> I willed my Keepsakes– Signed away
> What portion of me be
> Assignable– and then it was
> There interposed a Fly–

> With Blue– uncertain stumbling Buzz–
> Between the light– and me–
> And then the Windows failed– and then
> I could not see to see–

This poem operates in terms of all the standard religious assumptions of her New England, but with a difference. They are explicitly gathered up in one phrase for the moment of death, with distinct Biblical overtones, 'that last Onset– when the King / Be witnessed– in the Room.' But how is he witnessed?

As the poet dramatizes herself in a deathbed scene, with family and friends gathered round, her heightened senses report the crisis in flat domestic terms that bring to the reader's mind each of the traditional questions only to deny them without even asking them. Her last words were squandered in distributing her 'Keepsakes,' trivial tokens of this life rather than messages from the other. The only sound of heavenly music, or of wings taking flight, was the 'Blue– uncertain stumbling Buzz' of a fly that filled her dying ear. Instead of a final vision of the hereafter, this world simply faded from her eyes: the light in the windows failed and then she 'could not see to see.' The King witnessed in his power is physical death, not God. To take this poem literally as an attempted inside view of the gradual extinction of consciousness and the beginning of the soul's flight into eternity would be to distort its meaning, for this is not an imaginative projection of her own death. In structure, in language, in imagery it is simply an ironic reversal of the conventional attitudes of her time and place toward the significance of the moment of death. Yet mystery is evoked by a single word, that extraordinarily interposed color 'Blue.'

To misread such a poem would be to misunderstand the whole cast of Dickinson's mind. Few poets saw more clearly the boundary between what can and what cannot be comprehended, and so held the mind within its proper limitations. When she did indulge in fantasy it was often a deliberate strategy for dealing with the irrational, as in her humorous verses on this very subject of trying to imagine one's own death:

> We dream– it is good we are dreaming–
> It would hurt us– were we awake–
> But since it is playing– kill us,
> And we are playing– shriek–

What harm? Men die— externally—
It is a truth— of Blood—
But we— are dying in Drama—
And Drama— is never dead—

Cautious— We jar each other—
And either— open the eyes—
Lest the Phantasm— prove the Mistake—
And the livid Surprise

Cool us to Shafts of Granite—
With just an Age— and Name—
And perhaps a phrase in Egyptian—
It's prudenter— to dream—

For situational irony she chooses that absurd moment of the mind's reawakening when the conscious self and the unconscious self are simultaneously aware of nightmare and yet terrified by it. As she wrote to a friend on hearing of his recovery from a near-fatal illness: 'the fear that your life had ceased came, fresh, yet dim, like the horrid Monsters fled from in a Dream.' It would indeed be a ghastly joke, a 'livid Surprise,' if this drama of dying turned into the reality. A variant conclusion in the manuscript—'a phrase in Egyptian'>'a latin inscription'—brings the burial closer home, from obelisk to New England tombstone. But if the mind's mental image of its own extinction is 'Phantasm' in a dream, it is even more so in daydreaming. She could satirize her own attempt at an inside view of the moment of death as well as the orthodox belief about it.

Men do die 'externally,' however, and this 'truth of blood' can be observed and reported. Viewed from the outside, the crisis of dying challenged her creative powers seriously. The sudden violence that separates life from death teased her imagination to find terms for measuring it in both space and time. 'The distance that the dead have gone,' 'The overtakelessness of those/Who have accomplished Death,' and similar phrases recur throughout her poetry. Once she began with a fine image of the soul on 'Pinions of Disdain,' that can fly farther 'Than any feather specified in Ornithology,' but the infinite contrasted with the finite never furnished the controlling idea for an entirely successful poem on the distance between life and death. She made her most interesting use of it, perhaps, when she levied on the new astronomical concept of light-

years for measuring the vastness of interstellar space. Those who die
pass over the arc of the comet, she says, further than a giant's arm could
reach,

> Further than Sunshine could
> Were the Day Year long, . . .

For time was a more natural measurement of the moment of death to
one brought up in the Christian tradition, which emphasized immortality as the unending spiritual life contrasted with the mortal allotment
of three score and ten. Also immediately available to her was the poetic
tradition of transience, the brief human calendar set against eternity.
Seeking out the most startling extremes to render these opposites, she
reduced the fraction of the life span under consideration to its minimal
dimensions. As the crisis of death approaches, in one poem, all that remains between the mortal life and eternity is a 'Hair.' In another:

> The instant holding in its claw
> The privilege to live. . . .

A third method of measuring the difference between life and death was
that of movement versus immobility. She pleads eloquently for the inert
corpse:

> Oh give it Motion— deck it sweet
> With Artery and Vein— . . .

Such experiments were in fruitful directions.

When she hit upon man's best invention for measuring time by motion, she worked out a perfect conceit for the life-death crisis. Even the
figurative language applied to the clock in everyday speech could be
counted on to personify it with no need of being spelled out, from the
more obvious face and hands to the idea that its life is in its movements,
that it is running when it ticks off the minutes, that it dies down when
it stops. Motion and measurable time are synonymous with being alive,
stillness and eternity with being dead. The hourglass was too worn a
convention, and its mechanism too simple for her purposes. The grandfather clock so common in New England must have tempted her, its
dignity and ancestral quality lending it easily to personification, but for
her the old-fashioned was equated with belief. When she was analytical
her skepticism used a modern vocabulary, frequently drawn from tech-
nology. To fit the growing mechanistic temper of her age, though not
of Amherst village, she needed a timepiece that suggested intricate invention, so she seized upon the Swiss as masters of artifice:

A Clock stopped—
Not the Mantel's—
Geneva's farthest skill
Cant put the puppet bowing—
That just now dangled still—

An awe came on the Trinket!
The Figures hunched, with pain—
Then quivered out of Decimals—
Into Degreeless Noon—

It will not stir for Doctors—
This Pendulum of snow—
The Shopman importunes it—
While cool— concernless No—

Stares from the Gilded pointers—
Nods from the Seconds slim—
Decades of Arrogance between
The Dial life—
And Him—

The audible ticking of a clock, she says elsewhere, reassures those keeping the deathwatch that time is real and life is still there: ' 'Twas comfort in her Dying Room/To hear the living Clock.' But when it suddenly ceases the bottom drops out of things, as she puts it in a letter describing the aftermath of a thunderstorm, 'and the clock stopped— which made it seem like Judgment day.' The ingeniously sustained clock conceit in the present poem is so revealing there was no need, other than by denial ('Not the Mantel's'), to name the true subject of her poem. Man is a 'Pendulum,' a 'Dial,' better still a 'Trinket' or 'Puppet,' as he is renamed in successive stanzas. There is no evidence that the Dickinsons owned a Swiss clock, but she had certainly seen one with those animated figures that come out and bow as the hours strike, the exact personification of time suited to her needs. She had probably noted how tragicomically the life goes out of them if the clock happens to run down just as they are going through their proud motions. Whatever wonders 'Geneva's farthest skill' might be capable of with a mantel clock, the implied maker here is unequal to reviving this collapsed puppet. Her next image for man, a 'Trinket,' is not especially novel since the Christian vocabulary is filled with words belittling mortal significance in comparison to that of God. She extended this usage in a letter once by referring to 'that strange Trinket of Life, which each of us wear and none of us own.' But in her poem she gives the epithet shock value by placing it in conjunction with the only word in the text that has religious overtones ('An awe came on the Trinket!'), the awe on the face of the dead being connected with the belief that they get a glimpse of heaven at the moment of passing. Has the stopped clock seen God?

Instead of pursuing this question, the poem returns to the agony of physical dying. The 'Figures' that hunched with pain refer back to the dangled puppet as well as forward to the numerals on the clock's face that tell what hour it is, now the hour of death. If they do not literally 'quiver' with the death rattle, the sympathetic imagination can supply this infinitesimal motion from the excess of tension built up so far. Nor does it matter that the dial is not specifically calibrated to the decimal system; the years of man's history are so measured, in decades, centuries, millenia. When the hands of the clock have swung full circle around their three hundred and sixty degrees, at the exact moment that they point to the beginning of a new cycle they also strike the hour of 'Noon,' or midnight, which is there mathematically though not registered on the dial, and which is 'Degreeless' because the pointers are superimposed instead of separated at an angle. Twelve o'clock is zero as well as zenith, and if the clock stops then it escapes 'out of Decimals,' hence out of time. She habitually passed over the conventional middle of the night as the zero hour, when villagers are asleep and unaware of time, pre- ferring midday as the hour when eternity begins. Farmers, working in the fields all day, maintain that the sun stands still when directly over- head, the stopping of time being thus visible at noon through optical illusion. This was her recurring symbol for heaven. In one poem she describes it as 'Centuries of Noon'; in another, the zone 'Whose Sun constructs perpetual Noon.' In a third, after trying to define it as 'Light' and as bodiless 'Melody,' she returns to her time image:

> And the Everlasting Clocks—
> Chime— Noon!

This is the perfect gloss for the second stanza of the poem under consid- eration. The soul of the clock passes out of the decimals of human time into the 'Degreeless Noon' of eternity, unmeasurable by the calibrations of the dial, just as she once described her own flight to heaven as 'When I go out of Time.'

In the clock poem her chief concern is with the moment of death, however, not with the moment beyond. 'It will not stir for Doctors,' she continues, 'This Pendulum of snow.' The advantages of a clock with a visible symbol of its life, measuring time by the swinging of its pendulum, needs no comment except that the heart likewise sways in the breast, though warm and red instead of cold and white. Less obvious are the connotations of 'snow,' a word that appears frequently in her poetic vocabulary as the image of eternity, and so of death. When one remembers her plea for the corpse (give it motion and pumping arteries, marry it again to that 'Pink stranger we call Dust') the full meaning here emerges. 'Snow' connotes both the whiteness when blood drains away from the body and the freezing of motion into the stillness of death. But is this 'Doctor' an intruder, a medical man coming in rudely to remind the reader that this, too, is after all a corpse? His figure quickly merges with the 'Shopman' two lines below and with the Swiss clockmaker of the first stanza, so that he is more properly the clock-doctor called in vain to make repairs, and there is no real lapse in the controlling mechanistic conceit. All three may be taken as masks for the Great Artificer, with an irony bordering on blasphemy: the Lord giveth and the Lord taketh away, but he cannot repeat the performance with the same trinket.

The only answer to all efforts at reviving this puppet is 'No,' a verdict delivered with the unconcern of a machine, the coolness of the hands matching the snow of the pendulum. In the first draft she was at fault in letting a slight motion creep into the denial, '*Nods* from the Gilded pointers,' but she corrected this to 'Stares,' motionless and suggesting the glaze on the eyes of death. The drama of this puppet show has now moved to its climax. Dickinson's best poems, with every word vital, move from surprise to surprise until the accumulated tension explodes in a shock phrase, frequently a single unexpected word set in a flat context to heighten the effect, as here:

> Decades of *Arrogance* between
> The Dial life—
> And Him—

Just as living man stares down the idea of death until the crisis is at hand so, once it is past, death looks back defiantly at the very notion of being alive, or at any doctor who might attempt resurrection. The separation is immediate and irrevocable. As she phrased it in another poem, the eye 'Shuts arrogantly— in the Grave—/Another way— to see.' And, yet again, she asks of death:

> Was ever Arrogance like This?
> Within a Hut of Stone
> To bask the Centuries away—
> Nor once look up— for Noon?

'Arrogance' was her inspired word for defining the hostile encounter between life and death, the absoluteness of the distance between them both in time and in space.

Is this all? Does the poem end with the extinction of life by physical death? The explosion has left some fragments around that must be picked up. It should be remembered that the whole action has taken place in a split second, the recently animated puppet having 'just now' dangled still. Then how have 'Decades' of time elapsed? Knowing that eternity cannot be measured, she seeks to suggest its infinite duration by saying that one moment of it is equal to decades of mortal time, ten, a hundred, she does not specify. So 'Decades' leads on beyond the boundary of the grave and beyond the limits of the poem, but within the text they stand between 'The Dial life—/And *Him.*' Who is 'Him'? This pronoun cannot refer to the clock's body which is consistently represented by the neuter 'it,' whether she is naming the whole or its parts, puppet, pendulum, dial life. The grammatical antecedent might seem to be 'Shopman' or 'Doctor,' but that is impossible because they are both on the same side of death as the stopped clock, the mortal side. 'Him' can only refer to God or to the soul of the trinket man, which has now escaped into degreeless noon with decades of arrogance between him and his former brief life in human time. Only the soul, as she implies in one poem, can be 'More distant in an instant/Than Dawn in Timbuctoo.' In another, it is specifically named: 'The Second poised— debated— shot—' and then 'simultaneously, a Soul/Escaped the House unseen.' The clock poem is not thematically concerned with immortality but, as the concept of it is rarely absent from any of her serious treatments of death, it is invoked here ambiguously in the final word.

 What makes death fascinating to the poet is that, to borrow a term she used elsewhere, it is the 'Hyphen' between the mortal life and man's dream of immortality. However short the hyphen of death, however instantaneous the soul's passage from one world to another, the customs of society have habitually prolonged the interval with last rites, funeral procession, and burial service, perhaps to allow time for meditation on its meaning. In the village world of a century ago these ceremonies were carried off with far more solemnity and pomp than today, and they were an inescapable part of people's lives. The pageantry of that dark parade to the graveyard particularly caught the eye of Emily Dickinson, with its plumed horses, flower-decked hearse, and formal mourning attire. From her tenth to her twenty-fifth years, when she lived on Pleasant Street, it regularly passed her home on its way to the cemetery nearby. As a schoolgirl she reported in a letter: 'Yesterday as I sat by the north window the funeral train entered the open gate of the church yard, following the remains of Judge Dickinson's wife to her long home.' She then went on to recount at length her own first experience of death in the loss of a young friend, whom she frequently went to visit in her dying room and finally to see in her coffin. The seemingly obsessive concern with death in such an early letter is largely the result of her repeating formulas from the language of conventional piety, usually in a highly emotional context, as here, when she was discussing the problem of religious conversion with a schoolmate. Her extreme sensitiveness to death is indicated by the fact that on this occasion, at the age of thirteen, she 'gave way to a fixed melancholy' and had to be sent on a long visit to relatives in Boston to recuperate.

This incident is not brought up in order to imply that her personal attitude towards death was morbid, a strictly biographical problem, but as evidence of her familiarity with its solemn ceremonials from an early age and to serve as an introduction to several interesting poems that take the funeral procession as their subject. What she saw and brooded on in actual experience is one thing, what she made of it in her art quite another. The traditional decorum for facing death had proved inadequate to her, as had the faith of her fathers of which it was a part, but she created a new one through her poems that enabled her to master death rather than be mastered by it. In them, as contrasted with the letters, the agony of death and the sundering of ties rarely appear.

Another convention, one of the most hackneyed passed on by the Graveyard School of poetry, was that of death as the democratic leveler. She did not wholly escape it, threadbare as it was after a hundred years, any more than did Whitman, Tennyson, and the other major writers of her day. This final status is the 'Common Right' of all, she said in one poem that follows the mode closely; but even here she achieved freshness of phrasing: 'Of Earl and Midge/The privilege.' Perhaps she came nearest to novelty when she applied this trite idea to the great conflict over slavery; in her response to the Emancipation Proclamation, so different from that of Whittier and Lowell, she said that racial distinctions are 'Time's Affair' and will disappear in the large democracy of death: 'Chrysalis of Blonde– or Umber–/Equal Butterfly.' There was an opposite tradition of the grave's power, available to her from environment rather than from books, the Christian belief that it exalts the humble to royal rank. When she exploited this she achieved some measure of success. Of one lifted up by death from an undistinguished life, she wrote, 'No more her timid bonnet' on the village street, 'But Crowns instead, and Courtiers. . . .' And seizing upon the funeral itself as a ceremonial symbol of this elevation:

> Pompless no Life can pass away–
> The lowliest career
> To the same pageant wends it way
> As that exalted here. . . .

To follow this tradition slavishly would preclude originality just as surely as the imitation of a worn-out literary mode. When she did—as in the one beginning 'Wait till the Majesty of Death/Invests so mean a brow!'– the result reads all too much like a smoother version of one of Watts' hymns. But from the questioning secular view, which remained an unsubdued component of her mind, the same ceremony that may elevate the soul undeniably lays low the body of this life. It was this ambiguity that gave the characteristic stress to her treatment. The mixing of 'Bells and Palls,' according to one poem, makes a 'Lacerating Tune':

> 'Tis Coronal– and Funeral–
> Saluting– in the Road–

The funeral procession not only embodied the ambiguity of death that teased her, but dramatized it. These tensions give some distinction to an early poem:

> One dignity delays for all–
> One mitred Afternoon–
> None can avoid this purple–
> None evade this Crown!

Coach, it insures, and footmen—
Chamber, and state, and throng—
Bells, also, in the village
As we ride grand along!

What dignified Attendants!
What service when we pause!
How loyally at parting
Their hundred hats they raise!

How pomp surpassing ermine
When simple You, and I,
Present our meek escutcheon
And claim the rank to die!

The status words have a twofold reference throughout. The formal ceremony is both coronation and funeral service, the royal equipage is also the dark hearse that leads to the graveyard. Not all the pealing bells or pompous monosyllables 'As we ride grand along!' can conceal the fact that the occupant of this coach is a corpse looking out on its kingdom of death. The framing stanzas render the ambiguousness of the ceremony more subtly. The crown it confers at the beginning is quite properly a mitre, the symbol not of secular kingship but of spiritual rank. But the participial form in which it appears, 'One mitred Afternoon,' suggests that this is simply the occasion for joining together body and soul in that last instant before they fall apart into the death of this life and, for the faithful, the life of this death. At the end, the 'meek escutcheon' of the dead can only be a tombstone, hopefully to be exchanged for a shield of heavenly status but not in this poem, which concludes by claiming merely 'the rank to die!' The irony remains that man becomes a king only when he is dead. The surface coronation, despite all its pomp and circumstance, is swallowed up in the submerged funeral.

Her finest poem on the funeral ceremony uses the reverse technique. On the surface it seems like just another version of the procession to the grave, but this is a metaphor that can be probed for deeper levels of meaning, spiritual journeys of a very different sort:

Because I could not stop for Death—
He kindly stopped for me—
The Carriage held but just Ourselves—
And Immortality.

We slowly drove– He knew no haste
And I had put away
My labor and my leisure too,
For His Civility–

We passed the School, where Children strove
At Recess– in the Ring–
We passed the Fields of Gazing Grain–
We passed the Setting Sun–

Or rather– He passed Us–
The Dews drew quivering and chill–
For only Gossamer, my Gown–
My Tippet– only Tulle–

We paused before a House that seemed
A Swelling of the Ground–
The Roof was scarcely visible–
The Cornice– in the Ground–

Since then– 'tis Centuries– and yet
Feels shorter than the Day
I first surmised the Horses Heads
Were toward Eternity–

At first reading, the orthodox reassurance against the fear of death appears to be invoked, though with the novelty of a suitor replacing the traditional angel, by emphasizing his compassionate mission in taking her out of the woes of this world into the bliss of the next. 'Death,' usually rude, sudden, and impersonal, has been transformed into a kindly and leisurely gentleman. Although she was aware this is a last ride, since his 'Carriage' can only be a hearse, its terror is subdued by the 'Civility' of the driver who is merely serving the end of 'Immortality.' The loneliness of the journey, with Death on the driver's seat and her body laid out in the coach behind, is dispelled by the presence of her immortal part that rides with her as a co-passenger, this slight personification being justified by the separable concept of the soul. Too occupied with life herself to stop, like all busy mortals, Death 'kindly stopped for her. But this figure of a gentleman taking a lady for a carriage ride is carefully underplayed and then dropped after two stanzas.

The balanced parallelism of the first stanza is slightly quickened by the alliterating 'labor' and 'leisure' of the second, which encompass vividly all that must be renounced in order to ride 'toward Eternity.' So the deliberate slow-paced action that lies suspended behind the poem is charged with a forward movement by the sound pattern, taking on a kind of inevitability in the insistent reiteration of the following stanza:

> We passed the School, where Children strove
> At Recess— in the Ring—
> We passed the Fields of Gazing Grain—
> We passed the Setting Sun—

Here her intensely conscious leave-taking of the world is rendered with fine economy, and instead of the sentimental grief of parting there is an objectively presented scene. The seemingly disparate parts of this are fused into a vivid re-enactment of the mortal experience. It includes the three stages of youth, maturity, and age, the cycle of day from morning to evening, and even a suggestion of seasonal progression from the year's upspring through ripening to decline. The labor and leisure of life are made concrete in the joyous activity of children contrasted with the passivity of nature and again, by the optical illusion of the sun's setting, in the image of motion that has come to rest. Also the whole range of the earthly life is symbolized, first human nature, then animate, and finally inanimate nature. But, absorbed 'in the Ring' of childhood's games, the players at life do not even stop to look up at the passing carriage of death. And the indifference of nature is given a kind of cold vitality by transferring the stare in the dead traveler's eyes to the 'Gazing Grain.' This simple maneuver in grammar creates an involute paradox, giving the fixity of death to the living corn while the corpse itself passes by on its journey to immortality. Then with the westering sun, traditional symbol of the soul's passing, comes the obliterating darkness of eternity. Finally, the sequence follows the natural route of a funeral train, past the schoolhouse in the village, then the outlying fields, and on to the remote burying ground.

In the concluding stanzas the movement of the poem slows almost to a stop, 'We paused' contrasting with the successive sights 'We passed' in the earlier stages of the journey. For when the carriage arrives at the threshold of the house of death it has reached the spatial limits of mortality. To say that it 'passed the Setting Sun' is to take it out of bounds, beyond human time, so she quickly corrects herself by saying instead that the sun 'passed Us,' as it surely does all who are buried. Then, as the 'Dews' descend 'quivering and chill,' she projects her awareness of what it will be like to come to rest in the cold damp ground. The identification of her new 'House' with a grave is achieved by the use of only two details: a 'Roof' that is 'scarcely visible' and a 'Cornice,' the molding around the coffin's lid, that is 'in the Ground.' But the tomb's horror is absorbed by the emphasis on merely pausing here, as though this were a sort of tavern for the night. When she wanted to she could invoke the conventional Gothic atmosphere, and without being imitative, as in an early poem:

> What Inn is this
> Where for the night
> Peculiar Traveller comes?
> Who is the Landlord?
> Where the maids?
> Behold, what curious rooms!
> No ruddy fires on the hearth—
> No brimming Tankards flow—
> Necromancer! Landlord!
> Who are these below?

The image of the grave as a ghastly kind of inn is there built up to a climax which blasts all hopes of domestic coziness by the revelation that its landlord is a 'Necromancer,' a sorcerer who communicates with spirits.

In the poem under consideration, however, the house of death so lightly sketched is not her destination. That is clearly stated as 'Eternity,' though it is significant that she never reaches it:

> Since then— 'tis Centuries— and yet
> Feels shorter than the Day
> I first surmised the Horses Heads
> Were toward Eternity—

An eminent critic, after praising this as a remarkably beautiful poem, complains that it breaks down at this point because it goes beyond the 'Limits of Judgment'; in so far as it attempts to experience death and express the nature of posthumous beatitude, he says, it is 'fraudulent.'

But in addition to being a hyper-rational criticism, this is simply a failure to read the text. The poem does not in the least strive after the incomprehensible. It deals with the daily realization of the imminence of death, offset by man's yearning for immortality. These are intensely felt, but only as ideas, as the abstractions of time and eternity, not as something experienced. Being essentially inexpressible, they are rendered as metaphors. The idea of achieving immortality by a ride in the carriage of death is confronted by the concrete fact of physical disintegration as she pauses before a 'Swelling in the Ground.'

The final stanza is not an extension of knowledge beyond the grave but simply the most fitting coda for her poem. In projecting the last sensations of consciousness as the world fades out, she has employed progressively fewer visible objects until with fine dramatic skill she limits herself at the end to a single one, the 'Horses Heads,' recalled in a flash of memory as that on which her eyes had been fixed throughout the journey. These bring to mind the 'Carriage' of the opening stanza, and Death, who has receded as a person, is now by implication back in the driver's seat. 'Since then— 'tis Centuries,' she says, in an unexpected phrase for the transition from time to eternity, but this is a finite infinity; her consciousness is still operative and subject to temporal measurement. All of this poetically elapsed time 'Feels shorter than the Day,' the day of death brought to an end by the setting sun of the third stanza, when she first guessed the direction in which these apocalyptic horses were headed. 'Surmised,' carefully placed near the conclusion, is all the warranty one needs for reading this journey as one that has taken place entirely in her mind, 'imagined without certain knowledge,' as her Lexicon defined it. The last word may be 'Eternity' but it is strictly limited by the directional preposition 'toward.' So the poem returns to the very day, even the same instant, when it started. Its theme is a Christian one, yet unsupported by any of the customary rituals and without any final statement of Christian faith. The resolution is not mystical but dramatic.

Read in this way the poem is flawless to the last detail, each image precise and discrete even while it is unified in the central motif of the last journey. Yet another level of meaning has suggested itself faintly to two critics. One has described the driver as 'amorous but genteel'; the other has noted 'the subtly interfused erotic motive,' love having frequently been an idea linked with death for the romantic poets. Both of these astute guesses were made without benefit of the revealing fourth stanza, recently restored from the manuscript. But even in the well-known opening lines of the poem there are suggestive hints for anyone who remembers that the carriage drive was a standard mode of courtship a century ago. In the period of her normal social life, when Emily Dickinson took part in those occasions that give youthful love its chance, she frequently went on drives with young gentlemen. Some ten years before the date of this poem, for example, she wrote to her brother: 'I've been to ride twice since I wrote you, . . . last evening with *Sophomore Emmons,* alone'; and a few weeks later she confided to her future sister-in-law: 'I've found a beautiful, new, friend.' The figure of such a prospective suitor would inevitably have come to the minds of a contemporary audience as they read: 'He kindly stopped for me–/The Carriage held but just Ourselves. . . .' Such a young couple likewise would have driven beyond the village limits into the open country and then, romantically, past the 'Setting Sun.' Restraint kept her from pushing this parallel to the point of being ludicrous, and the suitor image quickly drops into the background.

The love-death symbolism, however, re-emerges with new implications in the now restored fourth stanza, probably omitted by previous editors because they were baffled by its meaning:

> For only Gossamer, my Gown–
> My Tippet– only Tulle–

This is certainly not a description of conventional burial clothes. It is instead a bridal dress, but of a very special sort. 'Gossamer' in her day was not yet applied to fine spun cloth but only to that filmy substance like cobwebs sometimes seen floating in the autumn air, as her Lexicon described it, probably formed by a species of spider. This brings to mind her cryptic poem on the spider whose web was his 'Strategy of Immortality.' And by transforming the bridal veil into a 'Tippet,' the flowing scarf-like part of the distinctive hood of holy orders, she is properly dressed for a celestial marriage. 'Death,' to be sure, is not the true bridegroom but a surrogate, which accounts for his minor role. He is the envoy taking her on this curiously premature wedding journey to the heavenly altar where she will be married to God. The whole idea of the Bride-of-the-Lamb is admittedly only latent in the text of this poem, but in view of the body of her writings it seems admissible to suggest it as another metaphor for the extension of meanings.

Most of her love poems, it has been shown in the chapter on 'Ecstasy,' are concerned with a celestial betrothal. Several of them combine this with the metaphor of a funeral as the wedding journey to eternity, like the one beginning: 'Tie the Strings to my Life, My Lord, ... Just a look at the Horses.' The most original, written late in life, is an explicit rendering of death as the lover who transports her in his carriage, the theme that is only implicit in the major poem just discussed:

> Death is the supple Suitor
> That wins at last—
> It is a stealthy Wooing
> Conducted first
> By pallid innuendoes
> And dim approach
> But brave at last with Bugles
> And a bisected Coach
> It bears away in triumph
> To Troth unknown
> And Kinsmen as divulgeless
> As Clans of Down—

The idea of Christ as the heavenly bridegroom with the Church or the Elect as his bride was available to her from the Book of Revelation and from the glosses to the Song of Solomon, though she shrewdly avoided imitating the Biblical phrasing. For all readers familiar with the Christian tradition it forms an unmistakable basis of reference in this poem, setting up a system of correspondences between the changes brought about by death and the changes in roles of the unnamed partners in this spiritual love game. When 'Death' first appears as a suitor she changes from a girl to a coy virgin. This must be a 'stealthy Wooing,' for though she knows it will result in a glorious new status for her, she is vaguely aware that it will mean a renunciation of all the world she has known. Her maidenly reserve is indicated by the manner in which he is forced to conduct his courtship, by 'pallid innuendoes' and a 'dim approach.' But he is a 'supple Suitor' and attains his goal at long last.

The second change comes with great suddenness for it is the kiss of death, transforming her from virgin to bride, or at least to the betrothed. Because of the protean character of 'Death,' who is both envoy and groom-to-be, the ceremony itself does not occur in the poem but falls between the first six lines and the last six. Then without more ado he bears her away 'in triumph,' both from a proxy wedding and towards a final one, to the sound of 'brave Bugles' such as would announce a royal marriage, or the Day of Doom. The strange duality of this journey is reflected by the odd vehicle in which they travel, 'a bisected Coach.' As a hearse it separates her body in the glass enclosure from the driver on his seat above, as a wedding coach it divides the wife-to-be from the virginal life left behind, as a heavenly chariot the mortal from the immortal. The third and final change of status lies beyond the poem because it lies beyond death. She only knows that she is going to a 'Troth unknown.' The impossibility of describing her spiritual marriage is put flatly in this phrase and in the vagueness of her projection of the glorious life to come, with 'Kinsmen as divulgeless/As Clans of Down'—or as the variant for these concluding lines reads: 'Pageants as impassive/As Porcelain.' The three stages of the poem, which also transform the suitor into bridegroom and prospective husband, correspond to the awareness of death, the act of death, and the state after death. The last, in relation to the Christian concept of entering heaven as the bride of Christ, is rendered with typical Dickinsonian obliqueness.

'Because I could not stop for Death' is incomparably the finest poem of this cluster. In it all the traditional modes are subdued so they can be assimilated to her purposes. For her theme there, as a final reading of its meaning will suggest, is not necessarily death or immortality in the literal sense of those terms. There are many ways of dying, as she once said:

> Death— is but one— and comes but once—
> And only nails the eyes—

One surely dies out of this world in the end, but one may also die away from the world by deliberate choice during this life. In her vocabulary 'immortal' is a value that can also attach to living this side of the grave:

> Some— Work for Immortality—
> The Chiefer part, for Time—

As an artist she ranked herself with that élite. At the time of her dedication to poetry, presumably in the early 1860's, someone 'kindly stopped' for her—lover, muse, God—and she willingly put away the labor and leisure of this world for the creative life of the spirit. Looking back on the affairs of 'Time' at any point after making such a momentous decision, she could easily feel 'Since then— 'tis Centuries.' Remembering what she had renounced, the happiness of a normal youth, sunshine and growing things, she could experience a momentary feeling of deprivation. But in another sense she had simply triumphed over them, passing beyond earthly trammels. Finally, this makes the most satisfactory reading of her reversible image of motion and stasis during the journey, passing the setting sun and being passed by it. For though in her withdrawal the events of the external world by-passed her, in the poetic life made possible by it she escaped the limitations of the mortal calendar. She was borne confidently, by her winged horse, 'toward Eternity' in the immortality of her poems.

Such a dying to the world and dedication to the spiritual life was readily acceptable in the medieval idea of the monastic life. No less a symbol would suffice to express her dedicatory service in the paradise of art. In another of those poems where an anonymous 'He' may stand for muse, unattainable lover, or God, she accepts serenely her status, 'No Wedlock— granted Me,' because of the invisible claim he presses upon her, concluding:

> I live with Him— I hear His Voice—
> I stand alive— Today—
> To witness to the Certainty
> Of Immortality—
>
> Taught Me— by Time— the lower Way—
> Conviction— Every day—
> That Life like This— is stopless—
> Be Judgment— what it may—

This is immortality achieved in time, whatever her chances of attaining it in the other paradise.

There is ample evidence that she cared deeply about immortality in the orthodox sense too. But whenever that is her theme, she is careful to define the absolute cleavage between the certainty of life on earth and man's dream about what lies beyond the grave:

> Our journey had advanced—
> Our feet were almost come
> To that odd Fork in Being's Road—
> Eternity— by Term—

> Our pace took sudden awe—
> Our feet— reluctant— led—
> Before— were Cities— but Between—
> The Forest of the Dead—
>
> Retreat— was out of Hope—
> Behind— a Sealed Route—
> Eternity's White Flag— Before—
> And God— at every Gate—

Having brought the soul at death to the brink of the incomprehensible, she leaves it there, knowing that any further advance is impossible to the mortal consciousness. For this, again, is not actual death but an adventure of the mind. This 'Fork in Being's Road' is her sharp awareness of the dilemma between faith in immortality and doubt of it. Having reached this point, 'Retreat' to the old life of happy indifference is a 'Sealed Route.' One's belief can now go only one of two ways: into the grave, the 'Forest of the Dead' being her bleak image of a cemetery with the white trees of its marble shafts, or towards the fabled City of God, with 'Eternity's White Flag' flying from every gate.

Either way the color is blank. No matter how one looks at it death is the 'White Exploit.' She did not conceal her uncertainty even from a young cousin who had just entered the ministry. 'I suppose we are all thinking of Immortality,' she wrote in a letter of consolation after his sister died, 'but . . . speculate with all our might, we cannot ascertain.' To his simple faith she could only oppose the ambiguous response of her questioning mind: 'It grieves me that you speak of Death with so much expectation. I know there is no pang like that for those we love, nor any leisure like the one they leave so closed behind them, but Dying is a wild Night and a new Road.'

I 2

IMMORTALITY

'You mention Immortality,' Emily Dickinson wrote to Higginson at the height of her powers. 'That is the Flood subject.' A series of metaphors followed, reaching a climax in the aphorism: 'Paradise is of the option.' Then she added, without stopping to catch her breath or complete her grammar, 'Whosoever will Own in Eden notwithstanding Adam and Repeal.' Is it here or there, man's vainest dream or the ultimate fact? Immortality was indeed her flood subject, overflowing into endless poems and letters. And since it challenges the symbol-making power of the imagination even as it provokes the reasoning mind to argument, more than any other subject in her writings it tends to break through the barriers of prose and verse. Witness the following, written as a paragraph yet with the formal devices of refrain and parallelism framing a perfectly patterned quatrain at the center:

> I hear robins a great way off, and wagons a great way off, and rivers a great way off, and all appear to be hurrying somewhere undisclosed to me. Remoteness is the founder of sweetness; could we see all we hope, or hear the whole we fear told tranquil, like another tale, there would be madness near. Each of us gives or takes heaven in corporeal person, for each of us has the skill of life.

As an effortless forerunner of polyphonic prose, supposedly invented by the *Imagistes* half a century later, it simply throws up a shower of metaphors revealing her preference for the heaven here and now over the one too remote to grasp. That the latter is not to be rejected merely because it is a mystery, however, is the theme of one of her latest jottings on a fragment of manuscript:

> We do not think enough of the Dead as exhilirants— they are not dissuaders but Lures— Keepers of that great Romance still to us foreclosed— while coveting their wisdom we lament their silence. Grace is still a secret. That they have existed none can take away. That they still exist is a trust so daring we thank thee that thou hast hid these things from us and hast revealed them to them. The power and the glory are the post mortuary gifts.

These lines begin like the germ of an unwritten poem and end like an unfinished private prayer.

The flood subject of immortality intrudes in her most casual correspondence. 'To live, and die, and mount again in triumphant body,' she wrote in the context of an otherwise flippant early letter, 'is no schoolboy's theme!' More seriously, she sought aid from those supposed to know, when trying to resolve the dilemma that had confronted her since childhood, as she recalled in a letter of 1877 to Higginson:

> When a few years old— I was taken to a Funeral which I now know was of peculiar distress, and the Clergyman asked 'Is the Arm of the Lord shortened that it cannot save?'
>
> He italicized the 'cannot.' I mistook the accent for a doubt of Immortality and not daring to ask, it besets me still, though we know that the mind of the Heart must live if its clerical part do not. Would you explain it to me?
>
> I was told you were once a Clergyman. It comforts an instinct if another have felt it too.

But as usual she was able to give more counsel than she ever received from her 'preceptor,' as in the note of consolation written to him after the death of his wife a few months later: 'We must be less than Death, to be lessened by it— for nothing is irrevocable but ourselves.'

Yet when death struck close she had no sure faith to lean on. After her father died she could only say, 'I am glad there is Immortality— but would have tested it myself— before entrusting him.' A sheet of letter paper found among her manuscripts contains the words 'Dear Father' at the top and at the bottom the signature 'Emily,' the blank space in between representing the vacuum she felt. After her mother's death she wrote: 'We don't know where she is, though so many tell us.' As she lost her closest friends one by one, the bombardment of doubts continued. To an intimate of the Reverend Mr. Wadsworth she wrote, following his death, 'Are you certain there is another life? When overwhelmed to know, I fear that few are sure.' She found some sort of comfort in Judge Lord's own ambiguous attitude towards immortality, when corresponding with his kinsman and executor: 'Perhaps to solidify his faith was for him impossible, and if for him, how more, for us! . . . Neither fearing Extinction, nor prizing Redemption, he believed alone. Victory was his Rendezvous.' An equally great blow had come with the untimely death of Samuel Bowles. How kindred a spirit he had been is revealed by her terse comment: 'That those have Immortality with whom we talked about it, makes it no more mighty— but perhaps more sudden.' This is immediately followed by the poem beginning:

> How brittle are the Piers
> On which our Faith doth tread—...

With the death of little children belief in immortality came more readily, for that central Christian doctrine 'of such is the kingdom of heaven' is almost irresistible in its appeal to the human heart. This found its way into her writings on several occasions but, as always, with characteristic novelty. When Higginson's baby girl died a few weeks after birth, she wrote:

> The flight of such a fraction takes all our Numbers Home— ...
> These sudden intimacies with Immortality, are expanse— not
> Peace— as Lightning at our feet, instills a foreign Landscape. ...
> The route of your little Fugitive must be a tender wonder— and yet
>> A Dimple in the Tomb
>> Makes that ferocious Room
>> A Home—

But it was the loss of her beloved nephew Gilbert that made belief a necessity. The response that welled up out of her heart, without premeditation, is one of her most confident statements of faith:

> The Vision of Immortal Life has been fulfilled—
> How simply at the last the Fathom comes! The Passenger and not

the Sea, we find surprises us– . ... Show us, prattling Preceptor, but the way to thee! ...

I see him in the Star, and meet his sweet velocity in everything that flies– His Life was like the Bugle, which winds itself away, his Elegy an echo– his Requiem ecstasy–

Dawn and Meridian in one.

Such certain faith in immortality could not be sustained for long. She knew that one of the strongest incentives to belief was the desperate desire of the heart not to be robbed by the grave, the pressure that had created her elegiac stanza on Gilbert quoted at the opening of the last chapter. This same idea could be expressed with involute irony. 'Immortal is an ample word' even when the loved one is nearby, she wrote; when he is taken by death it becomes a 'necessity.' This need, ironically, is the 'firmest proof' man has that the grave is a gateway to immortality. Yet this destruction of Eden is the work of God, who thus forces on us the necessity of believing in a 'Heaven above' to compensate for the loss of loved ones: 'Except for its marauding Hand/It had been Heaven below.' In another poem she declared that 'Drowning' in death should not be abhorred for our faith assures us we will be rescued by being 'grasped of God,' and yet

> The Maker's cordial visage,
> However good to see,
> Is shunned, we must admit it,
> Like an adversity.

Many of her apparent assertions of faith are merely part of her strategy of paradox. She makes the tacit assumption that heaven exists only in order to give this belief a twist asserting her preference for the mortal life, though the protest is usually in a lighter vein. 'The time to live is frugal,' she wrote to a friend, 'and good as is a better earth, it will not quite be this.' If immortality is achieved at all, she said in a poem, it will be at best an 'ablative estate,' giving a novel meaning to the Latin term for the case of deprivation; and 'Believing what we don't believe,' she concluded paradoxically, only increases our appetite for the solid sweetness of earthly life. 'Which is best?' she asked in another, the heaven-on-earth which is the 'Bird within the Hand' or the heaven-to-

come 'With that old Codicil of Doubt?' Once again, citing her mortal
limitations, 'I'm finite— I cant see,' she rendered that remote place in a
web of uncertainties: the 'House of Supposition,' the 'Glimmering Frontier' that skirts the 'Acres of Perhaps.' Eden may not be perfect but it
contents her. Its imperfection, on the other hand, is not necessarily an
affidavit that there will be a compensatory paradise beyond. The poem
ends in flat agnosticism:

> This timid life of Evidence
> Keeps pleading— 'I dont know.'

Another group of poems that have the ring of orthodoxy at the outset
are clearly experiments in fantasy that turn the worn images of conventional faith against themselves in the end. One begins with the language
of the gospel hymns:

> Going to Heaven!
> How dim it sounds!
> And yet it will be done
> As sure as flocks go home at night
> Unto the Shepherd's arm!

She continues by asking meekly for just a bit of 'Crown' and the smallest
'Robe,' then concludes abruptly:

> I'm glad I dont believe it
> For it w'd stop my breath—
> And I'd like to look a little more
> At such a curious Earth!
> I am glad they did believe it
> Whom I have never found
> Since the mighty Autumn afternoon
> I left them in the ground.

The balanced predications, 'I'm glad I dont . . . I am glad they did,'
separate her sharply from orthodox believers. And the double meaning
of 'it w'd stop my breath' emphasizes the power of death over and above
the glory of resurrection that is hinted at in the final phrase describing
their burial, 'the *mighty* Autumn afternoon.' She still prefers the wonder
of this life, which is amply embodied in 'such a curious Earth!'

A second version of the same theme resulted in a better poem, more compact and raised to distinction by wit:

> I went to Heaven—
> 'Twas a small Town—
> Lit— with a Ruby—
> Lathed— with Down—
> Stiller— than the fields
> At the full Dew—
> Beautiful— as Pictures—
> No Man drew.
> People— like the Moth—
> Of Mechlin— frames—
> Duties— of Gossamer—
> And Eider— names—
> Almost— contented—
> I— could be—
> 'Mong such unique
> Society—

The laconic second line, ' 'Twas a small Town,' brings heaven right down to old-fashioned New England. Since the Elect are few the City of God need not be large, no larger in fact than the village of Amherst. The diminutive size is even reflected in the reduced meter, two feet to the line. This restricted topography matches the narrow provincialism of the view that follows, a fanciful rendering of those Biblical descriptions that the pious took literally. As that 'great city, the holy Jerusalem' of the Book of Revelation was built on foundations 'garnished with all manner of precious stones,' so this small town is more modestly 'Lit with a Ruby.' For the ethereal nature of heaven and its inhabitants she ransacks the vocabulary of the fragile and impalpable: bodies of finest lace and duties of the filmiest cobweb, like eiderdown in both their abodes and their identities. The substitution of 'Moth' for the traditional butterfly as symbol of the soul gives it an even more dreamlike quality. To characterize the heavenly host, so described, as a 'unique Society' is a classic example of understatement. Her preference for earth over such an insubstantial place is sufficiently indicated by one limiting adverb, '*almost* contented.'

All the evidence from her writings points towards unresolved dilemma both as to her belief in immortality and that larger one encompassing it, belief in the existence of God. She was never able to find a solution in the religion of her heritage, nor was she content on the other hand to rest in the unbelief of the materialist. The tension between faith and doubt remained constant from an early age down to her death. A late poem sums up her lifelong problem as that of one who was cut off from simple faith by the new currents of thought in her day, mildly envious of the orthodox older generation:

> Those— dying then,
> Knew where they went—
> They went to God's Right Hand—
> That Hand is amputated now
> And God cannot be found—
>
> The abdication of Belief
> Makes the Behavior small—
> Better an ignis fatuus
> Than no illume at all—

The faithful then had been confident that their reward would be the same as Christ's, who after his resurrection was 'received up into heaven, and sat on the right hand of God.' That faith, embodied in her poem as a hand, is now 'amputated,' the violence of loss being rendered with shock by the surgical image in a Biblical context. In contrast with the harsh realism of her metaphor for unbelief is the folk superstition invoked for its opposite, 'ignis fatuus.' The older belief may have been a delusive light but it was better than none, and without it man has been reduced in size. 'Abdication' apparently suggested too positive an act of will in rejecting the faith of the fathers, because she marked it on the manuscript for revision, but she never found the proper word to express how this loss came about.

Her own drift away from orthodoxy began so early and was the result of such a complex reordering of her thinking it would be vain to seek a simple explanation. The problem is one for the biographer. But a few quotations from the letters, indicating some high points in her religious history, will throw light on the poems. As a young girl of seventeen she had resisted the pressures of a revival at Mount Holyoke Seminary, urging her to renounce the flesh for the spirit, because she was too honest to pretend that she could. But the two-way pull made her say in retrospect: 'I regret that last term, when that golden opportunity was mine, that I did not give up and become a Christian . . . , but it is hard for me to give up the world.' Two years later in Amherst, when there was another revival, she again reported: 'Christ is calling everyone here, . . . and I am standing alone in rebellion.' To a former school friend who had just been converted, she wrote: 'You are growing wiser than I am, and nipping in the bud fancies which I let blossom—perchance to bear no fruit, or if plucked, I may find it bitter. The shore is safer, Abiah, but I love to buffet the sea— . . . oh, I love the danger!' Her resistance was clearly connected with the discovery of selfhood, and with the dim awareness that she was an emergent artist. It seems not too farfetched to interpret these budding fancies as an intuition of the career that was to flower a decade later. At any rate, her conviction seems already formed that religion could never be acceptable to her as convention, but would have to be explored anew as a whole way of life. The poetic content of Christianity and the drama with which Puritan belief had once invested it she no longer found animating the services of the church, so that membership in it was incompatible with her deepest needs.

Another source of her strength to stand alone was undoubtedly the sturdy individualism she shared with other members of the Dickinson family. Though her mother had been converted as a young woman, and her sister likewise, her father did not join the church until the current revival of 1850 when he was forty-seven years old. Even then it was with distinct reservations, as indicated by the legalistic terms of his commitment, 'I hereby give myself to God,' written on a small card that he carried with him in his wallet till his death. In the next few years her brother also joined, apparently at the urging of his fiancée, but with both Dickinson men church membership was more a formal assumption of communal obligations than a matter of conversion. In this way they managed to keep religion a private affair while making a public profession of it.

Even more so Emily Dickinson maintained an independence of mind that enabled her to resist all importunings, including those of her future sister-in-law which had built up to a climax by 1854. Her reply makes it clear that her decision not to join the church was final, even if it meant the end of their friendship:

Sue– you can go or stay– There is but one alternative– We differ often lately, and this must be the last. . . . I shall remain alone, and though in that last day, the Jesus´Christ you love, remark he does not know me– there is a darker spirit will not disown its child. . . . We have walked very pleasantly– Perhaps this is the point at which our paths diverge– then pass on singing Sue, and up the distant hill I journey on.

A sense of anxiety over her spiritual intransigence remained, however, and occasionally it flared up in a lyric cry of pain:

> At least– to pray– is left– is left–
> Oh Jesus– in the Air–
> I know not which thy palaces–
> I'm knocking– everywhere–
>
> Thou stirrest Earthquake in the South–
> And Maelstrom, in the Sea–
> Say, Jesus Christ of Nazareth–
> Hast thou no Arm for Me?

Such an expression of being lost from the Christian community, though very rare in her writings, is significant to a full understanding of her spiritual history. What is even more significant is that, of all the Dickinson family, she is the only one whose entire career was devoted to a quest for religious truth, though always as an unflinching independent.

Her ability to make decisions, however arduous and irrevocable, is one of the clearest marks of her integrity. The language in which she dedicated herself to intellectual adventure and spiritual pioneering, as recorded in the letters just quoted, sounds remarkably close to that of Melville, though she was apparently unacquainted with his writings. Indeed, her decisions seem to have come exclusively from within. She continued to attend church services sporadically until the early 1860's, when she withdrew in all ways from the outer world into the inner world of poetry, but her reactions were always in the same vein. After the minister preached on Predestination one Sunday, she reported: 'I do not respect "doctrines," and did not listen to him'; but when he preached on unbelief she declared: 'Sermons on unbelief ever did attract me.' The theology of Puritanism no longer provided satisfactory answers for minds like hers. Coming to maturity at a time when its structure of dogmas was falling into collapse, she gradually realized her need to construct a private religion through the poetic imagination in order to revitalize in her personal experience what had formerly been kept alive by automatic belief.

Yet even after her retirement she maintained a cordial relation with the local pastors, especially with the Reverend Jonathan Jenkins, who was called to the First Church of Amherst in 1866. At some time after this he was requested by Edward Dickinson to interview his daughter, who he felt 'needed guidance in spiritual matters.' Jenkins left no account of this, but an imaginary reconstruction of the catechizing of Emily Dickinson by that broadminded clergyman has come down in the reminiscences of his son. After indulging in this play of fancy, with undisguised amusement at the incongruity of the occasion, he comments: 'All that is really known is that my father reported to the perplexed parent that Miss Emily was "sound," and let it go at that. . . . I am quite sure that, in his heart, he thought [her] rather less in need of spiritual light than any person he knew.' Orthodoxy, in a period of religious doldrums, can be another name for what is simply conventional and dead. Her position was both too new and too old, or rather too poetic and experimental, to be understood by most of her Amherst contemporaries. As she asked herself over and over, What are God and immortality to me? she came up with a new answer each time. Many of these suggest a kinship to New England's greatest religious thinker of the century before, Jonathan Edwards, though there is no real evidence of her acquaintance with his writings. Her most recent biographer sums the matter up succinctly: 'Not the least of the paradoxes in her life is the fact that she was closer to the Edwardsean core of thought than she ever really knew, or than were many of the orthodoxies preached in the Valley.' As applied to her concepts of God and nature, beauty and language and reality, this is true; but it does not hold for many of the theological doctrines he gave himself to the defense of. Puritan dogma she found an empty shell, though she exploited its dramatization of man's life and death and fashioned a new poetry by playing variations on some of its philosophical themes.

She was keenly aware of the decline of orthodoxy from the stern Calvinism of her grandfather to the growing secularism of her own day. Her poems leave no doubt that she was conscious of what this meant for her personally, but her occasional expressions of nostalgia for the good old days when belief was firm are those of the poet rather than the theologian. She knew instinctively that in any age the artist, as well as the philosopher, must go his own way. The new science and new thought about religion had broken into the stronghold of Amherst College, it is true, and she probably learned of them from the students who were friends of her brother as well as from a young Unitarian in her father's law office who presented her with a copy of Emerson's *Poems* as early as 1849. But her reading seems to have confirmed rather than initiated her revolt, for she had passed the crisis in her religious life and struck out on her own road of spiritual pioneering long before she knew the writings of Carlyle, Thoreau, and most of the other new lights. Of the influential liberal preacher, Theodore Parker, she said as late as 1859: 'I never read before what Mr Parker wrote. I heard that he was "poison." Then I like poison very well.' The relevance of this comment to her attitude towards orthodoxy is made clear by the remark that follows: 'I wish the "faith of the fathers" did'nt wear brogans, and carry blue umbrellas.' Emerson's essays she did not discover apparently until the 1860's, but what they meant to her after that may be inferred from her characterization of *Representative Men* as 'a little Granite Book you can lean upon.'

. It was clearly the discovery of a kindred spirit in such matters that drew her to George Eliot about this time. She followed her writings avidly during a period of two decades, and was deeply moved by her death. In a letter written shortly after this occasion, about 1881, referring to her as '*my* George Eliot,' she seems aware of the parallel in their careers: 'The gift of belief which her greatness denied her, I trust she receives in the childhood of the kingdom of heaven. As childhood is earth's confiding time, perhaps having no childhood, she lost her way to the early trust, and no later came.' This is close to one of her own poems, not a good one but significant for her religious history, recording the 'loss of something' poignantly felt throughout her life. Even as a child she had often thought of herself as a 'Prince cast out,' and in maturity is still searching for her 'Delinquent Palaces.' These vague images for the loss of some royal estate are clarified in the prosaic concluding stanza where she puts her finger on the problem at last, a 'Suspicion'

> That I am looking oppositely
> For the site of the Kingdom of Heaven—

'Oppositely' because the old way was through faith, but the only way left to her was through reason and the imagination. But the link between the two authors is less in the nostalgia over loss than in what lies behind the opening line of her tribute to George Eliot, 'The gift of belief which her greatness denied her.' For it was the particular area of their greatness that made orthodox belief impossible for both of them. Their genius was essentially religious, but it had been turned out of conventional channels by the new streams of thought in that period and the powerful originality of their minds. Such as they, the poets as well as the Kierkegaards and Henry Adamses, were especially sensitive to the upheavals in belief that marked the last half of the nineteenth century. One did not have to be in the thick of the fight, like Eliot, to be influenced by all this. From reading her novels, Dickinson in remote Amherst was sufficiently informed about such schools of thought as the Higher Criticism, which obviously played a part in her secular approach to the Bible, and was aware of the whole tide of modern doubt that was to sweep away the last foundations of the older orthodoxy.

From some equally available source she had also discovered enough of the new revolutionary scientific theories to feel their full impact. The disturbing implications of evolution for the fundamentalist belief in revealed religion are conveyed by the casual remark in a letter, 'we thought that Darwin had thrown "the Redeemer" away.' Again, one of the applications of Newton's *Principia* to astronomy gave her a new image of heaven:

> Eternity will be
> Velocity or Pause...

she wrote, depending on our understanding of the 'Fundamental Laws' of the cosmos. The general scientific principle of the conservation of matter and energy gave her another: the 'Chemical conviction' that nothing will be lost. If the 'Faces of the Atoms' will be preserved to eternity, she asked, how much more so the 'Finished Creatures' who have disappeared from this earth? But this conviction is broken by words of doubt. Her 'fractured Trust' in this poem could no more be healed by scientific theories than the amputated right hand of God could be restored in another. And here for the religious plight of moderns she used 'Disaster,' a stronger word than the 'Emergency' she had called upon science to rectify in an early poem, previously discussed in some detail. There she had posed the whole conflict between religion and science in a sententious quatrain, without taking sides:

> 'Faith' is a fine invention
> When Gentlemen can *see*—
> But *Microscopes* are prudent
> In an Emergency.

Is this her meaning when she wrote to a friend: 'God seems so much more friendly through a hearty Lens'? But these are mere sallies of wit. Though the emergency was very real for her, she sought no easy solution in the new faith in science.

The standard sources of comfort did not minister to her any more effectively. For example, the concept of God as a Heavenly Father only raised a series of questions in her mind. How does one envision this super-image of man, she asked: 'Hast thou a Hand or Foot/Or Mansion of Identity'? Equally unsatisfactory was the doctrine of indwelling spirit central to the Transcendentalist's revision: 'They say that God is everywhere, and yet we always think of Him as somewhat of a recluse.' Yet the orthodox one, that God is simply invisible, led to the skeptical query: Is He then nonexistent?

> I know that He exists.
> Somewhere— in Silence—
> He has hid his rare life
> From our gross eyes.
>
> 'Tis an instant's play.
> 'Tis a fond Ambush—
> Just to make Bliss
> Earn her own surprise!
>
> But— should the play
> Prove piercing earnest—
> Should the glee— glaze—
> In Death's— stiff— stare—
>
> Would not the Joke
> Look too expensive!
> Would not the jest—
> Have crawled too far!

The poem begins with a simple statement of faith, its positiveness reinforced by ending the first line with a period, an unusual form of punctuation for her even at the end of a poem. But this is merely the spring-board for her dialectic.

It is quite reasonable that such a 'rare' life should be invisible to such 'gross' eyes. The adjectives that separate God and man are chosen with great precision. In their root sense they define God as refined or rarefied into pure essence in comparison with man who is crude clay; in their derived sense they contrast uncommon excellence with dull stupidity. The second stanza toys with the idea that God's invisibility is a cosmic piece of wit, a game of hide-and-seek that will enhance the 'Bliss' of final discovery with the added delight of 'surprise.' But a devastating alternative is set up by the ambiguous phrase 'a *fond* Ambush.' The modern meaning of this adjective is loving; etymologically it means foolishly naive and credulous. Following out this original definition, as an epithet transferred to the speaker, the poem ends with a pretended nightmare of nihilism. The macabre effect is increased by supplementing the sparse rhymes with grotesquely insistent alliteration, especially in the climactic stanza. Should the 'glee– glaze' in death's 'stiff– stare' then the game is up in the grave; God is invisible because He does not exist. But she reassured herself in a late jotting on a fragment of manuscript: 'God cannot discontinue himself. This appalling trust is at times all that remains.'

These speculations threw her back on the metaphysical consideration that perhaps the heavenly reality, as well as the reality of the external world, exists only in the mind:

> The Brain– is wider than the Sky–
> For– put them side by side–
> The one the other will contain
> With ease– and You– beside–
>
> The Brain is deeper than the sea–
> For– hold them– Blue to Blue–
> The one the other will absorb–
> As Sponges– Buckets– do–
>
> The Brain is just the weight of God–
> For– Heft them– Pound for Pound–
> And they will differ– if they do–
> As Syllable from Sound–

The elaborate rhetorical devices, with balance and parallelism worked out to the last detail, give this such a logical structure as to make it more like a Euclidean theorem than a poem. But the images are memorable, particularly the final one. The mind's perceptions of reality, both spiritual and natural, are symbols; like the poet's words ('Syllable') they stand for the truths ('Sound') that can be grasped by it from outside. The effect of the poem is not to minimize the importance of God, or nature, but to magnify the value of the consciousness. 'It is solemn to remember that Vastness— is but the Shadow of the Brain which casts it,' she said elsewhere. So of the truth of immortality. Normally, it was enough for her that she had the idea. 'Heaven is so far of the Mind,' according to one poem, that if the mind were dissolved no architect could discover its site again; it is as 'vast' and as 'fair' as our idea of it, and for one with adequate perceptive powers: 'No further 'tis, than Here.' In a late prose aphorism she restated this idea, with a difference: 'Paradise is no Journey because it is within— but for that very cause though— it is the most Arduous of Journeys.' Her emphasis here is on the point that the heaven of this new faith is even more difficult of attainment than that of the old.

An imperious need to reorient herself in the universe is quite possibly what turned Emily Dickinson to writing poetry, just as in its deepest sense her withdrawal from the world may have been for the purpose of creating a religion she could live by. Her writings in prose and verse seem the record of such a search. Once, when temporarily deprived of her eyesight and so thrown back wholly on her inner world, she put her dedication in positive terms:

> The Only News I know
> Is Bulletins all Day
> From Immortality.
>
> The Only Shows I see—
> Tomorrow and Today—
> Perchance Eternity—
>
> The Only One I meet
> Is God— The Only Street—
> Existence— This traversed

> If Other News there be—
> Or Admirabler Show—
> I'll testify—

When her eyes were reopened to the world the old doubts assailed her again, but the explorations continued with unabated zest. When they engaged her full powers the results were invariably striking, in direct proportion to their ambivalence, for her religious experience was always more a seeking than a finding. Her final position may be summed up, that it is better to be in a state of unbelieving search than to accept a creed on the basis of habit or authority.

'The unknown is the largest need of the intellect,' she once said. In some verses written about the same time she tried to justify so many poems on the subject of heaven by calling it the most redoubtable mystery, the most fascinating 'Plot,' the mind can attempt to solve. Again, 'The Riddle that we guess/We speedily despise,' she began a letter to Higginson in verse, then continued in prose: 'The Risks of Immortality are perhaps its charm— A secure Delight suffers in enchantment— The larger Haunted House it seems, of maturer Childhood— distant, an alarm— entered intimate at last as a neighbor's Cottage.' But the passage concluded in an opposing key, 'even in Our Lord's "they that be with me where I am," I taste interrogation.' In midcareer she spoke to Samuel Bowles of 'the Balm of that Religion/That doubts— as fervently as it believes.' In a letter to her sister-in-law she made the paradox into an equation: 'Faith is *Doubt*,' and then reversed the emphasis in a late prose jotting: 'Doubt has the wisest men undone.' Lest vacillation be thought the sign of a small mind, she reminded Higginson that 'Hamlet wavered for all of us.' Near the end of her life she wrote to another intellectual friend, Judge Lord: 'On subjects of which we know nothing, . . . we both believe, and disbelieve a hundred times an Hour, which keeps Believing nimble.' With many great religious thinkers doubt is a constant ingredient of faith. These are the ones who know despair as well as ecstasy, and this is what keeps their believing 'nimble.' Such is the tension that marks the vitality of Dickinson's religious life and informs her best poems on immortality.

Whenever the formulas of conventional religion are invoked, the resistance of her inquiring mind rises to cancel them out or at least to balance them in a precarious equilibrium. Such is her strategy in an extremely interesting poem:

> This World is not Conclusion.
> A Species stands beyond—
> Invisible, as Music—
> But positive, as Sound—
> It beckons, and it baffles—
> Philosophy— dont know—
> And through a Riddle, at the last—
> Sagacity, must go—
> To guess it, puzzles scholars—
> To gain it, Men have borne
> Contempt of Generations
> And Crucifixion, shown—
> Faith slips— and laughs, and rallies—
> Blushes, if any see—
> Plucks at a twig of Evidence—
> And asks a Vane, the way—
> Much Gesture, from the Pulpit—
> Strong Hallelujahs roll—
> Narcotics cannot still the Tooth
> That nibbles at the soul—

Her private debate is framed by the public profession of faith, as in a church service remembered during her subsequent inner struggle to make this official belief personal. The poem begins with a resounding echo of the hymns she had sung out of Watts' *Christian Psalmody*. Heaven may be 'Invisible' but we hear it in the 'Music' of Sunday worship, answered at the end when 'Strong Hallelujahs roll.' Once again this positive assertion of belief is reinforced by her rare use of a period to punctuate the opening line, 'This World is not Conclusion.'—which lends an air of finality excluding all further discussion. But no sooner is a description of heaven attempted than doubts begin to proliferate, already planted in the second line by the scientific word 'Species' for the kind of world that stands beyond.

Following the initial quatrain each succeeding one modifies its flat statement of fact. (The poem clearly divides itself into five stanzas though there are no spacings to indicate this.) The structure of antitheses is set up by the fifth line, 'It beckons, and it baffles,' the two alliterating predications balanced on a fulcrum and weighted syllable against syllable. Throughout the center of the poem philosophy has usurped the role of faith, but the doubts are countered by a positive 'it' which continues to stand for the after life until lost in confusion at the end. 'Scholars' puzzle their heads here on earth because to solve the riddle of death 'Sagacity'—both mortal wisdom and sentience—'must go . . . *through*' the grave, presumably emerging vindicated on the other side. But to answer the questions raised by the rational mind requires something more than the calm assumption of immortality made at the beginning. The martyred saints of an earlier day bore the contempt of unbelievers, even to the point of crucifixion, because they were exalted by faith. Though this profound emotional assurance is exactly what has been missing from the poem so far, 'Faith' finally appears belatedly at the opening of the fourth stanza. But this shy young lady does not make a very dignified entrance into the august assemblage of scholars. She trips at the threshold, is covered with confusion ('Blushes'), fidgets with her hands ('Plucks'), and instead of offering any triumphant evidence asks the first inane question that enters her head. Can a weather vane, in default of a steeple, point the way to heaven today?

The last stanza is a final reversal of the first one, its quiet assertion having been gradually replaced by the noise of debate and then by the attempt to drown that out with rolling hallelujahs. But modern man is afflicted by doubts, and there is no drug to relieve his pain. 'Narcotics' is the sharpest epithet she ever applied to the sermons and hymns of an orthodoxy she found inadequate. The poem has moved steadily downward from a flat statement of belief to a confession of gnawing doubt that 'nibbles at the soul.' There is no attempt at a resolution of the debate, and this is the source of its special effect. There is even a suggestion that it has spread to the pulpit, where 'Much Gesture' implies too much for a faith that is firmly held, which adds a final irony. Such is the plight of the religious sensibility in an increasingly rational age, but the poet does not take sides.

A similar web of ambiguities was set up when she turned to traditional literary symbols for immortality, as foreshadowed in the poems on the worm-chrysalis-butterfly sequence discussed in an earlier chapter. For one who worked best in paradox it was most expeditious to stay strictly within the cocoon, and this maneuver produced her best poem on the silken cage:

> My Cocoon tightens— Colors teaze—
> I'm feeling for the Air—
> A dim capacity for Wings
> Degrades the Dress I wear—
>
> A power of Butterfly must be—
> The Aptitude to fly
> Meadows of Majesty implies
> And easy Sweeps of Sky—
>
> So I must baffle at the Hint
> And cipher at the Sign
> And make much blunder, if at last
> I take the clue divine—

Here, as in many of her finest poems taking off from a fact in nature, the cocoon is merely a conceit and the real theme is immortality. Similarly, the soul is locked in the body, during mortal life and to all mortal comprehension, though one may think he feels it tugging at the confining walls. True the metaphorical butterfly, in the second stanza, seems to escape in all its splendor and take wing to 'Meadows of Majesty.' But this is only an 'Aptitude' of the soul, not a known attribute. The poem does not offer an analogy confirming faith so much as a phenomenon in nature that raises the question: Is the body likewise only a cocoon from which there will be a glorious release? The poem is centered on the hope that the traditional butterfly 'must be' a symbol of the soul's power for flight. But words of doubt are scattered liberally through the opening and close: 'tease,' 'dim,' 'baffle,' 'blunder,' 'hint.' The tensions of unresolved conflict give the poem its strength. The concluding words are '*if* at last/I take the *clue* divine.'

Her search for new symbols of belief was as endless as the nibbling of old doubts was persistent. Being the kind of poet she was, she knew her best strategy was through the language of surprise, which might discover the meanings of her special religious experience. Once again she turned to the new scientific thought for effective terms to phrase her dilemma. For she was well aware that the supposed conflict between religion and science, which shook the Christian world at mid-century, dramatized the very real conflict between man's belief in immortality and his doubt of it. This split one of her best poems so irrevocably into two versions she could never decide which was her final choice. (See Plate II, p. 310.) Written several years apart, they have identical first stanzas but reach opposing conclusions in the second. In all collections of her poetry until the recent variorum edition, her editors have combined them into one poem of three stanzas, on the plausible grounds that they are parts of a larger whole she happened never to construct. Though there is no real authority for this familiar arrangement, it is a convenient one for launching a commentary and is temporarily adopted here:

> Safe in their Alabaster Chambers—
> Untouched by Morning
> And untouched by Noon—
> Sleep the meek members of the Resurrection—
> Rafter of satin,
> And Roof of stone.
>
> Light laughs the breeze
> In her Castle above them—
> Babbles the Bee in a stolid Ear,
> Pipe the Sweet Birds in ignorant cadence—
> Ah, what sagacity perished here!

* * *

> Grand go the Years— in the Crescent— above them—
> Worlds scoop their Arcs—
> And Firmaments— row—
> Diadems— drop— and Doges— surrender—
> Soundless as dots— on a Disc of Snow—

At first reading this seems like a structurally simple poem, each stanza self-contained, each giving a separate thought about the dead: the peaceful last sleep of the faithful, their exclusion from the world of the living, the possibility that they are swallowed up in the vastness of eternity. The poet stands on the earth's surface and looks down into the grave, around her at life, then up into the starry heavens. Stanza one gives a religious view of death, with a confident belief in personal immortality;

two, a humanist view of life in a world vibrant with sensations, but precariously enjoyed; three, a scientific view of cosmic peace achieved by extinction. But the several parts are intricately interrelated. At the beginning the possibility of immortal life is divorced from all wishful motivations, such as desire for reunion with the beloved, and made to stand on its own theological legs if it can. But this comes into conflict with the cold astronomical concept of eternity in the end. In between lies the poet's preference for the earth, signalized by the use of an exclamation point. Tension lines of irony, both within the stanzas and between them, complicate this simple structure by the strategy of verbal conflict.

The first stanza echoes the language of the Bible and of Protestant hymns, especially in the two long lines that establish with quiet assurance the coming Resurrection of the meek who lie 'Safe' in their 'Sleep.' But the short antiphonal lines undercut these orthodox affirmations of faith, by reminding that this is a cold white prison locking out the golden sunshine. As another poem proves, she could record with bleak accuracy the otherworldliness of her Puritan ancestors whose longing for heaven was such as to make them spurn the joys of this life. She even gave it a title, 'Country Burial,' suggesting that the old orthodoxy survived most narrowly in rural areas:

> Ample make this Bed—
> Make this Bed with Awe—
> In it wait till Judgment break
> Excellent and Fair.
>
> Be its Mattress straight—
> Be its Pillow round—
> Let no Sunrise' yellow Noise
> Interrupt this Ground—

The 'yellow Noise' of this world's sunrise they gladly rejected for that daybreak to come, far more 'Excellent and Fair.' But for herself she could not so easily renounce the Eden of this world. The gloominess of the older faith provoked her to irreverence in an early letter. After commenting on the impiety of mourning the death of the year as if there would be no spring, she exclaimed: 'Business enough indeed, our stately Resurrection! A special Courtesy, I judge, from what the Clergy say!

To the "natural man," Bumblebees would seem an improvement, and a spicing of Birds, but far be it from me, to impugn such majestic tastes.' Her treatment of the Resurrection is more responsible in the poem under consideration, though the emphasis is no more doctrinal than it is mortuary. She achieves objectivity by concentrating on the frozen expectancy of the tombstone, and irony by implying the skeletons beneath in terms of what they are deprived of. The peace of the grave, in one sense, results from the loss of sentience.

The second stanza spells this out with novel effect, by a linguistic strategy similar to her use of hymnal conventions in the first. The ecstasy of life on this earth is rendered in the banal language of popular literature, the poetry of the gift books: laughing breeze, piping birds, and babbling bees. But a few deftly placed words puncture the sentiment that this 'Castle' can be man's permanent home. Its sunshine was excluded in the first stanza. Now its sounds fall on 'stolid' ears that are as 'ignorant' of the bird's song as it is of them. These two words are sharply juxtaposed with 'sagacity' in the final line, standing for both the wisdom of living beings and, from its root meaning, their quickness of sense perceptions. For sagacity has 'perished' amid the emblems of life, and the green-gold-and-blue world evoked by them has been extinguished in the whiteness of death. Such was the original version of her poem. She thought well enough of it, apparently, to let her friend Samuel Bowles publish it in his newspaper (one of the very few poems to appear during her lifetime), where it was printed in the issue of 1 March 1862 with a title, 'The Sleeping.'

Yet six weeks later, when she sought a literary adviser in Higginson, she included among the poems sent for criticism a draft of the second version. When these two stanzas are brought together (the first and third as given above) a shattering question reverberates through the lines, especially if one bears in mind the 'Castle' of sunshine from the missing stanza. When sagacity has perished from this brightly colored earth, will it dwell in the white houses of death or in white cosmic space, 'Alabaster Chambers' or a 'Disc of Snow'? These two images are linked in much of her writing. 'White as alabaster' is used in a letter as a symbol of death, the snow that obliterates the life of the year in one poem is described as 'Alabaster Wool,' and when her mother died she used the image of a snowdrift for eternity: 'She slipped from our fingers like a flake gathered by the wind, and is now part of the drift called "the infinite."' In the present poem, while the humble dead 'sleep' in white silence in the first stanza the mighty dead 'surrender' and 'drop' in the last, 'untouched' by light at the beginning being echoed by 'soundless' at the end. The technical nicety of these concluding lines even suggests a falling snowflake. Both alabaster and snow are images of peace, but also of immobility and coldness. From the point of view of this world, the radiant world of the omitted stanza, they imply deprivation. Both are reinforced by royal attributes, 'Satin' at the beginning and 'Diadems' at the end, but only the sunny castle of the first version has warmth and human appeal. Life at its meekest is simply buried in the ground. Life at its most pompous, tottering thrones and the collapse of the most glamorous symbol of republican power in modern times (Napoleon's extinction of proud Venice), makes no impression on the blank cosmic immensity. On this earth, by implication, both had formerly shared the common glory of being alive.

Two clues in the final stanza, 'Crescent' and 'Disc,' seem ample warrant for an astronomical interpretation of its imagery. These words, in lieu of the old familiar phrase 'the dome of heaven,' suggest that Dickinson knew enough astronomy to be aware of the newer cosmology in her day: that the crescent-shaped Milky Way is what man sees when he looks upward from the earth's surface towards the furthest reaches of the universe, a crescent that would appear as a full disk if he were not an earthbound mortal limited to seeing only half of it at a time. There was a telescope in the Amherst College observatory through which she may well have stared in awe into its starry depths. For she had taken a course in astronomy at Mount Holyoke Seminary, and the textbooks used there had opened up this relatively new concept of the universe for her. More specifically, in a new encyclopedia added to the Dickinsons' library in 1860 the Galaxy is described as being shaped like 'a cloven disk.' Most pertinent to her poem was a little book by Felix Eberty, *The Stars and the Earth,* also in the family library, written for the avowed purpose of reconciling the latest scientific theories with religious belief. The picture of our universe he offered to her was that of 'a single lens-shaped canopy.' Then after a simple demonstration of how man, situated at its center, sees fewer stars when he looks out through the thickness of this disk than when he looks up towards its circumference, he continued: 'We may consider the Milky Way as the edge and furthermost limit of this set of fixed stars, where the infinitely distant crowds of stars are collected in such masses that their light flows together into a whitish cloud.' After pursuing his own contemplations as promised in the subtitle, 'Thoughts upon Space, Time, and Eternity,' to the effect that astronomy only adds to the vastness of man's conception of God, he concluded: 'We leave the further execution of the details ... to the poet.'

Probably taking off from this challenge, she created a trope for concluding her poem that would have startled the pious author. When 'Diadems drop,' she says, the souls of the mighty dead disappear in interstellar space 'Soundless as dots– on a Disc of Snow.' The Transcendental concept of death as the individual soul merging with the Oversoul was cheerless enough put in the abstract. In her poem, made concrete by an astronomical metaphor, it is chilling. By implication, the same destiny awaits the meek dead in stanza one. The small comfortable Puritan faith in a personal resurrection, with which the poem begins, is not pursued but simply allowed to hang in the air as a point from which to measure the cold immensity of infinite space and unending time, the comfortless view brought in by the new science. In his famous chapter on the meaning of whiteness, Melville had said of the Galaxy: 'Is it that by its indefiniteness it shadows forth the heartless voids and immensities of the universe, and thus stabs us from behind with the thought of annihilation, when beholding the white depths of the milky way.' As man's concept of the universe has continued expanding into an endless series of universes, in a time-space relationship that is ungraspable by the average mind, this view has grown even bleaker. One of the distinguished philosophers of today, in an essay on modern man's shrunken capacity for worship, concludes that 'all the labors of the ages, all the devotion, all the inspiration, all the noonday brightness of human genius, are destined to extinction in the vast death of the solar system.'

This is the direction towards which her poem moves. 'Science will not trust us with another World' was her explicit comment in a late letter. This does not mean that she, for her own part, trusted science on such a theme as immortality, any more than she could subscribe to the doctrine of a literal Resurrection. As a poet she felt no compunction to take sides between reason and faith. She merely used the conflicting ideologies of science and religion in her day as the materials for art, not to work out a philosophy. Here they furnish her with symbols, 'Alabaster Chambers' versus a 'Disc of Snow,' that render a poetic meaning without arguing it. 'Sleep the meek members of the Resurrection' is thus the key line that gives tension to the whole poem. Rather, in terms of the actual state in which the manuscripts have survived, it provides the contrast in the first version between what is in the grave and what is outside, physical death waiting to be raised up to immortality and mortal life perishing. In the second version, it provides the contrast between 'Safe' orthodox believers and lost modern man, though by one minute change in the opening stanza, 'Sleep' to 'Lie,' she reduced the chances that they will ever wake to a new life. It is only by comparing the two poems that the final contrast is brought out, between the brief life of 'sagacity' on earth and the change that comes with death, whether Resurrection or extinction. That she never made up her mind between the two, or composed them into a single three-stanza poem, is one of the disappointments encountered in reading a private poet.

Though immortality cannot be grasped by either theology or science, it can at least be rendered poetically as an aptitude of the soul, if the right images are found and maneuvered adroitly enough. Her best efforts are limited to this more modest end. In a poem subscribed 'Easter,' signifying the title or the date or possibly the pseudonymous author, she delivered herself of a strange symbolic sermon on the mighty theme:

> Those not live yet
> Who doubt to live again—
> 'Again' is of a twice
> But this— is one—
> The Ship beneath the Draw
> Aground— is he?
> Death— so— the Hyphen of the Sea—
> Deep is the Schedule
> Of the Disk to be—
> Costumeless Consciousness—
> That is he—

The first four lines announce her quasi-Biblical text, aiming it directly at doubters; the last two substitute for the conventional homily a startling pronouncement for the comfort of believers. All that lies between is her exegesis, written in a cryptic form of discourse, which if fathomed will initiate all who have ears to hear into an understanding of her special kind of faith. The 'scriptural' lesson itself is clear enough: those who doubt immortality are not even alive during their mortal existence. This is followed by a doctrinal correction: one must not say 'live *again*' for there is only one everlasting life; man carries his immortal soul with him from birth and does not live 'twice,' once in this world and again in the next. 'There is no first, or last, in Forever,' she once put the same point in a letter. Her poem about immortality is thus a poem about the continuity of 'Consciousness,' the term she explicitly uses at the end. And all three images centered between illustrate her concept of the one continuous life.

What makes them disconcerting at first is their seeming disparity. Perhaps the very illogic of this sequence—'Ship,' 'Hyphen,' 'Disk'—reflects her belief that immortality can only be conceived in flashes, metaphors thrown up at random, rather than by some rational ordering of argument. Yet, though discrete on the surface, they are subtly fused in that each is an unexpected image of burial as an illusory gap between existences. The first is put as a query. When a ship is seen from a distance passing through the narrows between two bodies of water, 'Draw' being used in its colloquial sense, it appears to have run aground half-buried in the land. This optical illusion, suggesting the confines of a grave, exactly matches the mortal perspective of death which seems to doubters simply a burial in the earth. But, 'Aground— is he?' Believers would answer with a resounding No. The second drops the ship image for the sea. Death is a 'Hyphen of the Sea,' a mere formal sign placed between the terms mortality-immortality, connecting them even while it seems to separate them. This has also been read as her image for the link between the river of life and the sea of eternity. 'So,' in the seventh line, does make a fleeting reference back to the preceding metaphor of the strait of death, through which the everlasting waters might be thought of as continuing to flow if one could only see 'beneath the Draw.' (The Greek root of *hyphen* actually carries the meaning of 'under.') With a little forcing it could be said further that the soul-ship is not really 'aground' but waiting momently for the tides to bear it out into the unfathomable eternal ocean. The 'Disk' in the baffling final image would then become the moon, controlling the tides in their 'Schedule' by some mysterious force. But by this time the meaning of her language has been made to wander off into uncharacteristic vagueness, for the moon has no connection with immortality and there are no tides actually in this poem.

Most attempts to push Dickinson into the Metaphysical School do violence to her text, as for example by treating these three images as the elaboration of a single conceit of the soul's voyage. In view of her proven precision with words, it seems best to keep them separate here, as she does, however bizarre the sequence may seem. Burial in the earth is merely the illusion that a mortal ship has run aground; the grave is a hyphen-sign which if read aright connects the two phases of the life everlasting; and the last figure is a still different way of simultaneously symbolizing the illusory quality of death and her certainty of some kind of survival. The image she uses here, as a matter of fact, is the well-known one of the setting and rising sun, though rendered as a cryptic notation ('Deep is the Schedule/Of the Disk to be'). No matter how deep its 'Disk' plunges into the earth, or sea, this is the necessary condition for its rising again, on a 'Schedule' that is 'Deep' in the sense of being profound, since it is the absolute measure of time. Or rather, since this motion too is an optical illusion, it is the necessary condition of its eternal repose, the sun's setting and rising being the result of mortal myopia. 'Disk' is also her metaphor for eternity in a vaster astronomical sense, as in her poem on 'Alabaster Chambers' and in another describing the heavenly circumference as 'the Stupendous Vision/Of His Diameters.' But more pertinently here it is the sun as a traditional image for the risen Christ, as her subscription 'Easter' calls to mind. Man's promise of a similar Resurrection she made the theme of an ambiguous quatrain written a few years later:

> Obtaining but our own Extent
> In whatsoever Realm—
> 'Twas Christ's own personal Expanse
> That bore him from the Tomb—

Easter, indeed, but with a difference. In the poem under consideration, she concludes with a more affirmative kind of unorthodoxy than this ambivalent epithet for heaven, 'whatsoever Realm.' Resurrection in the flesh may have been necessary for the doubting Thomases of old. But when she points ecstatically, 'That is he,' to the continuous life of her ship-hyphen-disk, she uses a surprising abstraction for immortality, 'Costumeless Consciousness.' This was a long way from the doctrines that prevailed in conservative Amherst.

She was well aware how heretical her speculations sounded in orthodox ears. 'Austin and I were talking the other Night about the Extension of Consciousness, after Death,' she reported in a letter of the same period, concluding: 'Mother told Vinnie, afterward, she thought it was "very improper." She forgets that we are past "Correction in Righteousness." ' The flippant tone here is only because of the impassable gulf she always recognized between her own beliefs and such literal ones as her mother's. She could turn the same concept into a serious statement of a new kind of faith: 'How unspeakably sweet and solemn— that whatever await us of Doom or Home, we are mentally permanent. "It is finished" can never be said of us.' Several years earlier, shortly after her father's death, she had written: 'I dream about father every night, ... wondering where he is. Without any body, I keep thinking. What kind can that be?' These passages from her letters confirm the reading of 'Costumeless Consciousness' as her shock image for immortality. During its earthly life the soul is visible because it wears 'corporeal clothes,' as she said elsewhere, but it is not finished when it sinks in the grave except for those who doubt. At death it merely discards its 'Overcoat of Clay,' its 'Sod Gown,' to borrow phrases from still other poems, and continues its everlasting life, dimly visible to the faithful and capable of being rendered metaphorically by the believing poet. The soul's essence does not change in its transition from one mode of existence to another, from mortality to immortality. Such is the meaning of all her imagery in this remarkable poem.

Another traditional symbol of immortality, and of deity as well, is pure light. It has both classical and Christian authority, but the latter is clearly the source of its use in a large number of her poems, associated as it frequently is with the opposite concept of darkness for the mortal state. She was familiar with its prominent place in Biblical writings, as for example in the Epistle of John: 'God is light, and in him is no darkness at all,' and in the Book of Revelation: 'The nations of them which are saved shall walk in the light.' In her churchgoing days she had quite likely sung from Watts' *Psalmody*:

> Though all created light decay,
>   And death close up our eyes;
> Thy presence makes eternal day,
>   Where clouds can never rise.

She did not normally equate the earthly life with darkness, far from it. But she made use of this as a dramatic contrast with the beatific vision to work out an interesting cluster of images in which night, often specifically midnight, stands for mortal existence, dawn for death, and noon for eternity.

The first two stages of this sequence appear in an early poem, one of a group using the figure of Bride-of-the-Lamb as the attainment of the immortal state. 'At Midnight, I am but a Maid,' she said, and then triumphantly: 'A Wife— at Daybreak I shall be.' The second and third are combined in the letter on her nephew's death, voicing her confident belief in his simultaneous translation to heaven: 'Dawn and Meridian in one.' For the last stage, her finest use of noon as the zenith of the soul's fulfillment begins like a hymn in praise of the dazzling light of the eternal day:

> There is a Zone whose even Years
> No Solstice interrupt—
> Whose Sun constructs perpetual Noon
> Whose perfect Seasons wait—
>
> Whose Summer set in Summer, till
> The Centuries of June
> And Centuries of August cease
> And Consciousness— is Noon.

The traditional symbolism of pure light informs this poem, but it is made strikingly new by complicating it with her unique theory of the mind's entrapment in time as the essence of the mortal condition, rather than the conventional one of the spirit imprisoned in the body. Since heaven is out of time it exists in 'perpetual Noon,' the point at which the 'soul' of a stopped clock escaped from its dial-life, in another poem.

Immortality is here envisioned as an escape from the seasonal as well as the diurnal clock into a 'Zone' that is timeless and motionless. To render the stasis of eternity she sets it against the terms of earthly flux, 'Solstice,' 'Seasons,' 'Summer,' and the whole cycle of hours around the dial. There such temporal divisions cease to function, and since its years are all 'even' they cannot be counted in 'Centuries.' Eternity is not only eternal summer, 'set in Summer' rather than in a changing year, but also 'perpetual Noon,' unmeasurable by any man-made timepiece. At first blush this seems indeed like an attempt to go beyond the limits of judgment. But she describes timelessness strictly in the accepted terms for reckoning human time, by naming these terms and then denying their applicability, without inventing new ones for a state mortal man cannot experience. Besides, such a zone is a well-established astronomical fact. When the mind removes itself theoretically from the surface of the rotating earth, the sun ceases to measure years and hours and one's speculation is quite simply out-of-time. The only leap beyond knowledge is in the last line, 'Consciousness– is Noon.' Yet even this makes perfect poetic sense, not as proof that costumeless consciousness does survive but as another metaphor for its ineffable qualities, if one has faith in its survival. In the motionlessness of eternity there will be no distinction between the soul and its setting, between perceiver and perceived. Just as the sun's disk sets only to rise again in visible splendor, so the soul's disk sinks only to rise again according to a schedule unfathomable from this side of the grave. But in the cosmic zone they will blaze indistinguishably. The pure light of noon will be both the immortal consciousness and the beatific vision. Her own faith, again beginning with an orthodox image, is expressed at the end in a most unorthodox way.

A final poem, the most impressive of the cluster and one of the finest she ever wrote, develops this light-dark imagery in a highly original way:

> Behind Me– dips Eternity–
> Before Me– Immortality–
> Myself– the Term between–
> Death but the Drift of Eastern Gray,
> Dissolving into Dawn away,
> Before the West begin–
>
> 'Tis Kingdoms– afterward– they say–
> In perfect– pauseless Monarchy–
> Whose Prince– is Son of None–
> Himself– His Dateless Dynasty–
> Himself– Himself diversify–
> In Duplicate divine–
>
> 'Tis Miracle before Me– then–
> 'Tis Miracle behind– between–
> A Crescent in the Sea–
> With Midnight to the North of Her–
> And Midnight to the South of Her–
> And Maelstrom– in the Sky–

The pure light of immortality shines behind this poem though it never fully materializes in the text. Taking advantage of an orientation traditional in her civilization, she looks back towards the east as the source of all light and life, glances towards the west as the soul's ultimate destination, then fixes her attention on the dark span that lies between. The first is transformed into her image of death as a 'Dissolving into Dawn,' the coming light of the heavenly life as the earthly one dies out. Yet this stanza has the tone of dealing with assured fact, for she is describing what she sees 'Before the West begin[s].' Over the horizon behind 'dips Eternity,' the timelessness before her consciousness existed; over the horizon in front looms 'Immortality,' the future timelessness into which her consciousness will survive. Her gaze is for the moment so fixed on these two radiant zones she has no words for the mortal existence she actually knows. This is lightly bypassed as the 'Term between,' the allotted three score and ten years of man, too insignificant to warrant further description now.

The central stanza presents an unabashed apocalypse, but she is careful to assign an anonymous authority for it, 'they say.' Having achieved the proper poetic distance by this device, she can then indulge in a vision of what it will be like 'afterward.' The language of royal estate in the succeeding lines conjures up the well-known picture of heaven as a 'Kingdom' in the Book of Revelation. The single word 'Dateless' suggests the eternal day of Christian sermons and hymns, but also her unique image of 'perpetual Noon,' the zone to which she will escape when she goes 'out of Time.' The over-image is entirely original. It is one of eternal repose in this 'perfect— pauseless Monarchy,' rendered superbly through the hypnotic repetition of sounds, both by alliteration and identical words:

> Himself— His Dateless Dynasty—
> Himself— Himself diversify—
> In Duplicate divine—

The triple use of 'Himself' faintly suggests the Trinity, but this hint of orthodoxy is undercut by the assertion that the heavenly Prince is 'Son of None.' This phrase surprises the ear, which would have expected the words of incarnation 'Son of Man,' and shocks the doctrinal mind that bases its faith on the literal birth of the 'Son of God' out of the trinitarian godhead. But in her poem He is son of none other than Himself, the internal rhyme being the phonetic counterpart of the idea that follows: her affirmation of multiplicity in unity and changeless change, without motion and without end. The words duplicate themselves even as He eternally duplicates Himself, and the King is one with both His 'Dynasty' and His 'Kingdoms.' These lines may well represent her greatest success in finding the words to that one thought she despaired of ever being able to express. Yet she shrewdly says them through another voice, not even admitting her costumeless consciousness into this part of the poem to behold her transcendent vision of immortality.

The concluding stanza does not deny this vision but relegates it to the status of 'Miracle,' something beyond mortal knowledge. It returns instead to the unfinished business of the first stanza, recapturing its tone of assurance by repeating its structure and word pattern but completely reversing its emphasis. The earthly life, there passed over as a mere 'Term between,' now becomes her whole concern, specifically described as 'A Crescent in the Sea.' This is the perfect counter-image for the dateless, pauseless, motionless perfection of the immortal vision. The restless surging of the sea and the perpetual changes of the moon represent a return to the world of flux. There may be some implication that this crescent, though a conventional symbol of mutability, will fulfill itself as a disk, reflecting the light of that mightier disk that makes perpetual noon. But the inversion that puts the moon in the sea and the whirlpool in the sky suggests instead a world of hopeless confusion. This is compounded by another reorientation. For the poet has turned in a new direction, away from the east-west axis of eternity-immortality, and faces toward the poles of her own planet. All she can see now is 'Midnight to the North of Her' and 'Midnight to the South of Her,' centers of mortal darkness instead of the miracles of light that lie beyond the horizons. The pronominal shift from 'Me' to 'Her' at the end might seem like a grammatical slip, but it actually represents a shift in perspective. The aspiration towards immortality at the beginning naturally led the poet to a personal emphasis, but as this vision fades she becomes the impersonal representative of the common lot of man. Even as she turns her eyes upward there is only 'Maelstrom– in the sky,' a nightmarish chaos in place of the cosmically ordered universe of stars that mirrors the 'perfect Monarchy' of the immortal world. Such is the 'Term between,' the poet's mortal life, which in the main comprises the world of her poetry.

The very shape of this poem, in a sense, symbolizes the pattern of all her best work. Its fine symmetry is achieved by balancing the certain change of death in the first stanza against the uncertain changes of life in the third, with irony in the echoing words and repetitive structure, and in between the attempt to rise into the splendid motionlessness of eternity. So in the rest of her poetry. Whichever pole she began with she found it intricately related to the other—death or life, the outer world of forms vanishing as the inner world comes to life in the consciousness. And both were starting points for her ascent to immortality, whether in the paradise of art or the other paradise.

The final direction of her poetry, and the pressures that created it, can only be described as religious, using that word in its 'dimension of depth.' As defined by one of the truly creative theologians of the twentieth century, Paul Tillich, this differs widely from what is conventionally understood by the term: it means 'asking passionately the question of the meaning of our existence, . . . and of *being* universally, . . . even if the answers hurt.' It is not necessarily connected with the creeds and activities of particular institutions dedicated to belief in the existence of God and devotion to His service. Indeed, many people who have been grasped by this infinite concern feel themselves far removed from historical religion because of its inadequacy in expressing their concern: 'They are religious while rejecting the religions.' Loss of the dimension of depth in religion, Tillich feels, is the result of modern man's estrangement from his world and from his self. As a consequence, the great religious symbols by which this concern has been expressed in Western civilization have lost their power. It is notable that this religious thinker concludes by finding painters and poets are the ones most sharply aware of the human predicament today—as revealed in their themes, their styles, their imagery—the ones most passionately searching to recover this lost dimension by revitalizing the traditional symbols or creating new ones that fit the particular modern dilemma. This is precisely the purpose of Dickinson's explorations of the self and external nature in her poetry, often beginning with Biblical language and metaphor, then transmuting these into new forms through the creative power of words, to render her experience of what it means to be human.

Another representative philosopher of our times, A. N. Whitehead, in describing the decay of religious values under the impact of science, fill out this area of relevance in her poetry for readers today. Religion will never regain its old power, he feels, until it can face change in the same spirit as science does. Noting that no belief can be contained permanently in the same mold, he emphasizes the need to 'preserve the life in a flux of form,' especially in an age when religion is degenerating into a mere formula to embellish a complacent society. Though Whitehead's own attempt at redefinition is offered diffidently, it has real pertinence to the present inquiry. 'Religion is the reaction of human nature to its search for God,' he says, and since this is chiefly manifested as worship, 'The worship of God . . . is an adventure of the spirit, a flight after the unattainable.' Then more fully:

> Religion is the vision of something which stands beyond, behind, and within, the passing flux of immediate things; something which is real, and yet waiting to be realized; something which is a remote possibility, and yet the greatest of present facts; something that gives meaning to all that passes, and yet eludes apprehension; something whose possession is the final good, and yet is beyond all reach; something which is the ultimate ideal, and the hopeless quest.

The most effective formulations of this quest, he also concludes, will come from the imagination of the artist rather than from philosophical or theological thought. And it is notable how closely his own definitions fit the creative vision Emily Dickinson tried to fix in her poetry. These modern analogies should make clear what is meant by the claim that she is a religious poet.

Her great talents, to be sure, are those of a highly original sayer, not a seer. To set this emphasis right one more analogy will be cited in conclusion, the literary one used at the beginning of this book. If significance in literature can be measured by the quantity of metaphor thrown up, as Henry James believed, then her poems on death and immortality represent the summit of her achievement. The novelty and brilliance of her imagery in these last two chapters are memorable. Within the context of the individual poems, old and new symbols are maneuvered by the language of surprise so as to illuminate the two profoundest themes that challenged her poetic powers. This reveals her kinship with another article of James' esthetic faith: if the creative writer pushes far enough into language he finds himself in the embrace of thought. By slant and surprise, by wit and a novel reworking of traditional modes, she evolved a way with words that became her instrument of knowing. Committed to nothing but dedicated to a search for truth and beauty, hers was a free spirit for whom living was a succession of intense experiences and art an endless exploration of their meanings. A poet rather than a systematic thinker, she never came up with dogmatic answers. Indeed her most effective verbal strategy was to exploit ambiguity, as in the conflicting attitudes towards her flood subject Immortality.

In her personal life, as well as in her poetry, alternating doubt and belief held her mind unresolved to the very end. Her next to last letter, according to the dating by her editors, was a brief note to Higginson: 'Deity– does He live now? My friend– does he breathe?' The very last letter she ever wrote, addressed to her Norcross cousins just before her death on May 15, 1886, was also her shortest: 'Called back.' And the smallest bit of manuscript that has come down, measuring one half by one and a half inches, records in her latest handwriting: 'Grasped by God.' The true ordering of these undated jottings can probably never be known, nor what her last words were on this mighty theme. But this is of no importance here. Her personal faith and the final destiny of her soul lie outside the bounds of a book concerned exclusively with her creative achievement. The tensions that created the great poems had been relaxed. In them, at least, she gained some measure of immortality. And in them she exemplified the travail and the fulfillment that Emerson ascribed to the bardic 'Merlin':

> He must aye climb
> For his rhyme ...
> But mount to paradise
> By the stairway of surprise.

APPENDIX

1 EMILY DICKINSON

The essential Emily Dickinson, the poet who should be the modern reader's chief interest, is now at last accessible in the six volumes of her collected writings. That 'life' has been the concern of the preceding chapters. The other Emily Dickinson, the figure familiar in Amherst a hundred years ago, is not so easy to know today. She kept no diary or other account of her outer history. Her letters were rarely concerned with straightforward autobiography. And since she enjoyed no fame during her lifetime little has come down in the way of those pen portraits and reminiscences by contemporaries that bring alive more fortunate authors. During the first half century after her death, gaps and obscurities in the record were filled in by hearsay, guesses, and deliberately fabricated legends. But several recent biographical studies have corrected all this, and taken together they establish with reasonable certainty the main outlines and most of the important facts in her career. These can be set down here in a summary sketch for those unacquainted with her life.

The world into which Emily Dickinson was born in 1830 was as propitious for a good life as it was unfavorable for a poetic career. It was remote from the great centers of culture, inhospitable to radical ideas and art, all but bare of literary companionship. But it offered her a high measure of economic security, social position, and devoted family life in a stable and attractive New England township. Her family on both sides was well connected throughout the region and prominent in local affairs. Their prestige in this provincial setting was roughly equivalent to that of the 'Brahmin' families in Boston society.

Edward Dickinson, the father, was a leading citizen during the long years of his active life. A graduate of Yale, he became a prosperous lawyer who provided amply for his household. As a civic-minded man he entered effectively into all phases of village affairs, as a pillar of the church, treasurer of the college, sponsor of a project that brought the railroad to Amherst, and so on. His outstanding abilities also took him beyond village limits, to the legislature of Massachusetts and to the national Congress for one term. In his stern sense of duty and the unbending integrity of his character he was a somewhat formidable man, but the notion of him as a repressive figure is largely the result of misreading his daughter's wit. He was, however, a dominant personality and one of the strongest shaping forces in her life. The mother image is more shadowy. All that comes clear in the picture of Emily Norcross Dickinson is that she was a simple woman with few interests beyond the domestic. She was sick a good deal, and a year after her husband's death in 1874 she was paralyzed by a stroke that left her a complete invalid until her own death seven years later. She seems to have been a rather ineffectual person, with little influence on the lives around her.

There were three children in the family, with Emily in the middle. Her brother Austin, only eighteen months her senior, was an intimate companion during the first twenty-five or thirty years of their lives, sharing with her an interest in books and ideas that tended to break with the conventions of their little world. In his outward life he followed in many of Edward Dickinson's footsteps. Educated at Amherst College and the Harvard Law School, he also became prominent as an attorney and as a supporter of the local church and college. Unlike his father, however, his interests included art and literature, and he had a lively personality as well as a flexible mind. Some years after his marriage in 1856, though he lived next door, intimacy between the two households slackened but not Austin's devotion to his gifted sister. Lavinia Dickinson, three years younger, was also close to Emily throughout her life. Like her Lavinia remained unmarried and, except for occasional visits, spent all of her life at home. The bond seems to have been purely sisterly, for though she had some reputation for wit there is little evidence of a community of interests outside family affairs.

In Austin Dickinson's wife, Susan Gilbert, Emily felt that she had found another sister, closer kin in spirit than any of her blood relations. For a number of years, beginning about 1850, no other friendship meant so much to her. Enchanted by her vivacity and her enthusiasm for reading, she made 'Sister Sue' a confidante of her poetic life, sending her in all between two and three hundred poems, far more than to any other person. This outpouring provided her with an encouraging audience if not a helpful critic. It also gave added zest to her life. But her sister-in-law was mercurial in temperament and she herself possessive. Differences arose between them, and their attachment suffered frictions and finally serious strain. The intensity of this friendship in the middle years and its zigzag course in the later are pertinent facts for an understanding of Emily Dickinson's poetic career, but the reasons for its decline are not and they are too complex to be entered into here.

With all allowances for clashes between personalities, the Dickinson family was a remarkably close-knit clan. It is indeed surprising that there was so much harmony in such an intimate circle. This extended beyond the immediate household to uncles, aunts, and cousins. The Dickinson house on Main Street, a small-scale brick mansion situated in spacious grounds on the edge of Amherst, was the homestead to which all the kin returned for renewal of family ties. This was the setting where Emily Dickinson acted out the whole of her life (except from her tenth to twenty-fourth years, when the family occupied a house on Pleasant Street). It was also a center of village hospitality, especially during the twenty years prior to Squire Dickinson's death, and frequently attracted prominent visitors from the larger outside world. Local ministers, professors, political figures and business promoters of the region were welcome here, and as time went on the circle was extended to include statesmen of larger caliber, judges, visiting lecturers at the college, leading journalists and magazine editors, even an occasional author. It was a stimulating group if not a notable one.

In childhood and youth Emily Dickinson enjoyed the usual experiences of friendship, though even then marked by the extraordinary intensity of her nature. There were exchanges of mutual devotion with relatives, especially with her two young Norcross cousins, sentimental friendships with schoolmates, comradeship with the young people of the village. None of these are important for the student of her poetry except indirectly: as recipients and preservers of her letters they offer proof of the normalcy of her early years. At maturity she had several attachments with young men, like that with a student in her father's law office, Ben Newton, who first guided her interests in literature, but none of them ripened into love. As she gradually passed into the status of spinsterhood, withdrawing more and more from a gregarious life, the important friendships of her career began to develop, all with people somewhat older than herself.

The first and longest lived of these was with J.G. Holland and more particularly with his wife, whom she called affectionately 'Sister.' A widely known journalist and writer of popular books, he was after 1870 the editor of *Scribner's Monthly*. A far closer friend than Dr. Holland and more stimulating as an intellectual companion was Samuel Bowles, editor of the Springfield *Republican,* which under his direction became one of the most influential newspapers in the country. He was a man of great mental vigor, wide interests, and unusual personal charm. Her lifelong friendship with both of these couples enriched the years of her seclusion by keeping her in touch with the world she had rejected.

Her most important literary friendship was with T.W. Higginson, inaugurated in 1862 by her request for criticism of her poems and continuing for nearly a quarter century, exclusively by letter except for two personal meetings. He had a varied career as minister, crusader for liberal causes, and professional man of letters. In her correspondence with him one finds most of her comments on art and on her own poetic career. But though he provided an audience of one, he never understood her mind or her poetry and clearly advised her against publication. (With Emerson and James unavailable, what contemporary would have understood her better?) She herself was by temperament a private person, aware of the revolutionary nature of her poems and offended by the editorial liberties taken with the few that found their way into print. The failure of Higginson to respond to her shy overtures was probably what finally persuaded her not to seek a public audience. Less influential on her as a poet was her only other literary friendship, the renewal in her last years of a childhood acquaintance with Helen Hunt Jackson, who had become widely known as a poet and novelist. The chief significance of this brief intimacy was the fact that a successful woman author (*Ramona* climaxed her career in 1884) admired her work and asked to be her literary executor.

The tenor of a large group of Emily Dickinson's poems coupled with the fact of her seclusion, has led to much speculation that she must have had an intense but thwarted love affair. One revelation has been recently made that is substantiated by evidence. A dozen surviving letters, written to Otis P. Lord between 1878 and 1883, indicate that she was very much in love with him and that the affection was returned. He was judge of the Supreme Court of Massachusetts at the time, a distinguished and unusually attractive man. But he was almost a generation her senior (one of her father's best friends), the attachment began late in her poetic career, and it never materialized though it undoubtedly brought her great joy.

The other person widely accepted as a man she was in love with was the Rev. Charles Wadsworth, pastor of a Presbyterian church in Philadelphia throughout her maturity, except for the years 1862-70 when he was in California. The facts about their relationship are all obscure and the evidence indirect or speculative, but there seems good reason to believe that this was an attachment of great importance to her. He was much older than she, however, apparently happily married and unaware of her adoration. On her side it is difficult to say whether the image she cherished of him was that of lover, muse, or spiritual guide. Her own phrase was simply, 'My closest earthly friend.' The record of their few meetings and exchanges of letters is tenuous in the extreme. But her devotion to him seems to have reached its crucial point at the very period when she withdrew from the outer world and dedicated herself to poetry; the major crisis in her life coincided with his departure for the West and her recovery with his return. It is unfortunate that a relationship of such potential significance should remain so dark. One might venture that an equally good case could be made out for Samuel Bowles as the hopelessly beloved man in her life, on the basis of circumstantial but suggestive evidence in the letters. One might further note that he had the most attractive personality of all her friends, the spirit most congenial to her own ('the most triumphant Face out of Paradise,' she said), and that he was the nearest in age. All of the others, including Higginson and Holland, were old enough to serve in the role of surrogate fathers. At any rate, these cherished friends are the ones that loom largest in her correspondence and throw the most light on her poetic career.

Up to the age of about twenty-five, Emily Dickinson's outward life followed the usual pattern for a New England village girl of the times, filled with school and friendships, church and parties. Her formal schooling, appropriate to a young lady of her position, consisted of six years at the Amherst Academy and one as a boarding student at nearby Mount Holyoke Seminary. Short as this period was, ending at the age of seventeen, it gave her a good basic education, especially in languages and sciences. In addition to a little French and German she received excellent training in Latin, and learned more than a smattering of Mathematics, Botany, Chemistry, and Astronomy. But she is chiefly remembered for her English compositions, her lively personality, and her writings for the school paper. For several years thereafter she was the leading spirit in a group of Amherst young people who read and discussed books, had a Shakespeare club, and explored the neighboring fields and forests as ardent nature lovers. Naturally, they also enjoyed considerable social life. There were dances, sleigh rides, Valentine verse-writing games, and the parties centering around college Commencement and the autumn fair or Cattle Show. All the testimony pictures her as a popular and outgoing member of this circle of friends. In such healthy and happy activity there is little sign of the future recluse.

Though she participated in all aspects of village life, she had little experience of the world beyond its limits. As a young lady she had visited Boston, where she enjoyed some of the advantages of city life, and about the age of twenty-four she made an extended trip to Washington and Philadelphia, combining sightseeing and the diversions of a more sophisticated society. But this was all—except for rare trips to see a friend in a neighboring town and two more visits of about six months each in 1864-65 to Boston, where she was confined to her cousin's home while taking eye treatments. For the rest, she spent her entire life in Amherst.

As one by one her young friends married, she withdrew more and more from an active part in village life. Somehow love and marriage passed her by, or she by-passed them, though there is evidence of a normal desire for them in several letters written in her early twenties. By 1854 she was refering to herself as quaint and old-fashioned and showing many signs of timid withdrawal, as when she declined an invitation to visit with 'I dont go from home, unless emergency leads me by the hand.' By the time her active career as a poet began, presumably about 1859, her tendency to seclusion was marked, and by 1869 it was complete: 'I do not cross my Father's ground to any House or Town.' But the stages by which she became a recluse were so gradual, as revealed in the new chronological arrangement of her letters, as to take much of the eccentricity out of such behavior. Certainly she herself was only dimly aware of how far her retreat was going to take her, and her contemporaries apparently accepted it by slow degrees as a familiar phenomenon. Yet the completeness of her final withdrawal—first to the village, then to her home and garden, in the end even avoiding calls from intimate friends—was such as to make it the most talked-of aspect of her life today and the springboard of many sensational legends. The most persistent and most romantic of these is that she turned away from the world because of a frustrated love, but there are simply not enough facts in the record to prove or disprove this.

Other explanations are possible. Perhaps modern theorizers, forgetful of village customs a century ago, have failed to take into account the fact that maiden ladies then were not considered eccentric because they stayed at home. Deprived of an escort they gradually made fewer public appearances. And within the home they often had a central place, managing the household, keeping in touch with kin and friends by correspondence, nursing the sick, sending flowers and delicacies to neighbors. Emily Dickinson was increasingly occupied with all these tasks. Her devoted service to family alone kept her busy, as she reported in 1869: 'I am so hurried with Parents that I run all Day with my tongue abroad, like a Summer Dog.' Again, her retirement might be thought of as an extreme extension of the clannish tendency in the Dickinsons, all of whom clung to each other and to home because, as she put it, 'We're all unlike most everyone, and are therefore more dependent on each other for delight.' The quality that drew them together also made them independent of the world outside. Finally, there was the artist's desire for privacy which, in a highly conventionalized society, always appears to some extent abnormal but is widely tolerated unless it takes an extreme form. As an unmarried gentlewoman she could not retire like Thoreau to Walden Pond. Instead, like Emily Brontë at Haworth, her only recourse was seclusion in her own home, which gave it undue emphasis by contrast with the surrounding clatter of village life.

It is quite another matter to deny her the claim to normalcy within the poet's license, even though she felt it necessary to be a poet all the time. It has been suggested with some cogency by her most recent biographer that there was deliberate self-dramatization in her behavior, that withdrawal was 'a device for staging her appearances before the world,' her life like her art being planned with careful strategy. But her eccentricity consisted largely in not doing what others did, rather than in any affirmative acts, though she did carry this to an extreme that is marked even among artists. Her rejection of society may have been gradual but in the end it was total. Her sensibility was such that she felt compelled to conserve her response to experience, since human encounters drained her energies. Hers was a flight from the events of living into the perception of intensely felt life, a deliberate economy of thought and emotion in order to focus on her inner world of values.

Such complete renunciation of the world and dedication to the life of the spirit was the traditional mode for certain religious orders in the Middle Ages. One is tempted to go the whole way and say that Emily Dickinson too was a religious recluse, devoting herself after the age of thirty almost exclusively to a pursuit of spiritual truths, like the nature of the soul and its chances of survival—to announce dramatically that the beloved of her poems is none other than God. But this would be an oversimplification. The terms of such an analogy need translation for a more secular age. The image in her poetry wavers between a celestial and an earthly lover, and the orthodox belief in immortality tends to be transmuted into the conviction that her spirit will endure in her poems. How far such ambiguities are peculiar to her, rather than deeply based in all religions, it is difficult to say. But it can be said without hesitation that she is the most profoundly religious poet this country has produced, though it was the esthetic rather than the moralistic aspects of religion that concerned her, the discipline of art replacing the rituals and doctrines of a church. More than any of her contemporaries, in America at least, she found poetry her only way to the spiritual life. After all qualifications have been made, the medieval concept of the holy life is a useful analogy for understanding both her withdrawal from the world and the poetry made possible by it.

The outer story of her religious life is amply told in her letters and is summarized in the final chapter of this book, where its pertinence to the poems is greatest. The briefest sketch will have to serve here, especially of her struggle with the problem of church membership which took place between the ages of fifteen and twenty-five. The role of organized religion in the life of a provincial New England town was still paramount in her day, and it was certainly a shaping influence on her career. Calvinistic orthodoxy, firmly established in the Connecticut

Valley from the beginning and given a special emphasis by Jonathan Edwards, remained entrenched there until the middle of the nineteenth century and beyond. The forces that were bringing about the gradual dissolution of Puritanism had been at work in urban areas like Boston for more than fifty years. When they finally reached secluded places like Amherst, as a revolution in thinking already accomplished, the old and the new were brought into dramatic juxtaposition. This turning point in religious history, so sudden and unlooked for as to be unrealized by all but the astute, coincided with the maturing of Emily Dickinson.

The pressures of evangelism were first brought to bear upon her in a crucial way at the age of seventeen, when a revival swept the seminary at Mount Holyoke, lasting through most of the fall term. The momentous fact is that she, almost alone among the students, definitely drew back from commitment. During the next few years as the wave of revivalism continued unabated she kept up her resistance, though with a distressing sense of anxiety as sister, father, and brother, each in his own way, yielded to the emotional fervor and joined the church. In her twenty-fourth year she made the final decision not to align herself with the orthodox establishment, and though she continued to attend church services sporadically until about the age of thirty, she never became a member.

Put in such bald outline her conduct might seem headstrong, but her poems bear testimony to a deeply religious nature that simply had to go its own way. She had thought at first that her intransigence was the result of spiritual inadequacy, her inability to give up the world for Christ. In the end, however, she renounced the world as few others have ever done. What she was unwilling to give up was the living spirit for the dry husks of doctrine embodied in the old theology, and she distrusted the lasting value of evangelical conversion. She found her true church in the creation of poetry, a continual act of spiritual discovery and renewal for her. It cannot be mere coincidence that her break with orthodoxy, her withdrawal from the world, and her dedication as a poet all followed each other in such close sequence during the period between 1854 and 1859. Then came the creative floodtide, more than a thousand poems in the next six years. In so far as this biographical pattern can be established, it supports the clear evidence of the poems themselves: that a search for religious truth, using that term in its dimension of depth, was the mainspring of her life as well as of her art.

The striking contrast between her meager life and the richness of her poetry raises a final question: How did such varied and profound understanding come out of such limited experience? One fumbles in vain at the biographical record in an attempt to discover the sources of her wisdom. There is little if any evidence that she attended concerts, went to theatres and operas, visited museums and art galleries. Most of her literary contemporaries, from Henry James to minor figures like Higginson, had access to these institutions of culture such as to make her residence in Amherst seem 'benighted' in the extreme, to use her own word. Yet one poem, sometimes a single line or a glancing reference in a letter, will testify without need of further proof to her precise understanding of some aspect of ballet, the higher criticism, mathematics, music, or Venetian painting. Her formal schooling, with whatever differences, was just about equivalent to that offered by a modern high school. In comparison with what Longfellow enjoyed it seems elementary and provincial, yet somehow she learned God's plenty.

Her education was greatly extended by reading, of course, for hers was a bookish household, at least by local standards. But the hundred or so books and authors mentioned in her letters do not make an impressive list. There are as many trivial as there are significant ones, and the references are usually so sidelong it is difficult to tell what they might have meant to her. This reading can be supplemented, conjecturally, by the list of books in the Dickinson family library as it was made available many years after her death. It contained in the neighborhood of a thousand volumes, a sizable collection for that time and place, but it offered thin nourishment for a mind like hers. The bulk of it falls in three large areas: religious and theological works of an orthodox sort, books of travel, and popular didactic fiction. From the rest may be culled another hundred or so volumes that she could have read with profit. There are only a few philosophers present—St. Augustine, Bacon, Locke, Plato, Dugald Stewart—and of these only one or two seem pertinent. There is some history and biography, a sprinkling of the older classics of literature, and a majority of the leading American and British authors of her own times. But except for a few volumes inscribed or dated on the fly-leaves, it is impossible to tell which of these books were a part of the family library during her lifetime.

If from all the evidence available one attempted to name the chief potential influences from her reading, the Bible and Shakespeare would stand out above all others; then would come Emerson, Thoreau, George Eliot, the Brownings and the Brontës; finally, the 'metaphysicals,' though her actual references are limited to Herbert, Vaughan, and Sir Thomas Browne. Even with these one finds a kinship of spirit rather than anything specific. A painstaking study of all possible sources might yield more than one would suspect. But, though she was a keen and discriminating reader, the best informed guess is that no poet was ever less indebted to books. By comparison many of her literary contemporaries were erudite, not only writers like Adams and Melville but such as Lowell, who had the range of a library beyond any she ever dreamed of. Yet true wisdom comes by a subtle chemistry not to be measured statistically, and hers outshone all but a few of them because she had one of the finest poetic minds of the century. It will not be assayed by the source hunter or the biographer, but by the close student of her poetry.

'Biography first convinces us of the fleeing of the Biographied,' she remarked near the end of her life, probably intending the double meaning. Not only has the body died, but the spirit that inhabited it eludes the biographer. What can be recovered of the person who was Emily Dickinson has been made available in half-a-dozen excellent studies, and is summarized here. But her essence, real as opposed to nominal, was embodied in her writings—she makes clear her belief on this point. To discover that, and to understand it, has been the purpose of this book.

2 A NOTE ON THE TEXT

With Emily Dickinson's poems, the achievement of a text which is both definitive and readable is beset with unusual difficulties. A brief summary of their publication history will provide the best introduction to this problem. At her death in 1886 she left nearly two thousand poems of which only seven had been published during her lifetime, and even these without her supervision. The undifferentiated mass of her manuscripts ranged from the most incomplete to apparently 'finished' compositions, but none of them had been really prepared for the printer. To the normal problem of deciphering handwriting was added the handicap of a complete lack of dates and titles, and above all the peculiarity of her system of notation in regard to punctuation, capitals, and the like. The task confronting her editors was formidable. In the decade of the 1890's three slender volumes of her poems, less than five hundred in all, were selected and published. During the following half century the rest of them found their way into print in a bewildering series of installments, edited by several hands and with varying degrees of accuracy and bowdlerization, though with one notable exception (*Bolts of Melody,* in 1945). It was not until 1955 that this deplorable state of the texts was rectified by a complete scholarly edition of the poems. The alterations of previous editors, long thought of as confined to smoothing a meter or regularizing a rhyme, now appear more serious than had been suspected. For in addition to misreadings of her handwriting, they involved deliberate changes in wording, mechanics, and arrangement that affected meaning—all through well-intentioned efforts to make the poems more acceptable to the reading public. But the Harvard Edition brought order out of this chaos. Within the covers of these three volumes Thomas H. Johnson provided the standard texts of 1775 poems, reproduced from the original manuscripts as exactly as scrupulous editing and the limitations of the printer's font made possible.

Readers rejoiced that the chief handicap to reading Emily Dickinson was overcome at last, by having the poems just as she had written them. Yet even as the jubilation sounded discerning critics saw that another obstacle loomed large, the problem of how to read a 'private poet.' For what meets the eye in these pages seems even more idiosyncratic and difficult to evaluate than in the texts familiar for over half a century. The causes of non-publication during her lifetime concern only the biographer, but the results of it concern everyone who tries to read her poetry. The inescapable fact is that she did not prepare any of her manuscripts to meet the publisher's stylebook. An honest confrontation of the resulting problems will be the purpose of the following pages.

When private writings are brought into print after the author's death, they tend to make a strange appearance on the page in several ways if not adjusted to formal usage. Some of these difficulties are without remedy, such as her failure to supply titles for her poems. That she may well have done so had she sought a larger public is suggested by her referring to a number of them by title when enclosing them in letters to friends. Her first editors bravely made up this deficiency, but this seems too presumptuous today. Modern practice is against such creative editing even if it means putting up with minor inconveniences, an occasional initial obscurity, and the awkwardness of referring to the poems by first lines (or by the official numbering in the Harvard Edition). A simpler matter to rectify would seem to be her misspellings. Though artists are notoriously indifferent to what they consider minor matters (she once remarked casually, 'Orthography always baffled me'), publishers are inclined to make them toe the line. But some of her apparent misspellings are simply old-fashioned forms like *begun,* for the past tense *began,* and others preserve the local pronunciation like *boquet;* these were undoubtedly part of her deliberate strategy for speaking, as well as seeing, 'New Englandly.' There are not many in all, and it seems better to leave in an occasional slip (without the obtrusive *sic*) than to risk tampering with her idiom. One allied error has been corrected silently throughout this book, her invariable spelling of *it's* for the possessive pronoun *its,* to avoid any risk of misreading her meaning.

Another irregularity is more disturbing to the reader, her apparent waywardness in the matter of stanza division and line arrangement. It shows up clearly since the basic pattern of her verse is well known to be the quatrain, though she plays endless variations on the long and short hymn meters that served as her point of departure and return. All this is discussed in Chapter 1 of the present book as it relates to her poetic art, but what must be reckoned with here is the appearance on the page of a certain wildness as the result of breaking these forms. Certainly one must respect her preference for separating the quatrains into stanzas, grouping them in larger units, or running them solid as one poem with no divisions, as the manuscripts dictate. But consider the poem 'Safe in their Alabaster Chambers,' where three metrically identical quatrains are broken into 6-5-5 lines respectively, each in a different way (see p. 270); in another manuscript, consisting of the first and third stanzas only, the first is regrouped as 5 lines (see Plate II); in yet another, the third is broken into 8 lines (see Plate III). Is this conscious experimentation or sheer indifference to form? Any temptation to rearrange this lineation according to a standard pattern, merely because one cannot follow her intentions, is countered by other poems where one can prove such irregularities are a part of her strategy of meaning. For example, in 'A Clock stopped–/Not the Mantel's,' both the first and last lines are cut in half with a shock effect that turns the mechanistic figure into a conceit for death (see p. 235). Again, in 'I read my sentence steadily,' the climactic quatrain is drawn out into a long couplet to underscore the agony of a soul in despair (see p. 204). When I could find meaning in these irregularities I have included them in my interpretations; when not, I have passed them by without comment. Purposeful or wayward, there is not enough unorthodoxy of line and stanza arrangement in the preceding pages to constitute a blemish except in the eyes of the fastidious. As concession to convention, in a very few poems some minor irregularity of this sort has been corrected if it is obviously a careless slip without significance, as where she begins one line without a capital or where she spaces the fourth line of a quatrain so as to make it appear as a separate stanza. But these are rare exceptions, and the corrections are duly pointed out in the notes.

There are two final idiosyncrases in the manuscripts—her apparently capricious use of capitals and dashes—which must be seriously considered as flaws that may call for editorial alteration. (The few texts not showing these characteristics are those of the 122 poems not surviving in manuscript, which had to be reproduced from other than original sources.) They have troubled all commentators on the Harvard Edition, including the editor himself. Johnson holds to a literal transcription for his own scholarly text, as demanded by the chaos he was rectifying; but then he adds: 'Quite properly such "punctuation" can be omitted in later editions, and the spelling and capitalization regularized, as surely she would have expected had her poems been published in her lifetime.' This simple formula becomes difficult to apply, however, as soon as one faces the method of such regularization and its possible results. In seeking the wisest solution I have turned for counsel to the most thoughtful essays prompted by the Harvard Edition.

R. P. Blackmur sees the next need as a text for readers of poetry, to supplement the variorum text for scholars, but he immediately recognizes the difficulty of 'finding within the general conventions of printing a style of presentation which will furnish a version conformable to the original notation which the poet employed.' The dashes may have been consistent in her practice, he points out by way of example, but she did not evolve enough of a system to indicate what they mean, grammatically and dramatically. Then Blackmur puts his finger deftly on the prime qualification for an ideal editor, which makes the possibility of finding one truly formidable: 'he must learn to notate the voice which in intimacy he has learned to hear' as well as notating 'what he has learned to understand.' A second critic, Newton Arvin, probably expresses the initial reaction of many when he declares that it is 'simply destructive of poetic pleasure' to read her poems in their present form, and then calls for a text edited by a poet-critic 'printed with the normal spelling and punctuation.' But he adds, parenthetically, 'unless when the other really matters.' There's the rub. Where is the editor who can decide for all readers when her peculiar dashes and capitals 'really matter'?

A more direct confrontation of the problem is made by two other commentators. Austin Warren, in a detailed analysis of the dashes in one poem, makes out a convincing case that although some are used in place of commas or semicolons, others mark the pauses of suspense or anticipation and still others are equivalent to the 'phrasing marks of music.' He concludes:

> I analyze this specimen to show both the oddity of Emily's pointing and also the difficulty of repunctuating it in any fashion which does not constitute an interpretation. . . . The best method I can propose is to omit—after the fashion of some contemporary poetry—all punctuation, or all save that of the period: a method which would not, in any case I can summon up, obscure the comprehension of her poetry.

But this seems more an evasion than a solution. If the over-all effect of the dashes is to reproduce the pauses in her own reading of the poems or to give the clauses and phrases 'a fluidity of transition' which would be lost by 'a rigid system,' as he says elsewhere, will these qualities be preserved by no-system?

Similarly, in setting forth the problems of a reader's text, J.C. Ransom recognizes the need for 'hard decisions' in order to bring the informalities of the manuscripts into line with modern standards of printing. The future editor, though sensitive to her notation, will yet have to reckon with certain conventions:

> He will respect those capitalizations, I think, even while he is removing them. They are honorable, and in their intention they are professional, and even the poet who does not practice them must have wanted to; as a way of conferring dignity upon his poetic objects, or as a mythopoetic device, to push them a little further into the fertile domain of myth. The editor will also feel obliged to substitute some degree of formal punctuation for the cryptic dashes which are sprinkled over the poet's lines; but again reluctantly, because he will know that the poet expected the sharp phrases to fall into their logical places for any reader who might be really capable of the quick intuitional processes of verse.

Even while preparing to dispense with these unique features of her poetry, he thus offers some of the most eloquent suggestions ever made as to their special value.

Ransom then proceeds forthwith to a sample editing of ten poems, 'altered with all possible forbearance.' In the matter of punctuation he is surprisingly conventional, merely substituting commas, semicolons, and periods for the dashes, except in a few instances where the dashes are simply omitted. This 'improvement' in mechanics is curiously circular, restoring the text almost exactly to its earliest state in the Todd-Higginson editions of the 1890's. Although it cannot be said that any of these alterations change the basic meanings of the poems, they do eliminate the very modulations he admired as one of the effects of her 'sharp phrases.' But her capitalization is even more an object of fascination for him, and his treatment of it deserves close attention. In the famous poem 'Because I could not stop for Death' (see p. 241), he omits all the capitals except five. Death, Immortality, and Eternity one might expect him to retain, as traditionally capitalized abstractions. But if he keeps 'Setting Sun' and 'House' (grave), why not the other symbols for death: 'carriage' (hearse) and 'gown' (both shroud and heavenly bridal robe in one)? In another well-known poem, 'The Soul selects her own Society' (see p. 170), he reverses his percentages and keeps all of the capitals except two. This is confusing enough in itself, but if words like 'Majority,' 'Chariots,' 'Door,' and 'Stone' are to remain capitalized why not the other two also, 'gate' and 'valves,' the last being the key image in the poem? Ransom's system is as baffling as Emily Dickinson's.

All of these poets and critics are agreed that something should be done, but they disagree as to the method and extent of the alteration needed. Yet where would one find more sympathetic or more objective counselors? Many attempts have been made in the past to regularize her punctuation and capitals, and they remain distracting to the reader today. (See, for example, 'I went to Heaven,' p. 256, a poem of only fifty words but with twenty-three dashes and eleven capitals not counting sixteen capitals at the beginning of lines.) But with each-man-his-own-editor, the texts would simply be returned to the chaos from which they have just emerged. These eccentricities in her art, as those in her life, have also provoked violent reactions, pro and con. Some have cherished them, making a cult of her oddity; others have been irritated by what they consider her downright perversities. Neither extreme is likely to lead very far into the poems. In default of an ideal editor or of some way to arrive at an 'official' compromise for the reader's text, both unlikely, it seems wisest to accept these flaws as inevitable in the legacy of a private poet. When her poems are put into print either they must be adjusted to the conventions the public is accustomed to, or readers must be asked to adjust to the poet's eccentricities, with some initial discomfort. I have chosen the latter course, trusting that those who really care about her poetry will gradually accommodate themselves to it on its own terms without demanding an 'improved' text.

For all such alterations would be in effect interpretations, however slight. Her special use of capitals and dashes was beyond question meaningful to her, part of her defiant experimentalism, seeking to break loose from formal mechanics as from all other formalities. (See p. 61 for her complaint about editorial tampering with her punctuation.) Had she herself come to terms with the publisher's stylebook, the resulting typography might have achieved clarity without losing uniqueness, as with the texts of G.M. Hopkins and e.e. cummings. But in working from the manuscripts of a private poet who left no clues, one can only guess at the meanings of her innovations. Like Blake, who used private symbols as if they were self-evident, Emily Dickinson capitalized a great many words apparently in an effort to express some special attitude towards them as entities. None of the older conventions explain her usage, for she did not always so emphasize important words nor limit her capitals to the abstract and general as was the practice of Sir Thomas Browne, an author she was familiar with. The most fruitful conjecture seems to be that capitalization was her way of conferring dignity on certain poetic objects in order to push them up into the domain of myth, her way of deliberately playing with magnitudes in irony or in earnest. But how can one interpret them with confidence?

As for punctuation she made little use of the standard marks, such as commas and periods, but relied mainly on a variety of pointings that will be called dashes for the sake of convenience. Their function cannot be explained by the rule of separating grammatical units, for they break them as often as not, coming between subject and verb as well as between predications. Indeed, one of the purposes of her dashes may be to underscore her unorthodox syntax, for it is clear she broke the rules deliberately to achieve special effects. (This strategy is not always successful nor is its effect always demonstrable, but when it is I have commented on it in the preceding chapters.) Certainly her dashes are not mere impressionistic signs for pauses and emphases. In their apparent consistency and the hints of meaning that come through to an attentive ear, they seem more like an attempt to create a new system of musical notation for reading her verse. All the forms she derived from had been sung—hymn, ballad, Mother Goose Rhyme—as was pointed out in Chapter 1. Perhaps her meanings, too, would profit from a surer knowledge of the inflections and speech tunes she intended. Many readers will be tempted to make their own interpretations of these signs, but in the present state of knowledge there is no real clue to her system and it seems presumptuous to be dogmatic.

Similarly, all those who go back to the manuscripts, as Johnson did, will be tempted to make their own transcriptions of her handwriting. For it often shows several degrees of bigness from small letters to capitals, as though she were discontent with the standard division into two classes, so that categorical decisions by an editor are often impossible. For example, in the manuscript of 'Safe in their Alabaster Chambers' (Plate II) note the words beginning with *s* and *c* and compare their renderings as capitals or small letters in the standard text (p. 270). In the sequence Safe-Satin-Stone-Snow one could argue that there are four different sizes; or is this simply the casualness of private composition? Again, in addition to standard length dashes (—) there are elongated periods (-), angular commas (,), stress-marks (ʋ), dividing verticals (ı), and numerous other variations of length and slant (see Plate I). It is impossible to say positively whether such differences are accidental or deliberate, and if the latter, what they mean. Though there is certainly some arbitrariness in the reduction of all these variations to a uniform use of capital and short dash, as in the Harvard Edition, that text has been followed to avoid confusion since no more satisfactory compromise could be devised. But the interested reader of Emily Dickinson's poetry should pore long over any manuscripts or facsimiles available in order to familiarize himself with the appearance of her poems exactly as she posted them to posterity.

Finally, one suspects that her unorthodoxies in mechanical matters are related to her experiments in more basic poetic techniques, though this is not often easy to prove. The broader aspects of her theory and practice are not included here, since it is unprofitable to discuss techniques abstractly and unrelated to their functioning in specific works of art. Instead, they are treated in the opening chapters of this book, where they can be illustrated in the analyses of her best poems. There, in connection with these larger issues, I have tried to point out whenever possible the relevant meaning of her punctuation, capitals, and those other devices that give her poems their special appearance on the page.

POEM FACSIMILES

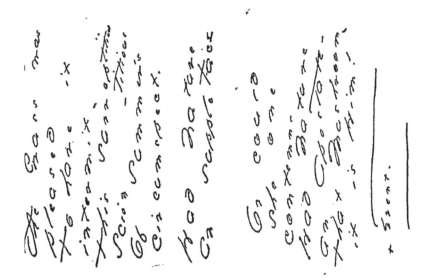

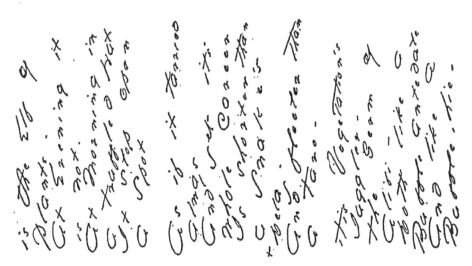

Plate I. Punctuation. The pointings, of various length and slant, are standardized as dashes in the Harvard text, page 123 above. (Manuscript in the Amherst College Library.)

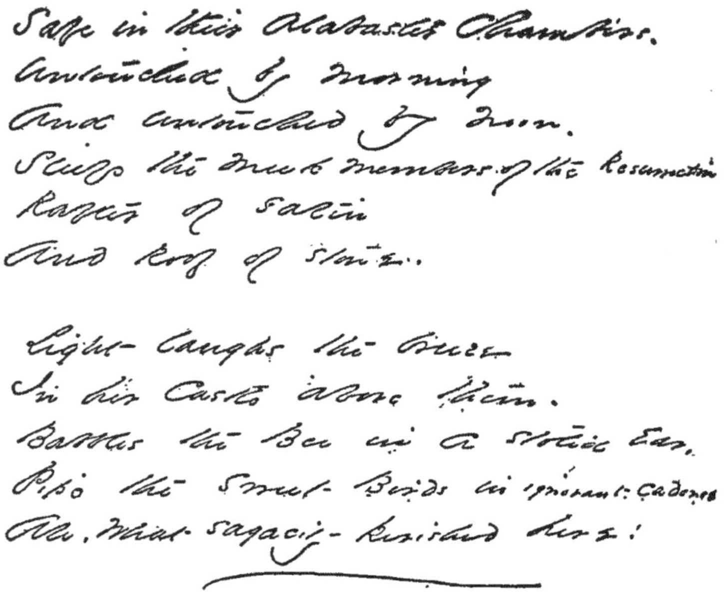

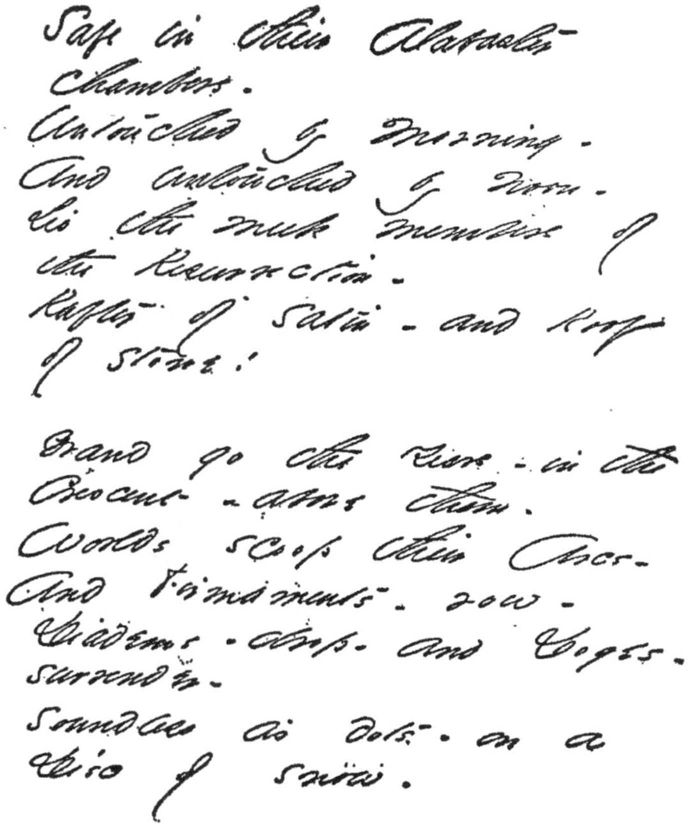

Plate II. CAPITALS. Note the words beginning with s and c and compare the Harvard text, page 270, above. (Manuscripts in the Houghton Library, Harvard.)

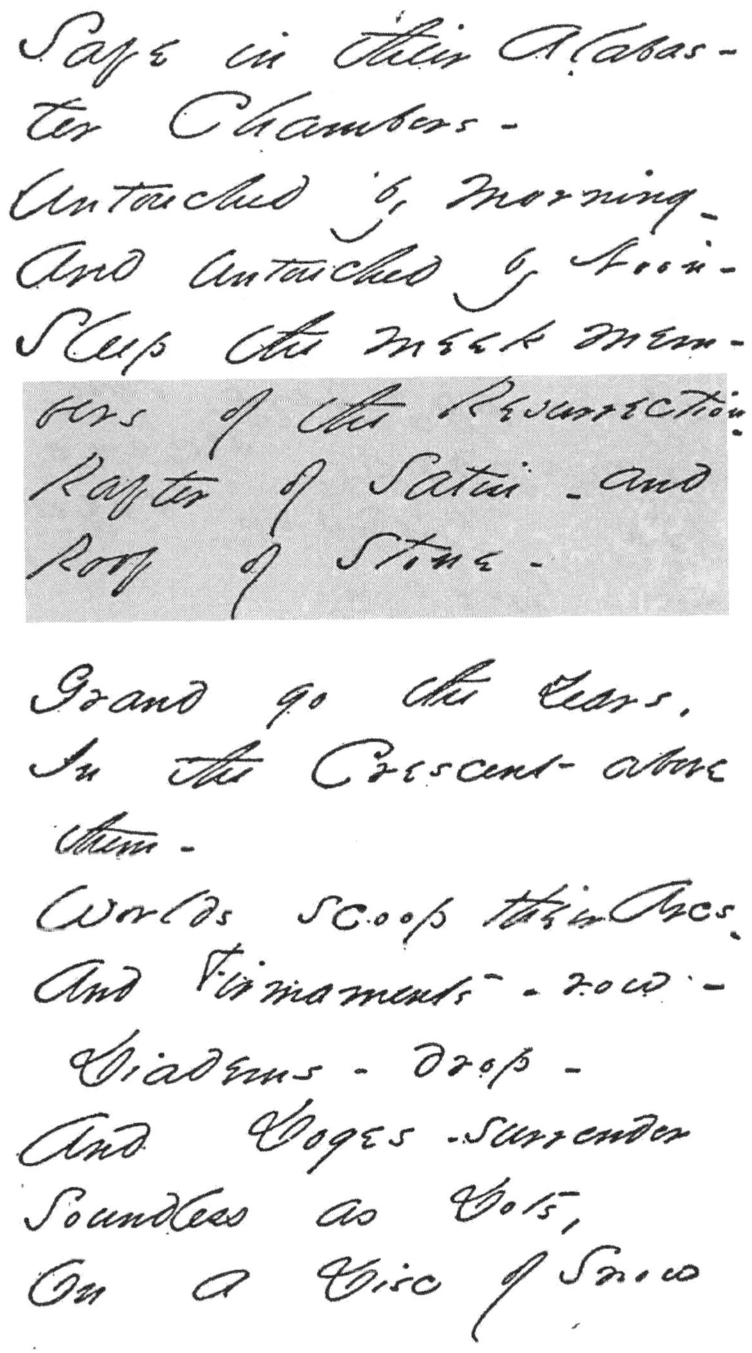

Safe in their Alabas-
ter Chambers -
Untouched by morning -
And untouched by Noon -
Sleep the meek mem-
bers of the Resurrection
Rafter of Satin - and
Roof of Stone -

Grand go the Years,
In the Crescent - above
them -
Worlds scoop their Arcs,
And Firmaments - row -
Diadems - drop -
And Doges - surrender
Soundless as dots,
On a Disc of Snow

Plate III. Lineation. Note that stanza one is divided into five lines and stanza two into eight lines here, but into six and five lines respectively in the versions on Plate II. (Manuscript in the Boston Public Library.)

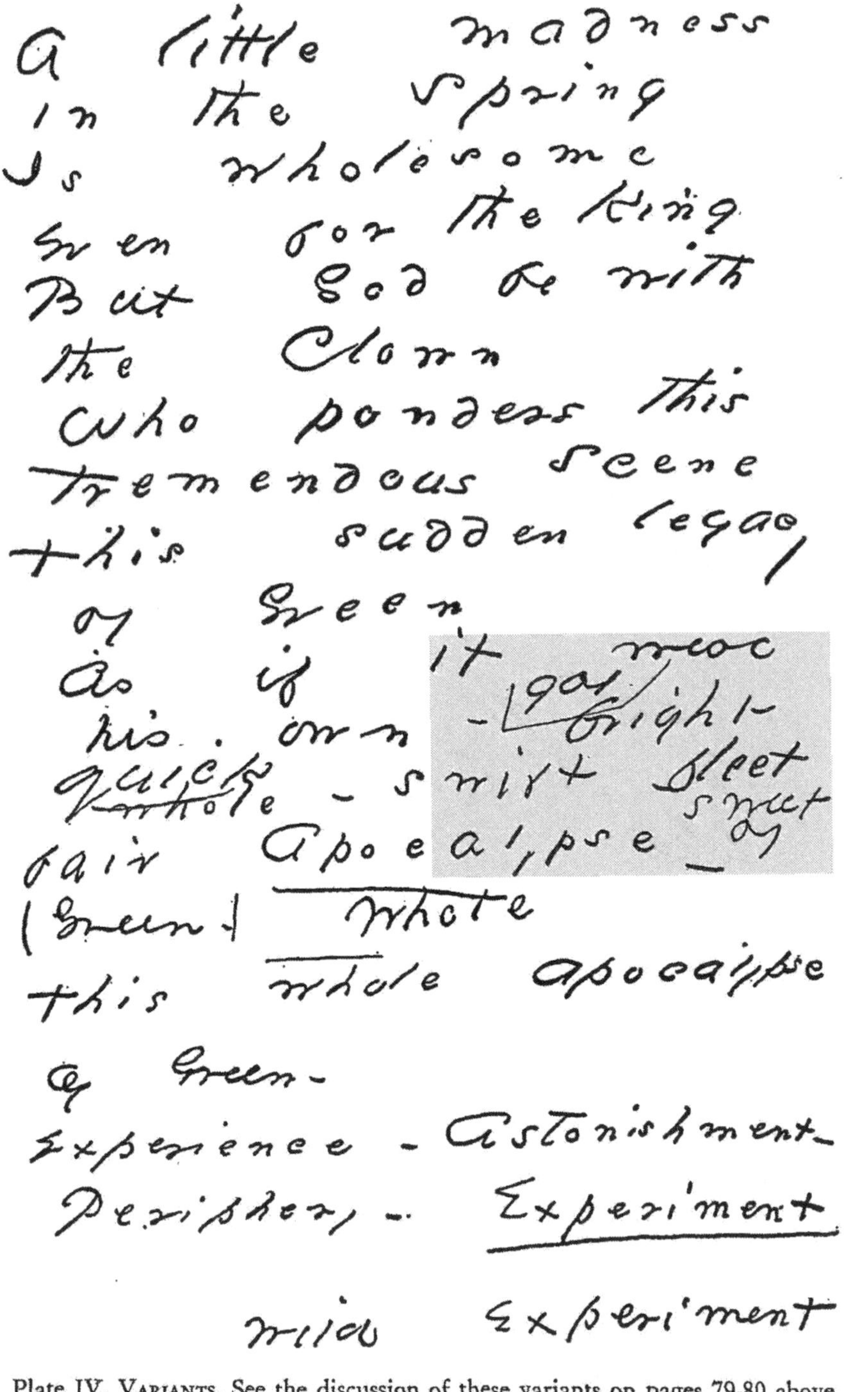

A little madness
in the spring
Is wholesome
Even for the King
But God be with
the Clown
Who ponders this
Tremendous scene
this sudden legacy
of Green
as if it were
his own
quick — smirk fleet
fair Apocalypse —

(Green) whole
this whole apocalypse
of Green —
Experience — Astonishment
Perishery — Experiment

wild Experiment

Plate IV. VARIANTS. See the discussion of these variants on pages 79-80 above, and compare the printing of them in the Harvard Edition of Poem No. 1333. (Manuscript in the Amherst College Library.)

312

NOTES

ABBREVIATIONS

ED	Emily Dickinson
P- (or *Poems*)	*The Poems of Emily Dickinson* (Harvard University Press, 1955), 3 vols., edited by Thomas H. Johnson
L- (or *Letters*)	*The Letters of Emily Dickinson* (Harvard University Press, 1958), 3 vols., edited by Thomas H. Johnson
PF-	'Prose Fragments,' printed as an appendix to *Letters* (1958)
Bianchi	Martha Dickinson Bianchi, *Emily Dickinson Face to Face* (Boston, 1932)
Bingham	Millicent Todd Bingham, *Emily Dickinson's Home* (New York, 1955)
Chase	Richard Chase, *Emily Dickinson* (New York, 1951)
Johnson	Thomas H. Johnson, *Emily Dickinson: An Interpretive Biography* (Cambridge, Mass., 1955)
Tate	Allen Tate, *The Man of Letters in the Modern World* (Meridian, 1955)
Whicher	George F. Whicher, *This Was a Poet: A Critical Biography of Emily Dickinson* (New York, 1939)

From the very nature of this book it had to be an independent study, for the most part. I have read everything that has been published on ED, to the best of my knowledge, in order to increase my understanding of her; but very little of it is concerned with a close reading of her poems. In addition to a general debt to my predecessors, I gratefully record a few specific debts in the following notes. References have been kept to a minimum by citing only those that proved helpful. In the interests of conciseness I have used a shortened form for those items listed in the table of abbreviations (opposite); also I have omitted the publisher and place for book titles, except when they were necessary to identify a particular edition, and the volume and page for magazine articles.

My greatest debt is to the poems and letters of ED, and citation of these constitutes the bulk of my notes. The texts of the Harvard Editions have been followed verbatim, with the qualifications noted below. They are referred to by the initial letter, P- or L- (and PF- for 'Prose Fragments'), followed by the official numbers assigned them in those editions. In a very few cases slips in mechanics have been corrected, but always with an explanation in the notes. In a few other cases my transcriptions from the MSS (which I have consulted when available) differ in slight particulars from the Harvard text, again duly noted. A more important matter concerns the fairly large number of poems that exist in more than one version, or with variant words at the bottom of the page. Since there is no evidence for ED's final preferences, I have felt at liberty to choose the text that struck me as best, though in no instance have I made a composite one out of two or more MSS. My choices are indicated in parentheses following the citation. When no such indication is made, the text used is the one printed first in the Harvard Edition. (But it must be remembered that these initial texts, though printed by Johnson in larger type, take no precedence over the others, being merely the 'earliest fair copy.')

The notes that follow are cued to the preceding pages of this book by page number and key phrase: the first line for poems; the last words of the quotation for letters; and several of the most important words for references other than the identification of quoted matter (as, for example, in the notes to the Preface).

NOTES FOR THE PREFACE

x Which text . . . preferred? See examples cited in *Poems*, I, xxxiv-xxxvi, lxi.

xii The chronological arrangement The dating in the Harvard Edition has been adopted when pertinent to my discussions, but with two warnings: (1) though probably as good as can be achieved (since none of the MSS are dated), it is only approximate, being based largely on the evidence of handwriting; (2) it is not an arrangement in the order of composition but a conjectured chronology of the known MSS, many of which may have existed in earlier drafts now lost.

xiv challenge to modern readers No previous book has been devoted exclusively to her poetry. Those by Chase, Johnson, Wells, and Whicher include some general commentary on the poems along with much biography; the other half dozen or so have been concerned with biographical and historical matters only. In the compendious *Literary History of the United States* (1948, 3 vols.) by Robert Spiller, et al., separate chapters were allotted to 25 American authors, but ED was not one of them. When the major American writers of the 19th century were chosen for treatment in a collaborative bibliography by Floyd Stovall, et al., *Eight American Authors: A Review of Research and Criticism* (1956), ED was not included.

NOTES FOR CHAPTER 1: 'WIT'

4 Locke•Essay Concerning the Human Understanding, chap. XI, 2. A copy of the 1768 edition was in the Dickinson family library, now at Harvard.

4 Eliot•Selected Essays (1932), 252, 254.

4 'hate to be common' L-5.

4-5 Her first experiments See L-34 and P-3 for examples; see also the reminiscences in *Letters* (1931), xix, 32, 127-28; Bianchi, 130; and Whicher, chap. X.

5 'Instincts for Dance' P-1046.

5 'a paradox, a riddle' Bianchi, 40. The conversation with Higginson, following, is from L-342a and L-342b.

6 'gazing bewildered after him' L-908.

7 'story fatigues you' L-261. The preceding quotation is from L-268; the following from L-330 and L-330a.

8 'The show is not the Show' P-1206 and L-381. The preceding quotation is from L-342a.

8 'and the Jacqueminots' L-473.

8-9 'the adjacent buildings' L-182 (paragraph divisions have not been kept).

9 Her pen-portraits . . . family circle The quotations in this paragraph are from L-261, -342b, -405, -339, and -792, respectively.

9-10 The father image The quotations in this and the following paragraphs are from L-342a, -418, -457, -58, -145,

-311, -315; -65, -339, -360, and -644, respectively.

11 *'a supposed person'* L-268.

11-2 *commentary on characters and events* The quotations in this and the following paragraph are from L-339, -389, -901; -691, -133, -318, respectively.

12 *'What Soft Cherubic Creatures'* P-401. These satires on contemporary America, pp. 12-16, above, are discussed more fully in my article in the *New England Quarterly*, June, 1958.

13-4 *'glory of his Father'* • *Mark* 8.38.

14-5 *'somebody would see me'* L-127; see also Bingham, 218, 295, and 285-300 *passim*.

15 *'I like to hear it'* P-585. (Variants adopted in lines 1, 9, 15.)

16 *'Sun of Thunder'* • *Mark* 3.17.

16 *'its flash of salute'* Bianchi, 129-30. See Nathalia Wright's article in *Modern Language Notes*, February, 1957, comparing ED's poem with Thoreau's iron horse in *Walden*.

17 *'embarrass my Dog'* L-271. The next quotation is from L-261.

17 *'please him, somehow'* L-175. The other quotations in this paragraph are from P-315, L-230, and P-1207.

18 *'Some keep the Sabbath'* P-324; see also P-1591.

18 *'in a godly village'* L-234. Whicher, chap. IX, coined the apt phrase, 'poked the Scriptures.'

19 *'The Bible is'* P-1545 ('bastinadoed,' line 11, is from an earlier draft).

19 *'Solution is insufficient'* L-794.

19 *'The Garment of Surprise'* P-1335. The next quotation is from P-1479; see also P-59, -597, -1317, -1459.

20 *'Elijah's Wagon'* P-1254. The preceding Biblical quotation is from 2 *Kings* 2.11.

20 *'Correction in Righteousness'* L-650. The next quotation is from L-750.

21 *'look alike, and numb'* L-261 and note.

21 *'I cannot dance'* P-326.

24 *'God moves in a mysterious way'* Watts's *Christian Psalmody*, No. 48. (A copy of the American edition, Boston, 1817, was in the Dickinson family library.) The next quotation is from L-278.

25 *'Alake and alas'* The ballad of 'Sir Patrick Spence.'

26 *'descant on Watts'* Austin Warren in *Sewanee Review*, Autumn, 1957. For a convenient summary of the hymn meters and ED's variations on them see Johnson, 84-86.

26 *'The pattern of the sun'* P-1550.

27 *'jingling cooled my tramp'* L-265.

28 *'Lightly stepped'* P-1672. Whicher, 184, first referred to this poem as a 'musical joke'. R.P. Adams's study of ED's sound techniques in relation to her meanings opens up a very important area, but the very lack of a precise esthetics of verse music handicaps his analyses of individual poems (*Tulane Studies in English*, 1957, 133-52).

29 *'We play at Paste'* P-320.

NOTES FOR CHAPTER 2: 'WORDS'

30 *Words* William Howard's 'ED's Poetic Vocabulary,' in *Publications of the Modern Language Association*, March, 1957, is the most ambitious study of this aspect of her poetry. But the author, aiming at a strictly objective survey, limits himself largely to quantitative measurements and con-

ventional meanings. Another limitation results from his tendency to treat words as if they existed in her poems inert and separable from the context, though he admits in conclusion: 'It is not in the words she uses but in the way she uses them that Emily Dickinson is most original.' For these reasons his findings have not proved useful for my book, which is concerned with evaluating only her best poems, by analyzing her special verbal strategies and exploring her poetic language as a system of words in contextual relations.

30 'my only companion' L-261. The next quotations are from P-728 and P-246.

31 'comes from the sea' L-965. The next quotation is from L-368.

31 'Auctioneer of Parting' The three poems here quoted from are discussed later.

32 distinguished linguist Margaret Schlauch, *The Gift of Language* (1955), 232; also 235, 239, 244, 246, 251, 252, 255, for the points discussed in the following paragraphs, but not in relation to ED. (See also R.P. Blackmur, *Language as Gesture*, 1952, 39 ff., for a discussion of the same problem applied specifically to ED but reaching conclusions opposite to mine.)

33 like Hopkins • *The Letters of Gerard Manley Hopkins to Robert Bridges*, ed. by C.C. Abbott (1955), 89.

33 'the wiles of words' L-555. The quotations in the next paragraph are from L-342b and L-271.

34 'Because I see New Englandly' P-285.

34 'Faith is a fine invention' P-185. (Both 'faith' and 'fine,' it is true, derive ultimately from Latin rather than Anglo-Saxon, but they were incorporated into English from French at an early period and with new meanings so that they are thought of as native words.)

35 'Capacity to Terminate' P-1196. The next quotation is from P-494.

35 'Tell all the Truth' P-1129. The similar lines in 'Uriel' are: 'knowledge grown too bright/To hit the nerve of feebler sight.'

36 'They shut me up in Prose' P-613. The next quotation is from L-56; see also L-65.

37 'I dwell in Possibility' P-657. The sequel, discussed following, is P-838.

37 'too soon for language' The three letters quoted in this paragraph are L-252, -330, and -730, respectively.

37 'Speech is one symptom' The five fragments of poems quoted in this paragraph are from P-1681, -1668, -1700, -420, and -581, respectively.

38 'Shall I take thee' P-1126. (Variants adopted in lines 4, 5, 6.)

39 'poems or songs' Emerson, 'The Poet,' *Works* (Centenary Ed., 1903), III, 23.

39 'Could mortal lip divine' P-1409. The next quotation is from P-276.

39 'a Voice but one' L-470. The poem cited at the end of this paragraph is P-318.

40 'thought that walks alone' L-330. The next quotations are from L-656, -1007 note, and -1011.

40 'feel quick gratitude' L-260.

41 'A Word that breathes' P-1651 (lines 9-12 only; the rest of the poem is quoted on p. 42, above).

41 'A word is dead' P-1212. (Third version adopted.) See also P-1261.

41 'Your thoughts dont have words' P-1452. (Variant adopted in line 4.)

42 '*A Word made Flesh*' P-1651. (Quotations marks are supplied at end of line 13.)

42 '*dwelt among us*' • *John* 1.14; also 1.1, 18, 31.

43 ' "*dwelt among us*" ' PF-4.

44 '*He ate and drank*' P-1587. The Biblical reference, preceding, is to *John* 6.51, 54, 63.

45 '*nations, and tongues*' • *Revelation* 10.10-11.

45 '*Strong draughts of*' P-711.

46 '*the embrace of thought*' Henry James, *Essays in London* (1893), 155.

NOTES FOR CHAPTER 3: 'CIRCUMFERENCE'

47-8 '*Of Bronze and Blaze*' P-290. (Variant adopted in line 19.)

48 '*Auroran widths*' The fragments quoted in this paragraph are from P-776 and P-710.

48-9 '*call attention to it*' L-53. The next quotation is from Gerard Manley Hopkins, *Selections* (Penguin, 1953), 123.

49 '*Celestial Face*' P-1002.

50 '*engrossed to Absolute*' Poem fragments in this paragraph are from P-629 and P-783.

51 '*world where bells toll*' L-269. The next quotation is from P-629.

52 '*Menagerie to me*' P-1206. (See p. 8, above. See also L-506, identifying a circus that came to Amherst in 1877 as 'Van Amburgh's Menagerie.')

53 '*After a hundred years*' P-1147.

55 '*take it away*' L-268; in a previous letter, L-261, she had asked: 'Could you tell me how to grow— or is it unconveyed— like Melody— or witchcraft?'

55 *Religio Medici* • *The Works of Sir Thomas Browne* (London, 1852), II, 333 and note. (This set was in the Dickinson family library.) Margery McKay was the first to point out this parallel (unpublished thesis, 'Amazing Sense', Swarthmore College, 1936; see also the article by H.E. Childs in *American Literature*, January, 1951). Browne and Dickinson were kindred spirits in many ways: intensely interested in all the minute phenomena of nature and death, combining an analytical skepticism with a generally spiritual orientation, employing a style marked by economy of expression and startling imagery. He was also, like her, a recluse who did not intend to publish, calling his *Religio Medici*, 'a private exercise directed to myself.' The concept of 'circumference' is central to his philosophy and gives unity to his vast system of circle imagery. The poetry of ED is likewise rich in wheels, arcs, axes, cycles, discs, spheres, and orbits. But there is an important difference. His use of 'circumference' has a strictly religious purpose, an attempt to define God; her emphasis is esthetic. (See also Johnson, chap. VI.)

55-6 '*A Coffin is a small Domain*' P-943. The next quotations are from P-515 and P-378.

56 '*new Circumference*' P-313 (see chap. 9, of the present book). The next quotation is from P-802.

57 '*Bride of Awe*' P-1620.

57 '*not with the Circumference*' L-950. (See Johnson, 140, 151-53; and L-261, where she lists 'the Revelations' among her six favorite books.)

57 '*By intuition Mightiest Things*' P-420. In her distinction between the center and circumference, ED seems closer

to the esthetic-religious positions of modern writers like Langer, Bergson, and Whitehead than to the Transcendentalism of Emerson.

58 *'The Poets light'* P-883. (Other poems on circumference are P-451, -633, -641, -680, -889.)

59 *'Fame is a fickle food'* P-1659. Other poems quoted in this paragraph are P-1763 and P-288.

59 *'Publication is the Auction'* P-709.

61 *'by the punctuation'* L-316. See P-986 and note; also the correction to this note by J.L. Spicer in *Boston Public Library Quarterly*, July, 1956.

61 *'use it for the World'* L-261. The next quotation is from L-265.

61-2 *Her attitude towards fame* Thornton Wilder in the *Atlantic Monthly*, November, 1952; see also Johnson, 110-20.

62 *'and less singular'* • *The Letters of Gerard Manley Hopkins to Robert Bridges*, ed. by C.C. Abbott (1955), 291.

62 *'Some Work for Immortality'* P-406. The next quotation is from P-441. Other poems on fame are P-250, -713, -855, -1226, -1232.

NOTES FOR CHAPTER 4: 'CENTER'

63 *'This is a Blossom'* P-945. (Variant adopted in line 5.)

64 *'Essential Oils are wrung'* P-675. (Second version adopted.)

65 *'My drop of India'* P-430; see also L-900.

65 *'This was a Poet'* P-448. These words form the title of Whicher's book on ED.

66 *Emerson . . . organicism* In 'The Problem' Emerson says of his poems: 'These temples grew as grows the grass.' (It would be mere quibbling to point out that attar of roses happens not to be one of the perfumes extracted by hydraulic presses, the process used being either distillation or maceration.)

67 *puzzling verb forms* My conjectured explanation of these verb forms that omit the final *s* is confirmed by an eminent linguish, Kemp Malone. Johnson, 93, offers an explanation in the same direction, that ED was trying to 'universalize her thought to embrace past, present, and future.' Whicher, 234, tried to explain similar

forms, amounting to almost a mannerism in her poetry, as subjunctives to express her 'chronic state of trepidation;' but this does not fit the present poem though it may apply in some other cases.

67 *'never Treason to Nature's'* L-1004.

68 *'What is inspiration?'* L-353.

68 *'ever I met in my life'* L-128. The next quotation is from P-593.

69 *As defined by Eliot* T.S. Eliot, *Selected Essays* (1932), 241-50, 'The Metaphysical Poets,' inspired by Herbert Grierson's introduction to *Metaphysical Lyrics and Poems of the 17th Century* (Oxford, 1921). See also Louis Martz, *The Poetry of Meditation* (1954), 324, who includes ED along with Hopkins, Yeats, and Eliot when naming later poets in this tradition.

69 *'leaves me bare and charred'* L-265 and L-271.

70 *'Is there any other way'* L-342a. The letter quoted at the end of this paragraph is L-390.

70-1 'On my volcano' P-1677. In 'The Problem' Emerson said: 'The litanies of nations came/Like the volcano's tongue of flame,/Up from the burning core below.'

71 'To pile like Thunder' P-1247. The phrases following are from Emerson's 'Merlin.'

71 'Bolts of Melody' P-505. Mrs. Bingham chose these words for her title when she edited a volume of ED's poetry in 1945.

71 'No man saw awe' P-1733.

72 'My business is to sing' L-269.

72 'Sang from the Heart' P-1059 (see also P-1005). The other poems from which fragments are quoted in this paragraph are P-544, -571, -963.

73 'The Verses just relieve' L-261 and L-265.

73 'worries one like a Wasp' L-220. The next two quotations are from L-342a and P-677.

73 'I taste a liquor' P-214. (Variants adopted in lines 3 and 16.) See Whicher, 187-88.

75 'So gay a Flower' P-1456. The other quotations in this paragraph are from L-759, L-965, and P-1654. The reference to Jonathan Edwards is in Chase, 195-96.

76 'tries to be haunted' L-459a.

NOTES FOR CHAPTER 5: 'PERCEPTION'

79-80 'This whole Experiment' P-1333. The arrangement of variants for this line on the original MS (Amherst College) differs considerably from the Harvard Edition. (See p. 312, above.)

80 'science . . . theoretical description' Josiah Royce, *The World and the Individual* (1901), 2nd Series, 214.

81 'A little Madness' P-1333.

81 'Vandykes Delineation' P-606. The other poems quoted in this paragraph are P-291 (variant adopted in line 21) and P-307.

82 ' "Nature" is what We see' P-668. (Second version adopted.)

83 'Nature and God I neither knew' P-835.

83 'We spy the Forests' P-1097. (Second version adopted.)

84 'Artist who drew me so' P-155. The other poems quoted in this paragraph are P-1748 and P-191.

85 'The Tint I cannot take' P-627. (Variants adopted in lines 16 and 19.)

86 'The Soul's Superior instants' P-306.

86-7 'What mystery pervades a well' P-1400.

88 'To hear an Oriole sing' P-526. (The variant in line 11 is cited following.)

89 'Split the Lark' P-861.

90 'Thomas's faith in Anatomy' Quoted from *Letters* (1931), 411. See *John* 20.24-25. The quotation from *Religio Medici*, following, may be found in *The Works of Sir Thomas Browne* (1852), II, 378, the set in the Dickinson family library.

90 'Perception of an Object' P-1071. (Second version adopted.)

91 the new theoretical physics See Werner Heisenberg, *The Physicist's Conception of Nature* (London, 1958), especially 7-31.

92 From Baudelaire to Surrealism See R.P. Blackmur's article in the *Sewanee Review*, Spring, 1956.

92 'tries to be haunted' L-459a; P-1400 was probably written in 1877.

93 'His own was ampler' P-308. The next poem quoted is P-766.

93 'I reckon when I count' P-569. (All variants adopted.)

NOTES FOR CHAPTER 6: 'FORMS'

96 'these lives of our's' L-80 and L-56.

97 'in their mild eyes, tears' L-161. The following quotation is from L-503. The two poems cited are P-142 and P-790.

97 'Christopher Robin' mode Chase, 111 ff.

97 'long white nightgowns' L-228. The quotations following are from L-340 and L-689.

98 'Babbles the Bee' The three poems quoted from in this paragraph are discussed on pp. 270, 108, 140 ff., of the present book, respectively.

98 'Pink small and punctual' P-1332. The following quotation is from Bianchi, 95.

99 'children of spring' L-23.

99 'as lightly from disdain' P-1586. The following quotation is from P-380.

100 'Consider the Lilies' L-904. See *Matthew* 6.28-30, for following quotation.

100 'The Grass so little' P-333.

101 The Bible . . . Solomon • Song of Songs 1.12.

101 'he was disgraceful' L-261. A scrap of MS written late in life contains a notation that seems superficially much closer to Whitman (compare PF-110 with 'Song of Myself,' lines 110-12) but his passage leads to the doctrine that grass is a microcosm of the universal soul, a philosophy alien to hers.

102 'dust might not terrify' L-182.

103 'How happy is the little Stone' P-1510. The following quotation is from P-629.

104 'Two Butterflies went out' P-533, and note.

104 'Bees are Black' P-1405. The imagery of stanza two suggests the passage in *King Lear*, III, ii, concluding 'Cracke Natures moulds, all germaines spill at once.'

105 'there— he is gone!' L-502.

106 'The Pillow of this' P-1561. The following quotations are from P-1279. The poem cited on the oriole is P-1466. (See also P-634, -1465, -1591.)

106 'If Nature smiles' P-1085.

107 'Those Cattle smaller' P-1388.

107 'The Rat is the concisest Tenant' P-1356.

108 'The Bat is dun' P-1575.

110 'left the little Angle Worm' P-885. The quotation at the end of the paragraph is from L-193.

110 'Nature ... perhaps a Puritan' L-706.

111 'Mr. Thomson's "sheaves" ' P-131. (See Whicher, 211, 250.) The poem cited next is P-128.

111 'Beauty be not caused' P-516. (The space between lines 3 and 4 has been closed up.)

112 'The Definition of Beauty' P-988. The next quotation is from P-1700.

NOTES FOR CHAPTER 7: 'EVANESCENCE'

113-4 'Within my Garden' P-500. The last two stanzas are quoted on pp. 115-16, above.

114 'A Route of Evanescence' P-1463. (See Grover Smith, *Explicator*, May, 1949.)

114 'Beauty is its Evanescence' L-781, in 1881; the poem was written 1879-82.

114 'With a delusive,' etc. The MS containing these variants for line 2 was not available to the editor of the

Harvard Edition. It has recently been found and is now in the Forbes Library, Northampton, Mass.

116 passage, The Tempest See II, i, 246-248. Kenneth MacLean first pointed out this specific source, but nothing more, in the *University of Toronto Quarterly,* October, 1950. ED's casual reference to 'Caliban's "clustering filberds" ' in a late letter seem sufficient evidence that she knew the play.

117 'please accept a Humming Bird' L-769 and L-770, inclosing copy of P-1463.

118 'A Bird came down' P-328.

119 'To Nowhere' P-354 (see also P-517). The next poem quoted is · P-1723.

119 'Demosthenes has vanished' P-1379. (Variant adopted in line 16.) The next quotations are from L-442.

120 'Several of Nature's People' P-986, last 2 stanzas. (Second version adopted.)

120 'A snake with mottles rare' P-1670.

121 'A narrow Fellow' P-986.

122 'A snake is summer's treason' P-1740. The next quotation is from L-271.

122 'Nature affects to be sedate' P-1170.

123 'The Mushroom is the Elf' P-1298. (Variants for the last stanza are given on p. 124, above.)

125-6 'A Spider sewed at Night' P-1138 (see also P-1275).

126 'The Spider . . . dancing' P-605. (Variant adopted in line 4.)

127 'On fine Arterial Canvas' P-451.

128 'He plies from Nought' P-605. The quotation in the previous sentence is from P-1275. ·

128 'Drab Habitation of Whom?' P-893. Other poems quoted in this paragraph are P-129, above, and P-517, below.

129 'Its little Ether Hood' P-1501.

130 'than other ones' avowals' L-479. The quotation in the next paragraph is from L-318.

NOTES FOR CHAPTER 8: 'PROCESS'

132 'The Day came slow' P-304.

133 'The Lilac is' P-1241. The quotation in line 17 is from *1 Corinthians* 2.9.

134 'our unfurnished eyes' L-280.

134 'Time's Analysis' See my article in *English Literary History,* September, 1959, bringing together conceptually all of ED's poems on 'The Trap of Time,' scattered through the present book under thematic headings, in chaps. 8, 11, and 12.

135 'The far Theatricals' P-595. The following quotation is from P-628 (see also P-265, -291, -1114, and -1349).

136 'Blazing in Gold' P-228. (Variants adopted in line 4 and 7. Two other

variant readings, for lines 5-6, are given on the next page.)

137 'Civilization spurns the Leopard' P-492.

138 'It rises— passes' P-1023; see also P-591 and P-1419.

138-9 'The Wind begun to rock' P-824. (Second version adopted.)

139 'It pulled the spigot' P-1235; see also P-1694.

139-40 'There came a Wind' P-1593. (Variants adopted in lines 2 and 12.)

140-1 'It sounded as if' P-1397. (Variants for line 7 are given two pages below.)

141 'Jehovah's Watch is wrong' P-415. The following quotation is from L-471.

141 'Again the smoke' P-1134; see also P-1327. (These seem like trial flights for P-1397, but neither employs the novel image of eclipse. For an analogy to that see John Donne's 'The Storme,' lines 37-50, rendered in terms of theology.)

142 'grows from the seed' L-690.

142 'call their "Father"' L-261. The following quotation is from P-1649.

143 'To pile like Thunder' P-1247.

143 as formulated by Whitehead • Dialogues of A.N. Whitehead, ed. by Lucien Price (New York, 1954), 61, 124, 371.

143 'assuring me they lived' L-488. (Edward Hitchcock, ardent botanist, was president of Amherst College when ED attended the Academy.) The following quotation is from L-520.

143 'The Dandelion's pallid tube' P-1519. The following quotation is from P-1682.

144 'It will be Summer' P-342. The preceding quotation is from L-948.

145 'and a new Road' L-332. The letter quoted in the next paragraph is L-57.

146 'These are the days' P-130. (See George Arms's reading, *Explicator*, February, 1944.)

148 'kingdom of heaven' • Matthew 18.3.

149 'As imperceptibly as Grief' P-1540. (Variant cited two pages below.)

150-1 'Further in Summer' P-1068. (Third version, sent to Niles in 1883, adopted because the punctuation clarifies several difficult passages; but the reading in the 1866 version of 'pensive' for 'gentle,' line 7, seems superior. I have corrected one error in the Harvard Edition's transcription of this MS, 'this' for 'the,' line

11.) Marshall Van Deusen's interpretation of the religious language in this poem (*Explicator*, March, 1955) has proved helpful.

153 'The earth has many keys' P-1775. These 8 lines, printed as a separate poem in the Harvard Edition, are actually the conclusion of the 'lost Vanderbilt version' of P-1068, now available in the Bingham Collection at Amherst College. The first 20 lines of this version are nearly identical with those of the 'Norcross transcript' of P-1068, reproduced by Johnson in his notes to this poem. Since the 'Vanderbilt' MS of this important poem has never been printed, it is given here entire, with thanks to Jay Leyda who called it to my attention:

Further in summer than the birds
Pathetic from the grass
A minor nation celebrates
Its unobtrusive mass.

Nor ordinance be seen,
So gradual the grace
A pensive custom it becomes,
Enlarging loneliness.

'Tis audibler at dusk
When day's attempt is done
And nature nothing waits to do
But terminate in tune;

Nor difference it knows
Of cadence or of pause
But simultaneous as sound
The service emphasize;

Nor know I when it cease,
At candles it is here;
When sunrise is, that is it not.
Than this, I know no more.

The earth has many keys—
Where melody is not
Is the unknown peninsula.
Beauty is nature's fact.

But witness for her land,
And witness for her sea,
The cricket is her utmost
Of elegy to me.

154 'both her Hands of Haze' P-574.
The poem cited following is discussed
on p. 146, above.

156 'no film on noon' L-235. The poem
quoted following is P-606.

156 'The Revelations of the Book' P-
1115. The next quotation is from
P-1422.

157 'That makes the Heart' P-1271.
(Punctuation corrected from the
MS.) The other quotations in this

paragraph are from P-1690, L-195,
and L-937.

157 ''Twas later when the summer' P-
1276.

158 'Apparently with no surprise' P-
1624. In another poem, P-724, the
same 'Perturbless Plan' is applied to
man, though with God taking a more
active role.

159 'frost is no respecter of persons'
L-227.

159-60 'It sifts from Leaden Sieves' P-
311. (First version, written in 1862.
The fourth version, written in 1883,
is reproduced two pages below.)

160 'Tumultuous privacy of storm' This
phrase was transcribed by ED on
PF-116. Even in the late superior
version of P-311, ED's last line ('Denying that it was') seems to echo line
24 of Emerson's 'Snow-Storm' ('re-
tiring, as he were not').

NOTES FOR CHAPTER 9: 'ECSTASY'

165 'living is joy enough' L-342a;
see also T.W. Higginson, *Atlantic
Monthly,* October, 1891.

166 'Soto! Explore thyself!' P-832. (See
the similar poem by Thoreau in
Walden, chap. XVIII.) The next
quotation is from P-1354.

166 A concordance to her poems Doc-
toral dissertation (unpublished) by
Louise Kelley, Pennsylvania State
College, 1951; written before the
Harvard Edition was available.

167 'Sang from the Heart' P-1059. The
next two quotations are from P-1005
and P-1765.

167 a parallel love affair See Appendix,
pp. 289-99, of the present book; and
L-187, -233, -248.

168 'a supposed person' L-268. The

poem cited in the next sentence is
P-322; for its literary source see the
Explicator for December, 1952, and
April, 1954.

169 'What would I give' P-247. The
other poems cited or quoted in this
paragraph are P-223, -815, -506, -809,
-1725, -480, respectively.

169 'Wild Nights— Wild Nights!' P-249.
Similar erotic imagery is employed in
P-211, -368, -506; and Eden is simi-
larly used in several letters.

170 'Adam taught her Thrift' P-1119.

170 'The Soul selects' P-303. (Variants
adopted in lines 3, 4, and 8.) For a
different interpretation, identifying
the 'One' as muse, see Johnson, 56,
146, 248.

171-2 'Of all the Souls' P-664.

172 'If certain, when this life' P-511. (Fourth stanza only.) See also P-366, -729, -961.

172-3 'My Life had stood' P-754. The next two quotations are from P-174 and L-575.

173 'With swiftness, as of Chariots' P-1053.

176 'You constituted Time' P-765.

177 'Because You saturated Sight' P-640. (Stanzas 6 and 9 only.) The letter quoted following is L-193.

178 'I'm ceded— I've stopped' P-508. (Variants adopted in lines 13 and 19.)

179 'Baptized this Day a Bride' P-473.

179 'Given in Marriage' P-817. The next quotation is from P-918. (See Sister Mary Power, _In the Name of the Bee_, 1943.)

180 'God is a distant' P-357. (See note for an account of its reception; also Whicher, 183.)

181 'crowns of gold' • _Revelation_ 4.2-4.

181 'I never knelt to other' L-750. The fragments of poems quoted in this paragraph are from P-493, -273, -704, and -336, respectively.

182 'the Lamb's wife' The quotations in this paragraph are from _Revelation_ 22.4, 2.17, 3.12, and 21.2, 9, respectively.

182 'Title divine— is mine!' P-1072.

183-4 'Mine— by the right' P-528. (The variant for line 9 is given on p. 186, above.)

185 'To put this World down' P-527.

185 'the White Exploit' P-922. The following quotation is from P-709.

185 'whiter than snow' • _Psalms_ 51.7. The next quotation is from _Isaiah_ 1.18.

186 'linen, clean and white' • _Revelation_ 19.7-8; the next quotation is from 7.3.

186 'itself as yet unknown' L-891.

187 'The Love a Life can show' P-673. (The variant for line 10 is given following.)

188-9 'The farthest Thunder' P-1581. (Second version adopted, with variants in lines 7, 10, 18, and 20.) The quotations about St. Paul are from _Acts_ 22.6-11.

189 'that waylaying Light' L-937.

190 'Its fervor the electric Oar' P-1597. The next quotation is from P-1556.

NOTES FOR CHAPTER 10: 'DESPAIR'

191 'The Heart asks Pleasure' P-536. The letter quoted following is L-523.

191 _pleasure-pain antithesis_ The poems quoted in illustration are P-135, -572, -207, and -125, respectively. On the last one, see Georges Poulet, _Studies in Human Time_ (1956), 347.

192 'because I am afraid' L-261. The biographer referred to is Theodora Ward, 'Ourself behind Ourself,' _Harvard Library Bulletin_, Winter, 1956.

193 'Not with a Club' P-1304. (The omitted fourth stanza seems extra-neous.) The preceding quotation is from P-850.

193-4 'I cannot live with you' P-640.

194-5 'I should have been' P-313. See my note for p. 301, below, 'Orthography.'

196 'till he had been human' L-519. The Biblical quotations following are from _Matthew_ 27.46 and _Luke_ 22.42.

197 'The Auctioneer of Parting' P-1612.

198 'One Crucifixion is recorded' P-553. The next quotation is from P-532.

199 'I dreaded that first Robin' P-348.

200 'excels my Piano' L-261. The poem cited following is P-620.

202 'Split lives— never "get well"' L-246. The poem quoted following is P-244. (A spelling error, 'Gimblets,' is corrected.)

203 'Safe Despair it is' P-1243. The other quotations in this paragraph are from P-686, L-311, P-967, and P-963 (with variants). See also P-241, -650, -745, -1064, and -1738.

204 'I read my sentence' P-412.

206 'As if your Sentence' P-414. The poem quoted in the next paragraph is P-859.

207 'There is a pain' P-599. The preceding quotation is from PF-67; the following one from *Genesis* 1.2 (Septuagint version).

208 'I felt a Funeral' P-280. (Variants adopted in lines 19 and 20.)

210 'Death wronged them' L-907. The next quotation is from L-792.

210-1 'After great pain' P-341. (Variant line arrangement, stanza 2, adopted.) The explication here summarized is by Frank Manley in *Modern Language Notes*, April, 1958, growing out of a seminar paper under my direction. See also the analysis by Brooks and Warren, *Understanding*

Poetry (1938), 468 ff.; it is interesting that Warren used the same image of 'quartz contentment' to describe Jack Burden at the depth of his despair in *All the King's Men* (1946).

213 'It was not Death' P-510. (Variants adopted in lines 5 and 7.)

215-6 'There's a certain Slant' P-258. See Laurence Perrine, *Explicator*, May, 1953.

218 two other poems The quotations in this paragraph are from P-764 and P-310.

219 'A perfect— paralyzing Bliss' P-756.

219 'It struck me every Day' P-362.

220 'The joy that has no' P-1744. The letter quoted following is L-522.

221 An eminent critic See Tate, 217-26 *passim*. For ED's aphoristic poems concerned with the conscious self, see my article in *American Literature*, November, 1959.

221 'As Firmament a Flame' P-1286. The next quotation is from L-13.

221 an eminent scientist Julian Huxley, *New Bottles for New Wine* (1957), 279-312 *passim*.

222 'Of God we ask one favor' P-1601 and L-976; see also L-566.

NOTES FOR CHAPTER 11: 'DEATH'

225 'tell me its name' L-873. The poem quoted following is P-1564; see also L-868 and L-972.

226 Her correspondence is filled The quotations in this paragraph and the following are from L-785, -788, -792, -940, -245, -280, and -298.

226 'The Bustle in a House' P-1078; see Whicher, 223.

227 Her best poems on death The quotations in this paragraph are from P-7, -856, -982, and -922.

228 'does not entice us more' PF-70.

The next two quotations are from L-575 and L-555.

228 Two light verses P-389 and P-457; these are fully treated in my article in the *New England Quarterly*, June, 1958.

229 'And We— We placed the Hair' P-1100. (Variant adopted in last line.)

229 'How many times' P-187. Phrases from P-677 are quoted in this and the following paragraphs. (See also P-422, -519, -1063, and -1135.)

230 '*its mortal signal*' L-318. The poems quoted are P-654, -795, and -146.

231 *in the traditional pattern* The letters here quoted are L-153, -263, -785. For poems in this convention see P-622, -158, -160, and -547.

231-2 '*I heard a Fly buzz*' P-465.

232-3 '*We dream— it is good*' P-531. (The variant for line 15 is given on the next page.)

233 *death . . . in time and space* The poems quoted in this paragraph are P-1742, -1691, -1431, -949, -948, -889, and -1527, respectively.

235 '*A Clock stopped*' P-287. (Variant adopted in line 14; 'Doctor's,' line 10, has been corrected.)

235 ''*Twas comfort*' P-1703. The letter quoted at the end of this paragraph is L-438.

236 *In one poem* The quotations that follow are from P-112, -1056, -297, and -336, respectively.

237 '*Pink stranger we call Dust*' P-1527.

238 '*Shuts arrogantly in the Grave*' P-627. The quotation immediately following is from P-654 (with both variants adopted).

238 '*More distant in an instant*' P-981. The next quotation is from P-948.

239 '*to her long home*' L-11, and note.

239 *Graveyard School* Poems quoted in this paragraph are P-583, -970, -144, and -1626 (second version), respectively.

240 '*Wait till the Majesty*' P-171. The next quotation is from P-735.

240-1 '*One dignity delays*' P-98. (The MS spelling 'escutscheon' has been corrected.)

241-2 '*Because I could not stop*' P-712.

244 '*What Inn is this*' P-115.

244 *An eminent critic* Yvor Winters, *In Defense of Reason* (1947), 283-99. His chapter on ED is titled 'The Limits of Judgment.'

245 *two critics* Chase, 250; and Tate, 219. Other analyses of this poem are by Johnson, 222-224, and by Eunice Glenn in the *Sewanee Review*, Autumn, 1943; see also T.C. Hoepfner in *American Literature*, March, 1957.

246 '*a beautiful new friend*' L-72 and L-77 (and note).

247 '*Tie the Strings*' P-279; see also P-649 and P-1496.

247 '*Death is the supple Suitor*' P-1445. (Variant adopted in line 12.)

248 '*Death is but one*' P-561. The next quotation is from P-406.

249 '*I live with Him*' P-463. (Stanzas 3 and 4 only.)

249-50 '*Our journey had advanced*' P-615.

250 '*and a new Road*' L-332.

NOTES FOR CHAPTER 12: 'IMMORTALITY'

251-4 *Immortality . . . in letters* The quotations in the first four paragraphs of this chapter are from the following: L-319, -388, and PF-50; L-184, -503, -519; L-418, -785, -827, -968, -553 (inclosing P-1433); L-641, -868. (The unwritten letter, 'Dear Father,' cited on p. 252, above, is in Millicent Bingham, *ED: A Revelation*, 1955, 71n.)

254 '*Immortal is an ample word*' P-1205. The next poem quoted is P-1718.

254 *Many . . . assertions of faith* The quotations in this paragraph are from L-498, P-1741, P-1012, P-696, respectively. (See also P-413, -575, -623, -1408, and -1411.)

255 '*Going to Heaven*' P-79. (Lines 6-10 and 20-27 only.)

256 '*I went to Heaven*' P-374. (See

P-665, a third pseudo-orthodox picture of heaven; it is a closer parody of John's vision of golden streets and pearly gates, but with the precious stones and metals deftly transferred from the celestial city to the vehicle by which it is reached.) The Biblical account is in *Revelation* 21.

257 *'Those dying then'* P-1551. ('Abdication' is marked 'x' on the MS, but this is not indicated in the Harvard Edition.) The Biblical quotation is from *Mark* 16.19.

257-9 *religious history . . . from the letters* The quotations on these three pages are from L-23, -35, -39, -173, -176, -200, respectively. Of previous accounts of ED's religious history the most helpful are Johnson, chap. I 'The Valley'; Chase, 53-65; and Tate, 211 ff.

259 *'At least to pray'* P-502. (Variants adopted in lines 3 and 5.)

260 *Rev. Jonathan Jenkins* See MacGregor Jenkins, *ED, Friend and Neighbor* (1930), 80-82, for an account of his father's 'catechizing' the poet.

260 *Jonathan Edwards* See Johnson, 19. R.H. Pearce also notes this similarity between ED and Edwards, but remarks 'this fact is not material to the working of any one of her poems' (*Hudson Review*, Winter, 1957-58). The only reference to him in all her writings is trivial (L-712).

261 *Theodore Parker, Emerson* The references to them are in L-213 and L-481. There are few mentions of these authors in her letters, and the dates of reading them must be inferred from the title pages of their volumes in the Dickinson family library, now at Harvard.

261 *George Eliot* L-710 (the poem quoted following is P-959). Aside from their religious history, and their break with orthodoxy, there seems little kinship between these two authors. Yet a key statement of GE's purpose as an artist seems strikingly applicable to ED: 'my writing is simply a set of experiments in life—an endeavor to see what our thought and emotion may be capable of' (*The George Eliot Letters*, Yale, 1955, VI, 216).

262 *new scientific theories* The letters and poems cited on these themes are L-750, P-1295, P-954, P-185, and L-492, respectively.

263 *'Hast thou a Hand'* P-1689. The letter quoted following is L-551.

263 *'I know that He exists'* P-338. (Variant adopted in line 13.)

264 *'all that remains'* PF-34.

264 *'The Brain is wider'* P-632. The next three quotations in this paragraph are from L-735, P-370, and PF-99, respectively.

265-6 *'The Only News I know'* P-827. (Variant adopted in line 12.) See L-290.

266 *'The unknown is'* The letters and poems quoted in this paragraph are L-471, P-1417, P-1222, L-353, L-489, L-912, PF-122, L-512, L-750, respectively.

267 *'This World is not Conclusion'* P-501.

269 *'My Cocoon tightens'* P-1099. (Variants adopted in lines 4 and 7.) See P-365, -976, -1142, -1482, and -1630 for other attempts to find images for the soul's escape from the body.

270 *'Safe in their Alabaster Chambers'* P-216. (Stanzas 1 and 2 are from the version of 1859; stanza 3 from that of 1861.)

271 *'Ample make this Bed'* P-829. ('Noise,' line 7, is clearly capitalized on the MS though not in the Harvard Edition.) The next quotation is from L-193.

272 *'The Sleeping'* This version, as printed in the Springfield *Republican,* is reproduced in the notes to P-216. For other poems closely similar to the early version of P-216 see the following: P-54, a comic version; P-475; P-813; P-1724; the reference in L-432 to her father sleeping 'in the Marl House,' followed by P-1334; and her plea for the corpse in P-1384: 'Warm this inclement Ear . . . Invest this alabaster Zest/In the Delights of Dust.'

272 *'White as alabaster'* L-609. The next two quotations are from P-311 and L-785.

273 *Felix Eberty • The Stars and the Earth; or Thoughts upon Space, Time, and Eternity* (1854), 15-16, 40. A copy of this book, Ripley and Dana's *The American Cyclopaedia* (1860), and Dennis Olmsted's *An Introduction to Astronomy* (1861) were all in the Dickinson family library, now at Harvard. The last named, in an earlier edition, was the text used by ED at Mount Holyoke Seminary.

274 *Melville • Moby-Dick* (Hendrick's House, 1952), 193.

274 *distinguished philosopher* Bertrand Russell, 'A Free Man's Worship,' in *Mysticism and Logic* (1929), 47.

274 *'Science will not trust us'* L-395.

275 *'Those not live yet'* P-1454. The following quotation is from L-288. The interpretation referred to in the next paragraph is by Dorothy Waugh, *Explicator,* January, 1957. (See also P-76.)

277 *'Obtaining but our own Extent'* P-1543. The preceding quotation is from P-802.

277-8 *heretical her speculations* The quotations in this paragraph are from L-650, -555, -471; P-1399, -976, and -665, respectively.

279 *'Though all created light'* Watts's *Christian Psalmody,* Psalm No. 36. The Biblical quotations, above, are from *1 John* 1.5 and *Revelation* 21.24.

279 *'A Wife— at Daybreak'* P-461. The letter quoted following is L-868.

279 *'There is a Zone'* P-1056. See P-906 for another extremely interesting treatment of immortality in terms of light.

280 *'Behind Me dips Eternity'* P-721. What is original in this poem is the imagery, the idea itself being as old as Boethius (see *The Consolation of Philosophy,* Liberal Arts Press, 1960, Prose 6, in the new translation by Richard Green).

283 *Paul Tillich* See *The Courage to Be* (Yale, 1959), 186-90; see also *The Religious Situation* (1956), *passim.* The quotations that follow are taken from his specific attempt at a definition in 'The Lost Dimension in Religion,' *Saturday Evening Post,* June 14, 1958.

283 *A. N. Whitehead • Science and the Modern World* (Mentor, 1948), 187-88, 190-92.

284 *Henry James • Essays in London* (1893), 155.

285 *last letters* The quotations in this paragraph are from L-1045, L-1046, and PF-76.

NOTES FOR APPENDIX 1: 'EMILY DICKINSON'

289 *Emily Dickinson* The data for this appendix have been drawn from the *Letters,* and from the standard bio-graphical works by Bingham, Johnson, and Whicher, cited in the table of abbreviations, p. 314, above.

293 letters to Lord First printed in Millicent T. Bingham, *ED: A Revelation* (1954).

293 'My closest earthly friend' L-765.

293 'Face out of Paradise' L-489.

294 timid withdrawal L-166 and L-330. See also L-127, -154, -159, -176, -202, -271, -342a, and -342b.

295 'like a Summer Dog' L-333. See also L-666.

295 'each other for delight' L-114.

295 most recent biographer See Johnson, 45-55.

296 story of her religious life Among the letters see especially L-10, -13, -23, -35, -36, -39, -46, -77, -88, -142, -173, -200, -213. See also chap. 12, pp. 357-62, of the present book.

298 Dickinson family library The list was kindly supplied to me by Miss Carolyn Jakeman of the Houghton Library, Harvard, where the most important books from this collection are now kept.

299 'fleeing of the Biographied' L-972, with a copy of Cross's *Life of George Eliot*, sent in 1885.

NOTES FOR APPENDIX 2: 'A NOTE ON THE TEXT'

300 deplorable state of the texts The 3 vols. edited in the 1890's by Mabel L. Todd and T.W. Higginson (the third by Mrs. Todd alone) contained 449 poems; their faults were largely deliberate, to make the poems more acceptable to the public. These were reprinted and others added to a total of 889 in the 6 vols. edited by Martha Dickinson Bianchi (the last two assisted by Alfred Hampson), 1914-37; their faults were chiefly accidental, through inability to read the handwriting or to understand the poetry. Some 200 further poems were first published in various early collections of letters, in biographies, and in magazine articles—all with considerable alteration. With the publication of 668 new poems in *Bolts of Melody* (1945) a new era of editorial fidelity was inaugurated by Millicent T. Bingham, though the mechanics were still regularized. A detailed account of this publication history is given in her *Ancestors' Brocades* (1945), and a summary account by Thomas H. Johnson in his introduction to *Poems* (1955). The canon of 1775 poems set up in this Harvard Edition should be taken as a flexible figure, however, as pointed out by Jay Leyda in his review (*New England Quarterly,* June, 1956).

301 titles for her poems Only a small fraction have them. ED referred to 19 by title in her letters, 2 more on copies of poems enclosed in letters, and 3 on poem MSS in the packets (see *Poems,* III, 1206, Appendix 8).

301 'Orthography always baffled me' L-806. A test case for not correcting her spelling may be found in P-313, where her form 'Sabacthini' seems obviously an error. Yet it is barely possible she may have known that this is the feminine form of the Hebrew *sabacthani* and was trying to make it apply to herself as the persona of the poem (though this would actually have involved a misunderstanding of the grammar, since the feminine form would apply to the subject, not the object, of the famous lament 'Thou hast forsaken me').

303 'punctuation can be omitted'•Poems, I, lxiii. But when Johnson edited a selection of her poems for an anthology, four years later, he reproduced the Harvard texts exactly (*Masters of American Literature,* Houghton Mifflin, 1959).

303 essays prompted by the Harvard Edition Those cited in the next three paragraphs are, respectively, by R.P. Blackmur in the *Kenyon Review* (Spring, 1956), Newton Arvin in *American Literature* (May, 1956), Austin Warren in the *Sewanee Review* (Autumn, 1957), and J.C. Ransom in *Perspectives USA* (Spring, 1956).

INDEX TO POEMS

(This list includes only poems fully quoted and discussed.)

333

CPSIA information can be obtained
at www.ICGtesting.com
Printed in the USA
BVHW040153090322
630991BV00009B/246

9 781014 634900